THE NEW HATE

ARTHUR GOLDWAG

THE NEW
HATE

Arthur Goldwag is the author of *Cults, Conspiracies, and Secret Societies,* and of *'Isms and 'Ologies.* He lives in Brooklyn, New York, with his wife and family.

THE NEW HATE

THE NEW HATE

A History of Fear and Loathing
on the Populist Right

ARTHUR GOLDWAG

VINTAGE BOOKS A Division of Random House, Inc. New York

The Library of Congress has cataloged the Pantheon edition as follows:
Goldwag, Arthur.
The new hate : a history of fear and loathing on the populist right / Arthur Goldwag.
p. cm.
Includes bibliographical references and index.
1. Right-wing extremists—United States. 2. Hate groups—Political aspects—
United States. 3. Conspiracy theories—Political aspects—United States.
4. Politics and culture—United States. I. Title.
HN90.R3G62 2012   306.20973'09051—dc23
2011028589

Vintage ISBN: 978-0-307-74251-3

146122990

This book is for Nathan and Eli

The ecumenicism of hatred is a great breaker-down
of precise intellectual discriminations.

—RICHARD HOFSTADTER,

THE PARANOID STYLE IN AMERICAN POLITICS

CONTENTS

THE NEW HATE

INTRODUCTION

Birthers, Birchers, and Death Panels

On February 18, 2010, *The New York Times* ran a story about a significant undercurrent within the Tea Party movement. "Urged on by conservative commentators," it said, "waves of newly minted activists are turning to once-obscure books and Web sites and discovering a set of ideas long dismissed as the preserve of conspiracy theorists. . . . In this view, Mr. Obama and many of his predecessors (including George W. Bush) have deliberately undermined the Constitution and free enterprise for the benefit of a shadowy international network of wealthy elites."

It wasn't exactly news to me. In the fall of 2009, I published a book called *Cults, Conspiracies, and Secret Societies*. I had written it to satisfy my curiosity about, as one of my blurbers put it, "the wilder reaches of human belief"—and, more particularly, about totalizing systems of thought and faith, a subject I had become interested in while I was researching my previous book, *'Isms & 'Ologies*. By the time I finished writing it, I'd learned all I thought I'd ever need to know about the New World Order and its demonic financiers, from the Templars of the twelfth century to the Illuminati, the Elders of Zion, and the Bilderberg elites today.

I delivered *Cults* to my publisher just after Election Day 2008.

When the copyedited manuscript came back to me in January, I couldn't help noticing that the controversy about the president-elect's birth certificate wasn't fading; in fact, it was beginning to gain some real traction. I considered adding a paragraph or two to bring the book up to date but after due reflection decided that references to such a transitory political derangement might just as easily date it. "Who will remember any of this in six months?" I thought.

Had I ventured to define birtherism back then, I would have called it the wishful notion, cherished by a hard core of Obama haters, that he is a citizen of Kenya or Indonesia and hence ineligible to be president. Birthers believe that a sinister cabal created a false identity for Obama that would enable him to be elected president despite his foreign birth, one that was sophisticated enough to pass muster at the highest levels yet so shoddy that anyone with a modem and a few minutes to spare could crack it. His Social Security number, for example, had originally been assigned to a Connecticut resident who was born in the 1890s,[1] and it was just one of the dozens that Obama was purported to have used;[2] the computer-generated short-form birth certificate that he did provide was said to lack the raised seal that would have ensured its authenticity. And why, they asked (until April 27, 2011, when he did), didn't he release the handwritten long-form certification of live birth that was signed by the doctor who delivered him?* Such a conspiracy would have required either supernatural forethought or time travel, as not only is a birth certificate with a raised seal and signature[3] on file in Hawaii's office of vital records but contemporaneous announcements of Obama's birth were printed in two Honolulu newspapers.[4]

But citizen or not, who's to say that Obama's not a Communist

---

* On May 8, 2011, Joseph Farah, the editor of WorldNetDaily, declared the long form a transparent forgery. "There are new facts being uncovered about Obama's birth and his life, his parentage, that would seemingly render moot the question of where he was born," he wrote. "In other words, I have moved from believing Obama has something to hide to believing what he has to hide is the fact that he is just plain constitutionally ineligible to be president" ("The Birth Certificate Debate—It's Not Over," http://www.wnd.com/index.php?fa=PAGE.view&pageId=296293). On May 21, Jerome R. Corsi dropped the other shoe when "'The Obama Code' Hidden Messages in Birth Document?" was published in WorldNetDaily (http://www.wnd.com/?pageId=301329). The article revealed that when Hawaii State Registrar Alvin T. Onaka's signature is magnified 800 percent, "the distinct form of a smiley face can be seen on the side of the 'a' in Onaka's first name." The implication is obvious: the forger is "laughing at those who take the document seriously."

sleeper, a Manchurian candidate who wasn't just destined for the presidency but literally bred for it? Lisa Schiffren—who made her name writing speeches for Dan Quayle when he was vice president, most famously the one that attacked television's Murphy Brown for having a child out of wedlock—played with these notions in a piece she wrote for *National Review Online* in February 2008. "I don't know how Barack Obama's parents met," she noted, before going on to pointedly assert that mixed-race children of Obama's age tend to be "the product of very culturally specific unions . . . For a white woman to marry a black man in 1958, or 60, there was almost inevitably a connection to explicit Communist politics. . . . It was, of course, an explicit tactic of the Communist party to stir up discontent among American blacks, with an eye toward using them as the leading edge of the revolution."[5] Other bloggers have speculated that Obama's real father was Malcolm X[6] or the Communist writer Frank Marshall Davis.[7]

By the time my book hit the stores, I'd seen the words "Where's the Birth Certificate?" printed in ten-foot-tall letters on a billboard beside Interstate 78, not far from Harrisburg, Pennsylvania.[*] Not just birthers but Tea Partiers were ubiquitous on talk radio, cable TV, and conservative Web sites like *Newsmax, Townhall,* and *World-NetDaily.* Rumors of one world government, creeping Socialism, and Latin American plots to conquer and annex the southwestern states, once the stuff of cheaply printed samizdat publications and shortwave radio broadcasts from backwoods compounds with biblical names, were being trumpeted by big-name pundits and even some elected officials. *The Five Thousand Year Leap: 28 Great Ideas That Changed the World,* a thirty-year-old book by the late anti-Communist conspiracy theorist W. Cleon Skousen, was perched atop the Amazon best-seller list with a new foreword by cable TV and talk radio's Glenn Beck.

Now best remembered in far-right-wing Mormon circles, Skousen drew a straight line from the biblical patriarchs through America's founding fathers and found them equally inspired, but in general he took a more dire view of things; most of the time he seemed con-

---

[*] The billboard campaign was the brainchild of Joseph Farah; see http://www.wnd.com/index .php?fa=PAGE.view&pageId=172125.

vinced that he was living in the Republic's last days. "There is an extremely high-powered, well-financed campaign afoot to abolish the United States Constitution," he wrote in 1971 in *Law & Order* (a trade magazine for policemen that he edited), sounding uncommonly then as Glenn Beck does now.[8] And as long as we're on the subject of the then hugely popular, agenda-setting Beck (with the expiration of his contract with Fox News, Beck's future as a TV personality is up in the air), most of his September 2, 2009, Fox News show was devoted to an exposé of the subliminal propaganda that he'd discerned embedded in art deco sculptures, murals, and wall friezes at Rockefeller Center—stunning proof, for those who know how to see it, that its builder, John D. Rockefeller, was a crypto-Communist. It was hardly a coincidence, Beck insinuated, that Fox News's archrival MSNBC—the employer of Beck's ideological adversaries and ratings rivals Keith Olbermann (who has since left the network) and Rachel Maddow—would be headquartered in a place so replete with images of hammers and sickles.[9] Oddly enough, Fox News's headquarters is also located in Rockefeller Center, albeit in a newer, more reliably capitalistic precinct of the vast complex. Walled off from its neighbors' insidious influences, 1221 Avenue of the Americas, one can only presume, is the West Berlin of television news.

But it wasn't just conspiracies that people were talking about as my book went out into the world; secret societies and cults were enjoying a renaissance too. Stewart Rhodes's Oath Keepers,* which enlists soldiers and policemen to swear to disobey any orders they

---

* Its motto is "Not on Our Watch." Here are the ten orders its members vow to disobey (abridged from the organization's Web site, http://oathkeepers.org/oath/):

1. We will NOT obey orders to disarm the American people.

2. . . . to conduct warrantless searches of the American people.

3. . . . to detain American citizens as "unlawful enemy combatants" or to subject them to military tribunal.

4. . . . to impose martial law or a "state of emergency" on a state.

5. . . . to invade and subjugate any state that asserts its sovereignty.

6. . . . to blockade American cities, thus turning them into giant concentration camps.

7. . . . to force American citizens into any form of detention camps under any pretext.

8. . . . to assist or support the use of any foreign troops on U.S. soil against the American people to "keep the peace" or to "maintain control."

9. . . . to confiscate the property of the American people, including food and other essential supplies.

10. We will NOT obey any orders which infringe on the right of the people to free speech, to peaceably assemble, and to petition their government for a redress of grievances.

deem unconstitutional, was just getting off the ground. Some of the most vociferous early opponents of health-care reform—the ones who first started painting Hitler mustaches on pictures of Barack Obama—turned out to be not Tea Partiers exactly but followers of Lyndon LaRouche.[10]

On the wider cultural front, the novelist Dan Brown, whose mega-best-selling *Angels & Demons* and *The Da Vinci Code* had revived some of the most egregious anti-Catholic stereotypes of the Know-Nothing era, was getting ready to launch his next blockbuster. Instead of scheming cardinals and Opus Dei hit men, *The Lost Symbol* focused on Freemasons in Washington, D.C., with all of their esoteric secrets and hidden histories. In Brown's telling, the awesomely powerful Masons—billionaires, politicians, and paradigm-changing scientists—not only quaff rare vintages from human skulls but are on the brink of discovering the secret of eternal life.

Ingenious deconstructions of videos by rappers like Jay-Z, Rihanna, and the cult star Lady Gaga were popping up all over the Internet, exposing their cultic and conspiratorial content. The 2009 MTV Music Awards, the Web site the *Vigilant Citizen* reported,* was "a large scale occult ceremony, complete with an initiation, a prayer and even a blood sacrifice." Millions of people were downloading documentaries like *Zeitgeist: The Movie* (2007) and *Zeitgeist: Addendum* (2008), which a reviewer for the Web aggregator Boing Boing likened to "the John Birch Society on acid."[11] We were living in strange times.

In his seminal essay of the same name, written in 1964, the historian Richard Hofstadter defined the "paranoid style of political thought" as the belief in "the existence of a vast, insidious, preternaturally effective international conspiratorial network designed to perpetrate acts of the most fiendish character."[12] In the months after *Cults, Con-*

---

* See http://vigilantcitizen.com. This snippet from "The Transhumanist and Police State Agenda in Pop Music," one of *Vigilant Citizen*'s typically well-written, impressively erudite articles, provides a fair sample of its preoccupations: "Articles on this site have explored the way Illuminati symbolism, based on secret society occultism, has been reflected in popular videos. Exposing and desensitizing the world to the elite's sacred symbols is, however, only one aspect of their agenda. Other aspects of Illuminati control are reflected in today's popular music as well, including: mass mind control, transhumanism (the 'robotization' of the human body) and the gradual introduction of a virtual police state. Through the news, movies and the music industry, this agenda is being insidiously presented to the masses, using various techniques."

spiracies, and Secret Societies came out, I was able to observe this "paranoid style" for myself, up close and personal.

For one thing, I had launched a blog.* Almost before I knew it, I found myself arguing with Birchers and birthers† on a fairly regular basis—many of whom had clicked on my URL in the expectation that I was a purveyor of conspiracy theories myself. What struck me, over and over again, was how *old* most of their causes turned out to be. Americans have been demonizing blacks, non-Protestant Christians, freethinkers, Asians, and Jews since colonial times. Our fear and resentment of central banks dates back to Alexander Hamilton's day. The Tea Party may be new, but most of the ideas that animate it have been in circulation for decades. The animosities toward Mexican immigrants, legal and illegal, that Tea Party candidates in southwestern states have been espousing rouse echoes of the Zoot Suit Riots in Los Angeles in 1943 or, reaching back even further, of the anti-coolie riots in the 1870s, which culminated in the Chinese Exclusion Act of 1882. From a comment posted by the independent researcher Ernie Lazar, I learned that Kent Courtney, the secretary of the segregationist States' Rights Party of Louisiana, had urged its members to mail tea bags to their congressmen as a protest against taxation as early as 1959.[13] Today's anti-Sharia movement bears a distinct resemblance to anti-Semitic movements of the past.

One day, as I was preparing my notes for a talk that I had been invited to give at a Masonic temple in Manhattan, I noticed this announcement on a 9/11 Truth Web site:

> Arthur Goldwag is a self styled "conspiracy debunker," who rather than vehemently attacking our movement claims we are sadly misinformed. . . . I urge all Patriots in NYC particularly Masons to join me in confronting this so called debunker and NWO apologist.

I spotted its author as soon as I took my place behind the lectern. He was seated in the middle of the second row, pointing a video camera at me—implicitly putting me on notice that any lies I told would

---

* My blog can be found at www.arthurgoldwag.com. All of my posts are archived, and there are links to pieces I've placed at Boing Boing, the Southern Poverty Law Center, and elsewhere.
† An op-ed piece I placed in the *Chicago Tribune* on September 23, 2009, was headlined "Birthers, Birchers, and the Paranoid Style of Politics."

be duly recorded and exposed. He was bearded and wore his hair in dreadlocks; his T-shirt was emblazoned with an image of the twin towers. When I opened the floor for questions, he introduced himself as a Mason, a member of the John Birch Society, and a constitutionalist. In the exchange that followed (which was surprisingly low-key, to my great relief), I told him that I didn't understand how he could accuse me of apologizing for a New World Order that I don't even believe exists.

He answered me with a question of his own. "How do you feel about the Bilderbergers holding their meetings in contravention of the Logan Act of 1799?"

I admitted that I wasn't familiar with the statute.* One of his cohorts asked me if I believed that "the Whore of Babylon" in the book of Revelation prophesied the Vatican. I told her that while I don't personally put much stock in prophecies, I acknowledge that there are those who do, some of whom do indeed interpret the Whore of Babylon in precisely that light.

"Do you know about the Club of Rome?" she asked.

"Not enough to talk about it in a public forum," I answered cautiously, but I knew where she was going. According to a significant body of conspiracist literature, the Club of Rome isn't the global think tank that it pretends to be, dedicated to the search for solutions to the problems of sustainability and managed growth. No, it is a neo-Malthusian front for the global elite's genocidal plan to exterminate nine-tenths of the world's population by means of starvation and forced sterilization—a project conceived by the eugenicists at the Rockefeller Foundation and Planned Parenthood and carried on today by Bill Gates, Warren Buffett, and Oprah Winfrey.[14]

And speaking of the John Birch Society, when the American Con-

---

* I know now that the Logan Act imposes a fine and up to three years' imprisonment on uncredentialed private American citizens who engage in unsanctioned negotiations with foreign officials about "any disputes or controversies with the United States." It was passed in 1799 after George Logan, a Philadelphia physician, persuaded Talleyrand to lift France's embargo on U.S. merchant ships and to release the sailors and ships it had seized—something that President Adams's official diplomatic envoys had manifestly failed to do. Though it has prompted a handful of indictments, no one has ever been prosecuted because of the Logan Act, never mind imprisoned or fined. The act was last amended in 1994; the Congressional Research Service published a concise history and analysis of it in 2006, which can be found at http://www.fas.org/sgp/crs/misc/RL33265.pdf.

servative Union Foundation announced that the JBS would be a co-sponsor of its 2010 Conservative Political Action Conference (CPAC), I commented on my blog about the group's spotty—not to mention morally and intellectually inconsistent—record on civil rights. Its characterization of Nelson Mandela as a "communist terrorist thug," for example, comported oddly with its supposed zeal for liberty. How is it, I asked, that hard-right conservatives, who threaten to rise up against their own government over such comparatively mild offenses as cap-and-trade legislation, can become so squeamish and legal-minded when a foreigner halfway around the world takes up arms against as patently indefensible a system as apartheid? Isn't it always a cause for celebration when the tree of liberty is refreshed with the blood of tyrants?* Hal Shurtleff, a JBS spokesman, took the trouble to post a reply. Mandela's "own writing and actions condemn him," he commented. "He was a proud communist revolutionary and his ANC engaged in horrible crimes including the 'necklace'—burning people alive. Is this what you condone?"

Apartheid itself, in other words, bore none of the onus for the hideous violence that engulfed South Africa for so many years; only the movement that arose to combat it. The logic might not be consistent, but the hatred is. The John Birch Society might not say so in so many words (in fact its Web site is replete with stock pictures of blacks, Asians, and other minorities), but it doesn't exactly perceive where the moral problem lies with a system that keeps the races confined to their own separate spheres. Many of its members deplore the loss of such an effective arrangement in this country. And it wasn't just the extremists of the John Birch Society. The International Freedom Foundation, a pro-apartheid advocacy group that was secretly funded by the government of South Africa in the late 1980s, whose advisory board included the U.S. senator Jesse Helms and congressmen Phil Crane, Bob Dornan, and James Inhofe, claimed to be "dedicated to the

---

* "What country can preserve its liberties if their rulers are not warned from time to time that their people preserve the spirit of resistance? Let them take arms. . . . What signify a few lives lost in a century or two? The tree of liberty must be refreshed from time to time with the blood of patriots & tyrants. It is its natural manure" (Thomas Jefferson to William Smith, November 13, 1787). The quotation was printed on the back of the T-shirt that Timothy McVeigh was wearing when he was arrested after the Oklahoma City bombing.

promotion of individual freedom throughout the world."[15] Apartheid and freedom. Try to square *that* circle.

Some of the same people who are so quick to compare Obama to Hitler also deny that the Holocaust happened—or allow that if some Jews did die at the Nazis' hands, it wasn't anything that they didn't deserve. "I submit, Arthur," my dreadlocked Masonic constitutionalist said when he buttonholed me after my talk, "that it's possible to be a Holocaust revisionist and not be an anti-Semite."

It would almost be comical if so many people didn't think that way—and if so many politicians weren't courting their votes.

In November 2009, the Anti-Defamation League issued a report called "Rage Grows in America," which, like the *New York Times* article I quoted earlier, noted the "intense strain of anti-government distrust and anger, colored by a streak of paranoia and belief in conspiracies," that had been sweeping the country in the wake of the Obama election.[16] It singled out such groups as the Tea Party, birthers, Oath Keepers, and Three Percenters (a radical gun owner's rights group "committed to the Restoration of the Founders' Republic" that takes its name from a widely reported but completely unfactual statistic—that only 3 percent of Americans participated in the Revolutionary War), as well as the syndicated radio host Alex Jones and Richard Poplawski, one of Jones's loyal listeners, "a budding white supremacist who became angry after the election of Obama" and killed three Pittsburgh policemen with an assault rifle. I blogged about the report, and someone calling himself Cliff posted a comment, expressing his outrage at the ADL's paranoid delusions. And then he proved that in this case at least, the ADL was on to something real.

"Sure Russia won the war; they (and the jews that run it) write the propaganda," he wrote. "Look at the holohoax. . . . I say burn every Judea concern to the ground and do not stop until they are smoldering hulks, TV stations, banks, the lot. A Chrystalnacht for the 21st century . . . believe it." He posted again the next day and again the day after that, until I finally blocked him from commenting. I was genuinely shocked and disturbed by the violence of his language; since then, I've become inured to it: he was the first of his kind to visit my blog but very far from the last.

The frontier of wing-nuttery where Cliff and his peers reside doesn't even begin until you've trekked miles beyond the farthest bounds of the lunatic fringe, but increasingly we find ourselves in this strange territory. What else is one to make of an article like the one that was posted on Andrew Breitbart's *Big Government* blog in the spring of 2010 by Frank Gaffney, a deputy secretary of defense under Ronald Reagan, the founder and president of the Center for Security Policy, and a member in good standing of the Republican Washington establishment? Headlined "Can This Possibly Be True? New Obama Missile Defense Logo Includes a Crescent," it uncritically endorsed a semiotic interpretation of the U.S. Missile Defense Agency's newly minted logo that had been advanced by a blogger named Christopher Logan,* as a conscious "morphing of the Islamic crescent and star with the Obama campaign logo"—stunning evidence, as Gaffney put it, of "various, ominous and far more clear-cut acts of submission to Shariah by President Obama and his team."

It is as ingenious a reading as anything that Dan Brown's symbologist hero Robert Langdon might have come up with, so long as you are willing to overlook the fact that the logo was redesigned and approved long before the 2008 election, when the man in the White House was still a born-again Christian and a Republican. To Gaffney's credit, he issued a retraction within a day or two, but this wild, unsubstantiated claim did little to undermine his credibility with the Right, which continues to cite him as an authority on the Islamist threat. On January 4, 2011, he issued his most paranoid warning yet, in an interview in *WorldNetDaily*, when he accused jihadist interests of infiltrating CPAC, of all things. "What's going on in conservative circles should give everyone real cause for concern. What it bespeaks," he continued, channeling *Dr. Strangelove*'s General Jack Ripper, "is an effort to penetrate and influence conservatives, who are the most likely and perhaps only community in America who will stand up to and ultimately help ensure the defeat of this seditious totalitarian program."[17]

---

* Gaffney's blog post is archived at http://biggovernment.com/fgaffney/2010/02/24/can-this-possibly-be-true-new-obama-missile-defense-logo-includes-a-crescent/. Logan's can be found at http://loganswarning.com/2010/02/23/us-missile-defense-agency-changes-%20logo-to-obama islamic-crescent-hybrid/. "I will never state that Obama is a Muslim until I see him on his knees praying to Allah," Logan's begins, "but even if he is not the results would be basically the same. He is as pro-Islamic as they come."

The JBS's reluctance to condemn apartheid, Gaffney's paranoia about Islam, Cliff's detestation of the Jews, and the demonization of the Club of Rome is ridiculous, hateful, cartoon-crazy stuff, but it's all of a piece. And it resonates beautifully with themes that putatively mainstream politicians also play for the general public, blatantly pandering to its lowest common denominator, like Sarah Palin's politicization of her baby, Trig, who has Down Syndrome (any liberal, she insinuates, would have cold-bloodedly aborted him) and her talk of Obama's "death panels" for the elderly and developmentally impaired.*

Their message is clear: Liberalism may present itself as compassionate and caring and enlightened, but don't be fooled. Not only do its nagging, overbearing followers presume to know what is best for you, but the philosophy they subscribe to is vicious and totalitarian, no different in kind from Stalinism or Nazism. The conservative writer Jonah Goldberg struck some of the same notes in his influential 2008 book, *Liberal Fascism: The Secret History of the American Left from Mussolini to the Politics of Meaning,* with its memorable cover illustration of a smiley face wearing a Hitler mustache. The nanny state is transcendentally *evil.* Left to its own devices, progressivism will carry us down the same slippery slope that led to Auschwitz and the gulags. Just listen to Judson Phillips, the founder of Tea Party Nation, speaking at a rally in Wisconsin on August 6, 2011: "I will tell you ladies and gentlemen, I detest and despise everything the left stands for. How anybody can endorse and embrace an ideology that has killed a billion people in the last century is beyond me."[18]

To quote Hofstadter again:

> The distinguishing thing about the paranoid style is not that its exponents see conspiracies or plots here and there in history, but that they regard a "vast" or "gigantic" conspiracy as *the motive force* in historical events. History *is* a conspiracy, set in motion by demonic forces of almost transcendent power, and what is felt to be needed to defeat it is not the usual methods of political give-and-

---

* Ironically, so-called Trig Truthers have created a body of conspiracy theory of their own, in which Palin faked her pregnancy in pursuit of political advantage. I will have more to say about this in chapter 2, "What Is 'Conspiracy Theory'?".

take, but an all-out crusade. The paranoid spokesman sees the fate of this conspiracy in apocalyptic terms—he traffics in the birth and death of whole worlds, whole political orders, whole systems of human values.[19]

When my book *'Isms & 'Ologies: All the Movements, Ideologies, & Doctrines That Have Shaped Our World* came out in 2007, Tavis Smiley had me on his radio show. His first question brought me up short. "I couldn't help noticing," he said, "that one very important 'ism' is missing from your book's index—racism."

"That's because," I improvised, "I confined myself to specific systems of thought. I wrote about racist philosophies, but racism in general signals the absence of thought." I could tell he wasn't convinced, and to tell you the truth, I wasn't either. For what it's worth, that was when the seed of this book was planted in my head. Its topic, as I first conceived it, would be the role of organized hatreds in the historical arc of American politics.

As it's turned out, *The New Hate* is less about prejudice than it is about America's long-standing penchant for conspiratorial thinking, its never-ending quest for scapegoats. Hate groups have been active on the periphery of American politics since colonial times; many of them have exerted a significant, albeit largely unacknowledged, influence on its mainstream. Their targets haven't just been people of other races, national origins, and religious faiths (or lack thereof). Income levels and years of schooling, sexual preference, gender, and political affiliation have all sufficed at one time or another to mark a person as belonging to a group that is dangerously "other."

The most salient feature of what I have come to call the New Hate is its sameness across time and space. The most depressing thing about the demagogues who tirelessly exploit it—in pamphlets and books and partisan newspapers two centuries ago, on Web sites, electronic social networks, and twenty-four-hour cable news today—is how much alike they all turn out to be.

1.

The Paranoid Style of Hatred

"T is surprising to see how rapidly a panic will sometimes run through a country," Thomas Paine wrote in *The Crisis* on December 23, 1776.

Their duration is always short; the mind soon grows through them, and acquires a firmer habit than before. But their peculiar advantage is, that they are the touchstones of sincerity and hypocrisy, and bring things and men to light, which might otherwise have lain forever undiscovered. . . . They sift out the hidden thoughts of man, and hold them up in public to the world.

Though our country might not be in quite such desperate straits today, these too are "times that try men's souls," to reprise *The Crisis*'s famous opening line. In 2008, a decades-long pseudo-boom, one that transferred billions of dollars into the coffers of the richest Americans while average Americans saw their income fall or barely keep track with inflation, ended with a spectacular bust. The economy has remained in a swoon ever since, and the working class and the poor have been hardest hit by far.* In addition to their rising economic insecurities, many white, native-born Americans have taken alarmed notice of the accelerating racial and cultural changes affecting regions of the country that were once insulated from them.

America's politics and culture are increasingly polarized. The people who attend exurban mega-churches and relate the *Dred Scott* decision to *Roe v. Wade* truly don't have many points of contact with big-city liberals who regard gay marriage as the nation's most burning civil rights issue. Wars in Afghanistan and Iraq, the threat of terrorism, rising gas prices, the off-shoring of manufacturing jobs, and the terminal decline of once-great industrial cities have raised the nation's level of anxiety and alienation to the breaking point. And through it all, the echo chamber of twenty-four-hour opinion-driven cable-TV news and Web sites ensures that people's political predispositions are constantly reinforced. As Bill Bishop wrote of this new epoch in American life in his book *The Big Sort: Why the Clustering of Like-Minded America Is Tearing Us Apart*, "Americans were forming tribes. . . . Social psychologists had studied like-minded groups and could predict how people living and worshiping in homogeneous groups would react: as people heard their beliefs reflected and amplified, they would become more extreme in their thinking. . . . Americans were busy creating social resonators, and the hum that filled the air was the reverberated and amplified sound of their own voices and beliefs."[1]

If the election of America's first African American president was a source of pride for many, it also, in Tom Paine's words, brought many hidden feelings to light, and not all of them have been edifying. Viral, Photoshopped images of President Obama in an African witch doctor's getup, of Mrs. Obama with her face morphed into an ape's, of watermelons growing on the White House lawn, and of the president and first lady dressed like a pimp and a prostitute have been popping up in in-boxes everywhere—some of them sent by political activists

---

* Between 1992 and 2007, when the average American household's income grew by just 13 percent, the income for the top 1 percent of American earners grew by 123 percent; the income for America's top four hundred households swelled 399 percent (Economic Policy Institute press release, April 14, 2011, http://www.epi.org/economic_snapshots/entry/taxes_on_the_wealthy _have_gone_down_dramatically/).

who would describe themselves as conservative and mainstream. The October 2008 newsletter of the Chaffey Community Republican Women of San Bernardino, California, for example, featured a mock food stamp emblazoned with Obama's image, surrounded by buckets of fried chicken and wedges of watermelon. The group's president, Diane Fedele, was devastated when an angry African American member went to the press and her joke was widely misinterpreted as racist. "I absolutely apologize to anyone who was offended. That clearly wasn't my attempt [sic]," she declared, adding for good measure that she had once supported Alan Keyes.[2]

"I am an imperfect Christian lady who tries her best to live a Christ-like honoring life. I would never do anything to intentionally harm or berate others regardless of ethnicity. Everyone who knows me knows that to be true," Marilyn Davenport of the Orange County Republican Central Committee contritely declared in an e-mail in April 2011, a few days after she'd forwarded a family portrait of chimps, with Obama's face superimposed over the baby's, to her fellow committee members. The caption under the picture read, "Now you know why no birth certificate."[3]

It's easy to dismiss the lapses of these political small-timers; but what about seasoned pros who should have known better (and who undoubtedly did)? Laura Ingraham's satiric book *The Obama Diaries* was replete with jabs about Michelle Obama's ravenous appetite for ribs. "I've designed a whole line of Michelle Obama Fitness Apparel with Under Armour," Ingraham's fictional version of the White House social secretary Desiree Rogers confided in the pages of her journal. "It uses an all-new material called Expandex. As Big Mama back in New Orleans used to say: 'If the gumbo tastes bitter, throw more sugar in the next roux.'"[4]

In September 2010, an excerpt from Dinesh D'Souza's book *The Roots of Obama's Rage* appeared in *Forbes*; it argued that Obama, "the most anti-business president in a generation, perhaps in American history," can be best understood in reference to an article that his father, who disappeared from Obama's life when he was two years old, published in the *East Africa Journal* in 1965, called "Problems Facing Our Socialism."

"Incredibly," D'Souza concludes, "the U.S. is being ruled according to the dreams of a Luo tribesman of the 1950s."

This philandering, inebriated African socialist, who raged against the world for denying him the realization of his anticolonial ambitions, is now setting the nation's agenda through the reincarnation of his dreams in his son. . . . The invisible father provides the inspiration, and the son dutifully gets the job done. America today is governed by a ghost.[5]

Never mind that the "anti-business" Obama, who surrounded himself with such Socialists as Paul Volcker, Larry Summers, Robert Rubin, and Timothy Geithner, was the same president who was widely castigated for bailing out banks and big corporations like GM (the TARP program was enacted during the Bush administration but mostly carried out by Obama's). In an interview in *National Review Online*, the former House Speaker and 2012 presidential hopeful Newt Gingrich applauded D'Souza's "stunning insight."

What if [Obama] is so outside our comprehension, that only if you understand Kenyan, anti-colonial behavior, can you begin to piece together [his actions]? . . . This is a person who is fundamentally out of touch with how the world works, who happened to have played a wonderful con, as a result of which he is now president.[6]

And here's radio talker Rush Limbaugh—who wields so much influence over his tens of millions of daily listeners that he's been called the "titular head of the Republican Party"—spouting off about an ugly incident that occurred on a school bus in September 2009, when a gang of black kids set upon one of their white schoolmates:

It's Obama's America, is it not? Obama's America, white kids getting beat up on school buses now. You put your kids on a school bus, you expect safety but in Obama's America the white kids now get beat up with the black kids cheering, "Yay, right on, right on, right on, right on," and, of course, everybody says the white kid deserved it, he was born a racist, he's white.[7]

On August 4, 2011, on the eve of Standard & Poor's historic downgrade of the United States' debt rating, the Dow Jones Industrial Average plunged some five hundred points. Rush Limbaugh explained to his listeners that it was all a part of Obama's plan. "This guy obviously has got a new role model," he quipped. "Robert Mugabe of Zimbabwe. The next thing to look out for is for Obama to take the farms. Well . . . that's what Mugabe did, he took the white people's farms."[8] A year earlier, on July 2, 2010, during a show that his Web site transcribed under the headline "It's Payback Time: The Obama Economy Is Purposeful Disaster," Limbaugh had told his audience, "What the Democrats are trying to do is create . . . a perpetual underclass enslaved to the Democrat Party."

> Many people ask me . . . Who is Obama? Why is he doing this? . . . We're now governed by people who do not like the country, who do not have the same reverence for it that we do. . . . I think that he's been raised, educated, and believes on his own that . . . we have become as large as we are not because of any uniqueness or exceptionalism or greatness but because we've simply discriminated against the real people that made the country work, all the minorities. . . . Now it's payback time.[9]

A perpetual underclass *enslaved* to the Democrats. The specter of "slavery" has been a perennial theme in American political polemics, from rants against the British during the run-up to the Revolutionary War to Henry Ford's *International Jew.* "The crisis is arrived when we must assert our rights, or submit to every imposition, that can be heaped upon us, till custom and use shall make us as tame and abject as slaves, as the blacks we rule over with such arbitrary sway," George Washington wrote in 1774, revealing, perhaps, a guilty ambivalence about the peculiar institution that kept his beloved Mount Vernon going.[10] "The inescapable truth," Ronald Reagan hyperbolized in 1960, "is that we are at war and we are losing that war simply because we don't or won't realize we are in it. We have ten years. Not ten years to make up our mind, but ten years to win or lose—by 1970 the world will be all slave or all free."[11] Speaking at the Western Conservative Summit in Denver, Colorado, on July 9, 2010, the Minnesota congresswoman Michele Bachmann quoted from a letter that John Jay had addressed to the "Oppressed Inhabitants of Canada" in 1775: "We are determined to live free or not at all. And we are resolved that posterity shall never reproach us with having brought slaves into the world."[12] "What has transpired in the last eighteen months," Bachmann continued, is "turning our country into a nation of slaves."[13]

To indulge in a bit of armchair psychologizing, I believe Limbaugh's use of the word "enslaved" is telling. Since his own thinking is over-determined by his racial animus, he presumes that his adversaries' minds work in much the same way. The historian David Brion Davis has noted how nativist writings gave their authors the opportunity to push "the sins of individuals, or of the nation as a whole . . . off upon the shoulders of the enemy," where they could be "punished in righteous anger."[14] Or maybe it's not personal at all; maybe Limbaugh is just tooting on a dog whistle, sending a not-so-subtle signal to those who are wired to hear it that the world has turned upside down, that while millions of white people struggle to make ends meet, a black man lords it over them in the White House.

This phenomenon, of course, isn't remotely new. The scene on Limbaugh's school bus evokes the nightmare vision of the South in the days of Reconstruction in Thomas Dixon's 1905 novel, *The Clansman*, where "a white man has no right a negro need respect" and "the children of the breed of men who speak the tongue of Burns and Shakespeare . . . have been disarmed and made subject to the black spawn of an African jungle."[15] The film it inspired, D. W. Griffith's *Birth of a Nation*, gave the Ku Klux Klan, which had been moribund since the 1870s, a second life. At its peak in the 1920s, the revived KKK claimed more than four million members nationwide. "Against us," a spokesman proclaimed, "are all the forces of the mixed alliance composed of alienism, Romanism, hyphenism, Bolshevism, and un-Americanism which aim to use this country as a dumping ground for the fermenting races of the Old World."[16] Not to mention the Negroes, of course. And the Jews.

I can remember my mother telling me about the night—this would have been in Brooklyn, in the late 1930s—that one of her neighbors got drunk and shouted "Heil Hitler!" out his window. After that, her family knew he was a Bundist and could no longer look him in the eye. Though he was far from a right-winger in his economic ideas, Father Coughlin's radio broadcasts (I will have much more to say about Charles Edward Coughlin and his social justice movement in later chapters) are often pointed to as the most notorious example of anti-Semitism in the FDR era, but other anti-Semitic writers and activists enjoyed sizable followings too. For example, there was William Dudley Pelley, the publisher of the magazine *Liberation* and the founder of the overtly Fascist, uniformed organization called the Silver Legion (also known as the Silver Shirts or SS). Here are a few choice lines from Pelley's pamphlet *The 45 Questions Most Frequently Asked About the Jews with the Answers by Pelley:*

> 37. *Why did the Jews deny Christ?* Christ was the outstanding "Jew-Baiter" of His day. . . . Christ was identified as an "enemy" of the Jews; and the Jews know of but one way in which to treat their enemies: *Kill them!*
>
> 42. *How can we condemn or persecute people who cannot help having been born into the Jewish race?* We should consider that we are neither condemning nor persecuting, when we look squarely at the Jewish Enigma in modern society, recognize its fundamentals for what they are, and declare that after due discrimination, we do not want them further materialized in a country which recognizes the Christian moral code as all that epitomizes true spiritual greatness. . . . If we want a clean country to live in, we've got to be willing to do our parts toward its constant sanitation.[17]

The patently bogus "Prophecy of Benjamin Franklin," ostensibly transcribed from a diary that the South Carolina delegate Charles Cotesworth Pinckney kept during the Constitutional Convention of 1787, appeared in Pelley's *Liberation* around 1934. "I fully agree with General Washington that we must protect this young nation from an insidious influence and penetration," an impassioned Franklin is said to have told the assembled delegates.

> That menace, gentlemen, is the Jews . . . they are vampires, and vampires do not live on vampires. . . . They must subsist on Christians and other people not of their race. If you do not exclude them from these United States, in this Constitution, in less than 200 years they will have swarmed here in such great numbers that they will dominate and devour the land.[18]

As transparent a forgery as it is, racist publications continue to cite it today (and not just in America; the late Osama bin Laden referred to it in his 2002 "Letter to America": "The Jews have taken control of your economy, through which they have then taken control of your media, and now control all aspects of your life making you their servants and achieving their aims at your expense; precisely what Benjamin Franklin warned you against").[19] Pelley also devised a new explanation for America's Civil War, which began, in his telling, when Lionel Rothschild ordered Judah Benjamin to exploit the slavery question. Pelley's biographer Scott Beekman summarizes the rest:

> Lincoln, who hated the international bankers, began issuing paper money to break their power and, therefore, had to be killed (by the Jewish John Wilkes Booth). England and France, following Rothschild dictates, sided with the south while Emperor Maximilian arrived in Mexico in 1864 with two hundred million francs provided by the Rothschilds to carry out their program of Western hemispheric domination. Benjamin Disraeli then worked out a deal by which Napoleon III could have Texas and Louisiana, with the Confederacy's consent, if he sent French troops against the Union. The plan was foiled at the last moment when America's great friend, the Russian czar, sent his fleets to New York and San Francisco and put them at Lincoln's disposal.[20]

The poet Ezra Pound subscribed to *Liberation*; Pelley's ideas had a profound influence on his own thinking about banks and the Jews, and their echoes can be discerned to this day in the writings of Lyndon LaRouche and even Ron Paul. I will have more to say about Pelley in a later chapter as well.

Then there was Elizabeth Kirkpatrick Dilling, whose many books included *The Plot Against Christianity* (reprinted as *The Jewish Religion: Its Influence Today* in 1964), an exposé of the secret precepts of Talmudism, a subject that Robert Edward Edmondson was also deeply interested in. "Knowing that pitiless publicity is the only cure for public evils," he wrote shortly after he was charged with "libeling all persons of the Jewish religion" (the case was thrown out of court in 1938), "I started on a campaign to expose Jewish Anti-

Americanism and Talmudic Communism which has been called the 'Code of Hell.' "[21] Kansas's Reverend Gerald Burton Winrod,* the "Jayhawk Nazi," published the widely distributed magazines *The Defender* and *The Revealer*. In 1936, *The Revealer* printed a genealogy of Franklin Roosevelt that traced his ancestry to the Jewish Rosenvelts in seventeenth-century Holland. "Roosevelt inevitably draws upon his Jewish ancestry," the accompanying article concluded. "It is, therefore, as natural for him to be a radical, as it is for others to be true Americans. . . . HE IS NOT ONE OF US! This may also explain why he attaches so little importance to his word of honor, and has no hesitation in breaking his promises."[22]

None of it was new then either. Just as in other times of great stress and transition, Depression-era Americans were breathing an atmosphere that was toxic with fear and anger and confusion. Many of them were seeking not just a comprehensible explanation for their very real problems but a scapegoat, a villain they could blame them on. If Obama haters today see blacks and Muslims and immigrants where FDR haters saw Jews, in earlier eras the enemy was just as likely to be Catholics or Freemasons.

Slightly more than a century before the stock market crash that ushered in the Great Depression (on September 11, 1826, for collectors of significant dates), a would-be revealer of Masonic secrets named William Morgan was arrested in upstate New York. After a stranger paid his bail, he was never seen again; almost certainly he was murdered by local Masons who were trying—in vain, as it turned out—to prevent his book, *Illustrations of Masonry*, from being published. "Masonry is to the modern world what the whore of Babylon was to the ancient," its introduction read. It "is the beast with seven heads and ten horns, ready to tear out our bowels and *scatter them to the four winds of heaven*."

> Masonry . . . works . . . unseen, at all silent hours, and secret times and places; and like *death,* when summoning his diseases, pounces upon its devoted subject, and lays him prostrate in the dust. Like

---

* The Fascist villain in Sinclair Lewis's novel *It Can't Happen Here* (1935) is named Berzelius "Buzz" Windrip.

the great enemy of man, it has shown its cloven foot, and put the public upon its guard against its secret machinations.[23]

The outrage inspired by Morgan's untimely fate was so intense and widespread that a national anti-Masonic political movement took wing. For collectors of eerie coincidences, its first national convention was held on September 11, 1830, in Philadelphia.

A few years later, in 1834, the portrait artist and telegraph inventor, Samuel F. B. Morse, became convinced that the Vienna-led Holy Alliance of Catholic nations was gearing up for an all-out crusade against American liberties. "Our institutions," he wrote, are "at the mercy of a body of foreigners, officered by foreigners, and held completely under the control of a foreign power."

> Is not the evidence I have exhibited . . . sufficiently strong to prove to my countrymen the existence of a *foreign conspiracy* against the liberties of the country? . . . Is not the enemy already organized in the land? . . . *We* may sleep, but the enemy is awake; he is straining every nerve to possess himself of our fair land.[24]

Morse's hatred was visceral, but there was nothing new about it. His fears of foreign subversion had been drummed into him since his earliest childhood; his father, Jedidiah, had fulminated against Adam Weishaupt's Illuminati (still the bane of conspiracists in our own day) from his Charlestown, Massachusetts, pulpit back in the 1790s.

Fifty years after Morse's nightmares about a Catholic fifth column had come to naught, populist Silverites were attributing the nation's social and economic ills to a Jewish/English bankers' conspiracy that had achieved its treacherous ends with the "Crime of 1873," the Fourth Coinage Act that effectively demonetized silver. "So secretly was this done," E. J. Farmer related in 1886, "that General Grant, who signed the law, did not know it."

> The parties who concocted that law understood its purpose, however, and no doubt received their reward, whether it was in 30 pieces of gold, or more. They as completely sold out the nation, as Judas sold out Christ. . . . These conspirators have kept up their Cataline

assemblages ever since, and, backed by England, have their daggers ever ready to strike down the silver dollar.[25]

We've already heard from some of Roosevelt's adversaries in the 1930s, so let's skip ahead to Senator Joseph McCarthy. "How can we account for our present position unless we believe that men high in this Government are concerting to deliver us to disaster?" he fulminated from the floor of the Senate on June 14, 1951. "This must be the product of a great conspiracy, a conspiracy on a scale so immense as to dwarf any previous such venture in the history of man." In 1960 the Tulsa-based Billy James Hargis, leader of the Christian Crusade, warned that "segregation and racism" were an artificial social crisis "instigated by the Communists within America to add racial hatred to class hatred." The Communists, he added, "have more freedom in America than do the non-Communist, patriotic Christian-American people of America."[26]

Two years later Dan Smoot, a former FBI man and radio pundit, published *The Invisible Government*, an exposé of the pro-Communist agenda of the Council on Foreign Relations, not to mention such other subversive organizations as the Advertising Council, the American Civil Liberties Union, the National Conference of Christians and Jews, the American Association for the United Nations, and the Foreign Policy Association. "Modern 'liberalism,'" he said, "has abandoned American constitutional government and replaced it with democratic centralism, which, in *fundamental theory, is identical* with the democratic centralism of the Soviet Union, and of every other major nation existing today."[27] The Communists had already won.

Reading all these quotations out of context (and I've hardly scratched the surface of what's out there; I said nothing about the Yellow Peril, Islamo-Fascism, Satanists, blue-eyed devils, or UFOs, to name a very few other objects of conspiracist obsession), you'd think that America had ever been the plaything of wicked interlopers—that its leaders were congenitally weak-minded and corrupt, its military timid and inept, its citizenry complacent and gullible, and its vaunted free enterprise system neither enterprising nor free.

Most people are at least vaguely aware of the miasma of paranoid ideas that swirl around the extreme ends of the American political spectrum. Neo-Nazi white supremacists are of one mind with Louis Farrakhan when it comes to their thinking about the monstrous avarice of Jewish financiers; gun-toting sovereign citizen survivalists and antiglobalist anarchists alike presume that the U.S. government is deliberately poisoning its citizens through fluoridated water, bogus vaccinations, and chemtrails in the sky. What's new today is how far into the mainstream many of those themes have penetrated—or to put it more precisely, how far to the right the whole political current has shifted.

The New Hate is the same as the Old Hate—only now it's hiding in plain sight. Some of its themes may be subtly updated: the Hungarian-born Jewish billionaire George Soros stands in for the Rothschilds; ACORN and the Service Employees International Union occupy a space that used to be reserved for anarcho-syndicalism or international Communism. The New Hate's appeals to racism and nativism and fear are often subtly coded; those egregious Photoshopped images notwithstanding, the Tea Party and its Republican fellow travelers are more likely to deride the president as the protégé of 1960s-vintage leftists, a thuggish Chicago pol, an anticolonialist alien, or a crypto-Muslim than as a black man per se. For the most part, Obama haters prefer to take a page out of their enemies' book and cast themselves as the victims of reverse racism, as Rush Limbaugh did in his response to the infamous "wise Latina" speech that Sonia Sotomayor delivered in Berkeley, California, in 2001. Sotomayor had unapologetically laid claim to the notion that "our gender and national origins may and will make a difference in our judging."[28] Rush Limbaugh, who judges men and women by the content of their characters rather than the color of their skin, was appalled. "How do you get promoted in a Barack Obama administration?" he asked.

> By hating white people. Or even saying you do. . . . Make white people a new oppressed minority. . . . They're moving to the back of the bus. . . . That's the modern day Republican party. The equivalent of the old South. The new oppressed minority.[29]

On the eve of the November 2010 midterms, Obama told a joke on the hustings about how the Republicans had steered the car of state into a ditch. Now they're asking for the keys back, he said, so they can drive it again. "They can come along for the ride," went his punch line, "but they have to sit in the back." A chorus of Fox News talking heads took extravagant offense, saying that Obama was consigning Republicans to the "back of the bus." "If this is a racial metaphor," Jon Stewart retorted acidly, "you aren't Rosa Parks; you're Miss Daisy."[30]

Chuck Baldwin is a preacher, politician, and radio talk show host who ran for president in 2008 on the ultraconservative Constitution Party ticket and received Ron Paul's endorsement. In the summer of 2009, he published a column that revived a theme that hadn't been much heard of since the heyday of the Patriot movement in the Clinton years, one that is also touched on in the Oath Keepers' sixth and seventh pledges—the notorious FEMA camps. "That our federal government is building large numbers of 'holding areas' or internment camps seems to be an established fact," he wrote. "The only questions that remain are 'Why?' and 'For whom?' "

> At this point, the imagination can take us anywhere, but it is not a little disconcerting when the same federal government that is building these internment camps begins categorizing Christians, conservatives, people who support the Second Amendment, people who oppose abortion and homosexual marriage, people who oppose the North American Union and the New World Order, people who oppose the United Nations and illegal immigration, and people who voted for Ron Paul or Chuck Baldwin as "extremists," or "potential dangerous militia members."[31]

It is beyond Orwellian: Barack Obama, America's first multiracial president, is a racist, a man who, in Glenn Beck's words, harbors a "deep-seated hatred of white people, of white culture."[32] Liberals, progressives—the people who protested the Patriot Act and who are still lobbying the government to close Gitmo, an all-too-real "holding area"—are constructing concentration camps for conservative, heterosexual, gun-owning Christian whites. But as outrageous as it may be, there is nothing new about the idea. As far back as 1956, the passage of the Alaska Mental Health Enabling Act gave rise to rumors that the government was laying the groundwork for a northern gulag where its conservative enemies could be confined and brainwashed. The meme originated with Leigh F. Burkeland of the anti-Communist Minute Women of the U.S.A., who, first in a mimeographed broadside and then in a much-reprinted editorial in the *Santa Ana Register*, claimed that "this legislation . . . will place every resident of the United States at the mercy of the whims and fancies of any person with whom they might have a disagreement, causing a charge of 'mental illness' to be placed against them with immediate deportation to SIBERIA, USA!" Conspiracists as far afield as Scientology's L. Ron Hubbard and Dan Smoot fanned the flames.[33] The senator who finally steered the act to passage was, of all people, Barry Goldwater.

People are pattern seekers and storytellers; it's a fundamental aspect of our nature. We ponder events and try to make sense of them; we transform otherwise dry chronicles into narratives, with beginnings, middles, and ends, heroes and villains, and, most important, universally applicable lessons and morals. This is where myths come from, with their answers to questions about how the world was created, the origin of mankind and the conquest of fire, how cities and nations came to be, and why the gods so often lose their tempers with us.

The stories the New Hate tells are concocted out of those same kinds of primal materials. They evoke the snake in the grass and the kiss in the garden of Gethsemane; they call forth echoes of Ahab and Jezebel, idol worshippers who subverted a holy kingdom and brought the wrath of God down upon it. They scold us for our lapses and show us what we need to do to get back in God's good graces; they confirm our worst instincts about people whom we have already been culturally programmed to dislike. As such, they have an irresistible emotional appeal, and self-sealing as they are, their very familiarity seems to confirm their truth.

In its more objective manifestations, the systematic study of causes and effects, that same proclivity for storytelling provides a foundation for philosophy and science. At its least rigorous, it gives rise to sexist and racist pseudoscience—to anecdote-driven studies that purport to prove that girls are bad at math or that black people are genetically disposed to low IQs. Thoroughly discredited by the horrors of the Third Reich, the American eugenics movement has been mostly forgotten today (except, as we have seen, when the Club of Rome, "death panels," or legal abortion is on the agenda). But it did exist, and its racist fallacies provided a basis for American policy.

"To admit the unchangeable differentiation of race in its modern scientific meaning is to admit inevitably the existence of superiority in one race and of inferiority in another," Madison Grant wrote in 1916, in his hugely influential *The Passing of the Great Race; or, The Racial Basis of European History.* "Neither the black, nor the brown, nor the yellow, nor the red will conquer the white in battle. But if the valuable elements in the Nordic race mix with inferior strains or die out through race suicide, then the citadel of civilization will fall for mere lack of defenders."[34]

In 1921, Vice President–elect Calvin Coolidge reflected on the necessity of immigration restrictions in the pages of *Good Housekeeping* magazine. "Biological laws tell us that certain divergent people will not mix or blend," he wrote. "The Nordics propagate themselves successfully. With other races, the outcome shows deterioration on both sides. Quality of mind and body suggests that observance of ethnic law is as great a necessity to a nation as immigration law."[35]

Grant's and other eugenicists' findings were used to justify the Immigration Act of 1924, which cut the country's quota of immigrants to a total of 164,667 per year (less than 20 percent of the annual average before World War I) and then to 150,000 in 1927. The proportionate share from each country was set at "two per centum of the number of foreign-born individuals of such nationality resident in the Continental United States as determined by the United States Census of 1890."[36] By pegging the percentages to a thirty-year-old census, it guaranteed that the flow of Italian immigrants, which had swelled dramatically in the early twentieth century, would be cut by more than 90 percent; Jewish immigration from Russia and eastern Europe was cut to a trickle as well. Since Asians were already barred from naturalization or landownership by existing laws, they were excluded outright.

Senator Ellison DuRant "Cotton Ed" Smith of South Carolina argued for the bill's passage from the floor of the Senate:

If you were to go abroad and someone were to meet you and say, "I met a typical American," what would flash into your mind as a typical American, the typical representative of that new Nation? Would it be the son of an Italian immigrant, the son of a German immigrant, the son of any of the breeds from the Orient, the son of the denizens of Africa? . . . I would like for the Members of the Senate to read that book just recently published by Madison Grant, *The Passing of a Great Race.* Thank God we have in America perhaps the largest percentage of any country in the world of the pure, unadulterated Anglo-Saxon stock; certainly the greatest of any nation in the Nordic breed. It is for the preservation of that splendid stock that has characterized us that I would make this not an asylum for the oppressed of all countries, but a country to assimilate and perfect that splendid type of manhood that has made America the foremost Nation in her progress and in her power, and yet the youngest of all the nations.[37]

Ayn Rand is not a writer I often agree with, but her words on racism seem particularly appropriate in this context; I wish I'd quoted them in *'Isms & 'Ologies.* Racism, she said, is "a doctrine of, by and for brutes . . . a barnyard or stock-farm version of collectivism, appropriate to a mentality that differentiates between various breeds of animals, but not between animals and men."[38]

Racially inflected conspiracism surely influenced the decision to intern California's Japanese Americans after the outbreak of World War II, whether they were citizens or not. Lieutenant General J. L. DeWitt's official report on the evacuation noted that "because of the ties of race, the intense feeling of filial piety and the strong bonds of common tradition, culture and customs, this population presented a tightly knit racial group. . . . While it is believed that some were loyal, it was known that many were not."

It could not be established, of course, that the location of thousands of Japanese adjacent to strategic points verified the existence of some vast conspiracy to which all of them were parties. Some of them doubtless resided there through mere coincidence. It seems equally beyond doubt, however, that the presence of others was not mere coincidence.[39]

Congressman John Elliott Rankin of Mississippi was less politic. "Do not forget that once a Japanese always a Japanese," he remarked. "I say it is of vital importance that we get rid of every Japanese whether in Hawaii or on the mainland. They violate every sacred promise, every canon of honor and decency."[40]

In 2004, as more and more stories about seemingly arbitrary detentions and extraordinary renditions of resident aliens were coming to light and the civil liberty implications of the Patriot Act were, however belatedly, finally being discussed in the media, the Asian American blogger Michelle Malkin asserted her Americanist bona fides with the publication of her book *In Defense of Internment: The Case for "Racial Profiling" in World War II and the War on Terror.* Roosevelt and his people thought long and hard before they interned the Japanese of California, she averred, in what is perhaps the only full-throated defense of an FDR program or policy that has ever been published by Regnery or favorably reviewed in the *National Review.* Malkin not only praised FDR; she criticized conservatism's most sacred of sacred cows. "The most damaging legacy" of the $1.65 billion compensation package and formal apology that Ronald Reagan delivered to the so-called victims of the Japanese internments, she wrote, "has been its impact on national security efforts" today:

> The ethnic grievance industry and civil liberties Chicken Littles wield the reparations law like a bludgeon over the War on Terror debate. No defensive wartime measure that takes into account race, ethnicity or nationality can be contemplated, let alone implemented, without government officials being likened to the "racist" overseers of America's World War II "concentration camps." . . . a nation paralyzed by political correctness in wartime is a nation in peril.[41]

Amusingly enough, when Obama's Department of Homeland Security issued its report on the potential security risks posed by right-wing extremist groups in April 2010 ("Rightwing Extremism: Current Economic and Political Climate Fueling Resurgence in Radicalization and Recruitment"), Malkin was downright apoplectic.[42] This "piece of crap report . . . is a sweeping indictment of conservatives," she sputtered, sounding for all the world like an outraged member of the ACLU. "In Obama land," she added, in a less judicious spirit than General DeWitt's, "there are no coincidences. It is no coincidence that this report echoes Tea Party–bashing left-wing blogs . . . and demonizes the very Americans who will be protesting in the thousands . . . for the nationwide Tax Day Tea Party."[43] While ethnicity and race are appropriate reasons to target American citizens for special scrutiny or even to preemptively deprive them of their rights and liberties, Malkin believes, membership in groups that openly advocate violent attacks on federal officials is nobody's business but one's own—so long as the groups describe themselves as "conservative" rather than Islamic.

Kowtowing to Tea Partyism, more and more mainstream Republicans are throwing around incendiary words and phrases like "tyranny" and "slavery" on the campaign trail; candidates are basing their whole "brands" on their opposition to Sharia or immigration. The energies that some of them are summoning are ungovernable; when the Republican Party does regain the White House—if not in 2012, then at some future date when the pendulum of political fortune swings in its direction again—its first order of business will be to coax those unruly genies back into their bottles. Not all of them will go quietly.

You can see what might be in store for them if you lurk in conspiracist chat rooms and read the comments about Congressman Ron Paul, whose appeal extends well beyond the economic libertarians who are his base. Don Black, the founder of the white supremacist Web site Stormfront, was an early supporter of Paul's 2008 presidential hopes, as was Alex Jones, who has tirelessly promoted his views on 9/11 and the New World Order on his radio show, in films and videos, in books, and on the Internet.* Paul is a sitting congressman; he can toss those groups rhetorical red meat from time to time, he can borrow their inflammatory rhetoric, but he can't ultimately give them what they want without putting himself beyond the pale, or at

---

* On July 25, 2001, Jones went on the air and predicted that a "Reichstag event" was imminent—an attack on American soil that would be falsely blamed on a "bogeyman" like bin Laden, providing a pretext for the declaration of martial law (http://video.google.com/videoplay?docid =-1222445722544874066#). Of course, this does not prove that 9/11 was an "inside job," but it does show that Jones is consistent in his thinking.

the very least getting himself effectively banned from network TV. Even so, he has been playing with fire.

Brother Nathanael Kapner, an enthusiastic proponent of *The Protocols of the Elders of Zion* who claims to have converted to Orthodox Christianity from Orthodox Judaism,* hailed Ron Paul in September 2008 for his courageous sallies against the Jewish money interests:

> The shadow government operating behind the scenes of America is an elitist cabal of Jewish banksters headquartered in London. This shadow government, run by Jacob Rothschild and his son & heir, Nathaniel Rothschild, has no code of ethics, no moral compass, no Christian sensibilities, and certainly, no loyalties but to worldwide Jewry.
>
> Ron Paul has got his finger right on the aorta of the problem. In his proposed bill, HR 2755, Congressman Ron Paul seeks to abolish the Board of Governors [mostly Jews] of the Federal Reserve System. This would have made Ron Paul subject to an assassination attempt had he been allowed by the Jewish occupied press to be a candidate for the US presidency.[44]

But blowback was inevitable. Here's what another anti-Semitic blogger, Christopher Jon Bjerknes, had to say six months later, when Paul hadn't gone as far as he'd hoped:

> Ron Paul is a snake nipping at our ankles, whispering in our ears to gnaw on the apple and know of our deaths. . . . Ron Paul should be pointing his old finger at the Jews and decrying their ruin of America. Instead, he advocates the ruin of America.[45]

Paul's son Rand experienced some of this back-and-forth for himself when, flush from his victory in the Kentucky Republican senatorial primary in 2010, he shared his reservations about the Civil

---

* "I recall my parents taking me to my cousin's Bar Mitzvah at a farther part of the City of Pittsburgh, where I grew up," he writes in an essay titled "Why I Left Judaism" that can be found at his Web site (http://www.realjewnews.com/?p=180). "We entered into an old, musty smelling synagogue which had the Jewish Star of David everywhere. After only 10 minutes of being inside, I got very nauseated and wanted to vomit. . . . It was then at the age of 8 . . . that I knew that Judaism was a religion of death."

Rights Act of 1964 with MSNBC's Rachel Maddow, particularly his concern that it violated the First Amendment rights of private businesses to choose their customers (his father had said much the same things in a speech from the floor of the House, when he voted against the act's renewal in 2004). Blindsided by the firestorm of criticism that erupted in the national media, he swiftly backpedaled; the very next day he assured CNN's Wolf Blitzer that the Civil Rights Act would have had his vote.

"Did you catch Rand Paul on TV with Miss Weirdo Rachel Maddow?" the white supremacist David Duke asked his followers a week or so later.

> Paul let himself be kicked around by this perverted creep for ten minutes. He whined like a little schoolgirl when she suggested he was a racist. Now this supposed libertarian . . . cravenly praised Martin Luther King. This is the same King that referred to himself as a Marxist. . . . Today it is European Americans who are the real victims of massive discrimination.[46]

As if that weren't enough, the Libertarian Party of Kentucky strongly condemned Paul's "hurtful comments" from the other end of the spectrum, lambasting him in an official statement for his support of military detentions at Guantánamo Bay and his opposition to gay marriage. "Rand Paul is not a libertarian. . . . Rand Paul does not speak for us or for our party. We condemn all bigotry based on any and all factors."[47] *Not a libertarian.* Strong stuff for a son of Ron Paul, whose given name inevitably evokes associations with Ayn Rand (though he wasn't literally named after her; the name on his birth certificate is Randal). Then word got out that Paul had belonged to an ad hoc stoner fraternity in college, the NoZe Brotherhood, which was banned by the Baylor University administration for mocking Christianity[48]—and which once carried out a bizarre prank on a female classmate.[49] Seizing the opportunity, his desperate, bottom-feeding Democratic opponent ran an ad that asked, "Why was Rand Paul a member of a secret society that called the Holy Bible 'a hoax'? . . . Why did Rand Paul once tie a woman up? Tell her to bow down before a false idol and say his God was 'Aqua Buddha'?" Despite all that, Paul was elected handily.

When Matthew Scully wrote the speech that Sarah Palin delivered at the 2008 Republican convention, he quoted Westbrook Pegler's adage about heartland values: "We grow good people in our small towns, with honesty, sincerity, and dignity." Scully might not have realized it, but he had called up a disreputable ghost from conservatism's past. Pegler's words referred to Harry Truman, whom he had elsewhere called "thin-lipped, a hater, and not above offering you his hand to yank you off balance and work you over with a chair leg, a pool cue or something out of his pocket."[50] Pegler was so outspokenly anti-Semitic that he was dismissed from the John Birch Society; he greeted Robert Kennedy's presidential run with the hope that "some white patriot of the Southern tier will spatter his spoonful of brains in public premises before the snow flies";[51] and he once famously avowed that "my hates have always occupied my mind much more actively and have given greater spiritual satisfactions than my friendships."[52]

Old or new, that's a lot of hatred to take in all at once. It might be salutary for us to take a deep breath, set aside our rancor, and summon up that halcyon moment of September 12, 2001, when the whole country was "united as Americans, standing together to protect the values and principles of the greatest nation ever created," as Glenn Beck put it when he announced his 9/12 Project.[53] Our founding fathers bequeathed us nine American principles and twelve values, Beck went on to explain. The twelve values are honesty, reverence, hope, thrift, humility, charity, sincerity, moderation, hard work, courage, personal responsibility, and gratitude. The nine principles include belief in God, in America's innate goodness, and in the sanctity of the family; the right of dissent; and the all-important idea that "I work hard for what I have and I will share it with who I want to. Government cannot force me to be charitable."

Except for that last one, which strikes kind of a sour note, Beck's principles and values are anodyne and uncontroversial. As mentioned earlier in these pages, he pressed a book on his listeners, W. Cleon Skousen's *Five Thousand Year Leap*, that puts a biblical spin on America's founding. "It's the book Ronald Reagan wanted taught in high schools and Ted Kennedy stopped it from happening," Beck explained. "That should tell you all you need to know."

But who was W. Cleon Skousen? A former FBI agent, a part-time theology teacher at Brigham Young University, and, for a few tumultuous years, the chief of police of Salt Lake City (he was fired for overzealousness), Skousen rose to national prominence as an anti-Communist lecturer and writer in the late 1950s (an internal FBI memorandum described him as "well known to the Bureau . . . In recent years he has been aligned closely with the extreme right-wing such as the John Birch Society and has been characterized as an *'unprincipled racketeer in anticommunism'* who is *'money mad'* and who is doing everything and anything to exploit the subject of anticommunism").* Skousen's *Naked Communist* (1958) retailed the shocking revelation that FDR's adviser Harry Hopkins had provided the Soviets with "fifty suitcases" of classified materials from the Manhattan Project, as well as a huge quantity of enriched uranium (an accusation he invented out of whole cloth). He enjoyed a close relationship with Ezra Taft Benson, Eisenhower's agriculture secretary and the president of the Church of Jesus Christ of Latter-Day Saints from 1985 to 1994; the two were at the center of what became known as the Church-Birch connection, a wedding of apocalyptic Mormon theology and John Birch Society–inspired conspiracism—a minority movement within Mormonism, to be sure, but one that has had a profound influence on Glenn Beck, who joined the LDS as an adult. Skousen's nephew and Benson's son were good friends too. Glenn Beck's biographer Alexander Zaitchik relates how the two stirred up a panic in 1965 when they spread a rumor that the NAACP had dispatched thousands of black Muslims to attack the temple in Salt Lake City.[54] Ironic that Mormons—who have borne the brunt of so much intolerance themselves—would traffic in such calumnies, but perhaps that's not so surprising either.

In *The Naked Capitalist*, published in 1970, Skousen revived the idea that the Bolshevik Revolution had been financed by the billionaire Rockefellers and the Rothschilds, and he engaged in some of the same demonization of progressives—in particular Colonel Edward Mandell House (we will hear much more about House later)—that

---

* Ernie Lazar's report on the mythology surrounding Skousen's FBI career can be found at http:// sites.google.com/site/ernie124102/skousen. Alexander Zaitchik's devastating profile of Skousen appeared in *Salon* on September 16, 2009 (http://www.salon.com/news/feature/2009/09/16/beck _skousen/print.html); it is also a chapter of his book *Common Nonsense: Glenn Beck and the Triumph of Ignorance.*

would become Glenn Beck's stock-in-trade. He also introduced the Far Right to the scholarship of Carroll Quigley, a Georgetown professor (Bill Clinton was perhaps his most successful student) who wrote a number of academic studies of the influential Anglo-American clique known as "the secret society of Cecil Rhodes," "Milner's Kindergarten," "the Round Table Group," "the Chatham House crowd," "the All Souls group," and "the Cliveden Set." In Skousen's telling, this "relatively small but powerful group . . . has succeeded in acquiring a choke-hold on the affairs of practically the entire human race."

Quigley was appalled by Skousen's misappropriations and distortions of his scholarship. Writing in *Dialogue: A Journal of Mormon Thought* in 1971, he accused Skousen of "inventing fantastic ideas and making inferences that go far beyond the bounds of honest commentary" and of espousing a politics that "seems to me perilously close to the 'exclusive uniformity' which I see in Nazism and in the Radical Right in this country."[55] Undeterred, the John Birch Society's Gary Allen also made generous use of Quigley's work when he wrote his best-selling *None Dare Call It Conspiracy*—a book that is constantly cited in conspiracist circles to this day.

Skousen's name appeared briefly in national headlines in 1987 when the California Bicentennial Commission endorsed—and then abruptly un-endorsed—his textbook *The Making of America: The Substance and Meaning of the Constitution* (1985), which quoted a 1934 essay on slavery by Fred Albert Shannon that referred to black children as "pickaninnies" and contained the observation that the "slave owners were the worst victims of the system," burdened as they were with the care and feeding of their shiftless chattel.

In the spring of 2010, Beck would provoke a brief backlash when he endorsed another dimly remembered anti-Communist author whom I mentioned earlier in these pages, Elizabeth Dilling. Beck raved about the book she self-published in the mid-1930s, *The Red Network: A "Who's Who" and Handbook of Radicalism for Patriots.* "McCarthy was absolutely right," he exclaimed, holding the volume up to the camera. "Now he may have used bad tactics or whatever, but he was absolutely right."

> This [book] is from 1936 and . . . it talks about "Who were the communists in America?" . . . You really want to know who the real

radical communists are? The NEA! That's 1936, and they're talking about this new organization that is really nasty, that you really
have to look out for, the NEA. But everything this book has talked
about, they have mainstreamed.[56]

As Media Matters and a host of other commentators noted at the
time, Dilling went on to call Eisenhower "Ike the Kike" and labeled
President Kennedy's New Frontier the "Jew Frontier." David Duke has
posted the full text of her book *The Plot Against Christianity* on his
Web site, in which she dismissed the very notion of anti-Semitism.
"The cry of 'persecution,'" she wrote, "has always been used to cover
the crimes of the only people on earth whose very religion teaches
them that murder and enslavement and cheating of all other peoples
is a sacred right."[57] And here's a revealing quotation from Dilling's
Roosevelt Red Record and Its Background (1936):

Just as Socialism proposes to enforce sex equality and rob mankind of its natural birthright of an individual mother and father
and home, of belief in God and His commandments, so it proposes
to obliterate racial lines everywhere by enforcing social equality
and social intermingling and promoting inter-breeding. . . . I have
never attended a Communist Party mass meeting without observ-
ing the public petting of Negroes and whites. This is a deliberate
and staged policy. At one meeting three burly Negroes were paw-
ing their white girl companion, a college-type blonde wearing a
squirrel coat. At the huge American League Against War and Fascism Congress in Chicago, a Negro in front of me sat with one arm
around his white girl companion; with his other hand he stroked
her leg. . . . The studied, insincere and obsequious flattery by the
Roosevelts and their radical supporters of the Negro people is
without precedent in any *American* political party. However, it is
no accident but follows, as closely as other parts of the Roosevelt
Socialist program, the old, well-laid, well-thought-out plan of the
Marxists to enlist and use the Negro to change the American system of government and the entire social order.[58]

Decades later, Ezra Taft Benson would still be delivering much
the same message. "There is no doubt that the so-called Civil Rights

movement as it exists today is used as a communist program for revolution in America," he wrote in his 1968 pamphlet, *Civil Rights, Tool of Communist Deception.*[59]

Beck himself regards any movement that purports to advance "social justice" with extreme skepticism:

> Here's my definition of social justice: Forced redistribution of wealth with a hostility toward individual property rights, under the guise of charity and/or justice. . . . Progressives are good at changing words—for instance: "Federal assistance" has replaced the word "welfare"; "Welfare" replaced the word "handout"; "Subsidy" has replaced the word "self-reliance."[60]

For all that, Beck unashamedly donned the mantle of Martin Luther King in his pitches for his 9/12 Project. "Do not sit down," he exhorted his listeners. "Do not take a seat in the back of the bus. Sit at the counter. Risk peacefully, risk."[61]

On August 28, 2010, the forty-seventh anniversary of Martin Luther King's "I Have a Dream" speech, Beck mounted the steps of the Lincoln Memorial and exhorted the crowd that had turned out for his "Restoring Honor" rally to "turn back to God." Sarah Palin spoke too, praising patriots for "knowing never to retreat." Though Beck insisted the date was a coincidence, the symbolism was unmistakable: today it's the insurgent, antigovernment Tea Party, not liberals, that occupies the moral high ground. "The most racist people to ever live in America were the Progressives," Beck declares, pretending that the people who call themselves progressive today take their cues on race from the likes of Woodrow Wilson.[62]

Beck has scrutinized Obama and the public records of his "czars" for anything, no matter how tenuous, that might be construed as providing aid and comfort to radicals and subversives. As told in John Amato and David Neiwert's *Over the Cliff: How Obama's Election Drove the American Right Insane,* when the White House communications director Anita Dunn facetiously linked the names of Chairman Mao and Mother Teresa together in a high school commencement address, Beck was reduced to tears. "Is it a concern to any American that so many people now in and around this administration and this president seem to love a communist revolutionary dictator?" he asked.[63] Even so, Beck didn't hesitate to invoke Chairman Mao himself when it suited his purposes. "I was amazed to find that what we're experiencing now is really a ticking time bomb," he told a live audience at a Florida retirement center on November 21, 2009, "that they designed about a hundred years ago, beginning in the progressive movement."

> They thought, "You know what, if we just do this and this and this and this, over time if we do it in both the Republican and the Democratic Parties, we will have our socialist utopia." Well, I say again, two can play at that game. I am drafting plans now to bring us back to an America that our founders would understand. . . . We need to start thinking like the Chinese. I'm developing a one-hundred-year plan for America. A hundred-year plan. We will plant this idea and it will sprout roots.[64]

Beck, of course, wasn't the only right-wing luminary who had exhorted his followers to march on Washington. On November 5, 2009, Congresswoman Michele Bachmann invited Tea Partiers to gather at the Capitol for a "Super Bowl of Freedom." Bachmann, then minority leader John Boehner, Republican whip Eric Cantor, and conference chairman Mike Pence all addressed the crowd. *Politico* described the scene:

> Inside, Democrats were working to finalize a trillion-dollar health care bill. . . . Outside, on the grassy lawn just steps from where Barack Obama took the oath of office, an endless lineup of rank-and-file lawmakers and conservative All Stars—Bachmann, Rep. Steve King (R-Iowa), Family Research Council President Tony Perkins, actor Jon Voigt and Mark Levin, author of "Liberty and Tyranny"—demanded that the health care bill be torn asunder.[65]

Banners held up by the protesters read, "If Obama's Birth Certificate Is Legal, Why Is He Spending $100,000 to Conceal It?"; "Obama Takes His Orders from the Rothschilds"; and "Obama and His Marxist Buddies Are After Your Freedom." "You Lie!" accused yet another, echoing the South Carolina representative Joe Wilson, who had become a folk hero for fifteen minutes a few weeks before, after he heckled the president from the floor of the House.

Though she wasn't present in the flesh, Sarah Palin had already done much to stir the protesters' ardor. "The Democrats promise that a government health care system will reduce the cost of health care, but as the economist Thomas Sowell has pointed out, government health care will not reduce the cost; it will simply refuse to pay the cost," she had written on her Facebook page a few months earlier.

And who will suffer the most when they ration care? The sick, the elderly, and the disabled, of course. The America I know and love is not one in which my parents or my baby with Down Syndrome will have to stand in front of Obama's "death panel" so his bureaucrats can decide, based on a subjective judgment of their "level of productivity in society," whether they are worthy of health care. Such a system is downright evil.[66]

Never mind that under a strictly private system, millions of men, women, and children can't afford even minimal, never mind heroic care, that even those who can afford to pay their premiums (or have employers who do it for them) have many of their claims disputed or denied. Forget that private insurers can and do refuse to cover pre-existing conditions (which they define as broadly as the law allows) and have all too often contrived reasons to cancel policies once a subscriber becomes seriously ill. America's for-profit insurance companies are run on a strictly nonbureaucratic, wholly altruistic basis, Palin seemed to be saying, yet somehow manage to make money for their shareholders. The government, on the other hand, is a ruthless cost cutter, as evidenced by its penchant for squandering the taxpayers' money. Obama was trying to pass health-care reform at a huge political cost specifically so that people would receive *less* coverage, so that he could replace quality health care that cost taxpayers nothing with mandatory euthanasia.

Of course it didn't make any logical sense, any more than the hue and cry to "keep your government hands off my Medicare" did.[67] But "logic" and "sense" are completely beside the point when the object isn't to make people think but to frighten and confuse them so they won't think but merely react. And speaking of Sarah Palin's Facebook page, I can't help but recall what the actress and writer Deb Hiett posted on her own Facebook page after paying Sarah Palin a visit: "Be warned: it's like wandering through a hate farm that's just been fertilized with fear."

In his book *What's the Matter with Kansas?*, Thomas Frank memorably compared George W. Bush's America to "a French Revolution in reverse—one in which the sans-culottes pour down the streets demanding more power for the aristocracy." How did it happen that the people who had benefited the most from a century's worth of progressive policies—from antitrust and banking regulations to Social Security, Medicare, voting rights, farm price supports, and workplace and consumer protections—were so avidly seeking their repeal? How had so many millions been inveigled into voting against their financial interests?

"The country seems . . . like a panorama of madness and delusion worthy of Hieronymus Bosch," Frank wrote,

> of small farmers proudly voting themselves off the land; of devoted family men carefully seeing to it that their children will never be able to afford college or proper health care; of working-class guys in midwestern cities cheering as they deliver up a landslide for a candidate whose policies will end their way of life, will transform their region into a "rust belt," will strike people like them blows from which they will never recover.[68]

Frank argued that the Right did it by waving the flag of the "culture war"—by tarring liberals as effete, overeducated, amoral, and even satanic; by pounding wedges into America's long-standing racial, cultural, ethnic, and religious divides.

Richard Hofstadter pondered the same question when he was trying to make sense of "the pseudo-conservative" revolt of the 1950s and 1960s. "Political life," he wrote, "is not simply an arena in which the conflicting interests of various social groups in concrete material gains are fought out; it is also an arena into which status aspirations and frustrations are, as the psychologists would say, projected."[69] Status politics can be understood as "the effort of Americans of diverse cultural and moral persuasions to win reassurance that their values are respected by the community at large . . . Status politics seeks not to advance perceived material interests but to express grievances and resentments about such matters, to press claims upon society to give deference to non-economic values."[70]

"It is the tendency of status politics," Hofstadter continued, "to be expressed more in vindictiveness, in sour memories, in the search for scapegoats, than in realistic proposals for positive action."[71] He presciently noted that the "growth of the mass media of communication" has "made politics a form of entertainment in which the spectators feel themselves involved."[72]

Which brings us back to Sarah Palin, Rush Limbaugh, Glenn Beck, Michelle Malkin, Ann Coulter, Michael Savage, Ben Stein, James O'Keefe, Andrew Breitbart, Joseph Farah, Laura Ingraham, Debbie Schlussel, and so many other right-wing performance artists and impresarios. These crowd-pleasers well know how to exacerbate and tap into their listeners' primitive fears and feelings, their tribalism, xenophobia, racism, bafflement at high finance, envy, fear of the Devil, and resentment of their own diminished status in a topsy-turvy world that confuses, offends, and seemingly excludes them. They do it by evoking a primal narrative: that all was well until "they" came along and ruined things, "they" being both the impoverished immigrants and minorities who are stealing the jobs that nobody else wants and the billionaire elites, cosmopolitan Jews, and supercilious "progressives" who have made off with everything else—protected, enabled, and even coddled by a government that has forgotten and betrayed its real citizens. "Indignation," wrote Thomas Frank, "is the great aesthetic principle of backlash culture; voicing the fury of the imposed-upon is to the backlash what the guitar solo is to heavy metal."[73]

People who get their news from *The New York Times* and NPR might think that Freemasonry—whether the esoteric, cerebral Freemasonry of Benjamin Franklin and Voltaire or the homelier varieties most commonly associated with Shriners parades and charities—is mostly a thing of the past, but the Craft is still regarded with intense suspicion in some precincts, where it is believed to be blasphemous, occult, or pagan. Illuminated Masonry looms large in the imaginations of many religious fundamentalists and in a host of conspiracy theories, from those promulgated by the Islamic fundamentalists in Hamas to David Icke's bizarre Draco-Reptilian conspiracy, in which the British royal family, Henry Kissinger, and the Bushes alike are really shape-shifting reptiles from a distant star system.

Anti-Semites maintain a much lower profile in America now than they did in the days of Henry Ford, Father Coughlin, and *Gentlemen's Agreement*, but you don't have to dig deep to find stubborn revenants of old-fashioned Jew hatred. The days of publicly avowed racism—of Klansmen parading through town squares, as they did in the 1920s, of governors planting themselves in the doorways of state universities to block the passage of African American students, as George Wallace famously did in the 1960s, of White Citizens' Councils functioning in the open, as they did in the 1950s ("The Citizens' Council is the South's answer to the mongrelizers," read a pamphlet from the Association of Citizens' Councils. "We are proud of our white blood and our white heritage of sixty centuries"[74])—are mostly a thing of the past.

Mostly. Not too long ago, Haley Barbour, the governor of Mississippi, the former chairman of the Republican Party, and at the time a much-talked-about prospect for the presidential race in 2012 (he bowed out a few months later), endured considerable embarrassment after waxing nostalgic to a reporter from *The Weekly Standard* about his hometown Yazoo City's Citizens' Council, which he described as a force for moderation and racial equity. "Up north they think it was like the KKK," he said. "Where I come from it was an organization of town leaders. In Yazoo City they passed a resolution that said anybody who started a chapter of the Klan would get their ass run out of town."[75] A few days later, as pundits pondered whether Barbour had just rendered himself unelectable, he issued a clarification: "My point was my town rejected the Ku Klux Klan, but nobody should construe that to mean I think the town leadership were saints. Their vehicle, called the 'Citizens Council,' is totally indefensible, as is segregation."[76] But it wasn't the first time that Barbour's name had been linked to Citizens' Councils in the national media. In 2003, he had come under fire when he was photographed at a fund-raising event for segregated private schools sponsored by the Citizens' Council's successor organization, the Council of Conservative Citizens. Gordon Baum, the council's national president, told the political reporter Max Blumenthal that the imbroglio actually helped Barbour politically. "In Mississippi, one of the biggest problems he had was they thought [he] was a scalawag. So [the photographs] didn't hurt him."[77]

Not that individual politicians can't change and grow, as the country as a whole so clearly has. The late Democratic senator Robert C. Byrd of West Virginia would endorse Barack Obama for president when he was ninety years old. Byrd began his career in public life as an Exalted Cyclops of his local chapter of the Ku Klux Klan and vowed in a 1944 letter to Senator Theodore Bilbo of Mississippi that he would rather "die a thousand times, and see Old Glory trampled in the dirt never to rise again, than to see this beloved land of ours become degraded by race mongrels."[78] "I know now I was wrong," Byrd told an interviewer in 2005. "Intolerance had no place in America. I apologized a thousand times . . . and I don't mind apologizing over and over again. I can't erase what happened."[79]

But for every Byrd, who, however belatedly, acknowledged his wrongs, there are unrepentant haters like Rush Limbaugh, who, styling himself as a long-suffering victim of an overweening political correctness, wins points from his followers by testing its limits, playing and singing Paul Shanklin's novelty song "Barack the Magic Negro" on his show. And then there is Pat Buchanan, who responded to Obama's call for a "national conversation about race" during the uproar over Jeremiah Wright with a defiant op-ed piece titled "A Brief for Whitey." "It is the same old con, the same old shakedown," he wrote. "America has been the best country on earth for black folks. It was here that 600,000 black people, brought from Africa in slave ships, grew into a community of 40 million, were introduced to Christian salvation, and reached the greatest levels of freedom and prosperity blacks have ever known."[80]

Buchanan feels as put upon by pushy Jews as he does by ungrateful blacks. Back in 1992, his intemperate words about Jewish neoconservatives earned him a forty-thousand-word rebuke from William F. Buckley, who reluctantly dubbed his old comrade an anti-Semite in the pages of the *National Review*. Buckley knew whereof he spoke when it came to anti-Semitism. In 1937, in an excess of high spirits, four of his siblings burned a cross outside a Jewish resort in Sharon, Connecticut.

No, not everyone on the right or even the far right is an anti-Semite, a neo-Know-Nothing, or a racist, but haters aren't particularly rare or exotic either. The paleo-libertarian Lew Rockwell, an economic adviser to Ron Paul and the director of the Ludwig von Mises Institute, divides his efforts between energetic advocacy of laissez-faire Austrian school economic ideas and neo-secessionist Civil War revisionism. Rockwell has been blamed for writing some of the un-bylined racist, homophobic, and conspiracist rants that cropped up in Ron Paul's newsletters in decades past, though this choice passage was apparently written by Paul himself:

> I've been told not to talk, but these stooges don't scare me. Threats or no threats, I've laid bare the coming race war in our big cities. The federal-homosexual cover-up on AIDS (my training as a physician helps me see through this one). The Bohemian Grove—perverted, pagan playground of the powerful. Skull & Bones: the demonic fraternity that includes George Bush and leftist Senator John Kerry, Congress's Mr. New Money. The Israeli lobby, which plays Congress like a cheap harmonica.[81]

So after all that, what *is* the New Hate? It is a toxic brew of racial, religious, gender, and nationalistic chauvinism, as often as not buttressed by foundational myths about wily Jewish moneylenders, Masonic freethinkers and occultists, and two-faced Jesuits. Nowadays Islamic jihadists are frequent antagonists as well. These outsiders, it is said, are seeking to subvert the white, heterosexual, Protestant consensus and replace it with one or another of a laundry list of imported tyrannies—secularism, relativism, progressivism, Talmudism, Communism, one worldism—that at bottom amount to pretty much the same thing. If the New Hate sounds a great deal like the Old Hate, that's because it is.

Immediately after JFK was assassinated, before Oswald's status as a man of the Left had been fully assimilated, Max Lerner editorialized in the then stalwartly liberal *New York Post* that "when right wing racist fanatics are told over and over again that the President is a traitor, a Red, a 'nigger-lover'; that he has traduced the Constitution and is handing America over to a mongrelized world-state, there are bound to be some fanatics dull-witted enough to follow the logic of the indictment all the way."[82] All of those accusations that were flung at JFK almost fifty years ago have a familiar ring today.

Here is the New Hate, in all of its ugliness: In July 2009, an article in *Investor's Business Daily* described health-care reform as slavery reparations in disguise—"affirmative action on steroids, deciding everything from who becomes a doctor to who gets treatment on the basis of skin color."[83]

On May 10, 2010, Michael Steele, the then chairman of the Republican Party, issued a statement condemning Obama's newest Supreme Court nominee. Elena Kagan, he said, was an activist judge, clearly far out of the mainstream of American jurisprudence, and further still from what the founding fathers envisioned when they conceived of the Supreme Court. Consider, he said, her "endorsement" of Thurgood Marshall's outrageous statement that the Constitution, "as originally drafted and conceived, was 'defective.'"[84]

The defect Marshall was referring to was the Constitution's recognition of slavery as a legitimate institution,* something that Steele, though an African American himself, apparently considered to be above criticism or correction, because—Civil War, emancipation, and the Thirteenth, Fourteenth, and Fifteenth Amendments to the Constitution notwithstanding—it fell within the purview of the founders' "original intent." Of course Steele didn't believe anything of the sort; he was presuming upon his listeners' ignorance. He assumed they knew as little about Thurgood Marshall's judicial philosophy as they did about John Marshall's or for that matter Elena Kagan's; he hoped they would believe that Thurgood Marshall was yet another angry, well-spoken black man in a suit, like Al Sharpton or Obama's albatross the Reverend Jeremiah Wright—and that they would assume the worst of Kagan because of her association with him. Steele's skin color provided cover for his implicitly racist appeal. If a black man can accuse a civil rights hero like Thurgood Marshall of Mau-Mauing the Constitution, then anyone else can too. Steele—who lost his

---

* More specifically, the rule that counted a slave as three-fifths of a person when apportioning representation. The quotation came from a tribute to Marshall, under whom she'd clerked, that Kagan had published in the *Texas Law Review* in 1993.

chairmanship after one tumultuous term—was campaigning to keep his job. For all his talk of recruiting minorities into the Republican Party, he knew full well that it is white Christian men who pull its levers of power.

But race and racism are only a part of the picture. Though there are subtle (and some not so subtle) ideological distinctions that can be drawn between them, the New Hate of Newt Gingrich and Glenn Beck, of Michelle Malkin and Michele Bachmann and Ron and Rand Paul, of Tom DeLay, Sarah Palin, and Donald Trump (to name a very few of its best-known names) bears a familial resemblance to the America First isolationism of the Great Depression, the McCarthyism of the 1950s, and the Bircherism of the 1960s. Many of its themes—the danger of foreign-born people and foreign-minted ideas, the perfidy of international financiers, and the put-upon virtue of society's producer class—were sounded first by nineteenth-century populists and, going back even earlier, in the reaction of the propertied classes around the world to the bloody horrors of the French Revolution.

But its historical roots extend even deeper than that. When the Puritans first came to America, they feared Jesuit conspiracies as much as they did Indian ambushes. The *Monita Secreta Societatis Jesu,* or *Secret Instructions of the Society of Jesus,* was published in Krakow, Poland, in 1614. An obvious forgery, its style and substance bear an uncanny resemblance to *The Protocols of the Elders of Zion.* "My son," its speaker addresses the order's novices, "heretofore you have been taught to act the dissembler . . . to believe no man, to trust no man. Among the Reformers, to be a reformer . . . among the Calvinists, to be a Calvinist . . . and even to descend so low as to become a Jew among Jews, that you might be enabled to gather together all information for the benefit of your Order as a faithful soldier of the Pope." The order's principal mission, it says, is "to create revolutions and civil wars in countries that were independent and prosperous" that "the Church might be the gainer in the end"; the novice is reminded that "the end justifies the means."[85]

"The Oath of Secrecy Devised by the Roman Clergy, as It Remaineth on Record at Paris, Amongst the Society of Jesus," another forgery dating back to a 1689 publication by Robert Ware called *Foxes and Firebrands,* was widely circulated in America in the nineteenth and twentieth centuries as "The Extreme Oath of the Jesuits" or "The Knights of Columbus Oath." A few lines will suffice to convey its flavor:

> I furthermore promise and declare that I will . . . wage relentless war, secretly or openly, against all heretics, Protestants and Liberals . . . I will spare neither age, sex or condition; and that I will hang, waste, boil, flay, strangle and bury alive these infamous heretics, rip up the stomachs and wombs of their women and crush their infants' heads against the walls, in order to annihilate forever their execrable race.[86]

If we go back even further, to the fourteenth century, there were the terrible rumors about the Knights Templars—that they worshipped the Devil, defiled the cross, were adepts in Arab magic, and committed unspeakable sexual acts. The Templars, of course, were more than an order of knights; they had evolved into Europe's most powerful bankers. Perhaps ironically, considering all the conspiratorial accusations that have been flung in the Templars' direction, Anders Breivik, the Norwegian mass murderer, claimed to have been a member of an international anti-Islamic crusade, the *Novae Militae Pauperes Commilitones Christi Templique Solomonici*—the New Poor Fellow-Soldiers of Christ and of the Temple of Solomon.

What's different about the New Hate—what makes it new—is its farther-reaching influence, its heightened impact. There have always been those who believe that Anglo-Saxon genes are being diluted by those of the lesser races, that Catholics take their marching orders from the pope, that Christ-killing Jews are manipulating the economy, or that it's in America's best interests to turn the clock back to some mythical golden age when godliness still held sway. Amplified by the World Wide Web and the echo chambers of twenty-four-hour cable news shows, their unsavory obsessions have now become talking points for putatively mainstream politicians, who don't really believe them but are all too willing to use them to gain whatever temporary advantage they can.

It's not just the Right, either, though that is the primary focus of this book. Antiglobalist anarchists, 9/11 denialists, Islamic fundamentalists, Kennedy assassination revisionists, and Trig Truthers alike draw on its memes in their YouTube documentaries, podcasts, Webzines, and books; black separatists cherry-pick from its invidious racialist assumptions to buttress their own. The idea that the unfamiliar other is intrinsically hateful and demonic has been with us forever in one form or another; most likely, it will never go completely away.

Evolutionary psychologists have argued that a tendency toward "generalized reciprocity," in which economic goods are freely shared within kin groups and tribes, conferred a genetic advantage to our ancient forebears by promoting social cohesion. The opposite side of the coin of in-group altruism is an instinctive distrust of strangers. But even if our xenophobia and prejudice are innate (a highly debatable proposition), they come from a primitive part of our brains; just because we have those feelings doesn't mean we have to act on them. Our educational and political institutions should be dedicated to overcoming them, not encouraging them.

Most right-wing politics isn't conspiratorial; such a thing as principled, Burkean conservatism does still exist. Most of the loudest proponents of the New Hate employ it no less opportunistically than they do other themes from the culture wars. Once elected, they can be counted on to push the New World Order to the back burner along with abortion, school prayer, and creationism, so they can get back to the serious business of protecting and promoting the interests of big corporations. Some of their real aims—the privatization of Social Security, the elimination of Medicare and Medicaid, the gutting of food and drug and environmental regulations, the fight against health-care reform, the push for more regressive tax policies, and the general unraveling of the social safety net—take their worst toll on the very people who fight for them the hardest, the ones you see dressed up in colonial garb at tax day protests, who send their hard-earned money to patriotic-sounding Astroturf organizations, enroll in Beck University, and loyally cast their votes for Sarah Palin's Mama Grizzlies. What reels them in isn't the specifics of this policy or that but the irresistible logic of the narratives they are embedded in—tales that evoke the impending erasure of white Christian heartland values (and, at their most highly wrought, of white heartland Christians themselves). Behind those stories are an even older set of meta-stories whose antagonists still lurk in the dark corners of the collective imagination: British redcoats lined up in columns, ready to recolonize America (if not by military force, then by the invisible and well-nigh-irresistible power of high finance); wandering Jews and angry black men, thirsty for revenge; women who have forgotten that they belong in the kitchen and gays who've emerged from their closets, like vampires from their coffins, in search of new blood. Peel back yet another layer and there are witches and devils and changelings.

Picture the proverbial iceberg. The 10 percent of it that looms above the waterline is plastered with stickers and banners that tout family values and a strong national defense, fiscal prudence, and of course the liberty to get rich without interference from the state. But the most dangerous part of it by far is the 90 percent of it that you can't see. Innate or learned, sincere or cynically manipulated, the New Hate poisons political discourse and polarizes us even more than we are already. But it operates most effectively beneath the threshold of consciousness; it does its worst when it is unacknowledged or undiscerned. Subject its premises to critical or historical analysis, or merely expose them to the cleansing light of day, and they lose much of their power.

2.

What Is "Conspiracy Theory"?

Before I continue, I want to underline something important: there is nothing inherently disreputable or nutty about a belief in conspiracies per se. Conspiracies are what you get when people come together in secret to plan and execute criminal and subversive acts—which is something that happens all the time, in both the political and the private realms. A skeptical, questioning attitude about the official line, a cognizance of different ways to connect the dots, is eminently reasonable and healthy-minded; it does not suffice to make one a conspiracy theorist.

Thomas Frank's brilliant book *The Wrecking Crew: How Conservatives Ruined Government, Enriched Themselves, and Beggared the Nation* accuses libertarian antigovernment crusaders of deliberately "defunding" the regulatory state during the Reagan and Bush eras. "The chief consequence of the conservatives' unrelenting faith in the badness of government is . . . bad government," he wrote. "It is a classic self-fulfilling prophecy, and today we behold its fulfillment all around us." Frank's exposé of the malign consequences of unrestrained laissez-faire is of course thoroughly informed by his liberal ideology, but it is based on a rational premise: that when ideologues find themselves in a position where they can put their ideas into practice, they do just that. As Frank puts it, "Ideas have consequences."[1] Frank is neither unbiased nor nonpartisan; he detests his political adversaries, but he knows who they are: he sees them not as the reification of a supernatural principle of evil but as a specific set of political actors, with a clearly identifiable and objectively verifiable agenda. He is a muckraker, not a conspiracy theorist.

Jerome Corsi's *America for Sale: Fighting the New World Order, Surviving a Global Depression, and Preserving USA Sovereignty*, on the other hand—a book that hit the stores a few months after Frank's—describes the dual threat to America's independence posed by both elite conservative globalists and leftist Socialists, who are manipulating the worldwide economic crisis to achieve their secret objectives. "The ultimate goal from both the Left and the Right is to create a global reality for the future of the United States, in which a one-world government with a one-world currency will be created to supersede the sovereignty of the United States of America," Corsi warns.[2] *America for Sale* adumbrates a hidden conspiracy that stretches back for decades and a cabal that numbers in the tens of thousands. Its author calls himself a "whistle-blower," but as even the far-right magazine *Human Events* (which agrees with much of his political agenda) admits, he is a conspiracy theorist. "When I see important groups like the Swift Boat Veterans for Truth and the Minutemen get entangled in wacky conspiracy theories via their relationship with Corsi, I worry that it will hurt their credibility," wrote John Hawkins.

> When I see people like Joseph Farah, Phyllis Schlafly and Lou Dobbs promoting a laughable conspiracy theory about as credible as the ones about the Illuminati and the Trilateral Commission, it disturbs me to see them damaging their reputations when we may need their influence on issues like illegal immigration over the next couple of years. Last but not least, after making fun of some of our "friends" on the left for the wild conspiracy theories they've indulged in over the last few years, "Bush let 9/11 happen on purpose, rigged the elections, and is going to stick us in camps and rule as dictator, etc.," it troubles me to see a new "black helicopter crowd" being created from scratch on the right that's just as bad as the worst conspiracy theorists on the left. We're supposed to be better and smarter than that.[3]

When the words "conspiracy" and "theorist" are wedded together, they mean something different than just the sum of their parts; they become an epithet for someone who views the world *solely* through a conspiratorial lens, who reflexively interprets the daily headlines as the inevitable fulfillment of a cosmic scheme that was deliberately set into motion by clandestine powers long ago. "I cannot and will not accept the theory that long sequences of unrelated accidents determine world events," wrote Milton William Cooper in 1991, in his conspiratorial classic *Behold a Pale Horse.*

> It is inconceivable that those with power and wealth would *not* band together with a common bond, a common interest, and a long-range plan to decide and direct the future of the world. . . . I believe, therefore, that a grand game of chess is being played on a level that we can barely imagine, and we are the pawns.[4]

As the philosopher of science Karl Popper put it, the "conspiracy theory of society" is "the view that an explanation of a social phenomenon consists in the discovery of the men or groups who are interested in the occurrence of this phenomenon . . . and who have planned and conspired to bring it about."[5] Ocean liners don't blunder into icebergs in such a person's view; they are sabotaged or attacked by submarines, or their traitorous captains deliberately steer them into harm's way. Plagues are inflicted on populations with pathogens that are cultivated in secret laboratories. Political leaders and celebrities don't die from natural causes; their "suicides" and "accidents" are planned and staged. "We don't know whether the peculiar cancer of which Bob Taft died was induced by a radium tube planted in the upholstery of his Senate seat, as has been so widely rumored," wrote the John Birch Society's founder Robert Welch in 1959.[6] Or see, for example, this possibly satirical comment—sometimes it can be hard to tell—from a pseudonymous poster called Rapier, under an announcement of Edward Kennedy's death on the Web site *NowPublic* in the summer of 2009:

> Edward Kennedy was murdered. He was poisoned at the Obama Inaugural banquet. It was probably the final "bio-hit" of many that

surreptitiously preceded it. The sophisticated murderers of the 21st Century use biological attacks of various pathogens (including metals, chemicals, virus and bacteria, such as protozoan—which can lead to cancer) to murder, which are surreptitiously placed in food and beverage by bribed and often ideologically corrupted food preparers. Medical screens do not pick up the bio-assaults because they are not acute enough. It's the culminating effect that does the dirty work for the Gangster-Terrorists.[7]

Lurking behind all these tragedies is a shadowy "they" who profit from them (materially, strategically, and/or ideologically)—and who as often as not signal their presence by leaving behind numerological and symbolic clues that are as obvious to those in the know as they are inscrutable or seemingly insignificant to nearly everybody else. Here's Milton William Cooper again:

> The numbers 3, 7, 9, 11, 13, 39 and any multiple of these numbers have special meaning to the Illuminati. Notice that the Bilderberg Group has a core of 39 members who are broken into 3 groups of 13 members in each group. Notice that the core of 39 answers to the 13 who make up the Policy Committee. Take special notice that the 13 members of the Policy Committee answer to the Round Table of Nine. You know that the original number of states in the United States of America was 13. The Constitution has 7 Articles and was signed by 39 members of the Constitutional Convention. The United States was born on July 4, 1776. July is the 7th month of the year. Add 7 (for July) and 4 and you have 11; 1 + 7 + 7 + 6 = 21, which is a multiple of 3 and 7. Add 2 + 1 and you get 3. Look at the numbers in 1776 and you see two 7s and a 6, which is a multiple of 3. Coincidence, you say?[8]

This "they" might be people who share the same ideology—Communism, say, or atheism or progressivism or statism; more often than not, they are identified as members of an ethnicity, a religion, a nationality, or a race.

"I'm telling you that everybody who runs CNN is a lot like [Jon] Stewart, and a lot of people who run all the other networks are a lot like Stewart, and to imply that somehow they—the people in this country who are Jewish—are an oppressed minority? Yeah," scoffed the soon-to-be-dismissed CNN anchor Rick Sanchez while promoting his unfortunately titled book *Conventional Idiocy* on a satellite radio show on September 30, 2010.[9] Factually, his assertion was correct: there are more Jews in visible positions in the American media than their demographic representation in the overall U.S. population can explain, an interesting phenomenon to be sure, and one that conspiracists from Hitler to David Duke have made much of. But the deeper implication (which Sanchez apologized for—"Despite what my tired and mangled words may have implied, they were never intended to suggest any sort of narrow-mindedness and should never have been made,"[10] he said a few days later)—that all people of Jewish birth share the same agenda and are consciously working together toward a common goal—is conspiratorial.

"It has never been my intent to defame Jews," writes JewWatch .com's Frank Weltner. But it is precisely his intent, and he does it over and over again, as he goes on to prove before the end of the next paragraph:

> I do not, however, believe that Jews have an inherent right to dominate entire industries, societies, and governments where they are not the majority but represent 2% or less of the people. To allow this would be to allow the colonization of these majority cultures merely through the power of Jewish money to corrupt. . . .
>
> I did not bring the United States into many wars in the 20th century, but the Jews have done so time and again. Their stories and how they manipulated us into wars are inside Jew Watch where they demonstrate their personal responsibility for many, many non-Jewish deaths.[11]

Jews may constitute a vanishingly small percentage of the world's population (somewhere between two-tenths and three-tenths of 1 percent, depending upon what definition of Judaism the statistician uses), but they are astoundingly ubiquitous in the world of conspiracy theory. Abbé Augustin Barruel was the author of the enormously influential *Memoirs Illustrating the History of Jacobinism*, a book that purported to prove that the French Revolution was the culmination of a conspiracy that had begun with the Templars in the twelfth century and was ultimately carried out by the Illuminati and their Masonic tools. "Barruel's *Mémoires*," Umberto Eco noted in an essay on *The Protocols of the Elders of Zion*, "did not contain any reference to the Jews."

> But in 1806 he received a letter from a certain Captain Simonini, who claimed that Mani (the founder of Manichaeism) and the Old Man of the Mountain (grand master of the secret order of Assassins and allegedly a notorious ally of the early Templars) were Jews, that Masonry had been founded by the Jews, and that the Jews had infiltrated all the existing secret societies.[12]

Though Barruel never published either the letter (which is widely considered to be a forgery, probably sent to him by the French police) or the manuscript he wrote based on it, the idea of a Jewish-Masonic nexus would become a staple of conspiracy theory, enshrined in *The Protocols of the Elders of Zion* and widely promoted by Nesta Webster's *Secret Societies and Subversive Movements* published in 1924. Webster influenced Robert Welch of the John Birch Society in his turn, who came to believe that the Illuminati were the real "Insiders"—that the Communists were just one of their front organizations. Freemasonry and Judaism are the canaries in the mine shaft of conspiracy theory; whenever you see them mentioned in close proximity, you tend to know what's coming next.

Organized homophobia is usually associated with Evangelicalism and the Catholic Church—or with aspirants for public office who are pandering for the votes of religious cultural conservatives—rather than *Protocols of the Elders of Zion*–style anti-Semitism. But the other day I stumbled on a link to a Web site that had compiled a database of prominent gays and lesbians with Jewish surnames, "an exhaustive list proving, once and for all," it said, "that the radical homosexual movement in the United States is a Jewish movement. Jews created it and run it from top to bottom. They are pushing the perversion and degeneracy that is spreading disease, sin and sickness through America like a wildfire."[13] And here's the money quote from an essay titled "Freemasonry's Connection to the Homosexual Movement." I found it on a Web site called Heterosexuals Organized for a Moral Environment (HOME):

Are Masons using their power and influence to try to spread homosexual "values"? In the following enigmatic words, Pike* seems to be saying that Masons engage in homosexual oral sex. He states that an initiate "commemorates in sacramental observance this mysterious passion; and while partaking of the raw flesh of the victim, seems to be invigorated by a fresh draught from the fountain of universal life . . . Hence the significance of the phallus." As is his wont, Pike does not explain these words. For example, he does not spell out what he means by "this mysterious passion." But elsewhere in the book he twice notes that phallic worship is a part of their "Ancient Mysteries."

Not only does homosexual sex apparently play a role in Masonry, but homosexual orgies evidently do too.[14]

"A certain level of scapegoating is endemic in most societies," Chip Berlet and Matthew N. Lyons observe in their book, *Right-Wing Populism in America: Too Close for Comfort*, "but it more readily becomes an important political force in times of social competition or upheaval. At such times, especially, scapegoating can be an effective way to mobilize mass support and activism."

Scapegoating is a key aspect of conspiracism, an overarching political philosophy that is based on conspiratorial premises. No matter what its specific content, such thought systems, Berlet and Lyons note, share three attributes: First, conspiracism "assigns tiny cabals of evildoers a superhuman power to control events; it regards such plots as the major motor of history." Second, it "tends to frame social conflict in terms of a transcendent struggle between Good and Evil." Third, and perhaps most important, "in its efforts to trace all wrongdoing to one vast plot, conspiracism plays fast and loose with the facts.

"While conspiracy theorists often start with a grain of truth and 'document' their claims exhaustively," they continue, "they make

---

* Albert Pike (1809–91) was a brigadier general for the Confederacy and the longtime grand commander of the Scottish Rite, Southern Jurisdiction. The author of *Morals and Dogma of the Ancient and Accepted Scottish Rite of Freemasonry* (1871); Pike was reputed to be the leader of Palladism, a supposed satanic cult embedded within Freemasonry that was revealed as a hoax in the 1890s.

leaps of logic in analyzing evidence, such as seeing guilt by association or treating allegations as proven fact."[15] Given its obsession with the malign influence of elites, conspiracism is frequently allied with political populism.

Once again, I hasten to emphasize that populism is not necessarily a bad or irrational stance in and of itself. There are elite groups in every society who enjoy outsize shares of wealth and influence and who work hard (and frequently behind the scenes) to keep things that way. Consider the Hunt brothers in Texas or the Koch family in Kansas, who have underwritten conservative causes for decades; Richard Mellon Scaife in Pittsburgh, a very public scourge of the Clintons; or Howard Ahmanson in California, the heir to a banking fortune, who has lavishly funded far-right evangelical initiatives. On the other side of the aisle, as it were, there's George Soros, whose Open Society Institute has helped underwrite a panoply of progressive causes. Corporations and other deep pockets routinely buy favorable treatment from Congress and other branches of the government, through political donations, cronyism, and lobbying. The man on the street is right to worry about who really owns the government.

But when members of the elites adopt populist postures themselves to advance their own interests, when billionaires spuriously identify themselves with the people and stir up resentment of a faceless but nonetheless ubiquitous adversary—the Jews, bankers, Communists, secularists, Islamo-Fascists, blacks with hypertrophied senses of entitlement, freeloading immigrants, even their fellow plutocrats—a judicious dose of skepticism is called for.

The manifestly paranoid, conspiracy-minded Henry Ford toyed with the idea of running for president in the early 1920s. In 1992, the Texas billionaire H. Ross Perot mounted a third-party run for the presidency with a grab bag of progressive and conservative nostrums. In Perot's case, it wasn't his politics that were paranoid but his personality: he fatally damaged his credibility when he temporarily dropped out of the race because of a purported Republican plot to sabotage his daughter's wedding.

On March 17, 2011, floating a trial balloon for a presidential run in an interview on ABC TV news, the billionaire real estate developer and reality show star Donald Trump raised his populist cred by waving the birther flag: "Everybody that even gives a hint of being a birther . . . even a little bit of a hint, like, gee, you know, maybe, just maybe this much of a chance, they label them as an idiot," he said.[16] Though Trump was widely ridiculed, perhaps most devastatingly by Gail Collins of *The New York Times*—"In a potential Republican field that includes Michele Bachmann, Sarah Palin and Newt Gingrich," she wrote, "it's hard to come up with a line of attack loopy enough to stand out from the pack. But darned if Trump didn't manage to find one"[17]—he doubled down, perhaps heartened by his rising poll numbers. "There is a very large segment of our society who believe that Barack Obama . . . was not born in the United States," he responded on April 8, 2011. "For some reason, the press protects President Obama beyond anything or anyone I have ever seen. . . . Open your eyes, Gail, there's at least a good chance that Barack Hussein Obama has made mincemeat out of our great and cherished Constitution!"[18]

Just weeks later, on April 30, 2011, Obama himself pawned Trump from the podium at the annual dinner of the White House Correspondents' Association. The day before, Obama had released his long-form birth certificate, taking much (but by no means all) of the air out of the birthers' sails; the next evening he would announce to the world that a mission he'd authorized had successfully targeted and killed Osama bin Laden. With Trump in the audience, Obama offered up a deadpan synopsis of a recent episode of his *Celebrity Apprentice* TV show for examples of the kinds of leadership decisions that must keep him up at night. "Well played, sir!" he said mockingly, while Trump grimaced for the cameras, trying to look as if he were taking the president's gibes in a spirit of good-natured fun. His poll numbers plummeted within a matter of days.

Not long before Trump waded into the birther controversy, the former Arkansas governor and Fox News personality Mike Huckabee also a talked-about presidential contender for 2012, had dropped hints that he too had his doubts about Obama's Americanism, if not precisely his citizenship. "Growing up in Kenya with a Kenyan father and grandfather," Huckabee opined on *The Steve Malzberg Show*, Obama would have been exposed to dubious and even dangerous ideas. His "view of the Mau Mau Revolution in Kenya is very different than ours," he explained, "because he probably grew up hearing that the British were a bunch of imperialists who persecuted his grandfather."[19] Never mind that Obama didn't grow up in Kenya, or that he hardly knew his father. Huckabee's insinuation that it is un-American to hold a negative view of the British Empire is disrespectful not only to millions of Americans of Irish descent, who also believe that their grandfathers were persecuted by the English, but to the founding fathers, who famously took up arms against English tyranny.

Conspiracy theories tend to be grandiose and unwieldy and inherently unfalsifiable. Correlation is mistaken for causality, causes are deduced from effects; the logical structure of their arguments is frequently circular or tautological. "One reason for concluding these three buildings were brought down by explosives," the theologian and 9/11 Truth activist David Ray Griffin wrote of the collapse of 1, 2, and 7 World Trade Center, "is the very fact that they did collapse."[20]

"How much the whole existence of these people is based on a permanent falsehood is proved in a unique way by *The Protocols of the Elders of Zion*, which are so violently repudiated by the Jews," Adolf Hitler wrote in *Mein Kampf*. "With groans and moans the *Frankfurter Zeitung* repeats again and again that these are forgeries. This alone is evidence in favor of their authenticity. What many Jews unconsciously wish to do is here clearly set forth."[21] If A, then B. If the Jews are wicked, murderous liars, then they would strenuously object to being characterized as wicked, murderous liars. QED. Never mind that the syllogism would work equally well if premise A were the abiding goodness and truthfulness of the Jews; the proposition is hatred, after all.

"A distinctive feature of conspiracy theories is their self-sealing quality," Cass Sunstein and Adrian Vermeule observed in their 2008 monograph, "Conspiracy Theories." "Conspiracy theorists are not likely to be persuaded by an attempt to dispel their theories; they may even characterize that very attempt as further proof of the conspiracy."[22] Sunstein and Vermeule proposed that one way governments could correct those groups' "crippled epistemologies" was by deploying surrogates to "cognitively infiltrate" them and introduce the antibodies of new ideas.

Sunstein was still a law professor when his paper was published, and it made a relatively small splash at the time, but after Obama appointed him administrator of the White House Office of Information and Regulatory Affairs, it began to attract considerable attention. The cognitive infiltration that he and his co-writer had proposed amounted to deploying chat room trolls and pseudonymous bloggers to chip away at the conspiratorial consensus—not exactly cloak-and-dagger stuff, but hardly aboveboard or ethical either. Bush's White House had deservedly taken flack when it paid friendly political columnists and conservative personalities such as Armstrong Williams and Maggie Gallagher under the table to tout policies that they would have supported anyway. Liberal commentators like *Salon*'s Glenn Greenwald understandably saw Sunstein's "spine-chilling proposal" in much the same light.[23] Not that there's any evidence that the plan was ever put into practice—but then again, there wouldn't be, would there? Inadvertently but completely predictably, the hapless academics had given birth to a new conspiracy theory: that the Obama administration was conspiring to quash conspiratorial thinking by any means. Right-leaning commentators, who regarded themselves as Sunstein's targets, took it personally. "Top Obama Czar: Infiltrate All 'Conspiracy Theorists,'" screamed the headline in *World NetDaily*. "Among the beliefs Sunstein would ban," *WND* continued, "is advocating that the theory of global warming is a deliberate fraud."[24]

And speaking of global climate change, few if any mainstream figures have signed on to the notion that the High Frequency Active Auroral Research Program, or HAARP, the array of antennas in Gakona, Alaska, that the military uses to study the ionosphere, could be responsible for devastating earthquakes in Sichuan, Haiti, Chile, and Japan, a nonsensical idea that sounds like an over-the-top conceit from a James Bond movie but that has cropped up in venues as far-flung as a Web site controlled by the leftist government of Hugo Chávez and in white supremacist chat rooms in the United States (I've blogged about the rumors and was interviewed about them on Russian TV). Many Republicans are so skeptical of environmentalists and their perceived antibusiness agenda that they dismiss the idea that human activities could even alter the weather, never mind cause earthquakes, as not only unscientific but a conspiracy in its own right.

That is because, like the conspiracy theorists that they insist they're not, they think in circles, conflating consequences and causes. If anthropogenic climate change were real, it would necessitate a global response, which would inevitably empower internationalist institutions. Anything that's a boon to one world government must be part of a one world conspiracy. That's how Glenn Beck sees it. In 2007, he produced a TV special called *Exposed: The Climate of Fear.* "Mr. Apocalypse," Alexander Zaitchik wrote, "saw the end of the world in everything from Mexican gang violence to Islamic extremism. But in climate change, Beck saw only media hype facilitating a fascistic liberal power grab that was pushing the world closer to the New World Order of his nightmares. . . . 'Al Gore's not going to be rounding up Jews and exterminating them,' Beck explained. 'It's the same tactic, however. The goal is different. The goal is globalization. The goal is global carbon tax. The goal is the United Nations running the world.' "[25]

Thus "Climategate"—the pseudo-scandal that erupted in the fall of 2009 when hacked e-mails between scientists at the Climatic Research Unit at the University of East Anglia were made public. Some of the e-mails singled out global-warming denialists by name and disparaged them. More embarrassing still, there was chatter about using statistical legerdemain to obfuscate the occasional odd trend or outlier that a denialist might seize on and present out of context to undermine a study's overall conclusions. Embarrassing stuff to be sure—and a boon to true believers (or nonbelievers).

As early as 2003, Senator James Inhofe of Oklahoma, then chairman of the Senate Committee on the Environment and Public Works, had reached the conclusion that global warming might be "the greatest hoax ever perpetrated on the American people."[26] Upon the release of the Climategate e-mails he swiftly demanded a congressional investigation of what he called "the greatest scientific scandal of our generation."[27]

Congresswoman Michele Bachmann's brother is a "certified" meteorologist, and "he said there is nothing to this global warming phenomenon. . . . The cap-and-trade legislation," Bachmann stated, "is something that we all need to be very worried about, because what it would do in effect is give government the right to control almost every aspect of our lives."[28] "I want people in Minnesota armed and dangerous on this issue of the energy tax because we need to fight back," she demagogued in a radio interview. "Thomas Jefferson told us 'having a revolution every now and then is a good thing,' and the people—we the people—are going to have to fight back hard if we're not going to lose our country. And I think this has the potential of changing the dynamic of freedom forever in the United States."[29]

Note how Bachmann uncategorically dismisses the conclusions of the majority of the world's climate scientists but still makes a point of emphasizing that her brother is a *certified* meteorologist.* Bachmann's selective deference to academic authority brings Richard Hofstadter to mind (as so much else does too when the subject is willful political irrationality). "One of the impressive things about paranoid literature," he wrote, "is the contrast between its fantasied conclusions and the almost touching concern with factuality it invariably shows. It produces heroic strivings for evidence to prove that the unbelievable is the only thing that can be believed."[30] The 9/11 Truthers pay extravagant obeisance to science too, touting the academic qualifications of the handful of physicists and structural engineers who have signed on to their movement and ignoring the 99.9 percent of their peers who disagree with them.

Conspiracists obsessively balance every equation and tie off every loose end; they have zero tolerance for gray spaces and lingering questions, for contingencies, accidents, and unintended consequences. The strange story that Sarah Palin told about the circumstances of her fifth child Trig's birth, involving as it did a long plane flight from Texas to Alaska *after* her water broke, combined with photographs taken near the birth date in which her stomach appears to be flat, prompted rumors that Trig was really her teenage daughter Bristol's child (Sarah Palin wouldn't have been the first mother to pass off an

---

* An article in the March 30, 2010, *New York Times* sheds some light on the matter. As it turns out, most meteorologists and climate scientists are not on the same page at all when it comes to global warming: "Climatologists, who study weather patterns over time, almost universally endorse the view that the earth is warming and that humans have contributed to climate change. There is less of a consensus among meteorologists, who predict short-term weather patterns. . . . A study released . . . by researchers at George Mason University and the University of Texas at Austin found that only about half of the 571 television weathercasters surveyed believed that global warming was occurring and fewer than a third believed that climate change was 'caused mostly by human activities.'"

illegitimate grandchild as her own). The story passed from the realm of idle gossip to potential political scandal after she was nominated as John McCain's running mate, even after the revelation that Bristol was pregnant made it seem much less likely that she could have given birth to Trig just months before. The blogger Andrew Sullivan in particular became a thorn in Palin's side, with his incessant demands that Palin release medical and other records that would confirm that the birth took place under precisely the circumstances that she said it did.*

By March 2011, when Professor Brad Scharlott of Northern Kentucky University released a pseudo-academic paper on the Internet, "Palin, the Press, and the Fake Pregnancy Rumor: Did a Spiral of Silence Shut Down the Story?," the gossip had graduated to a full-blown conspiracy theory, whose proponents had even been dubbed with a catchy name: Trig Truthers (many of whom, like 9/11 Truthers, are partisans of the Left—proof that conspiracy theories aren't an exclusive foible of conservatives).[31] If we apply Occam's razor, the simplest and hence most likely explanation of the inconsistencies in Palin's story is that it wasn't precisely true—that she exaggerated or invented details to make herself look more intrepid than she really was and her self-mythologizing went off the rails. But seeing what political hay she'd made out of Trig, Trig Truthers made the leap into conspiracy theory. Deriving causes from effects, they concluded that the whole matter must have been deliberately stage-managed from the very beginning, with the cooperation of countless doctors, journalists, neighbors, family members, and colleagues.

People who believe that government agents in blimps are tape-recording their innermost thoughts are usually trafficking in conspiracy theory; so are people who relate current events to the end-time prophecies of the New Testament book of Revelation (as in the mega-best-selling Left Behind series of novels by Tim LaHaye and Jerry Jenkins). In *Right-Wing Populism in America*, Berlet and Lyons describe

---

* Sullivan has written innumerable negative posts and articles about Palin. His November 22, 2009, *Sunday Times* review of her book *Going Rogue* provides a fair summary of his issues with her (http://www.timesonline.co.uk/tol/comment/columnists/andrew_sullivan/article6926728 .ece). As Ahab-like as Sullivan has been in Palin's pursuit, he is very far from a conspiracy theorist, in that he doesn't impose his own narrative on her story; he may be unchivalrous, but he is not at all delusional.

how the millennialist narrative provides a template for one familiar conspiracist scenario:

> A powerful and charismatic agent of the Devil—the Antichrist—comes to earth along with his ally—the False Prophet. They appear disguised in the form of widely respected political and religious leaders. Promising peace and prosperity, these leaders launch a popular campaign to build a one-world government and a one-world religion. Many Christians are fooled, but a few recognize that these leaders are the prophesied Antichrist and the False Prophet, and thus actually Satanic traitors. Agents of the Antichrist try to force devout Christians to accept the Mark of the Beast (sometimes the number 666) which would mean they reject Christ. A wave of political and religious repression sweeps the world, with devout Christians rounded up and persecuted for their beliefs. Christians with this view read the book of Revelation as a warning about a government conspiracy and betrayal by trusted political and religious leaders in the End Times. A secular version of this narrative appears in conspiracy theories about liberal collectivists building a global new world order through the United Nations.[32]

This is in large part the story that Pat Robertson told in his 1991 best seller, *The New World Order*, in which, seamlessly melding John Birch Society conspiracism with Christian eschatology, he described the "invisible cord" that bound together the last two hundred years of history, from the eighteenth-century secret society the Illuminati to the looming Communist takeover of the world:

> A single thread runs from the White House to the State Department to the Council on Foreign Relations to the Trilateral Commission to secret societies to extreme New Agers. There must be a new world order. It must eliminate national sovereignty. There must be world government, a world police force, world courts, world banking and currency, and a world elite in charge of it all. To some there must be a complete redistribution of wealth; to others there must be an elimination of Christianity, to some extreme New Agers there must be the deaths of two or three billion people in the Third World by the end of this decade.[33]

Conspiracy theory is moralistic; it describes an ongoing battle between the forces of wickedness and those of virtue (though the good are often so naive that they fail to realize that they are even at war). Conspiracy theory is monistic. As Seymour Martin Lipset and Earl Raab noted in their book *The Politics of Unreason*, it is "typically distinguished by its recurrent and explicit advocacy of 'simplism'; that is, the unambiguous ascription of single causes and remedies for multifactored phenomena."[34] Conspiracy theory is magical: its antagonists have superhuman powers of prognostication and the ability to influence at a distance; they make use of esoteric curses and spells and mysterious symbols and equations.

Conspiracy theory flatters, congratulates, and exalts the conspiracist, who is gutsy and clever enough to crack the code, to see things that others don't, to break out of the matrix. The conspiracist discerns the subtle interconnections between the Nizari Assassins and the Templars and the Masons, the Bilderbergers and the Rockefellers, the Jewish bankers and the UN; between Wilsonian Progressivism, 1960s radicalism, and Barack Obama. To do this, he or she employs the skills of the historian, the linguist, the librarian, the semiologist, the detective, the psychologist, and the philologist.

The conspiracist has a scholarly command of a vast alternative library of specialized literature—most of it written by his or her fellow conspiracists. In Richard Grenier's oft-quoted phrase, "Conspiracy theory is the sophistication of the ignorant." Writ large, the conspiracist regards him- or herself not only as a savant but as a savior, a political or religious messiah, whose knowledge can restore and redeem the world—one reason that conspiracism and cultism are such frequent consorts. Jane Kramer describes a militiaman's descent into grandiose delusions in her book *Lone Patriot: The Short Career of an American Militiaman*:

> He could sit in the woods, alone with his computer, and log on to the Patriot Web sites, and see his name. He could tap a key and learn everything he needed to know about the world from "experts" who were counting on him, as he often said, to "share the intel." The world, in fact, leapt out at him from his small screen. He was privy to David Rockefeller's dark strategies. He was an instant specialist on the Federal Reserve. He was on intimate terms with the

Joint Chiefs and the Jewish bankers. He was a ranking member of the global village and never mind *whose* village it was, or whether he had the experience or the education or the context or even the capacity to evaluate the words he read and the pictures he saw. The illusion held. He lived in a kind of unsourced-data fugue. . . . The more connected to the world he felt, the more isolated from the world he became.[35]

Writing about the origins of the John Birch Society in his book *Before the Storm*, Rick Perlstein described how Robert Welch painstakingly put the pieces together and came to the conclusion that the United States had knowingly "turned over rule of China's four hundred million people" to Mao, "Stalin's stooge"—and then to an even more distressing corollary truth: that President Eisenhower himself was a traitor. In 1958, in a privately circulated edition of his book *The Politician* (the line would be expurgated from its later editions), Welch wrote, "My firm belief that Dwight Eisenhower is a dedicated, conscious agent of the Communist conspiracy is based on an accumulation of detailed evidence so extensive and so palpable that it seems to me to put this conviction beyond any reasonable doubt."*

"If every American knew this story," Perlstein summarized Welch's thinking, "how ready everyone would be to do what was right! If he recruited enough people to *explain* the conspiracy . . . the conspiracy could not work."[36] Welch's blatant conspiracism disturbed his more pragmatic ally William F. Buckley. "I hope the Society thrives," Buckley editorialized in his *National Review* on April 22, 1961, "provided, of course, it resists such false assumptions as that a man's subjective motives can automatically be deduced from the objective consequences of his acts." Buckley would convince Barry Goldwater to repudiate Welch, if not the JBS, when he ran for president.

All that said—and as conspiracists are always quick to point out—events can and do occur that put even the wildest and most sangui-

---

* The independent researcher Ernie Lazar has amassed a huge database of material about the extreme right wing in America (http://sites.google.com/site/ernie124102/home). He provides comparisons of the published and unpublished texts of *The Politician* in a posting at http://www.freerepublic.com/focus/f-news/972500/posts.

nary imaginings of conspiracy theorists to shame. It wasn't so long ago that millions of Jews and hundreds of thousands of Romanies, Jehovah's Witnesses, homosexuals, mentally and physically disabled people, and other designated enemies of the Nazi regime were secretly exterminated in death factories. Once upon a time a semen stain on an intern's dress almost brought down the president of the United States. Tobacco companies cynically suppressed scientific evidence about the dangers of smoking for decades. Roman Catholic plotters tried to blow up the English king and parliament in 1605. Lucius Sergius Catilina's plots against the Roman state were dramatically exposed by Cicero in 63 B.C.E.

But when a conspiracy is said to unfold over centuries or millennia, when none of its myriads of preternaturally powerful participants ever betray their comrades or accidentally leave forensic or documentary traces behind, when its goals are as vague and amorphous as "the destruction of freedom," or to "rule the world," a line has been crossed. "The first distinctive element of conspiracy theory is its *comprehensive* nature," wrote Lipset and Raab. "The typical conspiracy theory extends in space: it is international in scope: it extends in time: it stretches back in history and promises to stretch ahead interminably."[37]

Conspiracy theories themselves often add up to a kind of misbegotten, debased form of theology—one that begins with a set of suppositions and then reverse engineers a fantastical version of reality that comports with them. History does not dispute, for example, the fact that Vladimir Lenin's mother's father was Jewish. But in Henry Ford's telling, this genealogical detail provides the key not only to Lenin's entire character and political philosophy but to the vicissitudes of the former Russian Empire circa 1920 and to the historical development of Bolshevism worldwide. Lenin's *wife* is Jewish, and his children all speak Yiddish, Ford insists, a little hysterically. Russia's yeshivas are the recipients of lavish subsidies from the Bolshevik state:

> The Bolsheviks immediately took over *all the Hebrew schools* and continued them as they were and laid down a rule that the *ancient Hebrew language* should be taught in them. The ancient Hebrew language is the vehicle of the deeper secrets of the World Program.

And for the Gentile Russian children? "Why," said these gentle Jewish educators, "we will teach them sex knowledge. We will brush out of their minds the cobwebs. They must learn the truth about things!" with consequences that are too pitiable to narrate.[38]

Viewed through Ford's monistic frame, Lenin's grandfather's one-eighth contribution of Jewish "genes" was sufficient to neutralize the very Russianness of the Russian Revolution, to reduce it to just another local skirmish in Judaism's global war against the Gentiles.

Richard Nixon was forced to resign his presidency because of a small-c conspiracy to cover up the illegal activities carried out by his reelection campaign. But to conspiracists on his right, his whole presidency had been the enactment of a long-standing conspiracy to destroy America's sovereignty; his breakthrough trip to China was just the latest in a long line of betrayals. "If Mr. Nixon has been only kidding about his devotion to forging the links in the chain of the World Superstate that is to be welded around America's wrists, then he is a consummate hypocrite," the John Birch Society's Gary Allen wrote in 1971, a year before Nixon's epochal meeting with Mao. "But his commitment to world government goes back nearly a quarter of a century and indeed he would not now be in the White House if he were not committed to this ultimate goal of the Insiders."[39]

Conspiracism, like racial bigotry, is almost always a murky undercurrent in the mainstream of politics, its propositions only glancingly acknowledged by the political establishment and summarily dismissed. But as cartoonish as its heroes and villains might be, as disordered and disreputable and deranged as its proponents and its premises so often are, they are rarely without pertinence to an understanding of the social and political environment that spawned them. If op-ed columns, position papers, think tank monographs, and State of the Union addresses are politics' superego, paranoid conspiracy theories and blind, irrational hatreds, as often as not, are its id. Politicians—even some sober, fair-minded, consensus-seeking public servants—know that and take full advantage of it when they have to on the campaign trail. Even a dyed-in-the-wool Communist like Richard Nixon engaged in Red-baiting when it suited his purposes.

Before the dust had even settled, the terrible events of September 11, 2001, gave birth to conspiracy theories that were every bit as labyrinthine and obsessive as the body of lore that has accreted around the Kennedy assassination. Nothing so devastating could have possibly been caused by a small band of Arabs armed with box cutters, so-called 9/11 Truthers insist. The government needed a Pearl Harbor to justify its imperialistic aims, one major strain of thinking goes (and there were plenty of frustrated isolationists back in the 1940s who believed that Pearl Harbor itself had been either "made to happen" or "allowed to happen" by the war-happy FDR administration). Though 9/11 denialism remains the one frontier where no public official—or even a right-wing cable-TV talk show host—can go, one can only wonder whether they would be so fastidious if the attacks had taken place a year earlier than they did, when Bill Clinton was still in office, or eight years later, after Bush had returned to Texas. Looking at what America First's John T. Flynn wrote about FDR in his pamphlets *The Truth About Pearl Harbor* (1944) and *The Final Secret of Pearl Harbor* (1945), it's not hard to guess what the answer might be.

If you don't believe that our government could stoop to a false-flag operation, the Truther argument goes, then just look at Operation Northwoods in 1962—a documented plan to carry out hijackings and terror bombings in the United States that could be falsely pinned on Castro in order to justify an invasion of Cuba. One might counter that Operation Northwoods never did get past the proposal stages, and that the secret was revealed in due course, but that doesn't mean that devastating facts about 9/11 aren't waiting to come out too. Besides, we know about other lies that our government has told to promote wars. The Tonkin Gulf Incident served LBJ's purposes quite admirably—though that analogy isn't altogether apt either, since the scandal in that case was that at least one of the two naval engagements that constituted the incident didn't actually occur. As discreditable as it is to exaggerate about an enemy attack or outright invent one, it isn't remotely the same thing as attacking one's own troops or civilians.

One 9/11 theory builds on the coincidence that Marvin Bush (brother of George W.) sat on the board of Securacom, a company that handled some of the security at the World Trade Center. If 9/11 really was an inside job, the thinking went, planned and executed with the White House's approval and connivance, then Marvin Bush was the inside man who saw to it that security guards looked the other way while sappers wired thermite explosives to the buildings' steel frames—a process that would have taken days or weeks to complete and caused considerable disruption to thousands of office workers' daily routines. But why the plotters would have used such an elaborately complicated belt-and-suspenders approach, airplanes plus bombs (except at the Pentagon, where, according to yet another theory, they disappeared a jet and its passengers and crew and substituted a cruise missile for it at the last minute; and over Shanksville, Pennsylvania, where military jets—so conspicuously absent in New York and D.C.—shot Flight 93 out of the sky), is not explained.

When the Web site Boing Boing invited me to be a guest blogger in November 2009, I dedicated one of my first posts to 9/11 Truth. Paraphrasing F. Scott Fitzgerald's famous dictum about the test of a first-rate intelligence, I noted that you don't have to be a genius to simultaneously hold two separate and not necessarily opposing ideas in your mind: (1) that the Bush administration told all kinds of untruths about 9/11, and (2) that the attacks on the World Trade Center and the Pentagon were not an "inside job."

It opened up a floodgate. Links to YouTube documentaries and interviews and articles by scientists, architects, engineers, physicists, political thinkers, actors, and at least one theologian* came pouring in, along with testimony from disillusioned combat veterans and survivors of the day's events. Discussion forums on 9/11 Web sites were buzzing for days. Many of the Truthers that I heard from (or 9/11 skeptics, as most of them now prefer to be called) were earnest and idealistic and driven by a missionary zeal. Some were openly hostile; others, I suspect, were quite insane.

But what took me by surprise was the outsize role that Jews played in the anecdotes that so many of them related: warmongering Jewish neoconservatives in Washington, D.C.; the World Trade Center's owner, Larry Silverstein; even well-known Jewish leftists like Noam Chomsky, Naomi Klein, and Amy Goodman, who have stubbornly

---

* The aforementioned David Ray Griffin is an eminent process theologian. I quoted him a few pages back to illustrate circular reasoning.

and, to their accusers' minds, unaccountably refused to endorse the agenda of 9/11 Truth. Binding them all together was the Zionist entity of Israel.

There were stories about the four thousand Jewish office workers who were supposedly told to stay home that day (just for the record, my brother-in-law, whose office was in WTC 7, didn't get the memo—Snopes.com traced the rumor back to Hezbollah's Al-Manar television station in Beirut, Lebanon[40]), and about the Israeli moving men with alleged links to Mossad who were seen celebrating the collapse of the twin towers, arrested, held incommunicado in a federal prison, and ultimately deported without a trial. A disconcerting number of links led to virtual bookstores that featured *The Protocols of the Elders of Zion.* By the end of the night Boing Boing's beleaguered moderator posted a comment himself, about "the moistly glistening comments and links that I have in my refuse bin. I assure you that they are studded with feculent tidbits of loathsome vileness, mostly in the form of links to websites explaining how Obama is *exactly* the same as Hitler and why it's important to defend white culture."

This isn't to say that all or even most 9/11 skeptics are anti-Semites and white supremacists. Surely they're not. But even after writing a whole book about fringe beliefs and organizations, I hadn't realized to what extent even fringes have fringes, and I had failed to appreciate how potent and dependable a driver of conspiracy theory old-fashioned bigotry continues to be.

Still, you don't have to be a conspiracy theorist to take a jaundiced view of the administration of George W. Bush. Adversaries descried and decried a pattern of small-c conspiracies throughout its eight-year reign, beginning with the fight over the vote recount in Florida. Many of their suspicions were directed at the office of Vice President Dick Cheney. The former Halliburton CEO's chairmanship of the shadowy National Energy Policy Development Group prompted any number of Freedom of Information Act requests; during the run-up to the war in Iraq, sources in his office fed problematic or altogether false intelligence about Iraq's weapons of mass destruction to reporters. Over in the Department of Justice, U.S. attorneys deemed insufficiently loyal to the president's political agenda were systematically dismissed.

But if the Bush administration was accused of behaving like a secretive cartel by the Left, the kind of black-helicopter, New World Order hysteria that had been such a hallmark of the Clinton years was notable mostly for its absence. That said, a not insignificant sector of the extreme Right has held serious reservations about the Bush family for decades. As an investment banker at Brown Brothers Harriman, an assiduous supporter of Planned Parenthood, and a liberal Republican U.S. senator from Connecticut, patriarch Prescott Bush had been a quintessential figure of the elite eastern internationalist establishment. His son George H. W. Bush's "New World Order" speech of September 11, 1991 (and yes, it was delivered precisely ten years to the day before the attacks on the World Trade Center and the Pentagon—and exactly fifty years to the day after the Pentagon's groundbreaking ceremony), remains a watershed for those who believe that America's sovereignty is being undermined by wealthy elites. While they were undergraduates at Yale, Prescott, George H. W., and George W. Bush were all tapped for Skull and Bones, a secret society that many conspiracists believe functions as a recruiting arm of the Illuminati. In June 2007, as Bush fatigue was beginning to set in across the whole breadth of the political spectrum, Accuracy in Media's Cliff Kincaid angrily accused George W. of "putting into place the New World Order that his father talked about."[41]

But for all that, the Patriot movement had mostly been in abeyance during the younger Bush's presidency. The election of Barack Obama gave it a whole new lease on life. A Southern Poverty Law Center report released in March 2010 reported a 244 percent increase in the number of Patriot groups between 2008 and 2009—from 149 to 512. "Militias—the paramilitary arm of the Patriot movement—were a major part of the increase, growing from 42 militias in 2008 to 127 in 2009."[42] According to an SPLC report released in the spring of 2011, the number of hate groups active in the United States had risen to just over one thousand—a 50 percent increase since 2000.[43]

The twin shocks of the worldwide economic meltdown of 2008 and the election shortly thereafter of America's first multiracial president had exposed a set of fault lines running through the Republic whose like hadn't been seen since the days of Bleeding Kansas, or if that is an exaggeration,* since Joe McCarthy, Bull Connor, and the Kent State shootings. As Bush's second term sputtered to its ignominious end, uncounted millions of 401(k)s and IRAs had melted into air; whole neighborhoods were being abandoned to foreclosures. The hugely unpopular TARP bailouts of the auto industry and financial institutions (many of whose appallingly impenitent executives used them to line their own pockets with bonuses) were inspiring gusts of populist outrage. John McCain and Sarah Palin had stoked their campaign against Obama with fear and hatred, accusing him of consorting with terrorists, radicals, racists, and other un-American types, but when it came time to pull the lever, more of the same was scarier to more voters than the prospect of change.

Still, the nation's mood as Barack H. Obama assumed office was skittish, to say the very least. On Election Day, one of the winning Pick 3 numbers in the Illinois state lottery was 666—a coincidence that gave serious pause to the superstitiously inclined. "Mat Staver, Dean of Liberty University's law school, says he does not believe Obama is the Antichrist," *Newsweek* noted shortly after the election. "But he can see how others might."†

Flash back half a century or so and you'll hear much of the same agitated rhetoric that we hear today. On February 9, 1950, Senator Joseph McCarthy stood before the Republican Women's Club in Wheeling, West Virginia, and declared that the United States was engaged in "a final, all-out battle between communistic atheism and Christianity." The odds, he intimated, were very much against us.

"The reason why we find ourselves in a position of impotency," he said, is "because of the traitorous actions of those who have been treated so well by this Nation."

---

* With Texas governor Rick Perry's (a 2012 presidential prospect) talk of secession, Sarah Palin's husband Todd's former membership in the Alaskan Independence Party, and the rising "Tenther" movement, in which state legislatures are formally asserting their sovereignty under the Tenth Amendment, it might not be.
† "Is Obama the Antichrist?" *Newsweek*, November 15, 2008. According to a widely discussed (and much-criticized) Harris Poll conducted in March 2010, 67 percent of Republicans believe Obama is a Socialist, 45 percent that he is not an American citizen, 57 percent that he is a Muslim, and 24 percent that he might be the Antichrist.

It has not been the less fortunate or members of minority groups who have been selling this Nation out, but rather those who have had all the benefits that the wealthiest nation on earth has had to offer—the finest homes, the finest college education, and the finest jobs in Government we can give. This is glaringly true in the State Department. . . . In my opinion the State Department . . . is thoroughly infested with Communists. I have in my hand 57 cases of individuals who would appear to be either card carrying members or certainly loyal to the Communist Party, but who nevertheless are still helping to shape our foreign policy.[44]

McCarthy was right about the high stakes of the Cold War; it was also true that of the handful of high-placed traitors who had been exposed, at least one of them had attended prestigious schools and won conspicuous honors (though he'd endured a childhood that was filled with privations and tragedies). History has not been kind to Alger Hiss; the overwhelming consensus today is that Whittaker Chambers told the truth about him. But if there was a whiff of factuality in some of McCarthy's accusations, he demagogued them shamelessly.* McCarthy's infamous list of State Department employees (which he initially claimed had more than two hundred names on it) was never made public and almost certainly never existed.

Six weeks after the Wheeling speech, at a press conference in Key West, Florida, a reporter asked Harry Truman if he thought that McCarthy could prove that "any disloyalty exists in the State Department." The president didn't mince his words. "I think the greatest asset the Kremlin has is Senator McCarthy," he said. When pressed, he explained himself further, sounding very much like one of the combative, center-left-leaning commentators on the political scene today—E. J. Dionne, perhaps, or Mark Shields:

The Republicans have been trying vainly to find an issue on which to make a bid for the control of the Congress for next year. They tried "statism." They tried "welfare state." They tried "socialism."

---

* It's worth noting that by the time McCarthy made this speech, Hiss had already been tried and found guilty of perjury. The clarion about Communist subversion had been sounded years before, and not by McCarthy.

And there are a certain number of members of the Republican Party who are trying to dig up that old malodorous dead horse called "isolationism." And in order to do that, they are perfectly willing to sabotage the bipartisan foreign policy of the United States. And this fiasco which has been going on in the Senate is the very best asset that the Kremlin could have in the operation of the cold war. And that is what I mean when I say that McCarthy's antics are the best asset that the Kremlin can have.[45]

Six decades later, Glenn Beck reminded his viewing audience that if McCarthy was "an imperfect vessel," the era he gave his name to was "America's turning point." "It's frightening. It's frightening," he emoted. As reviled and mistreated as McCarthy's memory may be, he might well have saved the Republic from its own worst elements. "It's the truth and here is why you need to know history, because it's repeating itself," Beck continued, wielding the tactic of guilt by association that was McCarthy's métier.

I want to talk a little bit about the parallels between the Obama administration and the FDR administration as it comes into play with communists. We have Marxists, Maoists, communists in and around the White House influencing and actually working with [it]. We had that with FDR. Both denied it at the time.[46]

On July 21, 2010, Glenn Beck appeared on the air with a copy of a "plan to destroy the United States of America." "If you want to understand what is happening in this country," Beck said, "if you want to understand how this is all coming together and what their designs are, all you have to do is read *You Don't Need a Weatherman to Know Which Way the Wind Blows.*" Surely the word "plan" excessively dignifies the Weathermen's manifesto, a pastiche of overheated revolutionary rhetoric, most of it channeled from the writings of Frantz Fanon, Che Guevara, and Mao Tse-tung, but there's no denying that its authors sought to fan the flames of revolution. The Weathermen were Marxist-Leninists; they preached and practiced violence.

But what relevance could this artifact of late-1960s campus radicalism have with anything that's happening today? It's simple: some of the people who wrote it are still alive, and active in politics. One of them—a Chicago academic—even had some dealings with Obama before he became president. "We see it was submitted by Bill Ayers," Beck explained, "who is friends with the president, no matter what they say."[47] And then he connected the rest of the dots, from Ayers's spouse, Bernardine Dohrn, all the way to the billionaire George Soros.

As long as we're on the subject of history repeating itself, it's worth pondering what Harry Truman might have made of the likes of Glenn Beck. Perhaps he would have pointed to this telling passage from the best-selling book *Glenn Beck's Common Sense:*

> If the Progressive cancer were limited to defined political systems, it would be fairly straightforward to isolate it, treat it, and eventually be free from the disease. But it's not. It's infiltrated both political parties and the entire political class. . . . The Progressives on the right believed in Statism and American expansion through military strength, while the Progressives on the left believed in Statism and expansion through transnationalist entities such as the League of Nations and then the United Nations. . . . One of the hallmarks of Progressive thought is the concept of redistribution: the idea that your money and property are only yours if the State doesn't determine that there is a higher or better use for it.[48]

Beck tells the same story that McCarthy did, and he harnesses it to the same political purposes. All of the Republican talking points that Truman identified back then are present in Beck's ostensibly nonpartisan rant today: the evils of statism and the welfare state, the virtues of isolationism, and the specter of internal subversion. Except in Beck's telling the enemy is Wilsonian Progressivism rather than international Communism (though to Beck they amount to essentially the same thing). Reading McCarthy's words out of context, you'd hardly know that the United States was flush from its enormous victory in World War II and well on its way to an enormous, decades-long economic expansion. Reading Beck's today, you might think that the world was still poised on a knife's edge, divided between "two vast, increasingly hostile armed camps."

Anyone can play six degrees of Kevin Bacon; it doesn't take many steps to connect Glenn Beck to political pariahs who were as subversive in their day as Bill Ayers and Bernardine Dohrn were in theirs.

If you wanted to smear Beck by association, you could start with the author of the original *Common Sense*. "Our churches, our synagogues, our mosques—we must stand for the things we know are true," Beck orated from the steps of the Lincoln Memorial in August 2010. But in *The Age of Reason, Part the First*, section 1, Beck's admitted idol Thomas Paine—a man he has called a "heroic patriot"—stated, "I do not believe in the creed professed by the Jewish church, by the Roman church, by the Greek church, by the Turkish church, by the Protestant church, nor by any church that I know of. My own mind is my own church."[49] Imagine if Barack Obama, Bill Ayers, or for that matter Woodrow Wilson or Teddy Roosevelt had formulated such an arrogant credo.

But perhaps all that Thomas Paine stuff was just a subterfuge. Maybe Beck was really paying a sly tribute to Conde McGinley's infamous magazine, also called *Common Sense*, which was active from about 1947 to 1972. "Anti-Semitism is the chief stock in trade of *Common Sense*," stated a preliminary report on neo-Fascist and hate groups that was prepared in 1954 for the House Un-American Activities Committee (not exactly a bastion of leftism). *Common Sense* "distortedly defines communism as 'a false face for Judaism,'" it continued.

> Typical of headlines which appear in the publication are: "Jewish Leaders Are Crazy for Power," "Zionists Threaten Russia with War," "'Brotherhood'-Jew Trap for Christianity," and "Invisible Government Rules Both Parties: Adlai and Ike Marxist Stooges." Articles in *Common Sense* have even attacked water fluoridation as a Red plot by "the Invisible rulers," aimed at mass destruction of the American people.[50]

Both Eustace Mullins* and Elizabeth Dilling were frequent contributors to *Common Sense*, and books by both authors have been touted on Glenn Beck's TV show. Tit for tat. If Glenn Beck can draw lines on a chalkboard, so can I.

Mind you, I don't for a moment believe that Beck endorses or emulates McGinley's brand of anti-Semitism. Most likely, he hasn't even

---

* A summary of Mullins's career can be found in the next chapter.

heard of him. It's not unlikely that Beck's firsthand knowledge of Thomas Paine's writings doesn't extend very far beyond the extracts that he and his co-writers padded out *Glenn Beck's Common Sense* with. He probably doesn't know about Paine's favorable views on progressive taxation or what Paine had to say about the Bible: "What is it the bible teaches us? Rapine, cruelty, and murder. What is it the testament teaches us? To believe that the Almighty committed debauchery with a woman engaged to be married and the belief of this debauchery is called faith."[51]

"Beck has successfully grown a mass following," Alexander Zaitchik marveled in *Common Nonsense: Glenn Beck and the Triumph of Ignorance*, "while stumbling through a remedial self-education in U.S. democracy, which reflects the carnival mirrors inside his mind as much as it does the reality he struggles, in ever-so-profitable futility and desperation, to comprehend."[52] For $9.95 a month, his fans can learn along with him, by taking online courses at Beck University, "a unique academic experience bringing together experts in the fields of religion, American history and economics."

Anyone can quote selectively; anyone can hurl irresponsible and inflammatory accusations. But I do admit that it puzzles me how, on the one hand, Beck can ascribe such awesome powers to Adam Smith's invisible hand of the marketplace while, on the other, believing that we live in a world that is almost entirely shaped by the machinations of a malign few, a world in which the likes of Bill Ayers—the leader of a fringe movement forty years ago that accomplished exactly none of its goals and a distinctly minor-league academic today—is supposed to be a formidable power behind the throne, in a community organizing group like ACORN (now defunct, thanks to Beck's and his peers' untiring efforts) can marshal enough strength to subvert our whole political process. But neither Beck nor his listeners are going to be swayed by anything I might write. To quote Thomas Paine again (*The Crisis*, no. 5), "To argue with a man who has renounced the use and authority of reason . . . is like administering medicine to the dead."

Though Beck will no longer be as visible on television now that his contract with Fox expired, his paranoia-fueled flag-waving has already earned him a fortune; the passion he puts behind his message—of "self-empowerment, entrepreneurial spirit and true Americanism— the way we were when we changed the world, when Edison was alone, failing his 2,000th time on the lightbulb," as he puts it—is clearly heartfelt.[53] But why does it resonate so powerfully with so many ordinary Americans who, lacking Beck's extraordinary vocal endowments and his vast talent for self-promotion, can ill afford to give up such government entitlements as Social Security and Medicare?

Richard Hofstadter provides historical perspective. In his essay "Pseudo-conservatism Revisited," he cited *Symbolic Crusade* (1963), Joseph R. Gusfield's study of the temperance movement, for its insights into politics that are driven by status values rather than economic ideas. Gusfield distinguished "between the political aims of those he calls 'cultural fundamentalists' and 'cultural modernists' . . . Both are engaged with politics, but the fundamentalists have a special edge because they want to restore the simple virtues of a bygone age and they feel themselves to be fighting in a losing cause."

> On many occasions they approach economic issues as matters of faith and morals rather than matters of fact. For example, people often oppose certain economic policies not because they have been or would be economically hurt by such policies, or even because they have any carefully calculated views about their economic efficacy, but because they disapprove *on moral grounds* of the assumptions on which they think the policies rest.
>
> A prominent case in point is the argument over fiscal policy. . . . As a matter of status politics, deficit spending is an affront to millions who have been raised to live (and in some cases have been forced by circumstances to live) abstemious, thrifty, prudential lives. . . . When society adopts a policy of deficit spending, thrifty small-businessmen, professionals, farmers, and white-collar workers who have been managing their affairs by the old rules feel that their way of life has been officially and insultingly repudiated.[54]

Like Father Coughlin, Billy James Hargis, Pat Robertson, James Dobson, and so many other right-wing media crusaders before them, Glenn Beck, Sean Hannity, Rush Limbaugh, and Ann Coulter understand that for many religious Americans, "evil" is not just an adjective but also a noun. The Pilgrims believed they were reclaiming a wilderness from Satan. Many traditionalists on the right, whether

Christian millennialists or not, feel much the same way. To them, godless Communism or secular humanism isn't the *absence* of a religious orientation so much as it is a satanic religion in and of itself, whose acolytes glorify evil, promote the slaughter of innocent, unborn babies, and persecute believing Christians. Blue-state America is Rome in the time of Christ. Whether its depravity is manifested in the form of sexual libertinage, income redistribution, spiritual or economic incontinence, blasphemy, women's and gay rights, or the threat of "race mixing," anathema and even violence are completely appropriate responses to it.

As melodramatic and overwrought as Glenn Beck's fears for the Constitution might be, I suspect they are informed by a Mormon prophecy that resonates with his sense of self-importance. "When the Constitution of the United States hangs, as it were, upon a single thread," Brigham Young wrote in 1855, referring to Joseph Smith's still earlier "White Horse" prophecy of 1843, "they will have to call for the 'Mormon' elders to save it from utter destruction; and they will step forth and do it."[55] Above and beyond that, I suspect that Beck's conspiracy theories serve an essential psychological purpose: they provide him with at least the illusion of control (something that was clearly missing from his life during his alcohol- and cocaine-addled years in the radio wilderness). Conspiracy theory has been a gold mine for Beck as an entertainer too, both figuratively and literally; not only has it made him rich, but it provides him with an inexhaustible source of material, no small thing for someone whose job requires him to extemporize for hours every day.

For politicians, conspiracy theory provides both a ready-made rallying cry (*I know who's responsible for your misery; follow me and we will bring them to grief*) and an all-purpose escape hatch (*how can we possibly prevail against an enemy that's so elusive and powerful?*). Cult leaders, dictators, and demagogues are all avid promoters of conspiracy theories; nothing fosters dependency on a leader and solidarity among followers like the expectation of an imminent threat. "Collective fear," Bertrand Russell wrote in "An Outline of Intellectual Rubbish" in 1943, "stimulates herd instinct, and tends to produce ferocity towards those who are not regarded as members of the herd. . . . Fear generates impulses of cruelty, and therefore promotes such superstitious beliefs as seem to justify cruelty. Neither a man nor a crowd nor a nation can be trusted to act humanely or to think sanely under the influence of a great fear."[56]

Whether a product of one's own forebodings or a cynical attempt to promote them in others, conspiracy theory creates a feedback loop that is almost impossible to escape from.

And thus it has always been.

3.

Henry Ford and
The Protocols of the Elders of Zion

On October 25, 1918, there was a mysterious killing on an ad hoc pistol range at Fort Lewis, near the city of Tacoma, Washington. According to the military's official report on the incident, Captain Robert Rosenbluth had been leading a column of soldiers on a march when he came across Major Alexander Pennington Cronkhite of the 213th Engineers and his orderly, Sergeant Bugler Roland R. Pothier, firing their pistols at a tobacco can. Captain Rosenbluth halted his soldiers and walked over to the two men.

"I got it that time, Captain," Cronkhite called out by way of greeting. Suddenly his pistol went off again. "My God, I'm shot," he cried, and fell to the ground. Though Rosenbluth attempted to revive him and a regimental doctor was swiftly called to the scene, Cronkhite was dead within minutes. A .45-caliber bullet had penetrated his chest, just below his right armpit. It had been fired from his own gun.

Cronkhite was a West Point graduate; he knew how to handle firearms. What could have caused his weapon to discharge? He had recently been hospitalized with influenza; in fact he had reported sick that morning, which was why Rosenbluth, his subordinate, was leading the march. Investigators speculated that perhaps, in his weakened condition, Cronkhite had momentarily lost his grip on his pistol and accidentally squeezed its trigger when he felt it slipping out of his grasp.

Cronkhite's grandfather on his mother's side was Major General Alexander C. M. Pennington, who'd fought for the Union in the Civil War. His father, General Adelbert Cronkhite, was commander of the Eightieth Division of the American Expeditionary Force in France (the newsman Walter Cronkite, as it happened, was his distant cousin). Neither of Cronkhite's parents put much stock in the military's account of the tragedy. It seemed to them that their son's autopsy had been pro forma and the formal inquiry peremptory and slipshod. Soon after his return from overseas, General Cronkhite launched an investigation of his own. He ordered his son's body exhumed and had it examined by an independent pathologist, who concluded that the fatal wound "could not have been self-inflicted with a firearm in the hand of the deceased."[1] Then the general took a long, hard look at the shooting's two witnesses. Pothier was generally unpopular and had been the subject of nasty rumors. Though Rosenbluth's reputation was spotless, the general wondered if he hadn't had it in for his son for some reason. Perhaps he'd killed him (or had Pothier kill him) to prevent him from writing up a career-ruining evaluation. Or maybe Rosenbluth was the leading edge of a wide-ranging conspiracy among Fort Lewis's senior officers. Not averse to bringing his considerable influence to bear, General Cronkhite enlisted the federal Department of Justice. Special Agent James J. Lee of the Secret Service agreed with him that something smelled fishy; he wondered if Rosenbluth wasn't a German spy.[2] Others thought that he might be a Bolshevik—why else would he have traveled to Russia after the war?

General Cronkhite's exertions on his son's behalf didn't exactly endear him to his superiors; he would be forcibly retired in 1923. But once the wheels were set in motion, they seemingly couldn't be stopped. William P. Conley, a private detective, tracked Pothier down in Rhode Island and interviewed him. Claiming to be an insurance investigator, he offered to "split a bonus with him" if he could help him prove "that Major Cronkhite met his death in such manner that his company would not have to pay the insurance which Major Cronkhite had carried." Conley's trial testimony would be reported in *The New York Times*:

I told him it was a matter of bread and butter with me and I would make a nice piece of money if I could get the truth. He replied that the only split he would get if he told anything would be a trip to jail. I said that this seemed to show there was something wrong, and if there was why couldn't he be a good fellow and tell me about it. He replied, suddenly, "No matter how it was, it was all an accident, and they can't hang a man for an accident."[3]

Pothier was taken into custody by the agents Lee and Thomas Callaghan. After numerous interviews, they were able to get him "twisted in his story," as Lee explained in a deposition.[4] Pothier confessed five times in all and finally admitted to killing Cronkhite on Captain Rosenbluth's direct orders. The former bugler sergeant had no idea what Rosenbluth's motives were; all Rosenbluth had told him, he recalled, was that "we want to get him out of the way."[5]

Rosenbluth had received his master's degree from the Yale Forest School in 1907, worked in remote Philippine jungles, in Utah timberland, and for the Conservation Commission of New York State, where he designed a woodcraft program for prison inmates. When war broke out, he enlisted in the Engineer Corps. Major Cronkhite met Rosenbluth at Camp Forrest in Georgia and personally selected him to work with the 213th Engineers. General Cronkhite's unsubstantiated suspicions about a bad report notwithstanding, by all accounts the two officers had been on excellent terms. Nothing in Rosenbluth's life before or after the shooting suggested any possibility, as the Yale Forest School alumni magazine put it, that he had "a Jekyll and Hyde double personality."[6]

The energetic and public-spirited Rosenbluth had indeed traveled to Russia, but he did so as a relief worker under the auspices of Herbert Hoover's American Relief Administration and the Joint Committee; Hoover readily attested to both his competence and his character. Rosenbluth was no Bolshevik either. While in Kharkov, he had sent thoughtful dispatches to a journal published by the Institute for Public Service, in which he reported on Bolshevism's manifest failures:

Thus the irony of the Bolsheviki: setting out to destroy parasitic capital and to make labor supreme, they destroyed labor and made of each a speculator, in which the possession, legitimate or not, of anything essential, gave one a corner on the market, in which he squeezed the man who had to have it, and so on *ad infinitum. . . .* Worst of all, of course, was the feeling of insecurity of life itself. As a refugee who just came from Moscow told me, it made a city where everyone was hungry and no one smiles.[7]

As federal agents prepared their case against Rosenbluth, he was working for the Legislative Commission of the State of Ohio, helping to reorganize the state's government. Later, he embarked on a long career as a social worker in New York and Chicago. Rosenbluth's son Marshall was a renowned plasma physicist; his father's manuscript autobiography, "The Many Lives of Robert Rosenbluth," is included among his collected papers. When Rosenbluth wrote it in 1962, he was still employed by the Cook County Department of Welfare as its assistant director, "because, fortunately among other things, there is no compulsory retirement here because of age" (he was seventy-five at the time).[8]

Rosenbluth and Pothier's prosecution would be a slow-motion train wreck. The U.S. attorney feared the case was unwinnable from the outset, but instead of cutting its losses, the Department of Justice took advantage of a technicality. Since Fort Lewis had not yet become federal property at the time of the shooting, jurisdiction was ceded to the State of Washington. The federal prosecutors turned their files over to J. W. Selden, the prosecuting attorney for Pierce County, and left the ball in his court. The appalled Selden summarily dismissed the case, explaining his reasoning in a strongly worded report that was published in the *Tacoma Sunday Ledger* and printed as a pamphlet by Rosenbluth's supporters.

"There is no reason shown why the findings of the military board of inquiry . . . should not be accepted as final and conclusive," he wrote. "All of the statements made by Pothier must be repudiated. They do not ring true. They would not be sufficient, independent of other evidence, to even justify the filing of any charge against him.

"As to Captain Rosenbluth," Selden continued,

he should be and is so far as we are able to do it, entirely exonerated from any connection whatever with the death of Major Cronkhite. From the records we do not find even a breath of suspicion pointing toward him from any source other than Pothier and Special Agent Lee. Lee's suspicion may be attributed to overzealousness and Pothier's statements to a determined effort to extricate himself from a bad entanglement into which he unwittingly allowed himself to be drawn. . . . A great injustice has been done him which should be righted. . . . There is nothing which in any manner approaches the dignity of evidence to connect [Rosenbluth] with the killing of Major Cronkhite.[9]

And yet the case dragged on for another three years. The federal government quietly resumed its jurisdiction but delayed taking the case to trial until it was compelled to do so by the Supreme Court. As the court date loomed, the U.S. attorney Thomas Revelle wrote a long letter to his superiors in which he protested that "we have indicted a man on the charge of first degree murder without a single fact to substantiate the charge." A trial, he said, would result "in a fiasco of a most shameful nature."[10]

Pothier and Rosenbluth's trial began in the fall of 1924—almost six years after the shooting—and all of Revelle's worst fears came true. Pothier had long since disavowed all five of his confessions; the testimony of many of the prosecution's witnesses proved less helpful to the prosecution than to the defense (for example, when Revelle's assistant was enlisted to demonstrate that it would have been impossible for Cronkhite to fire his pistol while holding it at an angle that matched his wound, he easily pulled the trigger—a prosecutorial backfire that foreshadowed O. J. Simpson's struggle to squeeze his hand into a bloody glove many decades later). The jury acquitted Pothier after just forty-five minutes of deliberation. Since Rosenbluth's prosecution was entirely dependent on Pothier's, the U.S. attorney had no choice but to dismiss his indictment.

Why had the government persisted in its folly for so long, and at such extravagant expense? Rosenbluth's prosecution cost the United States in the neighborhood of $200,000 ($2,492,822 in today's dollars, according to the consumer price index). Here's how the American Jewish Committee's Louis Marshall explained it in its 1924 annual report:

There is an even more sordid aspect of this case which should not be overlooked. There lives in Michigan one Henry Ford, who for several years past has been amusing himself by publishing a personal organ known as *The Dearborn Independent,* which likewise bears the caption "The Ford International Weekly." Learning that Rosenbluth is a Jew, that damning fact was enough. For weeks and months Ford's columns were filled with cunningly contrived appeals to passion and prejudice, with attacks upon those who ventured to stand at the side of the man who had been unjustly accused of a heinous crime. Felix M. Warburg and Colonel Herbert H. Lehman . . . were accused of being members of a Jewish conspiracy to cheat the gallows. Rosenbluth's counsel, who likewise happened to be Jews, and who came to his rescue as a matter of simple justice in recognition of their oaths of office, were showered with insults. . . . Other good citizens who came forward to give to Rosenbluth his due, were denounced, not only as malefactors, but as the tools of a Jewish conspiracy.[11]

Among those "other good citizens" were the faculty and administration of the Yale Forest School, which had graduated only a handful of Jews besides Rosenbluth in its history. A long article in its alumni magazine systematically presented extracts from *The Dearborn Independent* side by side with the documented facts of the case. *The Dearborn Independent* had implied that ten minutes passed between the time the shots were fired and when Rosenbluth was discovered with Cronkhite's body; in fact it was less than a minute, as confirmed by numerous witnesses. *The Dearborn Independent* implied that Cronkhite's principal duty "was the weeding out of officers who, as the result of examinations, were found not qualified to hold commissions for overseas service." Rosenbluth, it claimed, was on probation. *The Dearborn Independent* claimed that "such military training" as Rosenbluth possessed "he had obtained at the Plattsburg training camp, New York." Rosenbluth had in fact seen service in France and been promoted in the field; his service reports were exemplary. Finally, *The Dearborn Independent* had characterized the case as a critical test of the American justice system. Rosenbluth's fate, it said, rested on the larger question of "whether one race"—meaning Rosenbluth and his co-religionists—can be allowed to "overturn the laws of constitutional government, nullifying its legal procedure in criminal cases."

A forceful concluding statement, signed by the members of the Forest School's executive committee (none of whom were Jewish), responded in no uncertain terms:

> The "race" to whom this case is important is the American race, and the institutions are those founded by our forefathers, who sought to guarantee justice and the right to life, liberty and the pursuit of happiness to all without regard to creed, color, or previous condition of servitude. The charge of racial conspiracies and plotting, childish and contemptible, has been raised by the articles in *The Dearborn Independent*. We, as Americans, challenge it. The accused has never raised this issue but has stood for justice as an American and as a public servant, and as an officer with honorable and unblemished reputation in the World War.[12]

The Dearborn Independent fired back with an editorial of its own, headlined "Shall Rosenbluth Be 'an American Dreyfus'? Attempt of Propagandists to Use Influence of Colleges."[13] Apparently, Ford and his editors were unaware of the fact that Dreyfus was railroaded and ultimately exonerated (or more likely they believed that he'd eluded justice, thanks to the machinations of worldwide Jewry).

In fairness to Ford, it should be noted that most of the prose that appeared under his byline was ghostwritten, much of it by *The Dearborn Independent*'s editor, William J. Cameron. Ford's secretary Ernest Liebold kept a New York private detective agency on retainer, which apprised him of the activities of prominent Jews. Many of its operatives were former Secret Service agents; some were Russians in exile who had worked for the tsar's secret police. But by all accounts, nothing that Cameron, Liebold, or their informants wrote or said about the international Jewish conspiracy, in *The Dearborn Independent* or elsewhere, contradicted any of Ford's own views, which he expounded in innumerable newspaper interviews and private conversations over the years. Ford's surrogates knew exactly what their boss believed and why. And they knew who Rosenbluth would have been talking about had he really said that "*we* want to get him out of the way." "We" was the Jewish people, "the most closely organized power on earth . . . a State whose citizens are unconditionally loyal wherever they may be."

According to *The International Jew* (the bound collection of *The Dearborn Independent*'s columns on the Jewish question, which eventually totaled four volumes[14]):

> The Jew is the world's enigma. Poor in his masses, he yet controls the world's finances. Scattered abroad without country or government, he yet presents a unity of race continuity which no other people has achieved. Living under legal disabilities in almost every land, he has become the power behind many a throne. There are ancient prophecies to the effect that the Jew will return to his own land and from that center rule the world, though not until he has undergone an assault by the united nations of mankind.[15]

Ford believed that the Jews had orchestrated World War I. As he later told *The New York Times*, he'd first come to this realization when he sailed to Europe on a personal mission to negotiate an end to the war back in 1915. The "Peace Ship" wasn't two hundred miles at sea, he said, when a pair of prominent Jewish passengers bragged to him about "the power of the Jewish race, how they controlled the world through their control of gold, and that the Jew and no one but the Jew could end the war."[16]

Like many of his contemporaries, Ford believed that the Russian Revolution was also the handiwork of the Jews, so the murder of a Gentile West Point graduate would have been a comparatively trivial matter for them to arrange. Pothier's bogus confessions and the total lack of forensic evidence against him notwithstanding, Rosenbluth's Jewish ancestry—and the celerity with which prominent Jews had risen to his defense—were prima facie evidence of his guilt.

"Ford, the intellectual brother of the Ku Klux Klan, the inspirer of Hitler . . . persists, as one would expect a man of his low mentality to do, in his crusade against him upon whom he has inflicted so terrible a wrong," Marshall's AJC report concluded. "There is not a decent man who would not rather stand in the shoes of Captain Rosenbluth than in those of Ford, even though he be the richest man in all the world."[17]

Needless to say, Ford took a very different view of the matter. As he put it in *The International Jew,* "race hatred" and "race prejudice" played no part in his program to expose and frustrate the manifestly wicked designs of the Jewish race. "We prejudge what we do not know, and we hate what we do not understand," he wrote. Ford understood the Jewish plot perfectly; he only aimed to tell the truth about it. "There is a serious snare in all this plea for tolerance," he wrote. "There can be no tolerance until there is first a full understanding of what is tolerated. Ignorance, suppression, silence, collusion: these are not tolerance."[18]

American Jews might not have had much use for Ford or his *Dearborn Independent*—which was reaching hundreds of thousands of readers through the Ford dealerships that distributed it—but he was wildly popular in the country at large. In a poll of college students taken in 1920, Ford had been ranked the third-greatest man in history, behind Jesus and Napoleon.[19] By late 1923, while Rosenbluth's prosecution was still grinding on, a Ford for President groundswell was building. Though the Teapot Dome scandal had not yet broken, President Warren Harding was politically vulnerable; *Collier's* magazine sponsored a poll that showed Ford beating him for reelection by a margin of 14 percent. In a lengthy interview published alongside the poll, headlined "If I Were President" (by the time it ran, Harding had already died and been replaced by his vice president, Calvin Coolidge), Ford revealed himself as a patriot who had scant patience for the democratic process. In that respect, he was not dissimilar to Donald Trump or H. Ross Perot or any number of other wealthy, practical, politically unbeholden, can-do men of action of our own day who have publicly considered taking a temporary leave from private life to save the country from itself.

"I can't imagine myself today accepting any nomination," Ford coyly averred. "Of course I can't say what I will do tomorrow. There might be a war or some crisis of the sort, in which legalism and constitutionalism and all that wouldn't figure, and the nation wanted some person who could do things and do them quickly." Ford opined that the day would come when industry would "eventually absorb the political government"; he also identified the two greatest enemies of productivity and progress: international financiers and the labor movement. "Jew financiers are not building anything," he observed.

> You probably think the labor unions were organized by labor, but they weren't. They were organized by these Jew financiers. The labor union is a great scheme to interrupt work. It speeds up loafing. It's a great thing for the Jew to have on hand when he comes around to get his clutches on an industry.[20]

And not just labor. As Ford had written in *The Dearborn Independent*, "The real struggle in this country is not between labor and capital: the real struggle is between Jewish capital and Gentile capital, with the IWW leaders, the Socialist leaders, the Red leaders and the labor leaders almost a unit on the side of the Jewish capitalists."[21]

One of Ford's most ardent supporters wasn't even an American. "I wish that I could send some of my shock troops to Chicago and other big American cities to help in the elections," Adolf Hitler told the *Chicago Tribune*'s Raymond Fendrick. "We look on Heinrich Ford as the leader of the growing Fascisti movement in America. We admire particularly his anti-Jewish policy which is the Bavarian Fascisti platform. We have just had his anti-Jewish articles translated and published. The book is being circulated to millions throughout Germany."[22]

Ford's appeal extended beyond college students and the nascent Nazi movement abroad. Wisconsin's senator Robert La Follette was a Ford backer, the People's Progressive Party (a remnant of Teddy Roosevelt's Bull Moose Party) endorsed his candidacy, and a Ford-for-President Convention was scheduled to be held in Detroit before the end of the year. Ford himself would dash their hopes when he endorsed Calvin Coolidge.

Nineteen twenty-four, the year of Coolidge's election and of Rosenbluth's final exoneration, saw the passage of an immigration act that effectively eliminated America as a place of refuge for Europe's Jews; it was also the year that the second Ku Klux Klan reached its apogee, with a national membership of at least four million and clout enough to influence both the Democratic Party's slate of national candidates and its platform (it declined precipitously shortly thereafter). While it might give one pause to imagine the political and cultural consequences of a Ford presidency, or how things might have played out in the world at large over the next decades if Germany rather than England had enjoyed a special relationship with the United States (Ford was almost as ardent an Anglophobe as he was an anti-Semite), I haven't dwelled on Ford or Rosenbluth so long to make the point that America's Jews were in any real jeopardy. Country clubs, white-shoe law firms, Ivy League universities, and up-and-coming apartment buildings and housing developments might have excluded them, respected national figures like Ford might have libeled them, but there hadn't been another Leo Frank since 1915,* and there were no moves to criminalize Judaism itself, as there soon would be in Germany. Ford's popularity was in spite of, not because of, his anti-Semitism.

Still, many socially and economically ambitious Jews found it expedient to change their names. Ford noted this in the November 12, 1921, issue of *The Dearborn Independent*. His indignation at their imposture was such that his (or Cameron's) prose literally dissolved into a kind of free-form poetry. Incantatory and obsessive, it goes on for pages; what follows is just a tiny extract:

benjamin becomes lopez, seef, wolf (this is translation).

The Rev. Stephen S. Wise . . . booms his way across the country from one platform to the other, a wonder in his way, that such pomposity of sound should convey such paucity of sense. . . . This Rabbi, whose vocal exercise exhausts his other powers, was born in Hungary, his family name being Weisz. Sometimes this name is Germanized to Weiss. When S. S. Weisz became S. S. Wise, we do not know. If he had merely Americanized his Hungarian name it would have given him the name of White. Apparently "Wise" looked better. Truly it is better to be white than to be wise, but Dr. Stephen S. is a fresh point in the query of "what's in a name?"

benjamin becomes lopez, seef, wolf (this is translation) . . .

---

* Frank was a Jewish businessman who was convicted of murdering Mary Phagan, a thirteen-year-old Atlanta factory worker. He was pulled out of prison and lynched after his death sentence was commuted by Georgia's governor, John M. Slaton.

This passion for misleading people by names is deep and varied in its expression. Chiefly due to Jewish influences, we are giving the name of "liberalism" to looseness. We are dignifying with names that do not correctly name, many subversive movements. . . . Thus there are "reverends" who are both unreverend and irreverent, and there are shepherds who flock with the wolves. . . .

benjamin becomes lopez, seef, wolf (this is translation) . . .

But it is all a part of the Jewish practice of setting up a label pretending one thing, while quite another thing really exists.

benjamin becomes lopez, seef, wolf (this is translation).[23]

Ford's sideline as an anti-Jewish propagandist began just as the recession of 1920–21 took hold and automobile sales temporarily cratered. The timing couldn't have been worse for him, as he had just taken on a massive load of debt so he could secure personal control of his company. If anyone had reason to fear and resent the eastern money interests, Ford did in 1920; his fate was literally in their hands. But of course the roots of his anti-Semitism ran much deeper.

In *Henry Ford and the Jews: The Mass Production of Hate,* Neil Baldwin describes Ford's probable introduction to anti-Semitism in his earliest boyhood in rural Michigan. He would have heard it preached from the pulpit of the church he attended with his family and absorbed it from the pages of his beloved McGuffey Readers, which featured excerpts from *The Merchant of Venice,* "Paul's Defense Before King Agrippa," and "McGuffey's instructive tale of 'The Good Son,' in which 'a jeweler's child will not sell his diamonds to a group of Jewish elders because in order to obtain the key to the merchandise chest the lad would have to awaken his sleeping father.'"[24] Ford collected the primers and would republish and donate them to American schools so modern children could have the benefit of their moral instruction. Interestingly enough, later generations of conspiracists would fault John Dewey's progressive education movement for taking McGuffey Readers (and hence God) out of public school classrooms. Samuel Blumenfeld recommends them for homeschoolers; in *NEA: Trojan Horse in American Education* (1984) and other writings he argues that "American social engineers have systematically gone about destroying the intellect of millions of American children for the purpose of leading the American people into a socialist world government controlled by behavioral and social scientists."

Ford wouldn't have had much personal contact with Jews; anecdotal evidence suggests he didn't meet one personally before he was twenty. America's first Jews had arrived from the Netherlands via Brazil in the mid-1650s; by colonial times, their numbers were in the low thousands. Though not all colonial- and Revolutionary War–era Americans welcomed them, George Washington's 1790 letter to the Jews of the Touro congregation in Newport, Rhode Island, offers as expansive and inspiring a vindication of American religious pluralism as has ever been written:

> It is now no more that toleration is spoken of as if it were the indulgence of one class of people that another enjoyed the exercise of their inherent natural rights, for, happily, the Government of the United States, which gives to bigotry no factions, to persecution no assistance, requires only that they who live under its protection should demean themselves as good citizens in giving it on all occasions their effectual support.[25]

By the 1840s, America's Jewish population, most of them of German origin, had increased to about fifteen thousand. Though political anti-Semitism wouldn't become a force in American political life until Jews began to arrive in significant numbers from eastern Europe in the 1880s, it would be a mistake to assume that America was free from anti-Jewish prejudice until then. General Ulysses Grant's General Order No. 11 of 1862, which summarily expelled all Jews from the Department of the Tennessee, reflected the same deep-seated animus against Jews that Ford, who was born a year later, imbibed with his mother's milk. Grant justified his actions to Assistant Secretary of War C. P. Wolcott in words that eerily anticipate the editorial voice of *The Dearborn Independent* (and that are featured prominently on many anti-Semitic Web sites to this day):

> They come in with their carpet-sacks in spite of all that can be done to prevent it. The Jews seem to be a privileged class that can travel everywhere. They will land at any wood-yard on the river and make their way through the country. If not permitted to buy

cotton themselves they will act as agents for someone else, who will be at a military post with a Treasury permit to receive cotton and pay for it in Treasury notes which the Jew will buy up at an agreed rate, paying gold.[26]

It's important to remember that Grant's order was shocking even in its day. Though it had its partisans, resolutions against it were introduced in both the House and the Senate, and it would come back to haunt him when he ran for president in 1868. President Lincoln ultimately countermanded it.

By the time Ford was a young man, America's Jewish population had grown exponentially; between 1880 and 1900, it swelled from 200,000 to more than 1 million. By the 1920s, it had surpassed 4 million.[27] Not coincidentally, the agrarian populism that came to the fore in the later years of the nineteenth century contained a strong anti-Semitic component (it was also enduringly hostile to England). "In Populist thinking," wrote Albert Lee in *Henry Ford and the Jews*, "we find all of the fundamentals of Ford's economic anti-Semitism."

It was a childish assumption which linked all finance to Jewry. . . . In the Populist model, the quintessential American was a man who worked with his hands. The antithesis was the man who manipulated ideas and money—the financier, the creditor who makes his living "at the expense" of the toil of "real Americans."[28]

The Silverite movement of the 1880s and 1890s, which carried William Jennings Bryan to two bids for the U.S. presidency, attributed the nation's economic ills to the "Crime of 1873," the congressional Coinage Act that had effectively demonetized silver—the direct result, many believed, of a conspiracy of English and Jewish bankers, spearheaded by the Rothschilds. Should silver coinage be restored, the Silverites believed, it would not only be a boon for silver miners out west but would also allow farmers to pay back old debts with cheaper coin. But standing between the farmers and prosperity were the money interests. "The most direful part of this business between Rothschild and the United States Treasury," as Gordon Clark put it in 1894, "was not the *loss of money*, even by hundreds of millions. It was the resignation of the country itself INTO THE HANDS of

England, as England had long been resigned into the hands of HER JEWS."[29]

"It is not too much to say that the Greenback Populist tradition activated most of what we have of modern popular anti-Semitism in the United States," Richard Hofstadter wrote in *The Age of Reform* in 1955:

> From Thaddeus Stevens and Coin Harvey to Father Coughlin, and from Brooks and Henry Adams to Ezra Pound, there has been a curiously persistent linkage between anti-Semitism and money and credit obsessions. A full history of modern anti-Semitism in the United States would reveal, I believe, its substantial Populist lineage, but it may be sufficient to point out here that neither the informal connection between Bryan and the Klan in the twenties nor Thomas E. Watson's conduct in the Leo Frank case were altogether fortuitous. And Henry Ford's notorious anti-Semitism of the 1920's, along with his hatred of "Wall Street," were the foibles of a Michigan farm boy who had been liberally exposed to Populist notions.[30]

One prominent Silverite politician, Ignatius Donnelly, was also a popular writer on pseudoscientific subjects. His book *Atlantis: The Antediluvian World* (1882) laid the groundwork for the modern myth of the lost civilization; *Ragnarok: The Age of Fire and Gravel* (1883) anticipated Immanuel Velikovsky in its account of an ancient planetary collision with a comet. He wrote several books that argued that Shakespeare was really Francis Bacon, and that he'd sprinkled cryptogrammic clues to his authorship throughout the plays. In 1890, Donnelly published *Caesar's Column*, a dystopian science fiction novel set in the far-off 1980s, when the United States had become a capitalist tyranny controlled by a ruthless Jewish oligarchy.

"The aristocracy of the world is now almost altogether of Hebrew origin," one of the characters explains. "It was the old question of survival of the fittest."

> Christianity fell upon the Jews . . . and forced them, for many centuries, through the most terrible ordeal of persecution the history of mankind bears any record of. Only the strong of body, the cun-

ning of brain, the long-headed, the persistent, the men with the capacity to live where a dog would starve, survived the awful trial. Like breeds like; and now the Christian world is paying, in tears and blood, for the sufferings inflicted by their bigoted and ignorant ancestors upon a noble race. When the time came for liberty and fair play, the Jew was master in the contest with the Gentile, who hated and feared him.

They are the great money-getters of the world. They rose from dealers in old clothes and peddlers of hats to merchants, to bankers, to princes. They were as merciless to the Christian as the Christian had been to them.[31]

Donnelly's view of the Jews might not pass muster with today's canons of political correctness, but he wasn't a thoroughgoing hater. The Georgia populist Thomas E. Watson (who became a U.S. senator in 1921) most certainly was. Defending the Leo Frank lynching in the October 1915 issue of his eponymous *Watson's Magazine*, he took particular umbrage at the effrontery of S. Mason, the editor of *The Jewish Daily News* of New York, who had appealed to the Vatican to "arouse Christendom to a realization of the sufferings of millions of human beings—the Jews—so that they may be accorded, wherever they now lack these—full equal rights and treatments." The pope had responded warmly, through his apostolic delegate in Washington, D.C. Watson was indignant. How dare these Jews and the pope conduct their conversations through an ambassador, as though the Jews were a sovereign state? It was an outrageous breach of protocol. How dare they address the pope as if he were the chief of all Christendom— and how dare he answer them? It is as if, Watson raged, "there are no Christians save the Romanists. Waldensians, Greek Catholics, and Armenians—all more ancient than Romanists—are left with the heathen. Baptists, Methodists, Lutherans, Presbyterians, Adventists, etc. are mere trash."

With a fine display of scorn for our President and Secretary of State, the Three Million Jews slap the face of Diplomatic Etiquette; and with a noble exhibition of contempt for non-Catholic churches, they spit upon the creed of Christianity. Two years ago, I thought that there were evidences of a league between American priests and the rich Jews of our large cities, and our readers may remember my comments. There is no longer any doubt that the Roman priests and the opulent Jews are allies.[32]

Agrarian populism emerged in the late nineteenth century. But "conspiracism in the Jacksonian era offers striking parallels with antisemitism," Chip Berlet and Matthew N. Lyons note in *Right-Wing Populism in America*. The producerist ethos—which remains an undercurrent in right-wing populism to this day—would have also exerted a strong formative influence on Ford. Producerism offers up a vision of farmers, artisans, merchants, and industrialists—the people who actually *create* wealth—as victims of both the idle poor beneath them on the economic ladder (not to mention the not-so-idle immigrants and free blacks who sell their labor cheap) and the parasitic financiers who cluster at its top. Producerism featured many of the anti-elitist themes and scapegoating that would later be applied wholesale to the Jews. "The attack on Freemasons echoes descriptions of the Jew as a bloodthirsty, power-hungry threat to Christian morality," Berlet and Lyons observed:

> The Jacksonian dichotomy between "productive" entrepreneurs and "parasitic" bankers is almost identical to a basic tenet of modern anti-Semitism: that the abstract, parasitic power of money (embodied in the Jewish banker) threatens the concrete authenticity of productive activity (embodied in non-Jewish workers, farmers, and industrial capitalists). Other aspects of the hatred of Jews are mirrored in the nativist image of Catholics as agents of a foreign power secretly plotting to take over the country, as tools of Satan, and as rapists and prostitutes whose sexual corruption takes monstrous forms. When anti-Semitism did become an important tool of political movements later in U.S. history, it resonated and interacted with these distinct ideological traditions.[33]

I will have much more to say about anti-Masonry, anti-Catholic Know-Nothingism, and producerism in later chapters.

If the Jewish conspiracy was largely a figment of Ford's imagination, so too was the bucolic American ideal that he believed he was defending. Like many conspiracy theorists, Ford mourned the world he had known in his youth as an Edenic paradise lost. During the 1920s, Ford organized a number of village industries, rural developments that included water-powered factories where farmers could work when they weren't tilling their fields outdoors, which he hoped would stanch the flight to the cities. They didn't, but the idea inspired planners in both Nazi Germany and Roosevelt's New Deal. Greenfield Village, Ford's museum of Americana in Dearborn, Michigan (to which he transported McGuffey's log cabin birthplace in 1934), memorialized a way of life that was rapidly disappearing.

Of course Ford knew who was to blame. "The Jew is not an agriculturalist," he wrote. "The productive work of farming has not had, and does not now have, any appeal to him. His choice in land is this: land that produces gold from the mine, and land that produces rents. Land that produces mere potatoes and wheat has not directly interested him." In Ford's conspiratorial view, the Jew recognized that the independent farmer posed a serious threat to his power. "The farmer's strong advantage is that, owning the land, he is independent in his sources of livelihood. The land will feed him whether he pleases International Jewish Financiers or not."

> It was therefore necessary to do something to hinder this budding independence. [The farmer] was placed under a greater disadvantage than any other business man in borrowing capital. He was placed more ruthlessly than any other producer between the upper and nether stones of a thievish distribution system. Labor was drawn away from the farm. The Jewish-controlled melodrama made the farmer a "rube," and Jew-made fiction presented him as a "hick," causing his sons to be ashamed of farm life. The grain syndicates which operate against the farmer are Jew-controlled.[34]

Perhaps Ford was thinking of the 1906 George M. Cohan musical *Forty-Five Minutes from Broadway*, which featured this ditty:

> *If you want to see*
> *The real jay delegation,*
> *The place where the*
> *Real rubens dwell.*

Just hop on a train
At the Grand Central Station.
Get off when they shout
"New Rochelle."

But Cohan, of course, was no Jew: the tribe of Cohan is Hibernian, not Hebraic; the name is derived from the Gaelic Mac Giolla Chaoine. The idea that the rube is a Jewish literary invention is frankly risible; one need look no further than Shakespeare's rustic bumpkins to realize that it manifestly isn't so.

Whether or not Ford's agrarian sympathies were the cause of his anti-Semitism, it was because of them that his public crusade against the Jews came to its abrupt end. Starting in April 1924, *The Dearborn Independent* ran a series of twenty articles, many of them bylined Robert Morgan (a pseudonym for Harry H. Dunn,[35] a former baseball player who'd covered the Mexican Revolution as a freelance journalist in the second decade of the twentieth century), that purported to expose a wide-ranging Jewish plot against America's farmers:

> A band of Jews—bankers, lawyers, moneylenders, advertising agencies, fruit packers, produce buyers, professional office managers and book keeping experts—is on the back of the American farmer. . . .
> This organization was born in the fertile, fortune-seeking brain of a young Jew on the Pacific Coast a little more than five years ago.[36]

The Jew in question was Aaron Sapiro, a lawyer who'd organized a number of agricultural cooperatives around the country. Whether or not the cooperatives thrived or failed, *The Dearborn Independent* insinuated, Sapiro had always assiduously collected his fees, turning "millions away from the pockets of the men who till the soil and into the pockets of the Jews and their followers."

Sapiro sued the *Independent* and Ford himself for defamation, and the case was tried two years later. After many theatrics in and out of the courtroom, a mistrial was declared when Ford's attorneys accused a juror of accepting a bribe. A new trial was scheduled, but Ford unexpectedly settled before it began. Not only did he pay Sapiro $140,000 ($1.7 million in today's dollars, according to the consumer price index), but he shuttered *The Dearborn Independent* and vowed to remove *The International Jew* from circulation. He also issued an astounding letter of apology, drafted by, of all people, the American Jewish Committee's Louis Marshall (the same man who'd written of Ford's "low mentality" just three years previously).

"For some time I have given consideration to the series of articles concerning Jews which since 1920 have appeared in *The Dearborn Independent*," Ford's mea culpa began. "To my great regret I have learned that Jews generally, and particularly those of this country, not only resent these publications as promoting anti-Semitism, but regard me as their enemy." Ford had been too preoccupied by other matters even to read his newspaper, never mind to write the flood of books and articles that had appeared under his byline, the letter continued. He had delegated those duties "to men whom I placed in charge of them and upon whom I relied implicitly." He was flabbergasted by the words they'd put in his mouth:

I am deeply mortified that this journal, which is intended to be constructive and not destructive, has been made the medium for resurrecting exploded fictions, for giving currency to the so-called *Protocols of the Wise Men of Zion,* which have been demonstrated, as I learn, to be gross forgeries, and for contending that the Jews have been engaged in a conspiracy to control the capital and the industries of the world, besides laying at the door many offenses against decency, public order and good morals.

No one had more *Ahavat Yisrayel,* love of Israel, than he did, Ford averred (though not in those exact words):

Had I appreciated even the general nature, to say nothing of the details, of these utterances, I would have forbidden their circulation without a moment's hesitation, because I am fully aware of the virtues of the Jewish people as a whole, of what they and their ancestors have done for civilization and for mankind toward the development of commerce and industry, of their sobriety and diligence, their benevolence, and their unselfish interest in the public welfare.[37]

It was absurd, of course; Ford would continue to rail against Jewry in private for the rest of his life. Both Cameron (who would become active in British Israelism*) and Liebold, who made no secret of his Nazi sympathies, would continue to work for Ford, despite the "mortification" they had ostensibly caused him. Cameron would host *The Ford Sunday Evening Hour* on CBS radio between 1934 and 1942. Liebold didn't retire until 1944. *The International Jew* continued to sell briskly in Germany and other countries through the 1930s; Ford was only too happy to accept the Grand Cross of the Supreme Order of the German Eagle in 1938, the highest honor the Third Reich conferred on non-Germans (Mussolini was also a recipient of the decoration). So why the public about-face?

Gerald L. K. Smith, a Disciples of Christ minister, a co-founder with Huey Long of the Share Our Wealth movement, a leader of the isolationist America First Party, and an unabashed white supremacist and anti-Semite, would bring out an edition of *The International Jew* under his own imprint. In its introduction, he claimed that Ford, who had funded some of his projects, had privately told him that Harry Bennett, Ford's go-to man for rough assignments (spying on employees, union busting, and so on), had forged Ford's signature on the apology, which Ford hadn't even read before it was released to the press.[38]

In interviews and in *We Never Called Him Henry*, the as-told-to memoir he wrote in 1951, six years after Henry Ford II fired him, Bennett said much the same thing, though he insisted he'd acted with Ford senior's full knowledge and approval. According to Bennett's not entirely plausible account, Ford had told Herman Bernstein, the editor of *The Jewish Tribune*, that if he brought him solid proof that the articles in *The Dearborn Independent* had caused any material harm to any Jew, anywhere in the world, he would instantly repudiate them. Bernstein embarked on a fact-finding mission to Europe. When he returned with the incontrovertible evidence that Ford had asked for, Bennett was deputized to do whatever was necessary to make things right.[39]

---

* A religious movement premised on the notion that the Anglo-Saxon people are descended from the original Israelites, which later devolved, in the form of Christian Identity, into the white supremacist belief that the people who call themselves Jews today are really the descendants of Khazarite converts—or of Satan himself (and thus no kin to Jesus). Christian Identity also teaches that the dark races were created on the fifth day, along with the beasts.

In his roman à clef *The Flivver King: A Story of Ford-America* (1937), Upton Sinclair related a very different story, in which the Hollywood producer William Fox threatened to unleash a national newsreel campaign about fatal crashes involving Ford automobiles unless Ford immediately put a stop to his "Jew baiting." What's certain is that there was talk of boycotts and there were more lawsuits to come. Whether or not Ford would have prevailed against Sapiro on narrow legal grounds in a second trial, it had become increasingly clear that his anti-Jewish activities were jeopardizing his business. As Will Rogers quipped, "Ford used to have it in for the Jewish people until he saw them in Chevrolets, and then he said, 'Boys, I am all wrong.' "[40]

Ford issued his recantation just as the Model A—a new product that he had invested millions in—was ready to roll off the line. If the Jews were as wealthy as Ford said they were, then why discourage their business? "I was sad and I was blue, but now I'm just as good as you, since Henry Ford apologized to me," the Happiness Boys (of "Yes! We Have No Bananas" fame) sang, in broad Yiddish accents. They knew full well what he was up to.

Di mama said she'd feed him if he calls
Gefilte fish and matzo balls
And even if he runs for president I wouldn't charge a single cent
I'll cast my ballot absolutely free . . . maybe
He's got an aviator for his new machine
Instead of Cholly Lindboigz he's got Charles Levine.[41]

Funny that they linked Ford's and Lindbergh's names back then. When World War II broke out and Lindbergh was denied a commission in the army, his fellow isolationist Ford would hire him to test and design bombers at the Willow Run plant.

A marketer today would call Ford's apology a rebranding effort. Timing played an equally critical role in Ford's second disavowal of anti-Semitism, which was issued in 1942, just as the United States went to war with the Axis—and the prospect of limitless defense contracts beckoned. In a widely publicized open letter to Sigmund Livingston of the Anti-Defamation League, Ford opined that "the creation of hate against the Jew or any other racial or religious group, has been utilized to divide our American community and weaken our national unity." He offered up his heartfelt hope that "when this war is finished, hatred of the Jews, commonly known as anti-Semitism, and hatred against any other racial or religious groups, shall cease for all times." Needless to say, Ford didn't write that statement either.[42]

Ford was also responding to pressure from his family. Edsel Ford, who would die in 1943, didn't share his father's prejudices and made it clear that they embarrassed him. After his grandfather died in 1947, Henry Ford II would make the first of his many expiatory donations to Jewish causes and organizations. But the anecdotal evidence strongly suggests that Ford senior never did understand what he had had to apologize for. As far as he was concerned, the Jewish people owed him a debt of gratitude.

"The study of the Jewish Question will bring knowledge and insight, and not to the Gentile only, but also to the Jew," Ford had written. "The Jew needs this as much, even more than the Gentile. For if the Jew can be made to see, understand, and deal with certain matters, then a large part of the Question vanishes. . . . Awaking the Gentile to the facts about the Jew is only part of the work; awaking the Jew to the facts about the Question is an indispensable part."[43]

Back in 1920, when *The Dearborn Independent* began its crusade, Ford had been baffled when his neighbor Rabbi Leo Franklin refused his annual gift of a new car. "I cannot in self-respect continue to be the beneficiary of your well-meant courtesy," the rabbi had written to him. "You claim that you do not intend to attack all Jews, but whatever the thought in your own mind, it stands to reason that those who read these articles—inspired and sanctioned by you—will naturally infer that it is your purpose to include in your condemnation every person of the Jewish faith." Liebold penned an icy reply, in which he expressed his hope that conditions "will so adjust themselves as to eventually convince yourself that Mr. Ford's position is correct." Ford, however, picked up the phone and called the rabbi, plaintively asking, "Has something come between us?"[44]

"The Jews have gone along during the ages making themselves disliked, right?" Ford purportedly told a friend during a round of golf. "They ignored their own splendid teachers and statesmen. Even they could not get their people to mend their obnoxious habits. I thought by taking a club to them I might be able to do it."[45] An oft-told story, originating in an unpublished manuscript by Josephine Gomon, Ford's director of women personnel in the Willow Run bomber plant (and a prominent figure in Detroit political circles), relates how Ford suffered his third and most massive stroke after watching uncut newsreel footage that had been shot at the Majdanek concentration camp in May 1945.[46] The implication is that he was conscience-stricken.

Perhaps he was, but as sentimental as Ford could be (he and his wife co-authored a book about the historical Mary of "Mary Had a Little Lamb" fame after he purchased the Sudbury, Massachusetts, schoolhouse the lamb had followed her to), most of the time he seemed oblivious to the effects that his theories might be having on their flesh-and-blood objects: the wounded feelings of the rabbi next door, the Kafkaesque ordeal of the falsely accused Robert Rosenbluth, or the grim fates of the millions of European Jews who had fallen beneath the Nazis' sway. Like the visionary of mass production that he was, Ford kept his eye on the big picture. What ultimately mattered to him were the finished cars rolling off the assembly line under their own power, not the countless hands that had put their pieces together and tightened the bolts. So it was with the Jews.

If Ford's monomaniacal anti-Semitism weren't so deplorable, there would almost be something poignant about it. Because as ardently as Ford mourned America's lost rural innocence, deep down inside he must have realized that he himself—or the American automotive culture that is his greatest legacy—had done more to ruin it than anything else. Thanks to cars, sinful city pleasures (moving pictures, jazz, fashion, bathtub gin) were no longer impossibly remote and inaccessible for farm dwellers; dangerous citified ideas—about agricultural co-ops, for example—were more easily propagated and spread as well.

The lure of well-paid work on Ford's assembly lines drew far more farmworkers to cities than crude jokes about their fathers' uncouth ways. But even if they had chosen to stay and work the land, tractors and motorized harvesters swiftly rendered most of them redundant. According to the USDA's Economic Research Service, some 41 percent of Americans worked in agriculture in 1900. By 1930 that percentage had been halved. Less than 2 percent work on farms today.[47]

As the manufacturer of a mass-produced object of desire that his own workers could afford to purchase, Ford did more than anyone to create the credit-driven consumerist culture that he found so objectionable. Verdant landscapes were bulldozed to build the roads that cars drove on; their noisy engines frightened the livestock; the exhaust fumes they belched fouled the air. Bootleggers smuggled moonshine in the trunks of souped-up cars; young people clad in raccoon coats took full advantage of the mobile, parent-free zone of sexual experimentation that cars provided.

In "To the Puritan All Things Are Impure," an essay collected in *Music at Night* (1931), Aldous Huxley defined Fordism as the "philosophy of industrialism." "Rigorously practiced for a few generations," he wrote, "this dreadful religion of the machine will end by destroying the human race."[48] It is richly ironic that, abstemious and prudish as he was in real life, Ford would preside over the dystopian civilization that Huxley went on to create in his novel *Brave New World* as its deity and savior. Huxley's World State's history is divided into two great epochs, B.F. (Before Ford) and A.F. (After Ford); its shallow, sensual citizenry regularly offer up thanks to Ford for their good fortune and express their sense of self-satisfaction in clichés like "Ford's in his flivver. All's well with the world." "Our Ford himself did a great deal to shift the emphasis from truth and beauty to comfort and happiness," its World Controller observes. "Mass production demanded the shift."[49]

A psychologist might theorize that Ford's Jew hatred was a titanic act of displacement, from himself and his industrialist peers to a ready-made scapegoat that, like countless other people of his day, he had already been taught to hate. But as vicious and extreme as Ford's crusade was, his place in the American pantheon remains secure. He will be forever remembered as the small-town tinkerer who revolutionized our country's economy, his racist and conspiracist obsessions easily forgiven as the foibles of an eccentric genius who was occasionally given to bouts of endearing crankiness. *The Dearborn Independent*, like a bad dream, swiftly faded from America's collective consciousness.

Except it didn't. Scratch beneath the surface of virtually any anti-Semitic group—Willis Carto's Liberty Lobby, Hamas, Christian Identity, David Duke's white nationalism—and, like a palimpsest, traces of *The Dearborn Independent* will bleed through. That's because it's so infused with the spirit and substance of *The Protocols of the Elders of Zion.*

A host of other factors undoubtedly contributed to Ford's anti-Semitism, but the reagent that catalyzed it into a full-blown theory of everything was his discovery of the book called *The Protocols of the Elders of Zion.* "The only statement I care to make about the *PROTOCOLS* is that they fit in with what is going on," he declared in an interview with the New York *World* in 1921. "They are sixteen years old, and they have fitted the world situation up to this time. THEY FIT IT NOW."

There's a strange synchronicity here. Theodor Herzl organized and presided over the First Zionist Congress in Basel, Switzerland, in 1897 after he had come to believe that the Dreyfus affair was no mere miscarriage of justice but "contained the wish of the overwhelming majority in France to damn a Jew and in this one Jew, all Jews."[50] Herzl had seen the writing on the wall. He was personally present for Dreyfus's public humiliation after his first guilty verdict in 1894, when his epaulettes were torn off his uniform and his sword was ceremonially broken; he'd heard the spectators' bloodthirsty chants of "Death to the Jews!"

"We have sincerely tried everywhere to merge with the national communities in which we live, seeking only to preserve the faith of our fathers," Herzl wrote in *Der Judenstaat (The Jewish State)* in 1896. "In vain are we loyal patriots, sometimes super-loyal. . . . In our native lands where we have lived for centuries we are still decried as aliens."[51] For all the hopes that had been vested in emancipation, it had been an abject failure, he regretfully concluded. France—the first European country to extend the full rights of citizens to its Jews—had its Dreyfus; no sooner had Germany enfranchised its Jews than writers like Wilhelm Marr* (his *Der Sieg des Judenthums über das*

---

* For collectors of coincidences, I note without comment that Marr shares all but one letter of his surname with two of the most visible conspiracy theorists at work in America today, Jim Marrs, the best-selling author of *Crossfire, Alien Agenda,* and *Rule by Secrecy,* and Texe Marrs, an apocalyptic preacher and anti-Semite who has published extensively about the Illuminati, the Zionist conspiracy, and satanic secret societies. His Web site is currently promoting a two-hour taped lecture called *Are Lesbians and Homosexuals Demon-Possessed?*

Germanenthum [The conquest of the world by the Jews] appeared in 1879) stirred a violent backlash. In 1897, the same year that the First Zionist Congress convened in Basel, Switzerland, the anti-Semitic Karl Lueger became mayor of Vienna.

"The Jewish question persists wherever Jews live in appreciable number," Herzl wrote.

> Wherever it does not exist, it is brought in together with Jewish immigrants. We are naturally drawn into those places where we are not persecuted, and our appearance there gives rise to persecution. This is the case, and will inevitably be so, everywhere, even in highly civilized countries—see, for instance, France—so long as the Jewish question is not solved on the political level. The unfortunate Jews are now carrying the seeds of anti-Semitism into England; they have already introduced it into America.[52]

Europe's Jews, Herzl concluded, had no choice but to form a nation of their own. For all its high aspirations, for all its pomp and self-importance—its delegates dressed in top hats and tails, its dinners and balls—the very fact that a Zionist congress needed to be held at all was an admission of Jewish failure and weakness—and a foreshadowing of the horrors that awaited in the next century. How ironic that Ford—who did his utmost to bring European-style anti-Semitism to America and who labored mightily to create a Dreyfus of his own in Major Rosenbluth—would seize on a document that was purported to have been created at that very Congress as the forensic proof for his conviction that Jewry "holds the sinews of world power in its hand and it apportions them among the nations in such ways as will best support All-Judaan's plan."[53]

Published first in a shorter form in 1903, in a Russian-language newspaper called *Znamia* (The Banner), and then in a longer version in 1905, as an appendix to the second edition of the Russian mystic Sergei Alexandrovich Nilus's apocalyptic book *Velikoe v Malom* (The great in the small; or, The advent of the Antichrist and the approaching rule of the Devil on earth), *The Protocols of the Elders of Zion* was said to contain the transcripts of twenty-four meetings among world Jewry's innermost circle. While a secretary took careful notes, they reviewed the tactics and stratagems they had been using since the time of Solomon to debauch, impoverish, enervate, and otherwise destroy the unsuspecting *Goyim** of the world.

The supposed discovery of the manuscript—which, according to various accounts, had been written in French or Hebrew and stolen from or leaked by a high Masonic official in Switzerland, France, or Germany (the original has never surfaced)—vindicated every conspiracist theme and meme of the past millennium. "Those who had the privilege of being initiated into the Great Mystery revealed by the book were thunderstruck," wrote Danilo Kiš in his short story "The Book of Kings and Fools," which treats the origins and influences of the *Protocols* in much the same donnish manner and tone as Jorge Luis Borges's *ficciones* about such fanciful literary specimens as the "*Don Quixote* of Pierre Menard" and the one hundred volumes of the *Second Encyclopedia of Tlön*. But if the contents of the *Protocols* were as incredible as anything that the great Argentine fabulist ever dreamed up, the book itself was all too real. As Kiš noted, many of its readers received it as a revelation—the master key that not only explained the reasons behind all of the miseries and dislocations that had occurred over the past century, but identified the villains who were responsible for them:

> The workings of European history, more or less from the French Revolution on, were laid out before them. Everything that had previously seemed the result of chance and heavenly machination, a battle of sublime principles and fate, all of it—this murky history as capricious as the gods on Olympus—was now clear as day: someone here below was pulling the strings. Here was proof not only that the Antichrist exists (which no one had doubted) but also that the Evil One has his earthly acolytes.[54]

For Kiš, the most awful thing about the *Protocols* wasn't its programmatic anti-Semitism, or even that it was used to justify pogroms and the Shoah. The *Protocols* was a symptom of Jew hatred, after all, not its cause. Worse was the fact that the Machiavellian philosophy it falsely ascribed to the Jews ("By the law of nature right lies in

---

* *Goy* is the Hebrew word for "nation"; its plural form *Goyim* is a pejorative for "Gentiles." Diaspora Jews were by definition sojourners in other people's lands.

force. . . . The result justifies the means") made such an "impression on the amateur painter who wrote the infamous *Mein Kampf* [and] also influenced an anonymous Georgian seminary student"—that the *Protocols* would become "a manual for contemporary despots."[55] Borges's "Tlön, Uqbar, Orbis Tertius" is the story of a secret society of philosophical idealists who permanently alter the real world by writing about an alternative universe that they'd imagined. So too, in Kiš's telling, did the anonymous authors of the *Protocols*. Their lurid fantasies about absolute evil became all too real when the Third Reich and the Soviet Union were modeled on the example of its fictitious Jewish superstate.

As brilliant and chilling as Kiš's conceit is, in Hitler's case it might have been literally true. *A Lie and a Libel: The History of the Protocols of the Elders of Zion* was one of several books that Binjamin W. Segel wrote in the 1920s to debunk the *Protocols*. In the introduction to his extensively annotated translation, Richard S. Levy quotes from the ex-Nazi Hermann Rauschning's *Gespräche mit Hitler* (Hitler Speaks), which was published in 1940:

> "In those [early] days [of our movement] I read *The Protocols of the Elders of Zion*—I was really shocked," said Hitler. "The perilous stealth of the enemy, and his omnipresence! I saw at once that we would have to imitate this—in our own way, of course. . . . We must strike the Jews with their own weapons. That was clear to me as soon as I read the book."
>
> I asked, "Were you inspired by the *Protocols* in your [political struggle]?"
>
> "Yes, indeed, and in detail. I learned enormously from these *Protocols*."[56]

"The *Goyim* are a flock of sheep, and we are their wolves," the unnamed narrator of the *Protocols* cackles. "And you know what happens when the wolves get hold of the flock?"* In his fourth edi-

---

* Quotations from the *Protocols* are drawn from the Victor Marsden translation, which can easily be found online (though not always at the most salubrious of Web sites).

tion of the *Protocols*, published in 1917, Nilus at long last identified the chief Elder as Herzl himself.

Like a super-villain in a James Bond movie, taking time out from his evildoing to explain himself to the hero, he laid out the conspiracy in all its dreadful details. Relying on the absolute control that the Jews exert over the media and their outsize influence in the academic and intellectual world, the Jews first corrupted the *goyim*'s minds. ("Think carefully of the successes we arranged for Darwinism, Marxism, Nietzsche-ism," he says. "To us Jews, at any rate, it should be plain to see what a disintegrating importance these directives have had upon the minds of the *Goyim*.")

Next, they tricked the cattlelike Gentiles into rejecting the kings, aristocrats, and priests who were their truest friends and protectors and adopting dangerously unstable liberal institutions.

> In all corners of the earth the words "Liberty, Equality, Fraternity" brought to our ranks, thanks to our blind agents, whole legions who bore our banners with enthusiasm. And all the time these words were canker-worms at work boring into the well-being of the *Goyim*, putting an end everywhere to peace, quiet, solidarity and destroying all the foundations of the *Goy* States.
>
> As you will see later, this helped us to our triumph; it gave us the possibility, among other things, of getting into our hands the master card—the destruction of the privileges, or in other words of the very existence of the aristocracy of the *Goyim*, that class which was the only defense peoples and countries had against us.

Preying on their insatiable greed, the Jews taught their victims to value money more than religion ("It is indispensable for us to undermine all faith, to tear out of the mind of the *Goyim* the very principle of God-head and the spirit, and to put in its place arithmetical calculations and material needs"). From there, it was a simple matter to ensnare their poorly led states in debt:

> Foreign loans are leeches which there is no possibility of removing from the body of the State until they fall off of themselves or the State flings them off. But the *Goy* States do not tear them off; they

go on in persisting in putting more on to themselves so that they must inevitably perish, drained by voluntary blood-letting.

It's not just the usurious interest the Rothschilds, their Jewish colleagues, and their various Gentile proxies charge that's so ruinous, but the taxes that states are compelled to levy to pay it down. When the Jewish superstate is established, the Elder confides, its activities will be financed by innovative new modes of taxation: "a progressive tax on property," a "tax increasing in a percentage ratio to capital," and levies on "receipt of money," such as retail sales and inheritances. Thanks to the Jewish money interests, the Gentile nations are driven to adopt such dangerously inflationary expedients as paper money, since "economic crises have been produced by us . . . by no other means than the withdrawal of money from circulation"—for example, by the demonetization of silver.

By manipulating the money supply, by seeing to it that some countries remain poorer than others, the Jews foment wars and other miseries. By promoting labor unions and compulsory public education, they raise the aspirations of the lower classes beyond their capabilities or deserts, guaranteeing the eventual establishment of Socialist and Communist regimes that will inevitably collapse into chaos, allowing the Davidic king of the Jews to openly seize power:

> This Chosen One of God is chosen from above to demolish the senseless forces moved by instinct and not reason, by brutishness and not humanness. These forces now triumph in manifestations of robbery and every kind of violence under the mask of principles of freedom and rights. They have overthrown all forms of social order to erect on the ruins the throne of the King of the Jews; but their part will be played out the moment he enters into his kingdom. Then it will be necessary to sweep them away from his path, on which must be left no knot, no splinter.
>
> Once his absolute iron rule is imposed, he will ruthlessly purge the anarchic forces that made his usurpation possible.

As preternaturally powerful as they are, the Jews cannot create their New World Order without their victims' unwitting assistance. Secret societies—particularly those of the Freemasons (whom conspiracists had long blamed for such social and political eruptions as the French Revolution and, through such related groups as the Carbonari, the Italian Risorgimento)—have all been infiltrated and co-opted by Jews. "Until we come into our kingdom, we shall create and multiply free Masonic lodges in all the countries of the world, absorb into them all who may become or who are prominent in public activity, for these lodges we shall find our principal intelligence office and means of influence." Once they have served their purpose, they too will be disposed of:

> When we at last definitely come into our kingdom by the aid of coups d'etat prepared everywhere for one and the same day, . . . we shall make it our task to see that against us such things as plots shall no longer exist. With this purpose we shall slay without mercy all who take arms . . . to oppose our coming into our kingdom. Every kind of new institution of anything like a secret society will also be punished with death; those of them which are now in existence, are known to us, serve us and have served us, we shall disband and send into exile to continents far removed from Europe. In this way we shall proceed with those *Goy* Masons who know too much; such of these as we may for some reason spare will be kept in constant fear of exile. We shall promulgate a law making all former members of secret societies liable to exile from Europe as the center of rule.

The *Protocols* passed through a number of editions in its first decade and a half and was widely circulated among the Russian aristocracy and officer class. Its first German translation appeared in 1919, published by Gottfried zur Beek (a pen name for Captain Ludwig Müller von Hausen, a former leader of a group called the Alliance Against the Arrogance of Jewry) as a chapter of a longer work called *Die Geheimnisse der Weisen von Zion* ("The secrets of the Elders of Zion"). Von Hausen quietly added explicit references to World War I and the League of Nations to its text, making it seem that much more prescient, and two additional rabbinical speeches, one supposedly delivered at the Zionist Congress of Lwow in 1912 (which never took place). Von Hausen's enlarged version of the *Protocols* was swiftly translated into Polish, French, Italian, and English (its first English-language title was *The Jewish Peril*). In 1925, an Arabic translation appeared in Damascus; in the 1930s, it was published in Portuguese and Spanish in Brazil and Spain. The *Protocols'* effect on a world that was still reeling from the political, social, and economic aftershocks of World War I and Russia's Bolshevik Revolution—and by the rise of Fascism—was electric.

"Have we," a correspondent for *The Times* of London wrote on May 8, 1920, "by straining every fibre of our national body, escaped a 'Pax Germanica' only to fall into a 'Pax Judaica'?" A few months later, the London *Morning Post* examined the *Protocols* in a series of eighteen articles, under the general title "The Cause of World Unrest." America's *Christian Science Monitor* considered the implications of *The Jewish Peril* on June 19, 1920, pointedly noting the sinister resemblance of the Elders' program to that of the eighteenth-century Illuminati:

> Anybody who will for a moment turn to the outpourings of Adam Weishaupt and the Illuminati may satisfy himself of that. . . . John Robison, who studied the gyrations of this order, in the spurious Masonic lodges of France and Germany, has summed up its ideals as the obliteration of Christianity; the deification of sensuality; the proscription of property; the abjuration of all religion and morality; the repudiation of marriage, and as a necessary corollary the state adoption of children; universal license; and the wrecking of civilization and giving over of society to general plunder.

"What is important," the *Monitor's* editor soberly concluded, "is to dwell upon the increasing evidence of the existence of a secret conspiracy, throughout the world, for the destruction of organized government and the letting loose of evil."

According to some accounts, Henry Ford was introduced to the *Protocols* by Boris L. Brasol, a White Russian lawyer, military officer, criminologist, and literary critic who immigrated to the United States in 1916, after winning distinction for himself by gathering evidence against Mendel Beylis, a Ukrainian Jew who was tried for the ritual murder of a Gentile child. Brasol is generally credited with the translation of the first American edition of the *Protocols*, which was published in Boston in 1920. In other accounts Ford received a copy of the *Protocols* from Paquita de Shishmareff, the American widow of a Russian aristocrat who was murdered by Bolsheviks. In 1931, under the pen name L. Fry, she would publish *Waters Flowing Eastward: The War Against the Kingship of Christ*, a book-length analysis and defense of the authenticity of the *Protocols* that warned that the present British and American governments were "Jewish radical, or to use plain language, Jewish-bolshevist."

> Both governments are run by men who are merely puppets in the hands of Jews highly placed in the secret councils of the central Jewish Kahal, the present-day Zionist World organization, whose object is the ultimate destruction of all our religious, social and industrial institutions and the annihilation of our freedom.[57]

As Hitler had in *Mein Kampf*, Shishmareff argued that the very fact that Jews were protesting and attempting to suppress the *Protocols* was stark evidence of the book's truth. After all, it wasn't as though Jews had anything to fear from such a scurrilous document; no one in Europe intended them any harm; no one was making plans to strip them of their rights and citizenship and execute them—men, women, and children. No, if anyone was guilty of unjustifiable violence, it was the Jews themselves.

> There is a saying in several languages that only the truth hurts. . . . If the evidence were false, then it would be ignored by those concerned and pass quickly into the realm of forgotten things. But if the evidence is genuine and open to verification from many angles, then the truth will hurt, and thus not be ignored.
>
> If this reasoning is correct, the violent methods used by the Jews, particularly those affiliated with the Zionist movement, to discredit and suppress the document entitled *The Protocols of the Elders of Zion*, would alone constitute a proof of its authenticity.[58]

The *Protocols* hadn't come out of nowhere. As witnessed by *The Christian Science Monitor*'s editorial, it drew on a long tradition of anti-Masonic, anti-Catholic, and anti-Semitic conspiracism. In fact, as we shall soon see, it's possible to trace pretty much precisely where it *did* come from; it is a tissue of plagiarisms, crudely cut and pasted together. And it was planted in fertile ground.

In 1869, a Frenchman named Henri Roger Gougenot des Mousseaux had published a book called *Le juif: Le judaïsme et la judaisation des peuples chrétiens* ("The Jew: Judaism and the Jewification of Christian peoples"). Binjamin W. Segel described it succinctly in *A Lie and a Libel:*

> This far-fetched piece of trash . . . is a wondrous mixture of absurd fantasy, infantile politics, and pathological Jew-hatred. According to Gougenot des Mousseaux, the entire existing state system of the nineteenth century was the creation of the Jews, who took it into their heads to "Jewify" the world. As liberal demands for the rule of law, constitutionalism, separation of powers, parliamentarism, ministerial responsibility, trial by jury, social reform, and compulsory education came closer to reality, so too did the Christian world come closer to Jewification.[59]

Cultural and political anti-Semitism had been rife in Europe throughout the whole of the nineteenth century; the emancipation movement only intensified it. A quip in Richard Wagner's 1850 essay "Judaism in Music" anticipates the principal burden of the *Protocols:* "According to the present constitution of this world, the Jew in truth is already more than emancipate: he rules, and will rule, so long as Money remains the power before which all our doings and our dealings lose their force."[60] Theodor Fritsch's *Antisemiten-Katechismus* ("Anti-Semitic catechism") was published in 1893.

By the time the *Protocols* appeared, conspiracist paranoia about secret societies had been comporting with racial and political anti-Semitism for a century. As early as 1806, Abbé Augustin Barruel had received the Simonini letter that connected the Jews to the Illuminati and Masonry. Ironically, some of the worst conspiratorial calumnies against the Jews came from the pen of the famously philo-Semitic Benjamin Disraeli. "You never observe a great intellectual movement in Europe in which the Jews do not greatly participate," a character in his novel *Coningsby* remarks.

The first Jesuits were Jews. That mysterious Russian Diplomacy which so alarms western Europe is organized and principally carried on by Jews. That mighty revolution which is at this moment preparing in Germany, and which will be, in fact, a second and greater Reformation, and of which so little is yet known in England, is entirely developing under the auspices of Jews who almost monopolize the professorial chairs of Germany. . . . The world is governed by very different personages from what is imagined by those who are not behind the scenes.[61]

In his *Lord George Bentinck: A Political Biography* (1852), Disraeli angrily condemned a certain contingent of ultraprogressive Jews, participants in the revolutions of 1848, who'd made common cause with their bitterest enemies to destroy Christianity:

The influence of the Jews may be traced in the last outbreak of the destructive principle in Europe. An insurrection takes place against tradition and aristocracy, against religion and property. Destruction of the Semitic principles, extirpation of the Jewish religion, whether in the Mosaic or the Christian form, the natural equality of men and the abrogation of property are proclaimed by the Secret Societies which form Provisional Governments and men of the Jewish race are found at the head of every one of them. The people of God cooperate with atheists; the most skillful accumulators of property ally themselves with Communists; the peculiar and chosen Race touch the hand of all the scum and low castes of Europe; and all this because they wish to destroy that ungrateful Christendom which owes to them its name, and whose tyranny they can no longer endure.

This outrageous and disturbing circumstance Disraeli blamed not on the native duplicity, evil, and vindictiveness of the Jews but on Christian society's wrongheaded insistence on persecuting them. Left to their own devices, Disraeli noted a few paragraphs later, the Jews would have been a potent force for conservatism:

The native tendency of the Jewish race, who are justly proud of their blood, is against the doctrine of the equality of man. They have also another characteristic, the faculty of acquisition. Although the European laws have endeavoured to prevent their obtaining property, they have nevertheless become remarkable for their accumulated wealth. Thus it will be seen that all the tendencies of the Jewish race are conservative. Their bias is to religion, property, and natural aristocracy: and it should be the interest of statesmen that this bias of a great race should be encouraged, and their energies and creative powers enlisted in the cause of existing society. . . . Thus it will be seen, that the persecution of the Jewish race has deprived European society of an important conservative element, and added to the destructive party an influential ally.[62]

I suspect that there are few Jews today, liberal or conservative, who wouldn't be troubled and embarrassed by the specifics, if not the spirit, of Disraeli's ethnic cheerleading. It's easy to imagine how defenders of the *Protocols* might seize on any or all of those quotations as evidence of Jewish perfidy (as they did—Nesta Webster's *Secret Societies and Subversive Movements* begins with an epigraph from Disraeli; Google the words "the world is governed by very different personages" and Jew Watch, BibleBelievers, and David Icke's Web site are among the first to pop up). Whether rich, moneygrubbing Jews are plotting to squash the common man or supplant the Christian aristocracy is all the same to them. In either or both cases the preferred Jewish strategy, they say, is to form tactical alliances, the better to play one side against the other, just as the *Protocols* explains.

Disraeli, of course, was a Jew himself (albeit a baptized one), and that was all Henry Ford needed to know:

The Jew says that the *Protocols* are inventions. Is Benjamin Disraeli an invention? Was this Jewish Prime Minister of Great Britain misrepresenting his people? . . . Disraeli told the truth. He presented his people before the world with correctness. He described Jewish power, Jewish purpose and Jewish method with a certainty of touch that betokens more than knowledge—he shows racial sympathy and understanding. Why did he do it? Disraeli the flamboyant, most oriental of courtiers and suave of politicians, with a keen financial ability. Was it that typically racial boastfulness, that dangerous, aggressive conceit in which the Jew gives up most of his secrets? No matter; he is the one man who told the truth about the Jews without being accused of "misrepresenting the Jews."[63]

When one reads the *Protocols* at the distance of a century and through the clarifying lens of the Holocaust, it seems incredible from a literary standpoint alone that anyone could believe in its authenticity—or that Americans, who, after all, have been generally hostile to priests and titled aristocrats and who take intense pride in their commercial abilities, wouldn't be nonplussed by its intrinsically undemocratic appeal.

"In the *Goy* societies, in which we have planted and deeply rooted discord and protestantism," Protocol 15 declares, "the only possible way of restoring order is to employ merciless measures that prove the direct force of authority: no regard must be paid to the victims who fall, they suffer for the well-being of the future." By "protestantism" does the Elder simply mean "protest movements" (an uncommon usage to be sure), or is he claiming that the Jews are responsible for the Protestant Reformation itself? "The principal guarantee of stability of rule," he continues, "is to confirm the aureole of power, and this aureole is attained only by such a majestic inflexibility of might as shall carry on its face the emblems of inviolability from mystical causes—from the choice of God. Such was, until recent times, the Russian autocracy, the one and only serious foe we had in the world, without counting the papacy."

If you assume the *Protocols'* authenticity—that it is an accurate transcript of a secret meeting of evil Jews, who have been plotting to impose a one world government on the unsuspecting countries of the world for centuries—must you also believe that the world's hereditary aristocracies were humanity's divinely appointed protectors? What does that say about America's own Revolution?

Did Henry Ford really pine for the restoration of the Catholic monarchies? Did Father Coughlin believe that America's liberal institutions were a Jewish Trojan horse, doomed by design to fail from their very inception—that America's founding fathers (many of them

Masons) were a bunch of saps, manipulated to do their will by wily Jews? Did the Liberty Lobby's Willis Carto believe that representative government is a pitfall that inevitably leads to chaos? Did Elizabeth Dilling believe that commercial pursuits are intrinsically degrading and that capitalism is inherently corrupt? How could they believe all those things and still call themselves patriots? As Richard Hofstadter wrote, "The ecumenicism of hatred is a great breaker-down of precise intellectual discriminations."

It is important to remember that in 1920, when the *Protocols* first exploded into general view, the established order of the Old World was literally coming apart at the seams: Weimar Germany was devastated and impoverished; the Austro-Hungarian Empire had been shattered; the Ottoman Empire was on its last legs; the tsar and his family were dead and their former empire in the control of the Bolsheviks. There was a disturbingly widespread consensus that the Jews—and not just overt revolutionaries like Trotsky but plutocrats like the Rothschilds in Europe and Paul Warburg and Jacob Schiff in the United States—were responsible for the Russian Revolution. "There is no need to exaggerate the part played in the creation of Bolshevism and in the actual bringing about of the Russian Revolution by these international and for the most part atheistical Jews," Winston Churchill wrote in the London *Illustrated Sunday Herald* in February 1920. "It is certainly a very great one; it probably outweighs all others."

So-called Judeo-Bolshevism, wrote Richard S. Levy, "rescued the *Protocols* from obscurity and has proved the most effective basis for its spread and its credibility." Judeo-Bolshevism does much more than acknowledge the long-standing affinity for progressive causes among the mostly secular Jews of the *haskala* (the Jewish Enlightenment of the eighteenth and nineteenth centuries). To the anti-Semitic way of thinking, the connection was transmitted in the blood, like a bacteria or a virus:

> Jews as a group, as a "race," according to anti-Semitic ideology, were intrinsically Bolshevik, instinctively destructive, no matter the outward, superficial differences among them. Reverting to form, the Christ-killing, well-poisoning, internationally connected Jew had once again unleashed a new affliction upon humanity.[64]

As a matter of historical fact, many more Russian Jews were involved with bourgeois Menshevism than radical Bolshevism. By the 1920s, when Stalin seized control of the state, most of Bolshevism's Jewish leaders were on the way out. Within a decade or so, many of them had been murdered.

But by identifying Jewry with the worst excesses of both liberal capitalism and revolutionary Communism, the *Protocols* rationalized a biblically mandated hatred that had been seething for almost two thousand years—and, not accidentally, directed resentment away from the representatives of the failed or failing old regimes, the very people who had the most to lose from the rising tide of liberalism. Anti-Semitism was already the default stance in most places; the Holocaust was still decades away. In the popular imagination the Jews were more likely to be Shylocks and Christ killers than innocent victims like Anne Frank.

Infinitely adaptable, the *Protocols* provided a one-size-fits-all template for every other conspiracy theory that had gone before it. As Umberto Eco wrote in his novel *Foucault's Pendulum*, "It was, again, the Plan of the Jesuits and, before that, of the Ordonation of the Templars. Few variations, few changes: the Protocols were self-generating; a blueprint that migrated from one conspiracy to another."[65] If the *Protocols* didn't already exist, as the saying goes, someone would have had to invent it. In fact someone did.

The *Protocols* was exposed as a hoax in August 1921, when the Constantinople correspondent of the London *Times*, Philip Graves, published a series of articles that revealed that a large part of its text had been lifted virtually intact from Maurice Joly's *Dialogue aux enfers entre Machiavel et Montesquieu (The Dialogue in Hell Between Machiavelli and Montesquieu)*. A thinly disguised satire of Napoleon III, who, Joly believed, cloaked his illegitimate despotism in the trappings of the liberal state, the *Dialogue* was printed in Geneva and Brussels in 1864 and 1868 and smuggled into France. Joly was arrested for sedition and served eighteen months in prison; virtually every copy of the *Dialogue* was confiscated by the authorities and destroyed. He committed suicide in 1878.

A former Russian landowner, diplomat, and officer of the White Army told Graves about Joly's long-forgotten volume. He'd purchased a rare copy of it, along with several other old books, from an indigent fellow exile who was a former member of the Okhrana, the tsar's secret police. He didn't know its title or author when he began to read it, as it was missing its cover, he said, but its similarities to the *Protocols*—a book he knew well—struck him forcibly. Virtually all of the *Elders of Zion*'s philosophy seemed to have been cribbed from Joly's Machiavelli; not only that, but, as Graves writes, "fully 50 paragraphs in the *Protocols* are simply paraphrases of passages in the *Dialogues*." Graves provided many examples of parallel passages; two will have to suffice here:

DIALOGUE	PROTOCOLS
After covering Italy with blood, Sulla reappeared as a simple citizen in Rome: no one durst touch a hair of his head.	Remember at the time when Italy was streaming with blood, she did not touch a hair of Silla's head, and he was the man who made her blood pour out.
You do not know the unbounded meanness of the peoples . . . groveling before force, pitiless towards the weak, implacable to faults, indulgent to crimes, incapable of supporting the contradictions of a free regime, and patient to the point of martyrdom under the violence of an audacious despotism.	In their intense meanness the Christian peoples help our independence—when kneeling they crouch before power; then they are pitiless towards the weak; merciless in dealing with faults, and lenient to crimes; when they refuse to recognize the contradictions of freedom; when they are patient to the degree of martyrdom in bearing with the violence of an audacious despotism.[66]

Oscar Wilde's former companion Lord Alfred Douglas published one of the first English translations of the *Protocols*. An avid anti-Semite—in 1924 he would be convicted of libel and serve time in prison for accusing Winston Churchill of participating in a Jewish plot to murder Lord Kitchener—Douglas announced that Joly himself was a Jew whose name was really Moses Joel. "Lord Douglas claims to have discovered this," Binjamin W. Segel wrote, "in the obscure memoirs of a French government official, who was supposedly 'intimately acquainted with revolutionaries and their Jewish wire-pullers.' "[67] In fact Joly was a Catholic and a monarchist; his father and grandfather were civil servants. Not surprisingly, Joly's Jewishness would nonetheless become an article of faith among conspiracists, even after his baptismal certificate turned up. Paraphrasing Kerry Bolton's monograph *The Protocols of Zion in Context* (2003), the Canadian conspiracy theorist Henry Makow confidently told his readers that "Joly, a Jew whose real name was Joseph Levy, was a lifelong Mason and member of the 'Lodge of Mizraim' where the Protocols document originated." If anyone was a plagiarist it was Joly himself, Makow insisted; he copied his *Dialogue* from an ur-*Protocol* that predated the Zionist convention.[68]

Joly's was neither the first nor the last deadpan satire that would be misappropriated for an altogether different purpose. Consider the strange case of Léo Taxil. Taxil was the pen name of Marie Joseph Gabriel Antoine Jogand-Pagès, an ex-freethinker and a highly public convert to Catholicism who, in a series of sensational books in the 1880s and 1890s, claimed to have discovered the existence of Palladism, a Devil-worshipping Masonic sect associated with Albert Pike and the Scottish Rite. But then in 1897, Taxil called a press conference in Paris and admitted that he had made the whole thing up. Not just Palladism—*everything*, starting with his conversion. For more than a decade, Taxil had been telling the Catholic Church exactly what it wanted to hear, setting it up for a stupendous fall when "the most colossal hoax of modern times," as he put it, was exposed. Already an incorrigible prankster as a teenager, Taxil had created a panic about fictitious shark attacks in the waters off Marseilles (shark attacks remain a staple of the sensationalistic media to this day); a few years later he fed Swiss newspapers a bogus story about a sunken city beneath Lake Geneva. But despite his spectacular confession, to this day conspiracists continue to cite Taxil's nonsense about Luciferian Masonry as though it were factual. "The only Taxil Hoax," the Web site Freemasonry Watch declares, "is the one Freemasonry is playing on anyone who brings up what High Level Masons have written about God, Satan and Lucifer. It's all just another one of the Masonic sect's 'divert the discourse' disinformation strawman illusions designed to 'hoodwink' the 'profane' (as they derisively refer to all non-Masons)."[69] The *Protocols* was most likely concocted in Paris, just a few years after Taxil's self-exposure; it isn't such a stretch to imagine that its creators might have been partly inspired by his example.

In 1967 in New York, Victor Navasky, the future editor of *The Nation*, who had lately been editor of a left-leaning humor magazine called *Monocle* that he founded with Calvin Trillin and others when they were students at Yale, noticed a news item about a stock market dip that was precipitated by a "peace scare." What would happen, he wondered, if the government were to commission a think tank to consider the dire economic implications of a permanent peace? He talked his friend Leonard C. Lewin, a former labor organizer and free-lance writer, into writing a book based on that very premise. Lewin dreamed up a top secret, blue-ribbon interdisciplinary Special Study Group that met in "an underground nuclear hideout for hundreds of large American corporations" near Hudson, New York. Its fifteen members included a distinguished historian, an economist, a sociologist, a cultural anthropologist, a mathematician, a literary critic, a systems planner, a businessman, and a physical chemist. Then he concocted a copiously footnoted Rand Corporation–style report, written in dense, cold-blooded bureaucratese, which promoted the political, cultural, and economic benefits of war. Here, for example, is the silver lining that the SSG discerned in the cloud of supposedly wasteful military expenditures:

> In the case of military "waste," there is indeed a larger social utility. It derives from the fact that the "wastefulness" of war production is exercised entirely outside the framework of the economy of supply and demand. As such, it provides the only critically large segment of the total economy that is subject to complete and arbitrary central control. If modern industrial societies can be defined as those which have developed the capacity to produce more than is required for their economic survival (regardless of the equities of distribution of goods within them), military spending can be said to furnish the only balance wheel with sufficient inertia to stabilize the advance of their economies. The fact that war is "wasteful" is what enables it to serve this function. And the faster the economy advances, the heavier this balance wheel must be.[70]

The report was ostensibly "leaked" by its primary author, a professor at a Midwestern college who was only identified as "John Doe," and published by the Dial Press as *Report from Iron Mountain: On the Possibility and Desirability of Peace* (its editor, E. L. Doctorow, was in on the joke). John Kenneth Galbraith (also an insider) pseudonymously reviewed it in *The Washington Post,* and it hit the best-seller lists soon after.

In 1972, when *The Pentagon Papers* was published, Lewin went public with the imposture. *The Pentagon Papers,* he said, was "'as outrageous, morally and intellectually' as his own invention. 'The charade is over,' he wrote. 'Some of the documents read like parodies of *Iron Mountain* rather than the reverse.'"[71] Strangely (and appropriately) enough, Lewin's book was reprinted by the far-right Liberty Lobby's Noontide Press in the 1990s as nonfiction; Lewin sued them for copyright infringement and won. Undeterred, conspiracist Web sites continue to post the full text of the book to this day. One appends a brief note mentioning Lewin's claim that the book was a hoax. "The only problem with this 'hoax,'" it demurs, "is that everything in the original book has worked out to be true. So whether the original title is a hoax or not is irrelevant. The original book is a blueprint for the present and the future."[72]

But I have strayed very far from the topic at hand. Joly's forgotten satire was not the only book that the *Protocols* borrowed from. More than a year before Graves dropped his bombshell in the London *Times,* a Berlin monthly had noted that the scenario of the *Protocols*—the convocation of the Jewish conspirators—bore a distinct resemblance to a scene in a German novel written by a virulently anti-Semitic former postal official and journalist named Hermann Goedsche. Published in 1868 under the pen name Sir John Retcliffe, *Biarritz* begins with a chapter titled "In the Jewish Cemetery of Prague," in which the leaders of the twelve tribes of Israel meet, as they do every hundred years on the last day of Sukkot, or the Feast of the Tabernacles, to report on the progress of their long-standing conspiracy to destroy Christendom (the chapter was also published as a stand-alone pamphlet in Russian translation). Drawing on the research of the German researcher O. Friedrich, Benjamin W. Segel presented passages from the two books side by side. Though perhaps not as striking or numerous as the examples from the

Dialogue, they make an undoubted impression. I reproduce two of them below:

PROTOCOLS	BIARRITZ
Every war, every revolution, every political and religious alteration brings us ever closer to attainment of our highest goal.	The instability of thrones lets our power and influence grow. To this end, we see to continuing unrest. Every revolution yields interest for our capital and takes us forward to our goal.
Commerce and speculation, two rich sources of our profit, we may never allow to be snatched from the hands of Israelites. Above all, we must protect our trade in alcohol, butter, bread, and wine because in this way we become the absolute lords of agriculture.	All trade that involves speculation and earnings must be in our hands. Above all, we must own the trade in liquor, oil, wool, and grain because then we will control agriculture and the land.[73]

Clearly the *Protocols* wasn't dictated by Herzl at the First Zionist Congress in Basel (or by the scholar and Zionist Asher Ginzberg or the banker Mayer Rothschild, two other candidates frequently cited by anti-Semitic conspiracists). But who forged it? A number of candidates have been put forward over the years. In 1999, the historian Mikhail Lepekhin fingered Matvei Golovinskii, a reactionary journalist who was based in Paris at the turn of the century and who carried out assignments for Piotr Rachkovskii, the head of the foreign branch of the Okhrana. Whether or not Golovinskii was the culprit (and there are reasons to question the veracity of many of his accusers), most investigators—going back to Philip Graves and Binjamin W. Segel in the 1920s—suspect that the Okhrana was involved in some way. Segel speculates that the *Protocols'* intended audience was none other than Tsar Nicholas II; that it was created to strengthen his resolve during the Revolution of 1905, to dissuade him from making the concessions that led to the adoption of the liberal Russian Constitution in 1906.

Writing in the spring 2008 issue of the journal *New German Critique*, the historian Michael Hagemeister observed that much of the research into the origins of the *Protocols*, even that of skeptics, debunkers, and legitimate academics like Lepekhin, devolves into a kind of demonology of its own. "What we hear," he writes, "is a narrative—to be precise, a conspiracy narrative. The actors this time are not Jews, however, but cunning secret agents, fanatical anti-Semites, and sinister reactionaries. The myth of the Jewish conspiracy has been responded to with a counter myth, which is no less mysterious than the one it aims to counter."[74]

It's no wonder that the *Protocols* and its mysterious authors would be regarded with such fear. Jews have been called the "people of the book." The Jewish mystics who are known as Kabbalists believe that God literally created the world out of Hebrew letters and numbers. But if words can be used to create in the Jewish imagination, they can also be wielded to destroy. Speaking to an interviewer from *The New York Times Book Review* about his novel *The Portage to San Cristóbal of A.H.*, George Steiner said that Hitler accomplished "all that he did by his incomparable command of language, by the almost unimaginable control and power he had over German speech."

Central to everything I am and believe and have written is my astonishment, naive as it seems to people, that you can use human speech both to bless, to love, to build, to forgive and also to torture, to hate, to destroy and to annihilate. In the gospel we read: "In the beginning was the word." And I am asking: Could there be a word at the end? If there is a divine word, a word of creation and forgiveness, is there by the same token a word of final destruction, a word which un-mans man? And did Hitler come very near to knowing that word?[75]

Still, Hagemeister's note of caution should be heeded. As ghastly and despicable as it is, the *Protocols* is neither demonic nor even unique: a vast library exists of equally spurious and destructive calls to hatred. But unlike many of those other titles, the *Protocols* is directly associated with an unparalleled bloodletting. Though countless books slander races, religions, and nations, few of their champions acted on their theories to the same extent as some of the

Protocols' did. If "Heinrich" Ford's anti-Jewish policies were a great inspiration to the up-and-coming Adolf Hitler, the Reich chancellor's Final Solution was carried out under Fordist principles as well: his killing factories were high volume and brutally efficient.

The *Protocols* was literally put on trial in Switzerland and South Africa in the 1930s and was declared a forgery in both cases (one of the Swiss judges dismissed it as "ridiculous nonsense"). But revelations of its dubious provenance have done little to change the minds of those who are already convinced of its premises. In her monumental *Secret Societies and Subversive Movements,* the English conspiracy theorist Nesta Webster admitted that the parallels between Joly's book and the *Protocols* were too obvious to ignore. But the reason they existed, she argued, echoing Lord Douglas, was that Joly was a familiar of the actual conspirators. The authors of the *Protocols* might not have been Jews, but that they were part of "an international circle of world revolutionaries working on the lines of the Illuminati . . . offers a perfectly possible alternative," she avers.

> The *Protocols* are either a mere plagiarism . . . in which case the prophetic passages added by Nilus or another remain unexplained, or they are a revised edition of the plan communicated to Joly in 1864, brought up to date and supplemented so as to suit modern conditions by the continuers of the plot.[76]

In *Pawns in the Game,* William Guy Carr, a retired Canadian naval officer, argued that what fell into Nilus's hands in 1901 were the transcripts of a meeting of wealthy Jews convened by Mayer Rothschild in Frankfurt in 1773. "His purpose was to convince them that if they agreed to pool their resources, they could then finance and control the World Revolutionary Movement and use it as their *Manual of Action* to win ultimate control of the wealth, natural resources, and man-power of the entire world." Rothschild enlisted the *goy* Adam Weishaupt to form the Illuminati, Carr relates; Rothschild himself took his marching orders from Lucifer, who has been striving to enslave mankind since the beginning of time. Christ, in Carr's telling, was the original conspiracy theorist:

He identified the Money-Changers (Bankers) the Scribes, and the Pharisees as the Illuminati of his day. What so many people seem to forget, is the fact that Christ came on earth to release us from the bonds of Satan with which we were being bound tighter and tighter as the years rolled by. Christ gave us the solution to our problem when he told us we must go forth and teach the truth, regarding this conspiracy (John 8. 31:59), to all people of all nations.[77]

William Luther Pierce, the American white supremacist who wrote *The Turner Diaries*, a novel about the coming race war in America (a great favorite of Tim McVeigh's, who was inspired by its hero's detonation of a parked truck loaded with fertilizer outside FBI headquarters in Washington, D.C., to rent a Ryder truck and blow it up outside the Alfred P. Murrah Federal Building in Oklahoma City,* also conceded that the *Protocols* "very likely are not what they purport to be." But that, he said, had no bearing on the book's ultimate truth:

In the first place the text of *The Protocols* doesn't ring true. It's too straightforward, too open. It doesn't use the sort of deceptive, weasel-worded, self-justifying language that Jews customarily use. . . . When a group of Jewish leaders get together to discuss their plans for the destruction of a host nation, they don't use straightforward expressions such as "encouraging miscegenation" and "leading the *goyim* to the slaughter." They use weasel-expressions, such as "building tolerance," "increasing diversity," and "eliminating inequality." . . . I'm inclined to believe Professor Nilus was an astute observer of the Jews and also was a patriot. He wanted to warn the Russian people of what the Jews were planning to do to them, and so he imagined how the Jews' plan might look if it were all laid out in straightforward language. I believe that he wrote the text he published, but that he believed it was a reasonably accurate description of what the Jews actually were doing.[78]

But when one considers the Jewish race's bottomless capacity for deceit, who's to say that the Jews didn't cynically arrange for Joly's

---

* For collectors of coincidences, Pierce was born on September 11, 1933.

and Goedsche's books to be written and published as insurance against the eventual discovery of an incriminating document like the *Protocols*? The Jews, remember, control all of the printing presses in the world (except the ones that publish anti-Semitic books and tracts). Besides, as any number of conspiracists have pointed out, it is perfectly possible to believe in the message of the *Protocols* and not believe that it condemns *all* Jews. Robert Welch was no anti-Semite, but his John Birch Society summoned the spirit of the *Protocols* in its depiction of the all-pervasive Communist/Illuminist conspiracy. Milton William Cooper cited the *Protocols* repeatedly in his writings—he included its entire text in the appendix to his *Behold a Pale Horse*—but with the caveat that his readers should substitute the word "Illuminati" for "Jews" and "cattle" for "Gentiles." The contemporary conspiracy theorist Jim Marrs proposes that the secret societies themselves, not their scapegoats the Jews, are the real actors; the *Protocols* may actually be "an Illuminati document with Jewish elements added for disinformation purposes."[79] The English conspiracy writer David Icke believes that the *Protocols* documents a conspiracy of shape-shifting lizards from outer space or perhaps another dimension (though Icke also believes that the lizards are closely allied with Khazarite impostors—a staple of the Christian Identity religion, which believes that most European Jews aren't descended from the biblical Hebrews at all, but from the Khazars, who converted to Judaism in medieval times). The anti–New Age Christian writer Constance Cumbey has argued that the real authors of the *Protocols* were Theosophical occultists.[80] "The Czarist Okhrana's 'Protocols of Zion' include a hard kernel of truth," wrote the arch-conspiracist Lyndon LaRouche. "The fallacy of the 'Protocols of Zion' is that it misattributes the alleged conspiracy to Jews generally, to *Judaism*. A corrected version of the Protocols would stipulate that the evil oaths cited were actually the practices of variously a Paris branch of B'nai B'rith."[81]

Or you can accept them bag and baggage. Not surprisingly, the *Protocols* is widely circulated and read in the Islamic world today. Book buyers in Ahmadinejad's Iran can read a Persian translation of the *Protocols* that includes four hundred additional pages, covering the Zionists' hostile designs on Iran, among other things. The *Protocols* is explicitly alluded to in Hamas's charter ("For Zionist scheming has no end, and after Palestine they will covet expansion from the Nile to the Euphrates. . . . Their scheme has been laid out in the *Protocols of the Elders of Zion,* and their present [conduct] is the best proof of what is said there"[82]), and it inspired a forty-one-part miniseries, *Horseman Without a Horse,* a history of the Middle East from 1855 to 1917, that was broadcast on Egyptian television in 2002. "This work of sublime hatred," Stephen Eric Bronner wrote in *A Rumor About the Jews: Antisemitism, Conspiracy, and the Protocols of Zion,* "celebrated the existence of a Jewish conspiracy, scenes of the Elders of Zion plotting their strategy, and the supposed discovery of *The Protocols of the Elders of Zion.*"

> The old justification for employing the forgery was rolled out once again: it is not a pedantic matter of whether the tract is authentic since—according to what the star of the series, Muhammed Sobhi, told *The New York Times* (10/26/02)—"Zionism exists and it has controlled the world since the dawn of history."[83]

A similar twenty-one-part series was produced in Syria and aired on a Hezbollah-owned satellite network a year later. As each episode of this second series began, the following text scrolled down the screen (the seemingly awkward translation is provided by the Anti-Defamation League):

> Two thousand years ago the Jewish Rabbis established an international government aiming at maintaining the world under its control and suppressing it under the Talmudic commands, and totally isolating them from all of the people.
>
> Then the Jews started to incite wars and conflicts, while those countries disclaimed them. They falsely pretended to be persecuted, awaiting their savior, the Messiah, who will terminate the revenge against the Goyim that their God, Jehovah, started.
>
> In the beginning of the 19th century, the international government decided to increase the conspiracies and the Jewish international secret government was established, headed by Amschel Rothschild.[84]

Which brings us back to Henry Ford, who wrote extensively about "the international Jewish banker who has no country but plays them all against one another." The *Protocols* sheds a dazzling light on this frightening figure's ultimate aims—which, in America, included "the creation of a banking aristocracy within an already existing autocracy": the Federal Reserve.

Though Morgans and Rockefellers and other non-Jewish bankers presided over its creation, representatives of organized Jewry were its foremost architects, Ford insisted. Especially Paul Warburg, "who admits that it was his ambition from the moment he came here an alien Jewish-German banker, to change our financial affairs more to his liking. More than that, he has succeeded; he has succeeded, he himself says, more than most men do in a lifetime; he has succeeded . . . to such an extent that throughout history the name of Paul M. Warburg and that of the Federal Reserve System shall be united."[85]

On June 10, 1932, the Republican congressman Louis Thomas McFadden took to the floor of the House to condemn the Federal Reserve:

> Mr. Speaker, it is a monstrous thing for this great Nation of people to have its destinies presided over by a traitorous Government board acting in secret concert with international usurers. Every effort has been made by the Federal Reserve Board to conceal its power but the truth is the Federal Reserve Board has usurped the Government of the United States. It controls everything here and it controls all our foreign relations. It makes and breaks governments at will. No man and no body of men is more entrenched in power than the arrogant credit monopoly which operates the Federal Reserve Board and the Federal Reserve banks.[86]

Moving to impeach Herbert Hoover, the secretary of the Treasury, and two assistant secretaries, McFadden also accused the Fed of financing the Bolsheviks and of deliberately causing the Great Depression. It was no mystery where he got his ideas from; he read long passages from *The Dearborn Independent* into the *Congressional Record*. "Mr. Chairman," he said in another stem-winder, this one delivered on January 24, 1934, "do you not see the *Protocols of*

Zion manifested in the appointment of Henry Morgenthau as Secretary of the Treasury? It is not by accident, is it, that a representative and a relative of the money Jews of Wall Street and foreign parts has been so elevated?"[87]

Seventy years later Congressman Ron Paul introduced legislation to eliminate the same Federal Reserve:

> From the Great Depression, to the stagflation of the seventies, to the burst of the dotcom bubble last year, every economic downturn suffered by the country over the last 80 years can be traced to Federal Reserve policy. . . . Though the Federal Reserve policy harms the average *American*, it benefits those in a position to take advantage of the cycles in monetary policy. The main beneficiaries are those who receive access to artificially inflated money and/or credit before the inflationary effects of the policy impact the entire economy. Federal Reserve policies also benefit big spending politicians who use the inflated currency created by the Fed to hide the true costs of the welfare-warfare state.[88]

It's basic Austrian school economics. . . . Except for its insidious hints that a certain class or category of people benefits from the "welfare-warfare" state. Paul himself—a sitting congressman and a once and future presidential candidate—parses his words carefully. His followers are often less circumspect. Here's Paul Joseph Watson and Steve Watson, writing on Alex Jones's Prison Planet Web site in June 2009:

> President Obama's plan to give the privately owned and unaccountable Federal Reserve complete regulatory oversight across the entire U.S. economy, which is likely to be enacted before the end of the year, will officially herald the beginning of a new form of government in the United States—an ultra-powerful banking dictatorship controlled by a small gaggle of shadowy and corrupt elitists. . . . Proof that the agenda of implementing overt financial dictatorship is being carefully coordinated can be seen in the fact that an almost identical scheme is also being set up in the United Kingdom.[89]

Though there is nothing overtly anti-Semitic in their report, its tone and its substance owe much to the *Protocols.* In the words of Nilus himself, writing in his epilogue:

> All countries are indebted to the Jews for sums which they will never be able to pay. All affairs—industry, commerce, and diplomacy—are in the hands of Zion. It is by means of its capital loans that it has enslaved all nations.

In 1952, a speech was delivered in Budapest that received wide play in racist and anti-Semitic newspapers in the United States. Its title was "Our Race Will Rule Undisputed over the World."

"As you know," Rabbi Emanuel Rabinovitch told the Emergency Council of European Rabbis, "we had hoped to have twenty years between wars to consolidate the great gains which we made from World War II, but our increasing numbers in certain vital areas are arousing opposition to us, and we must now work with every means at our disposal to precipitate World War III within five years." The Holocaust, it was revealed, was a regrettable stratagem, necessary to achieve the Jews' current position of strength. Though the rabbis had been "forced to let the Hitlerite bandits sacrifice some of our people" in order to bring their plans to fruition, "sacrifice has always been the watchword of our people, and the death of a few thousand lesser Jews in exchange for world leadership is indeed a small price to pay."

Then the rabbi spoke frankly about the conspiracy's pièce de résistance, the crowning glory of all of its historical efforts. Once they had seized power, they would "forbid the Whites to mate with Whites."

> The White Women must cohabit with members of the dark races, the White Men with black women. Thus the White Race will disappear, for the mixing of the dark with the White means the end of the White Man, and our most dangerous enemy will become only a memory. We shall embark upon an era of ten thousand years of peace and plenty, the Pax Judaica, and our race will rule undisputed over the world. Our superior intelligence will easily enable us to retain mastery over a world of dark peoples.[90]

The revelation that the Jews had knowingly brought the Holocaust down upon themselves—and that it had only made them stronger—must have come as a relief to those anti-Semites who were harboring any lingering feelings of guilt about the death camps. And the discovery that the Jews were seeking to mongrelize the white race (a detail they'd left out of their original *Protocols*) gave America's arch-segregationists new ammunition in their ongoing battle against civil rights. But unfortunately for both groups, Rabbi Rabinovitch, the Emergency Council of European Rabbis, and the speech itself were all fictions. As long rumored and recently confirmed by the independent researcher Ernie Lazar, they were all concocted by Eustace Mullins.

Not long afterward, another viral quotation that laid bare a different, albeit not unrelated, facet of the Jewish conspiracy began making the rounds of the hate sheets. It was drawn from *A Racial Program for the Twentieth Century*, a book ostensibly authored in 1912 by a Marxist Zionist Englishman named Israel Cohen. In 1957, the Mississippi congressman Thomas G. Abernethy read it into the *Congressional Record*. "We must realize that our party's most powerful weapon is racial tension," it began.

> By pounding into the consciousness of the dark races that for centuries they have been oppressed by the whites, we can mold them to the program of the Communist Party. In America we will aim for subtle victory. While inflaming the Negro minority against the whites, we will endeavor to instill in the whites a guilt complex for their exploitation of the Negroes. We will aid the Negroes to rise in prominence in every walk of life, in the professions and in the world of sports and entertainment. With this prestige, the Negroes will be able to intermarry with the whites and begin a process which will deliver America to our cause.[91]

Cohen's words confirmed an old conviction of the racist Right that's already been referred to in these pages more than once: that the civil rights movement was entirely the creation of Jewish Communists; that without their promptings, American blacks would have had no reason to feel any discontent. As the poet Ezra Pound put it, "It is perfectly well know that the fuss a bout [sic] 'de-segregation' in the

U.S. has been started by the jews. Plenty of americans have been getting on quite nicely with coloured people for nearly a century."[92] The only problem was that the Communist Party didn't exist in 1912, in either England or the United States—it came into being after the Russian Revolution—and no book with the title *A Racial Program for the Twentieth Century* was ever published. An article that appeared in the Washington *Star* on February 18, 1958, traced the story back to Eustace Mullins, who claimed to have encountered the quotation in a book he found in the Library of Congress. Around the same time, Mullins was also promoting a rumor that Eisenhower's mother was black.

Lazar's database of right-wing conspiracism is filled with fascinating and often galling snippets about Mullins's long career as a racial and political provocateur. In 1968, an internal FBI memo characterized him as a "depraved, warped degenerate . . . Since it would be inconceivable that any rational person would consider seriously Mullins' demented allegations and outrageous distortions we have previously considered it unwise to dignify his work with any kind of response."[93] Needless to say, the FBI has not always been the most credible source; its Counter Intelligence Program (the notorious COINTELPRO) unfairly smeared many political dissidents. But this was a private, intra-agency communication to J. Edgar Hoover himself; it wasn't intended for public release.

Starting in the late 1940s, Mullins issued a steady stream of articles, books, and pamphlets about conspiratorial subjects. He was a frequent contributor to *Women's Voice*, which, another FBI report noted, was "the official publication of an organization known as We, the Mothers, Mobilize for America, Inc., established in Chicago in 1941 . . . This organization is violently anti–Eisenhower Administration, anti-Semitic, anti-Masonic, anti-Catholic, anticommunist and opposed to all foreign elements in the United States."[94] We, the Mothers' leader Lyrl Clark Van Hyning maintained that Woodrow Wilson was a Sephardic Jew named Wohlson, that Roosevelt was a Jew named Rosenvelt, and that Eisenhower was a Swedish Jew, though he hadn't changed his name. Truman was Jewish too; his middle initial, she said, stood for Solomon.[95]

In 1955, Mullins warned the mobilized mothers of the nation about a new peril facing their children, pioneering the conspiracist meme of "vaccine denialism," which reemerged in our own day with some force with the H1N1 virus:[*]

> Jonas Salk, Yiddish inventor of a so-called polio vaccine, is direct-ing the inoculation of millions of American children with this sinister concoction of *live* polio germs. All that is known is that it CAUSES polio in an alarming percentage of children injected with it, while its effectiveness in preventing polio is a myth of Jewish propaganda. . . . [T]he nation's press refuses to carry these warnings, preferring to see children die rather than criticize the sacred Jew vaccine. Instead, the press prints testimonial after testi-monial in FAVOR of the Jew vaccine from the filthy immoral rats in the U.S. Public Health Service in Washington which is noth-ing but a publicity bureau for Jewish poisons such as fluorine in water.[96]

Mullins's *Murder by Injection: The Story of the Medical Conspir-acy Against America* (1988), offered a full-blown exposé of the AMA/Rockefeller/Rothschild stranglehold on American medicine:

> When the Rockefeller Syndicate began its takeover of our medical profession in 1910, our citizens went into a sharp decline. Today, we suffer from a host of debilitating ailments, both mental and physical, nearly all of which can be traced directly to the opera-tions of the chemical and drug monopoly, and which pose the great-est threat to our continued existence as a nation.[97]

In *The Biological Jew*, published in 1968, Mullins explained how the Jew was a parasite on civilization. The root of Jewish identity, he

---

[*] For example, on September 15, 2009, a press release headlined "Drug Cartel Exposed Creat-ing, Releasing, Injecting, Infecting, and Depopulating Planet with Pandemic H1N1 Swine Flu Viruses and Vaccines" was issued by a group called Tetrahedron, LLC (http://www.fluscam.com /Affidavit.html), a nonprofit that promotes the conspiratorial theories of Dr. Leonard G. Horo-witz. "Among the most stunning revelations from the Horowitz-Kane research are those linking Larry Silverstein of Silverstein Properties, Inc., and the 9-11 terrorist attacks, to the drug cartel's geopolitical, economic, and population reduction activities. Mr. Silverstein, leaser of the World Trade Center who authorized to have building 7 'pulled,' meaning detonated, is a chief suspect in the '9-11 truth' investigation. Silverstein is currently landlord and co-partner in the biotechnol-ogy trust founded by David Rockefeller and implicated by these new discoveries."

revealed, lies in the custom of the blood sacrifice (or blood *libel*, as non-anti-Semites call it):

> This religious ceremony of drinking the blood of an innocent gentile child is basic to the Jew's entire concept of his existence as a parasite, living off of the blood of the host. That is why he refuses to abandon this custom, even though it has brought him close to extinction many times.
>
> When the Jew can no longer symbolize his role by kidnapping a perfectly formed gentile child, spiriting him away to a synagogue, and ritually puncturing his body in the places which they boasted they had wounded the Body of Christ, and drinking the blood of the dying child, then, according to Jewish belief, he is doomed.[98]

Mullins was a frequent visitor to Ezra Pound when he was a political prisoner in St. Elizabeths Hospital (he would publish a biography and memoir of their friendship, *This Difficult Individual: Ezra Pound*, in 1961), and his best-known book, *The Secrets of the Federal Reserve*, was written at the poet's behest and with his material and intellectual support. "You must work on it as a detective story," Pound exhorted him. Every morning for two years, as Mullins told it, he conducted hours of research in the stacks of the Library of Congress. In the afternoon he and Pound would go over his notes; then he had dinner with the newspaperman George Stimpson, who offered insights of his own.

The fruit of their collaboration was published in 1952 as *Mullins on the Federal Reserve*. Mullins continually revised the book throughout the next three decades; at one point his labors were subsidized by the ultraconservative Texas oilman H. L. Hunt. By the time its 1983 edition was released, it included references to Carroll Quigley's writings on the Round Table Group via *Dope, Inc.* (a publication of the LaRouche organization), which wasn't issued until 1978; it's hard to discern what Mullins learned from later generations of conspiracy theorists and what he taught them himself. It's worth noting that the conservative political activist G. Edward Griffin, a biographer of Robert Welch and the author of the best-selling *The Creature from Jekyll Island: A Second Look at the Federal Reserve* (1994), a book that is much cited by Ron Paul, has scrupulously distanced himself from Mullins. Mullins, in turn, claimed that Griffin plagiarized his research.

Boiled down to its essence, Mullins's story is about the autocracy behind the aristocracy, to borrow Henry Ford's phrase. The Federal Reserve was the creation of an immensely wealthy American elite who used the powers it granted them to foment two world wars and innumerable recessions and depressions so they could profit off the nation's resulting misery. But as rich and powerful as they were and are, they don't call the shots. "The most powerful men in the United States were themselves answerable to another power, a foreign power, and a power which had been steadfastly seeking to extend its control over the young republic of the United States since its very inception," Mullins wrote. Its identity will surprise no one who has read this far:

> This power was the financial power of England, centered in the London Branch of the House of Rothschild. The fact was that in 1910, the United States was for all practical purposes being ruled from England, and so it is today.[99]

The Rothschilds' American agents made sure that Woodrow Wilson would be elected president by financing Teddy Roosevelt's Bull Moose insurgency in 1912. Once installed in the White House, Wilson oversaw the passage not just of the legislation that created the Federal Reserve but of the federal income tax. Wilson's chief adviser was Colonel Edward Mandell House, the arch-internationalist who went on to found the hated Council on Foreign Relations.

House was the author of a utopian novel called *Philip Dru, Administrator,* which he published pseudonymously in 1912. As dated and unreadable today as most books of its sort turn out to be (one can only wonder what it would be like to read the political parable set in the world of ants that Robert Welch was working on in the early 1950s,[100] or what future generations of readers will make of Glenn Beck's novel, *The Overton Window*), *Philip Dru* was "actually a detailed plan for the future government of the United States, 'which would establish Socialism as dreamed by Karl Marx,'" Mullins reveals.

This "novel" predicted the enactment of the graduated income tax, excess profits tax, unemployment insurance, social security, and a flexible currency system. In short, it was the blueprint which was later followed by the Woodrow Wilson and Franklin D. Roosevelt administrations. . . . This pensive dreamer who imagined himself a dictator actually managed to place himself in the position of the confidential advisor to the President of the United States, and then to have many of his desires enacted into law! On page 227, he lists some of the laws he wishes to enact as dictator. Among them are an old age pension law, laborers insurance compensation, cooperative markets, a federal reserve banking system, cooperative loans, national employment bureaus, and other "social legislation," some of which was enacted during Wilson's administration, and others during the Franklin D. Roosevelt's [sic] administration. The latter was actually a continuation of the Wilson Administration.[101]

A reader who actually takes the trouble to read the novel will quickly discern that House's elitism, his noblesse oblige, and his militarism—he foresaw a vast extension of the Monroe Doctrine that would result in "the amalgamation of Mexico and the Central American Republics into one government, even though separate states were maintained"—had much more in common with TR's big-stick Progressivism than with Marxism-Leninism.[102] But as anyone who reads John Birch Society publications or listens to Glenn Beck well knows, Theodore Roosevelt was a crypto-Communist too.

Mullins wasn't the only one who connected the dots. Robert Welch spoke about House and his novel in a filmed 1966 speech titled "The Truth in Time"; the novel was reprinted in 1998 by Robert Welch University Press. In his introduction, William N. Grigg calls it "a detailed schematic for subversion," comparing it to *Mein Kampf, The Communist Manifesto*, and Machiavelli's *Prince*, and quotes Westbrook Pegler's characterization of its author as "Wilson's Rasputin, the most influential private citizen in America and indeed one of the most powerful human beings in the world," who "copyrighted Fascism at a time when Mussolini was just a loud-mouthed, hand-to-mouth Communist in Milan [and] Lenin and Trotsky were unknown vermin hiding in dark corners of Geneva and New York." John F. McManus's *Insiders* says more:

In *Philip Dru: Administrator,* Edward Mandell House laid out a fictionalized plan for the conquest of America. He told of a "conspiracy" (the word is his) which would gain control of both the Democratic and Republican parties, and use them as instruments in the creation of a socialistic world government. . . . The House plan called for the United States to give up its sovereignty to the League of Nations at the close of World War I. But when the U.S. Senate refused to ratify America's entry into the League, Edward Mandell House's drive toward world government was slowed down. Disappointed, but not beaten, House and his friends then formed the Council on Foreign Relations, whose purpose right from its inception was to destroy the freedom and independence of the United States.[103]

During the spring and summer of 2010, Glenn Beck urged his listeners to seek out House's book online and read it to learn the ugly truth about progressivism. Woodrow Wilson, "the worst president this country has ever had—he *hated* America," read it three or four times, Beck commented.[104] For what it's worth, on September 22, 2010, while Beck regaled his television audience with an account of House's efforts to subtly alter details of the Federal Reserve legislation to make it even less democratic than it already was, the better to subvert the people's will, a quotation from Eustace Mullins's *Secrets of the Federal Reserve* flashed across the screen—providing, at the very least, an intriguing insight into Beck's reading preferences.[105]

But enough about Glenn Beck. In the spirit of *The Protocols of the Elders of Zion* and Henry Ford, of Gordon Clark and Conde McGinley, of Elizabeth Dilling and Ezra Pound and Eustace Mullins himself, the question that really needs to be asked and answered is this: Was Colonel House a member of the Hebrew race?

Not surprisingly, the conspiracist literature features considerable speculation along those very lines. In the pamphlet *Zionism: The Hidden Tyranny*, Benjamin H. Freedman, the millionaire owner of the Woodbury Soap Company who, before he converted to Catholicism and took up the cause of anti-Communism and anti-Zionism in 1945, was a self-styled "highly placed insider" in the Jewish establishment, noted gratuitously that House "did not claim or disclaim his Talmudist ancestry to this author."[106] In *The Controversy of Zion,* the English anti-Semite Douglas Reed expatiates on the mystery of House's origins, pointedly quoting his biographer Arthur D. Howden Smith, who wrote that House's "middle name, Mandell, was that of 'a Jewish merchant in Houston, who was one of his father's most intimate friends; the fact that the elder House conferred a Jewish name upon his son *indicates the family's attitude towards the race.'*"[107] John Coleman has contended that House, who was born in Houston, Texas, in 1858, was really Mandell Huis, a Dutch Jew.[108]

But wait, there's more: The Jewish financier and all-around Washington wise man Bernard M. Baruch attended the City College of New York. "This college," Henry Ford wrote in the November 20, 1920, installment of *The International Jew*, "is one of the favorite educational institutions with the Jews, its president being Dr. S. E. Mezes, a brother-in-law of Colonel E. M. House, the colonel whose influence . . . at the White House has for a long time been a favorite subject of wondering speculation on the part of the American people." A figure like Baruch, with the ear of the president and his connections in banking and industry, already wielded frightening power. But could a Jew seize the very reins of the state and become an American Disraeli? Ford feared that something even worse might happen.

> The Jews could do greater things in the United States than even Baruch has done, if the opportunity offered, acts of superb ease and mastery—but what would it signify? The ideal of a dictator of the United States has never been absent from the group in which Baruch is found—witness the work, "Philip Dru, Administrator," commonly attributed to Colonel E. M. House, and never denied by him.[109]

Not long ago, the blogger Hume's Ghost[110] e-mailed me a link to an article that began, "Is Barack Obama the product of a vast socialist conspiracy designed to undermine the fundamental tenets established by our Founding Fathers, all bankrolled and organized by Jewish financiers? The answer is unequivocally yes."[111]

"I came across this the other day," he explained. "It's from David Duke's website and is almost verbatim the conspiracy theory that Beck posits on a daily basis about the Soros/Obama/ACORN/SEIU/ Apollo Alliance/Van Jones/SDS nexus of evil, but with the added level of it also being a Rothschild's conspiracy. It's the same conspiracy but presented in its naked racist form. . . . I also noticed that the article talks about the tentacles of Soros organizations ruining the country and what not; Bill O'Reilly just said virtually the same thing on Fox the other day. It's why I've taken to describing such attacks on Soros as para-antisemitic." On November 9 and 10, 2010, Beck dedicated two entire shows to Soros. "The program," Michelle Goldberg wrote in *The Daily Beast*, "was a symphony of anti-Semitic dog-whistles. Nothing like it has ever been on American television before."[112] In retrospect, that might have been when Beck jumped the proverbial shark, rendering himself too offensive even for Fox News. Not long after four hundred rabbis addressed an open letter of protest to Roger Ailes, Beck defended himself by equating the Reform rabbinate with Wahhabists and other radical Muslims on his radio show, declaring that "Reformed rabbis are generally political in nature. It's almost like Islam—radicalized Islam—in a way to where radicalized Islam is less about religion than it is about politics." The ADL's Abe Fox-man issued a formal protest the next day, condemning Beck's words as "beyond the pale."[113]

Most mainstream avatars of the New Hate scrupulously avoid ref-erencing the *Protocols* directly; it is too poisonous, too anti-Semitic, too discredited. But the story that the Tea Partiers tell echoes its implied narrative in any number of ways. Liberal political institu-tions are a honey trap for the unwary, a secret invitation to tyranny and immorality. Paper money, deficit spending, and the graduated income tax are designed to impoverish the nation. Foreigners—if not Jews, then "an Indonesian Muslim turned welfare thug," America's "racist in chief" (as the radio talk show host and former Tea Party Express leader Mark Williams once characterized Barack Obama)— are using their influence to rot the country from within.[114]

As terrifying as the *Protocols* may be, it is also deeply reassuring. No matter what the burning problem of the day—the loss of religious certainty, immorality in popular culture, creeping Socialism, rising levels of public debt, war, recession, gay marriage—the *Protocols* tells us that there is a satanic someone we can blame. Someone foreign and non-Christian and undeservedly wealthy who sucks, vampire-like, at our country's very lifeblood. Hatred, under such dire circum-stances, is hardly a vice; surely it is one's patriotic duty.

4.

The Apron, the Trowel, and the Knife in the Back— Freemasonry and the Great Conspiracy

In 1797, John Robison, a professor of natural philosophy at the University of Edinburgh, published a book with the imposing title *Proofs of a Conspiracy Against All the Religions and Governments of Europe, Carried on in the Secret Meetings of Free Masons, Illuminati, and Reading Societies.* Later that year—an instance of the same sort of serendipitous synchronicity that had Alfred Wallace and Charles Darwin putting the finishing touches on their theories of natural selection at almost exactly the same moment, or, less momentously, that brought *A Bug's Life* and *Antz,* two blockbuster animated movies about talking insects, into theaters in one and the same season—Augustin Barruel, a French Jesuit who was living in exile in London, published *Mémoires pour servir à l'histoire du Jacobinisme (Memoirs Illustrating the History of Jacobinism).*

Both books stipulated that the French Revolution was the result of an immense international conspiracy spearheaded by Freemasons in the thrall of the Bavarian Illuminati, a secret society that Adam Weishaupt, a Jesuit-trained professor of canon law at the University of Ingolstadt, had founded in 1776. And both books warned that the

Illuminists posed an imminent threat to the New World. "As the plague flies on the wings of the wind," wrote Barruel, "so do their triumphant legions infect America. God grant that the United States may not learn to their cost that Republics are equally menaced with Monarchies; and that the immensity of the Ocean is but a feeble barrier against the universal conspiracy of the sect!"[1]

Barruel's opus is more encyclopedic and scholarly than Robison's comparatively brief jeremiad: its four volumes painstakingly trace the antecedents of Illuminism back to the Manichaeans and the Knights Templars and show how the ideas that animate it emerged from the mainstreams of Reformation and Enlightenment thought; only then does it map the specific paths that Illuminism traveled on its journey from Germany to France, and from the salons of the philosophes to the tumbrels of the Terror. His *Memoirs*, writes Daniel Pipes, in his book *Conspiracy*, "was the first attempt to present conspiracy theories in an orderly and intellectually punctilious fashion. In the words of a twentieth-century historian [René Le Forestier], 'the work by Barruel is a masterpiece, hatred and fear made him a poet.'"[2]

A little more than a century later, *The Protocols of the Elders of Zion* would insert the newly emancipated Jews and the engines of international finance that they supposedly controlled into a framework that was largely Barruel's and Robison's invention. The world they bequeathed us—for all intents and purposes, the model for every major conspiracy theory that has been proposed ever since—was both more complicated and vastly simpler than had been previously supposed. On the one hand, there were kingdoms and principalities and republics, ruled, for better or worse, by their divinely appointed or humanly elected sovereigns. On the other, there was a rootless cadre of non-Christian parasites who pretended to be other than they were, who preached a gospel of freedom and enlightenment, but whose real goal was the destruction of all order.

Though Weishaupt claimed to be as high-minded as the American founders—the goal of the Illuminati, as he put it, was "to regain Reason her rights . . . to restore the rights of man, original liberty and independence"—Barruel and Robison saw through his charade.[3] Drawing on candid letters and other revealing documents that had fallen into the hands of the Bavarian authorities, they used

Weishaupt's and his co-conspirators' own words against them to devastating effect.

Just as the *Protocols* would purport the Jews to do, the Illuminati inveigled the lower orders, hypocritically pretending to be their friends:

> We must win the common people in every corner. This will be obtained chiefly by means of the schools, and by open, hearty behaviour, show, condescension, popularity, and toleration of their prejudices, which we shall at leisure root out and dispel.[4]

But that was just a first step. Exactly as the Jews would be said to do in the *Protocols*, Weishaupt's minions systematically corrupted Masonic lodges, transforming them into revolutionary cells that not only propagated the Illuminati's nihilistic teachings to a wider public but carried out acts of sabotage and subversion.

Never mind that Weishaupt paid lip service to a higher, truer form of Christianity. The real aim of the Order of the Illuminati, Robison averred, "is not to enlighten the mind of man, and show him his moral obligations, and by the practice of his duties to make society peaceable." The Illuminati's ambitions were as vast as they were venal:

> Their first and immediate aim is to get the possession of riches, power, and influence, without industry; and, to accomplish this, they want to abolish Christianity; and then dissolute manners and universal profligacy will procure them the adherence of all the wicked, and enable them to overturn all the civil governments of Europe; after which they will think of farther conquests, and extend their operations to the other quarters of the globe, till they have reduced mankind to the state of one undistinguishable chaotic mass.[5]

The Illuminati held out the promise of a peaceable transnationalist New World Order, governed solely by the benign power of reason, of a utopian "Cosmo-Politism" in which the trappings of the traditional state would wither away. But what its leaders really aspired to, Barruel explained, was universal mayhem—and their own elevation and self-aggrandizement:

> It is not a new Empire they are seeking to establish; it is at the annihilation of every Empire, of all order, rank, distinction, property, and social ties, that they aim. Such is the ultimate view of its mysteries of Equality and Liberty. Such is that reign of anarchy and absolute independence proclaimed in the subterraneous lurking-places, under the appellations of patriarchal reign, of the reign of reason and nature.[6]

Just as the *Protocols* gained much of its credibility from the historical context that it emerged from—the unraveling of the old Europe on the brink of World War I and the Bolshevik Revolution—Robison's and Barruel's books were published into a world that was still reeling from the very real horrors unleashed by the French Revolution.

But unlike the Elders of Zion, the Illuminati really existed.

"We shall demonstrate that, even to the most horrid deeds perpetrated during the French Revolution," Barruel wrote, "everything was foreseen and resolved on, was combined and premeditated."

> They were the offspring of deep-thought villainy, since they had been prepared and were produced by men, who alone held the clue of those plots and conspiracies, lurking in the secret meetings where they had been conceived, and only watching the favorable moment of bursting forth. Though the events of each day may not appear to have been combined, there nevertheless existed a secret agent and a secret cause, giving rise to each event, and turning each circumstance to the long-sought-for end. . . . The grand cause of the revolution, its leading features, its atrocious crimes, will still remain one continued chain of deep-laid and premeditated villainy.[7]

Everything was foreseen and resolved on. If a French king and queen were beheaded, it could only be because a vicious, godless handful of foreigners convinced the Gallic masses that they were unhappy. If American blacks rose up and demanded the right to vote, to eat at the same lunch counters as whites, and to relieve themselves in the same public restrooms, foreign-born Communist provocateurs, enabled by homegrown traitors, must have convinced them to act against their better interests and inclinations. And lest you think this analogy is strained or hyperbolic, here is the John Birch Society's Robert Welch saying almost exactly the same thing in a 1964 speech: "It is not our duty nor our need tonight to explore the extent to which the *Illuminati* were responsible for, or contributed to, bringing on the French Revolution," he said. But "the evidence increases that their influence was powerful and extensive."

> The French people under Louis XVI had as little cause to let themselves be led by conspiratorial destructivists into insane horrors and a murderous clamor for "liberty" as the Negroes in America have today in a demand for "freedom." Both are being stirred and led into the same kind of cruel idiocy by exactly the same kind of revolutionary criminals, for exactly the same megalomaniacal purposes on the part of the real instigators of these monstrous crimes against God and country.[8]

Conspiracism insists on simplism—a coherent, consistent, easily digestible explanation for complex, often chaotic circumstances and events. It requires a "secret agent"—the Devil, often quite literally—and it never fails to find him. Here's Gerald Winrod, the Jayhawk Nazi, in his 1935 pamphlet *Adam Weishaupt: A Human Devil:*

> There is a white light of spiritual illumination. And there is a black light of Satanic illumination. "Satan himself is transformed into an angel of light." Illuminism is rooted in black magic. It produced a mighty wave of occultism in the eighteenth century which even swept governments from their foundations. And the end is not yet! . . . No matter where we find Illuminism or how we trace its ramifications, Satan is always the Master Mind behind it.[9]

Winrod goes on to reveal that the Illuminists' worldly sponsors were the Jews: "The whole scheme was a Jewish plot to the core."

It has been aptly remarked that the Russian Revolution began where the French Revolution ended. . . . Karl Marx, the recognized father of modern Communism, edited his teachings out of the writings of Adam Weishaupt. . . . Communism . . . resulted from centuries of under-cover Jewish planning. Its final objective is to exhaust the human family in suffering and misery until the whole world can be brought under the heel of the merciless Jewocracy of Moscow.[10]

This isn't to say, of course, that conspiracies and conspirators don't play a key role in political insurgencies. And it's certainly not to deny that for a time, the Illuminati posed a potential threat to the kings and priests of the Old World. But it's important to remember that there are essentially two Freemasonries and two Illuminati—one that resides in the perfervid fantasies of conspiracy theorists, and one that exists (or existed, in the case of the Illuminati) in the real world.

Reality often bears a faint, familial resemblance to conspiracy theory, but its texture is much thicker; truth has a tendency to get blurry around the edges and its stories can take unexpected turns, lapsing into incoherence, or ending in anticlimactic thuds. Real-life revolutionary cadres, often working in secret, almost always have an elaborately thought-out agenda. Their leaders are often intellectuals. But every action they take is subject to the vicissitudes of chance. Conflicts with rival conspirators, blowback, and unintended consequences exact steep tolls; history may ascribe to them very different motives than they did themselves. While the likes of Voltaire, Rousseau, and Diderot didn't man the barricades, their thinking certainly provided one impetus for the French Revolution. But so did the exigent circumstances of French society—the inequities of wealth and power, the corruption of its church, the venality of its rulers.

Many French Masons, rationalist and idealist as they were, *did* participate in the French Revolution, just as many Jews—outsiders by definition, without a stake in traditional Russian culture, bound up in the church and aristocratic landownership as it was—would throw themselves into the Russian Revolution more than a century later. The comte de Mirabeau might well have been exposed to Illuminist literature and the Illuminists themselves. But most of the impetus for the French Revolution boiled up from below: the intellectuals and ideologues who led it could no more control the forces it unleashed than they could have dammed the lava spewing out of a volcano (or put a match to its fuse). The French Revolution was not merely "Masonry in action,"[11] as Lombard de Langres would write in 1820, any more than the tsar and his family were victims of "Judeo-Bolshevism." Both revolutions were much larger than the sum of their parts.

The phrase "Masonry in action" might have a strange ring to it for an American reader, who might well think of Masons simply as those guys who dress up in fezzes and drive little cars in small-town parades, and of Freemasonry as a benevolent social institution whose members are wont to engage in harmless mummery—as a more venerable version of the International Order of Friendly Sons of the Raccoons, whose Bensonhurst, Brooklyn, lodge provided *The Honeymooners'* Ralph Kramden and Ed Norton with a refuge from their wives. Most Americans would be surprised to learn that anyone would have ever regarded the Masons as a threat to the established order, never mind that some still do today. But they do. Here's the arch-conspiracist Milton William Cooper, writing in 1991:

> I tell you now that Freemasonry is one of the most wicked and terrible organizations upon this earth. The Masons are major players in the struggle for world domination. . . . Unlike authors who out of fear have acted as apologists for the Freemasons, I decline to absolve them of responsibility and guilt. The Freemasons, like everyone else, are responsible for the cleanliness of their house. The occupant of a secret house within a secret house within a secret house cannot clean if he cannot see the number of rooms or what they contain. Their house is a stinking cesspool. Look to the Masons for the guilty party if anything happens to me.[12]

But wasn't George Washington a Mason? And General Douglas MacArthur and Gerald Ford, not to mention Roy Acuff, Audie Murphy, and John Wayne—and Count Basie and Kit Carson? What did they all have in common? According to Dan Brown's megabest-selling *The Lost Symbol*, the Freemasons—at least those who are initiated into the Craft's highest degrees—are the original New

Agers. More than that, they are magi, the keepers and proponents of an arcane philosophical technology, a noetic science dating back to ancient times that bids fair to bring us wonders like ESP and teleportation, and that one day might even conquer death. Heirs of the builders of the Tower of Babel, the Temple of Solomon, and the great Gothic cathedrals, close relatives of the Knights Templars, the Priory of Sion, and the Rosicrucians, the Masons hold occult secrets and wield vast powers—political, financial, and mystical.

Some of the Masonic mythology comes from its own "Legends of the Craft"; some of it was invented by its enemies. Stripped of its pageantry and mumbo jumbo, Freemasonry (which, despite its claims of ancient provenance and its adaptation of Templar rites and lore, can't be dated any earlier than the seventeenth century as a formal organization) celebrates the rational, nondogmatic, individualistic values of the Enlightenment. God the Architect is a Deist idea. The Masonic openness to Rosicrucian arcana, to alchemy, and to Egyptian Hermeticism is an attribute of the same unfettered, nonjudgmental curiosity that led to the scientific and technological breakthroughs of the early industrial era—and for that matter, to the rise of the bourgeois merchant class and the overthrow of the entrenched aristocracy.

Masonry's ideal human being can study and work his own way toward wisdom and happiness and spiritual perfection—a very different view of the human condition from that of Calvin, who believed that humanity was innately depraved and doomed without Christ's salvation (which can't be achieved by one's own efforts). It went against the grain of the Catholic Church as well, which saw itself and its sacraments as humanity's sole vehicle of grace. Masonic lodges are privileged communities, bound together by secret oaths and obligations, separate from the communion of the church and from the larger polity. Masonic oaths take the Lord's name in vain; Masonic secrecy violates the sacrament of the confession, which is one of the many reasons that the Catholic Church condemned it. It also makes it harder for a police state to exercise its authority.

In its way, Masonry epitomizes the myriad contradictions and tensions of American identity: it espouses brotherhood and democracy yet divides its members by degrees; it requires its members to believe in God yet implicitly questions religious and secular authority. Benjamin Franklin—a reluctant but eventually an ardent revolutionist—is the very type of the American Freemason (he was a member of St. John's Lodge in Philadelphia—the first in the New World). An inventor, scientist, and entrepreneur, he was a mass of contradictions: a sententious moralizer and codifier of bourgeois virtues, he attended séances and possibly orgies at the hedonistic Hellfire Club in England; homespun and self-educated, he was a familiar in the royal courts and academies of Europe. He was America's Leonardo da Vinci, except he couldn't paint or sculpt (and no one has ever accused him of being gay). Though oddly enough, Franklin *has* been accused of being a serial killer.

"In 1998," a post on the conspiratorial Web site Above Top Secret breathlessly began, "workmen dug up the remains of ten bodies hidden beneath the former London home of Benjamin Franklin. This incident was reported on February 11, 1998 by the Sunday-Times news company in the United Kingdom. . . . Although it never was reported in the United States, where Franklin is practically an icon."[13] In fact the find was widely covered. The bones—twelve hundred of them, some of them sawed and drilled—were disinterred in December 1997. Franklin's landlady's son-in-law ran an illegal school of anatomy at the same address, according to a story in *American Heritage*.[14]

Back in the eighteenth century, the boundaries between religion and science and magic were porous; chemists were still trying to transform lead into gold; physicians were practicing medicine without the benefit of germ theory (though medical students were so eager to learn anatomy that they rifled graveyards for corpses, as Franklin's neighbor undoubtedly did). Physicists were only just beginning to move away from Aristotle's worldview toward one that we would now call Newtonian; Newton himself, a devout, mystically inclined Christian and a practicing alchemist, lived into the 1720s. The fact that the early Masons were as intrigued by ancient esoterica as they were doesn't mean that they were Gnostics or Zoroastrians, any more than their familiarity with Latin and Greek authors made them pagans.

But for royalists and the conventionally pious, the Masons represented a clear and present danger. The nineteenth-century Republican politician and orator Robert Green Ingersoll, who famously declared, "If a man would follow, today, the teachings of the Old Testament, he would be a criminal. If he would follow strictly the teachings of the New, he would be insane," was a Mason.[15] In a posthumously published pamphlet, Ingersoll's great hero Thomas Paine had written of Masonry that it "is derived, and is the remains of the religion of the ancient Druids; who, like the Magi of Persia and the priests of Heliopolis in Egypt, were Priests of the sun." Blasphemously, Paine assigned the same pagan origins to Christianity:

> The Christian religion and Masonry have one and the same common origin: both are derived from the worship of the sun. The difference between their origin is, that the Christian religion is a parody on the worship of the sun, in which they put a man whom they call Christ, in the place of the sun, and pay him the same adoration which was originally paid to the sun.[16]

While most British and American Freemasons have tended to stay within the bounds of the mainstream, espousing a belief in God if not in religious orthodoxy, European Freemasons have sometimes embraced radical rightist and leftist doctrines—and in the notorious case of Weishaupt's contemporary Giuseppe Balsamo (a.k.a. Alessandro Cagliostro), the founder of so-called Egyptian Freemasonry, magical and other mystical arts.

Europe's Freemasons were at the forefront of the revolutions of 1848; anticlerical Freemasons spearheaded the revolts against Spanish colonialism in Latin America, and they were deeply involved in Italy's Risorgimento. In 1878, the Grand Orient de France waived its requirement that its members believe in a Supreme Being.

The Confederate Civil War general Albert Pike, a long-serving sovereign grand commander of the Ancient and Accepted Scottish Rite, Southern Jurisdiction, was wrongly accused of founding a Devil-worshipping religion (as noted earlier, Palladism was a canard dreamed up by a French trickster). But Pike did celebrate Lucifer the Light Bearer in his opus *Morals and Dogma of the First Three Degrees of the Ancient and Accepted Scottish Rite of Freemasonry:*

> Lucifer, the Son of the Morning! Is it *he* who bears the *Light,* and with its splendors intolerable blinds feeble, sensual, or selfish

Souls? Doubt it not! For traditions are full of Divine Revelations and Inspirations: and Inspiration is not of one Age nor of one Creed. Plato and Philo, also, were inspired.[17]

Aleister Crowley, a.k.a. "the wickedest man in the world"—a drug addict, an adept in sex magic, and an unapologetic Satanist—would emerge from esoteric Freemasonry at the turn of the twentieth century. He purported to live by what he called the Law of Thelema (also the motto of the Hellfire Club): "Do what thou wilt is the whole of the law."[18]

Theosophy and other allied forms of spiritualism that rose to the fore in the late nineteenth and early twentieth centuries had strong Masonic associations. Annie Besant would establish the International Order of Co-Freemasonry in England in 1902; C. W. Leadbeater would be initiated as a Co-Freemason in 1915. Manly P. Hall, who wrote *The Secret Teachings of All Ages: An Encyclopedic Outline of Masonic, Hermetic, Qabbalistic, and Rosicrucian Symbolical Philosophy* (1928), among dozens of other books on spiritual subjects, would become a thirty-third-degree Mason in 1973, when he was seventy-two years old. In 1941, the seer Edgar Cayce was said to have issued the gnomic prophecy that "Americanism—the ism—with the universal thought that is expressed and manifested in the brotherhood of man into group thought, as expressed by the Masonic Order, will be the eventual rule in the settlement of affairs in the world. Not that the world is to become a Masonic order, but the principles that are embraced in same will be the basis upon which the new order of peace is to be established in '44 and '45."[19]

One legacy of the Enlightenment is our ability to unravel science from superstition, to draw distinctions between theology and natural science and between ancient wisdom and ancient ignorance. But if curiosity about science and toleration of religious pluralism are abiding characteristics of the American character, so too are obscurantism and dogmatism. For fundamentalists who believe that the Bible is literally true in all of its particulars, and for Dominionists and Reconstructionists who believe that America once was and should be a "Christian nation" again, the Masons were dangerous freethinkers, or, even worse, occultists or Devil worshippers. For the congenitally conspiratorial-minded, Weishaupt's Illuminati, a secret society that secreted itself within the already-secret Masons and that sought to transform society wholesale, to undo the traditional bulwarks of faith and obedience, is the seeming incarnation of all that they fear—a precursor of the Comintern, with its secret cells carved out of the timbers of the state like so many nests of termites, and the same godless, world-spanning agenda.

Robert Anton Wilson, the erudite co-author of *The Illuminatus! Trilogy* (1975), summarized the range of contemporary beliefs about Adam Weishaupt and Illuminism in his memoir *Cosmic Trigger 1: Final Secret of the Illuminati:*

> It has been claimed that Dr. Weishaupt was an atheist, a Cabalistic magician, a rationalist, a mystic; a democrat, a socialist, an anarchist, a fascist; a Machiavellian amoralist, an alchemist, a totalitarian and an "enthusiastic philanthropist." (The last was the verdict of Thomas Jefferson, by the way.) The Illuminati have also been credited with managing the French and American revolutions behind the scenes, taking over the world, being the brains behind Communism, continuing underground up to the 1970s, secretly worshipping the Devil, and mopery with intent to gawk. Some claim that Weishaupt didn't even invent the Illuminati, but only revived it. The Order of Illuminati has been traced back to the Knights Templar, to the Greek and Gnostic initiatory cults, to Egypt, even to Atlantis. The one safe generalization one can make is that Weishaupt's intent to maintain secrecy has worked; no two students of Illuminology have ever agreed totally about what the "inner secret" or purpose of the Order actually was (or is . . .). There is endless room for spooky speculation, and for pedantic paranoia, once one really gets into the literature of the subject; and there has been a wave of sensational "exposés" of the Illuminati every generation since 1776. If you were to believe all this sensational literature, the damned Bavarian conspirators were responsible for everything wrong with the world, including the energy crises and the fact that you can't even get a plumber on weekends.[20]

Nesta Webster's *Secret Societies and Subversive Movements*, with its time line that stretches back into the mists of antiquity, its learned excursions on the Eleusinian mysteries, Gnosticism, Kabbalah, and the obscure byways of heretical Islam, its manifest fear of European Freemasonry, and its loathing of the Jews, was clearly influenced by Barruel; Robert Welch, as we have seen, bit off and swallowed chunks of Robison whole. The John Birch Society's Western Islands publishing arm would reprint *Proofs of a Conspiracy* in 1967.

Interestingly enough, just as Robison, a Freemason himself, defended England's lodges from his own worst imputations about Illuminism, Robert Welch would staunchly defend American Freemasonry as a bastion of anti-Communism. Rumors that Welch was a Mason himself would spark a schism on his right (if such a place can be imagined) and give birth to a new conspiracy theory that still has some currency in right-wing Christian circles—that of the so-called Belmont Brotherhood.

"Welch is on the side of Freemasonry," a group of insurgent Birchers wrote in the mid-1970s:

> No other explanation is possible. To try to explain away these passages in The Blue Book and Welch's nebulous position on Freemasonry is like insisting the earth is flat. But, unfortunately for Welch, we know that it is not. You may object: "Look at all the great things Welch has done—he has exposed the Illuminati." Baloney. The Illuminati was merely a branch of the Conspiracy. How can one attack the Illuminati without attacking the diabolical power behind it: organized Freemasonry? Welch has provided the most valuable service of all time to the Conspiracy. He founded an organization to neutralize millions of Americans from discovering what the true power behind the Illuminati really was. And we concede the Masons chose an extremely clever man to do the job. . . . There is entirely too much likelihood . . . that in a few short years we shall all be hanging from the same lamp posts, while MASONIC TERROR reigns around us.[21]

The myth of the Belmont Brotherhood provides a specific sort of poetic justice for Robert Welch, who was so quick to accuse others of treasonous designs, and offers an invaluable moral for everyone else: with depressing predictability, conspiracists turn their suspicions on their own; they swallow their tails, and they choke on them. They overreach, too. Just as Robert Welch accused Eisenhower of being a Communist, eighteenth-century American conspiracists turned their guns on the likes of Thomas Jefferson. "If I were about to make proselytes to Illuminatism in the United States," Theodore Dwight pointedly speechified in the 1790s, "I should in the first place apply to Thomas Jefferson."[22]

So who were the real Illuminati? They might not have been the out-and-out hallucination that the Belmont Brotherhood was, but neither were they the juggernaut of Barruel's and Robison's imaginings. Though trained by Jesuits, Weishaupt established himself as anticlerical early in his academic career. He conceived the Illuminati on the model of the ancient Pythagoreans as a "model secret organization . . . concealed from the gaze of the world behind walls of seclusion and mystery, wherein those truths which the folly and egotism of the priests banned from the public chairs of education might be taught with perfect freedom to susceptible youths," as Vernon Stauffer put it in his Columbia University doctoral thesis, which was published as *New England and the Bavarian Illuminati* in 1918.[23]

Weishaupt's first "school of wisdom" was organized with five members in the banner year of 1776. As its initiates learned the secrets of the order, they ascended through three grades of membership: Novice, Minerval, and Illuminated Minerval. By 1780, when the movement had grown to about sixty adherents, the diplomat and author Baron Adolf Franz Friedrich Knigge became a power in it. Knigge added several new grades of membership, among them Priest, Prince, and Magus, and began to recruit his fellow Masons to the ranks. Over the next few years, the membership of the Illuminati swelled into the thousands, including a number of titled aristocrats and distinguished men of letters, such as Goethe and Johann Gottfried von Herder. But then, in 1784, it all came to a crashing halt. Knigge and Weishaupt quarreled and split; then Duke Charles Theodore, the elector of Bavaria, alarmed by reports he had received from Illuminist defectors, issued the first of three edicts banning all societies and associations that weren't licensed by the state.

Though Knigge and Weishaupt eluded the Duke's dragnet (Weishaupt remained an exile in Gotha until his death in 1830; he wrote a number of books defending himself and his ex-order), many prominent Illuminati were arrested, among them Franz Xaver von Zwack, whose papers were confiscated. In 1786, the Bavarian government published a number of the incriminating documents it had seized in a book titled *Einige Originalschriften des Illuminaten-Ordens* (The original writings of the Order of the Illuminati). A second volume followed a year later. Letters from Weishaupt, in which he detailed his efforts to procure an abortion for his sister-in-law, whom he had impregnated, were especially damaging. Some of the most damning documents, according to Barruel—a story that sounds as if it should be apocryphal but that originated in Weishaupt's own *Apology*—had been sewn into the clothing of a courier, an apostate priest named Lanz, who was struck dead by lightning while he was leaving for a journey to Silesia. Weishaupt himself was right next to him when the incident occurred, but "the Brethren, in their first fright, had not recourse to their ordinary means for diverting the papers of the deceased adept from the inspection of the magistrates."[24]

Miraculously, much of the organization's official archive was preserved; at first mixed in with the papers of the Illuminist Duke Ernst II of Saxe-Gotha, and then at the Grand Lodge of Sweden and the Gotha lodge Ernst Zum Kompass. It was confiscated by the Nazis in the 1930s and seized by the Soviet Union in the 1940s, but it has since been reassembled and is now available to scholars. After examining the papers, one contemporary researcher described the Illuminati as the "executive arm of the Aufklärung (the German Enlightenment)."[25] Webster, Welch, Gerald Winrod, William Guy Carr, Cleon Skousen, and a welter of other writers who have perceived the dark hand of the Illuminati in everything from world Communism to the Club of Rome and the Council on Foreign Relations notwithstanding, no historical traces of organized Illuminism have ever been found dating any later than 1800.

None of this is meant to imply that Illuminism wasn't something to be feared, at least if you were one of Europe's sovereigns or priests. As events in France very quickly bore out, there was indeed a violent spirit of revolution in the air. Plus, there are cultic and totalitarian aspects of the group that might have disturbed anyone. "The Superiors of Illuminism are to be looked upon as the most perfect and the most enlightened of men," Professors Utzschneider, Grünberger, and Cosandey, three ex-Illuminists, revealed in their confession to the Bavarian authorities. "No doubts are to be entertained even of their infallibility."[26] Conspiracists might be intemperate on the subject of mind control, seeing evidence of its workings in everything from pop songs to fluoridated water and progressive education, but brainwashing—especially of the young and impressionable, whom Weishaupt most avidly sought as his recruits—is a real phenomenon, well-known to students of cults and political totalitarianism.

But why would Americans, who had after all just thrown off a European monarchy themselves and whose freshly ratified Constitution included a Bill of Rights that forbade Congress to make any "law respecting an establishment of religion," have supposed they had anything to fear from the Illuminati, whose exoteric rhetoric, at least, bore more than a passing resemblance to their own? A number of reasons leap to mind. Jesuits—secretive, ruthless, organized in cells, and whose Machiavellian "ends justify the means" ethos was adopted by the Illuminists (which would later be attributed to the Elders of Zion)—had long been figures of dread in Protestant New England. And the 1790s had been a harrowing decade, in which the young Republic was ceaselessly roiled by tax revolts, political infighting, and the threat of new international wars.

America's revolution was nothing as violent as France's, and it was middle class to its core: it never threatened the sanctity of private property, even when it was in the form of human beings. America's Constitution turned out to be a model of compromise and moderation. But there were significant and growing tensions in the fledgling nation—political, sectional, cultural, and religious. If Benjamin Franklin, George Washington, Thomas Paine, and Thomas Jefferson espoused Deist ideas, many clerics—especially in New England, which, though no longer a Congregationalist theocracy, was still intensely religious—were scandalized by them. America was becoming more secular, but both the established churches and the dissenting sects were pushing back. Vernon Stauffer described the growing backlash:

> On all sides the positions of traditional orthodoxy were being called
> in question. The cause of revealed religion had found new enemies,

and the cause of natural religion new agencies for its promotion. The French Revolution had given a terrifying exhibition of what might be expected to happen to a nation in which radical and skeptical opinions were allowed to have complete expression. As for the progress of impiety at home, the youth of the land were contaminated, the state of public morals was unsound, opposition to measures of government was increasing in power and virulence, the institutions of religion were commanding less and less respect, the clergy were treated with a coldness and criticalness of spirit they had never faced before. Seeking for the causes of this baneful condition of affairs, the clergy believed they were to be found mainly in the dissemination of revolutionary opinions issuing from France, but in part also in native tendencies to exalt reason and throw off the restraints of government in church and state.[27]

By 1798, Jay's Treaty had narrowly averted a second war with England, but in the aftermath of the XYZ Affair (a crisis that was precipitated by three French diplomats' blunt demands for unilateral concessions and bribes before they would even sit at a negotiating table) the maritime Quasi-War with France was heating up. And just as the authors of *The Federalist* had predicted they would be, factional forces were rife. President John Adams's Federalist Party, which was strongest in the North, was at loggerheads with the mostly southern Democratic-Republican Party. Federalist newspapers, which advocated a stronger national government and which promoted the interests of merchants, manufacturers, and cities, accused Adams's vice president and political archrival, Thomas Jefferson, of harboring Jacobin sympathies. A few years later, in 1802, a partisan newspaper would even level the outrageous accusation—which we now know to have been true—that Jefferson had fathered a family of mulattoes by one of his slaves, who happened to have been his dead wife's half sister.

Jefferson's fellow Democratic-Republicans, who envisioned America as a loosely knit republic of yeoman farmers, fired back in kind; they branded the Federalists as crypto-monarchists and accused them of plotting to deliver the United States back to the English. As rumors of war and French subversion reached a fever pitch, the imposition

of the Alien and Sedition Acts—which increased the naturalization period from five to fourteen years, granted the president discre-
tion to deport resident aliens from hostile countries, and made it a
crime "to write, print, utter or publish, or cause it to be done, or assist
in it, any false, scandalous, and malicious writing against the government of the United States . . . or to stir up sedition, or to excite
unlawful combinations against the government"—ratcheted up the
tension even more.[28]

As sensationalistic, alarmist, and over-the-top as Robison's and
Barruel's books might have been, they landed on fertile ground, sparking a genuine—if transient—panic. Ministers inveighed against the
Illuminati from their pulpits; journalists and political hacks fanned
the flames of rumor and suspicion. As mentioned earlier in these
pages, the Reverend Jedidiah Morse, best remembered today as the
father of Samuel Morse but well-known in his own day not just for
his preaching but for his books on geography, warned that the poison
had already been introduced into the veins of the body politic. In an
eerie foreshadowing of Joseph McCarthy, he even claimed to possess
a roster of Illuminist traitors:

> I have, my brethren, an official, authenticated list of the names,
> ages, places of nativity, professions, &c. of the officers and members
> of a Society of Illuminati (or as they are now more generally and
> properly styled Illuminees) consisting of one hundred members,
> instituted in Virginia, by the Grand Orient of FRANCE. . . . A let-
> ter which enclosed this list, an authentic copy of which I also pos-
> sess, contains evidence of a society of like nature, and probably of
> more ancient date, at New York, out of which have sprung fourteen
> others, scattered we know not whereover the United States. . . .
> Among these fruits may be reckoned our unhappy and threatening
> political divisions; the increasing abuse of our wise and faithful
> rulers; the virulent opposition to some of the laws of our coun-
> try; and the measures of the Supreme Executive; the Pennsylvania
> insurrection, the industrious circulation of baneful and corrupting
> books, and the consequent wonderful spread of infidelity, impiety,
> and immorality; the arts made use of to revive ancient prejudices
> and cherish party spirit, by concealing or disguising the truth, and

propagating falsehoods; and lastly, the apparent systematic endeavors made to destroy, not only the influence and support, but the official existence of the Clergy.[29]

A contributor to *The Hartford Courant* wrote that Thomas Jefferson is "the real Jacobin, the child of modern illumination, the foe of man, and the enemy of his country." Writing of Democratic-Republican electioneering, another claimed it was part and parcel of the Illuminist plan to "worm its votaries into all offices of trust and importance, that the weapon of government, upon signal given, may be turned against itself."[30]

Rumors of plots and conspiracies flew. Agents of the French Directory were said to have set sail for America; fortunately, the documents that betrayed them were discovered concealed in the false bottoms of two tubs. A tailor in Philadelphia was said to have received orders for the uniforms that would clothe the French invasion force; Frenchmen were said to have massacred the crew of an American vessel called the *Ocean*.[31] When Democratic-Republican papers traced those rumors back to Federalist sources, an indignant pamphleteer complained:

> The people have been continually agitated by false alarms and without even the apparition of a foe. They have been made to believe that their government and their religion were upon the eve of annihilation. The ridiculous fabrications of plots, which have been crushed out of being by the weight of their own absurdity; and the perpetration of massacres which never existed, but in the distempered malevolence which preached them, have been artfully employed to excite an indignation which might be played off for the purposes of party. Tubs have arrived at Charlestown. The crews of the Ocean and Pickering have been murdered. . . . No falsehood which depravity could invent, has passed unpropagated by credulity; and innocence which virtue could render respectable and amiable has escaped unassailed by federal malignity. Bigotry has cried down toleration, and royalism everything Republican.[32]

Within a matter of months, the Democratic-Republicans had seized the upper hand. Anti-Federalist polemicists contemptuously dismissed "the Arabian tales of Robison and Barruel" while turning their adversaries' own rhetoric against them, accusing them of acting more like the Illuminati than the Illuminati themselves.[33] In a pamphlet titled *A View of the New-England Illuminati: Who Are Indefatigably Engaged in Destroying the Religion and Government of the United States; Under a Feigned Regard for Their Safety—and Under an Impious Abuse of True Religion,* John Cosens Ogden dubbed Theodore Dwight's brother Timothy, the president of Yale University, as "the head of the Illuminati."

> In his sermon preached on the fourth of July, 1798, in New-Haven, he has given us a perfect picture of the Illuminati of Connecticut, under his control, in the representation he has made of the Illuminati of Europe. . . . Birth, education, elevation, and connections have placed Doctor Dwight at the head of the Edwardean* sect and Illuminati. . . . Science he forsakes, and her institutions he prostrates, to promote party, bigotry, and terror.[34]

Dismissive European reviews of Robison's book, which pointed out its exaggerations and inaccuracies, began to circulate in the United States; the eagerly awaited English translation of Barruel's *Memoirs,* whose very existence was presumed to provide independent verification of Robison's claims, turned out to be something of a dud. Barruel's book was too long, too obsessive, and too overwrought for most American readers, and it was too foreign to their current experience, which, for all its not inconsiderable Sturm und Drang, was still a far cry from France's. Upon George Washington's death in 1799, Masons eagerly reclaimed him as one of their own, doing much to restore their tarnished reputations; when Thomas Jefferson was elected to the presidency in 1800, the panic—if not the partisan warfare—slowly began to subside.

On January 31, 1800, Jefferson wrote a letter to Bishop James Madison, president of the College of William and Mary. "I have lately by accident got a sight of a single volume (the 3d.) of the Abbe Barruel's 'Antisocial conspiracy,' which gives me the first idea I have ever

---

* "Edwardean" refers to Jonathan Edwards's soteriology, which presumes mankind's innate depravity.

had of what is meant by the Illuminatism against which 'illuminate Morse' as he is now called, & his ecclesiastical & monarchical associates have been making such a hue and cry," he blandly informed his friend.

Tossed off as they are, Jefferson's impressions of Weishaupt and the Illuminati (and of Robison, Barruel, and Morse) are worth quoting at some length. Jefferson, remember, had been at the eye of the storm:

> Barruel's own parts of the book are perfectly the ravings of a Bedlamite. But he quotes largely from Wishaupt. . . . I will give you the idea I have formed from only an hour's reading of Barruel's quotations from him, which you may be sure are not the most favorable. Wishaupt seems to be an enthusiastic Philanthropist. He is among those (as you know the excellent Price and Priestley also are) who believe in the indefinite perfectibility of man. He thinks he may in time be rendered so perfect that he will be able to govern himself in every circumstance so as to injure none, to do all the good he can, to leave government no occasion to exercise their powers over him, & of course to render political government useless. This you know is Godwin's doctrine, and this is what Robinson, Barruel & Morse had called a conspiracy against all government. Wishaupt believes that to promote this perfection of the human character was the object of Jesus Christ. . . . As Wishaupt lived under the tyranny of a despot & priests, he knew that caution was necessary. . . . This has given an air of mystery to his views, was the foundation of his banishment, the subversion of the masonic order, & is the colour for the ravings against him of Robinson, Barruel & Morse. . . . This subject being new to me, I have imagined that if it be so to you also . . . I believe you will think with me that if Wishaupt had written here, where no secrecy is necessary in our endeavors to render men wise & virtuous, he would not have thought of any secret machinery for that purpose. As Godwin, if he had written in Germany, might probably also have thought secrecy & mysticism prudent.[35]

Twenty-six years later, in the northwest corner of New York state that would become known as the Burned-Over District because of its preternatural religious intensity (apocalyptic Millerism, from which Seventh-Day Adventism and the Jehovah's Witnesses were spun off, and Mormonism all started there), a fifty-two-year-old bricklayer named William Morgan, a transplanted Virginian, formed a partnership with David Cade Miller, the publisher of the Batavia *Republican Advocate*, and two other men, John Davids and Russel Dyer, to write an exposé of Masonic secrets on the model of Samuel Prichard's *Masonry Dissected* (1730) and *Jachin and Boaz* (1762).

Morgan needed the money. He had been ruined when the brewery he owned in Canada burned down; also he was nursing a grudge against the Masons of Batavia, who had blackballed him from membership in their new lodge. Once he began to publicize the book, a concerted campaign of harassment began. Local Masons took out a newspaper advertisement calling Morgan a swindler and a "dangerous man"; Miller's offices were torched. Then, on September 11, 1826, Morgan was arrested and imprisoned for a complaint about a trivial debt. No sooner was he acquitted than he was arrested again, about a matter of some stolen clothes (Morgan insisted they were borrowed). After an unidentified "friend" posted his bail, he was seen being forced into a coach; another eyewitness claimed he'd heard him crying "Murder!" as a band of men bearing torches led him away. In either case, Morgan was never seen again. Authorities later traced the coach as far as Fort Niagara, where Morgan had apparently been held prisoner for a time, but his trail ran cold after that.

If Morgan had indeed been "silenced," the plan backfired egregiously. *The Mysteries of Freemasonry, Containing All the Degrees of the Order Conferred in a Master's Lodge* was published on schedule and received much more attention than it would have otherwise. Morgan's disappearance became a cause célèbre, not just in western New York, but all over the United States.

New York's governor, De Witt Clinton, a high-ranking Mason, offered a $2,000 reward for information about his whereabouts, "that, if living, Morgan might be returned to his family; if murdered, that the perpetrators might be brought to condign punishment."[36] A year later, when a bloated corpse washed up on the shore of Lake Ontario, it was widely presumed to be Morgan's. Three separate inquests were held. The first declared the corpse "unidentified"; in the course of the second it was positively identified by Morgan's widow, Lucinda.

Less than half her husband's age, Lucinda Morgan would lead an eventful life herself, becoming something of a female Zelig. After she remarried in 1830 (to the great disappointment of the burgeoning anti-Masonic movement, which had been trotting her out at its conventions), she moved to Terre Haute, Indiana, where she and her new husband joined the Church of Latter-Day Saints. On January 22, 1846, two years after the death of Joseph Smith, Lucinda was sealed to him for eternity, which lent credence to the rumors that she had been one of his plural wives (which, if true, made Smith a plural husband too—a sin I've yet to hear him accused of). In 1856 the former Mrs. Morgan formally divorced her second husband; around 1860 she was reported to have joined the Catholic Sisters of Charity in Memphis, Tennessee. What are the odds that one woman would have found herself at the red-hot center of two signal national religious/political movements—and that she would have then converted to Catholicism, just as the anti-Papist Know-Nothing movement was reaching its peak?

After the third inquest, the body was released to the widow of Timothy Monro. Monro had been heavier and taller than Morgan, as was the corpse; Morgan was bald, and the corpse's scalp had hair on it. When her husband had gone missing, Mrs. Monro had described exactly the clothing he was wearing, and the clothing found on the body precisely matched her description, down to the places where his surtout coat and pantaloons had been mended and the manner in which they had been stitched. Skeptics were not convinced; cries of cover-up were heard.

A handful of Masons would be arrested and prosecuted for Morgan's kidnapping, but not for his murder, since there wasn't a corpse. Five were convicted and served light sentences—proof, to an increasingly outraged public, that a Masonic elite of judges, lawyers, sheriffs, jailers, newspaper publishers, and politicians did indeed control the criminal justice system. The Masonic line was that a band of overzealous, low-level members of the Craft had paid Morgan $500 to destroy his manuscript and make himself scarce in Canada. Few believed the story or put much stock in the periodic Morgan sightings that were reported (in places as far afield as Smyrna, in Asia Minor, where he was dressed in the costume of a Turk; in Antwerp, Holland, plying a respectable trade as a merchant; in Arizona, in the guise of an Indian chief; in Canada and Kentucky; sailing the Atlantic as a sea captain; and hanged for piracy in Havana, Cuba), and before long there were fewer and fewer Masons to tell it.

In his book *The Character, Claims, and Practical Workings of Freemasonry*, written some four decades later, during another wave of anti-Masonic feeling, the ex-Mason and renowned revivalist Charles Grandison Finney described the fallout of the Morgan Affair:

> In consequence of the publication of Morgan's book, and the revelations that were made in regard to the kidnapping and murdering of Mr. Morgan, great numbers of Masons were led to consider the subject more fully than they had done; and the conscientious among them almost universally renounced Masonry altogether. I believe that about two thousand lodges, as a consequence of these revelations, were suspended.
>
> The ex-president of a Western college, who is himself a Freemason, has recently published some very important information on the subject though he justifies Masonry. He says that, out of a little more than fifty thousand Masons in the United States at that time, forty-five thousand turned their backs upon the lodge to enter the lodge no more.[37]

One collateral casualty was the collegiate secret society Phi Beta Kappa. When the Reverend Peter Sanborn accused its members of collaborating with the Masons, it swiftly dispensed with its secret handshakes and ceremonials and transformed itself into an academic honor society. The Odd Fellows suffered a drop in membership as well.

Over the years, a number of gruesome confessions came to light that seemed to confirm the worst fears about Morgan's fate. Finney quoted the deathbed testimony of Henry L. Valance at length; his source was a pamphlet titled *Confession of the Murder of William Morgan, as Taken Down by Dr. John L. Emery, of Racine County, Wisconsin, in the Summer of 1848, Now First Given to the Public*:

> They . . . laid hold of their victim, "bound his hands behind him, and placed a gag in his mouth." They then led him forth to execu-

tion. "A short time," says this murderer, "brought us to the boat, and we all entered it—Morgan being placed in the bow with myself, along side of him. My comrades took the oars, and the boat was rapidly forced out into the river. The night was pitch dark, we could scarcely see a yard before us, and therefore was the time admirably adapted to our hellish purpose." Having reached a proper distance from the shore, the oarsmen ceased their labors. The weights were all secured together by a strong cord, and another cord of equal strength, and of several yards in length, proceeded from that. "This cord," says Mr. V., "I took in my hand [did not that hand tremble?] and fastened it around the body of Morgan, just above his hips, using all my skill to make it fast, so that it would hold. Then, in a whisper, I bade the unhappy man to stand up, and after a momentary hesitation he complied with my order. He stood close to the head of the boat. . . . I approached him, and gave him a strong push with both my hands, which were placed on the middle of his back. He fell forward, carrying the weights with him, and the waters closed over the mass. We remained quiet for two or three minutes, when my companions, without saying a word, resumed their places, and rowed the boat to the place from which they had taken it."[38]

Finney's portentous tone, gothic asides and all, is altogether fitting. Though by most accounts Morgan hadn't cut a very broad swath through the world when he was still breathing—Robert Morris, for example, while researching his pro-Mason *William Morgan* (admittedly a hatchet job), interviewed dozens of people who were willing to attest that Morgan drank to excess, that he was a braggart and a bully, had trouble holding on to a job, was a poor husband and provider, and hadn't even written the book that cost him his life—he would be mourned as a martyr nationwide. And the repercussions of his vanishing would permanently alter the face of the American political landscape.

The anti-Masonic movement "was a crusade," as Whitney R. Cross put it in his classic micro-history *The Burned-Over District: The Social and Intellectual History of Enthusiastic Religion in Western New York, 1800–1850.*

Masonry was believed to have committed a crime. Its members had put their fraternal obligations ahead of their duty to state and society, sanctioning both a lawless violation of personal security and a corrupt plot to frustrate the normal constitutional guarantees of justice.[39]

"You first arrested William Morgan as a debtor; next you put your fiendish claws on him; then you joined your hellish forces to abduct him; finally you murdered him," the politician and newspaper publisher Solomon Southwick declaimed. A remarkable string of invective followed:

> You are all banditti brethren, vile imposters, hypocrites, time-fools, time-fuddlers, sharpers, knaves, noodles, charlatans, blackguards, ignoramuses, wolves, drunkards, vile imposters, gullers, gullies, coxcombs, noodle-nobility, debauchees, a motley, nocturnal crew, blasphemers, bacchanalians, deceptive hearts, imposters, dumpling heads, nincompoops, blockheads.

And he was just getting started. Freemasonry is "atheism and infidelity," he continued.

> A degrading mummery, a genuine academy of Satan, a sink of iniquity and corruption; it maintains midnight revels; it is the legitimate offspring of hell; the modern whore of Babylon; it is naught but darkness, falsehood, fiction, corruption, and licentiousness; its temples contain dissipation and delusion; its mysteries are false and wicked; it is a bloodstained order, a monster, the offspring of the meanest motives; its Grand Lodge is a focus of iniquity, mystery, and mountain school of old Nick; its altars are altars of infidelity; it protects fraud and villainy, quackery, mummery, trumpery, fraud, and falsehood; it is emphatically the manufactory of noodles![40]

Anti-Masonry was in some ways a corollary of the Second Great Awakening. As the tide of religious enthusiasm rose, the stock of Freemasonry—ecumenical, intellectual, as ritualized as the hated Roman Church, and as exclusive and secretive as the mass revival meetings were public—naturally fell. Within a matter of months, the free-floating sense of outrage against the Masons had coalesced (and been cannily managed by political professionals like the Albany newspaper publisher Thurlow Weed) into a full-blown political movement. By 1830, 140 anti-Masonic newspapers were being published around the country, and anti-Masonic almanacs were being sold by the cartload; anti-Masonic nominating conventions—an innovation in American politics that was quickly taken up by rival political parties—were organized locally and statewide in New York, Massachusetts, Connecticut, Vermont, Rhode Island, and Pennsylvania. Typical of the resolutions they passed were these, from a Pennsylvania convention in Harrisburg in 1832:

> RESOLVED, That it is satisfactorily ascertained that direct Masonic influence has been used in this and other states to promote the political preferment of the Fraternity to the exclusion of others not Masons, equally well qualified, by filling nearly all offices of trust, honor, and emolument, with Masons and their supporters, thereby developing its political character; Anti-Masons are therefore necessarily compelled to resort to the elective franchise, in order to protect their rights and their liberties.
>
> RESOLVED, That this convention recommend to the people the propriety of political opposition to all adherents, and supporters of Masonry, whether oath-bound or otherwise.[41]

The first national anti-Masonic convention was convened in Philadelphia in 1830; among the speakers were Samuel W. Dexter of Michigan. "Free-masonry is an empire of itself," he warned, "distinct from every government within whose limits it exists. . . . it has its laws paramount to all other laws, its altars and its priests exalted above the religion of the land."[42]

Only a handful of anti-Masons actually attained to statewide office—William A. Palmer and Joseph Ritner were elected governors of Vermont and Pennsylvania in 1831 and 1835, respectively. But since Andrew Jackson was a high-ranking Freemason, the Anti-Masonic Party would become a major locus of anti-Jackson energies for the first few years of its existence.

John Quincy Adams, who had prevailed over Jackson for the U.S. presidency in 1824 when the election was thrown into the House of

Representatives, received substantial support from the anti-Masons during his unsuccessful reelection campaign in 1828. After his defeat, Adams threw himself into the anti-Masonic movement with a vengeance. Though he had been elected to Congress in 1830 as a National Republican, he ran an unsuccessful campaign for governor of Massachusetts on the Anti-Masonic ticket in 1834. Adams's book *Letters on Freemasonry* (1833) reflects the intensity of his obsession. Surely one of the most repetitious books ever published, its principal burden is that Masonry is "a conspiracy of the few against the equal rights of the many" and that it is an institution that "ought forever to be abolished. It is wrong—essentially wrong—a seed of evil, which can never produce any good."[43]

To fill up its pages, Adams compels poor Morgan to relive his martyrdom over and over again while morbidly cataloging the blood-curdling penalties that Masonry reserves for those who violate its oaths of secrecy—"cutting throats from ear to ear"; "cutting the body in two by the middle"; "opening the left breast and tearing out the heart and vitals"; "smiting off the skull to serve as a cup for the fifth libation"—for all the world as if he genuinely believed that the lawyers, aldermen, sheriffs, judges, and landowners who constituted the Masonic elite of the 1830s routinely inflicted such medieval torments upon their wayward brethren. Adams summons up the same level of moral outrage against the Freemasons as a later writer might against a Pol Pot or an Idi Amin—tyrants who casually slaughtered whole populations as a cold-blooded matter of policy—even though Freemasonry's confirmed body count was exactly zero (though I suspect that most Freemasons, even then, would have conceded that Morgan was murdered).

In fairness to Adams, most of the anti-Masonic literature of the day makes for equally tedious reading. Morgan himself was no Barruel or, for that matter, no Milton William Cooper. His book, true to its title, merely provided transcriptions of Masonry's ceremonials and described its secret grips and shibboleths: it didn't trace the pentagrams on the street map of Washington, D.C., or deconstruct the national seal; it didn't tie the Masons into a grand narrative of international conquest or implicate them in Devil worship. For the Bible-believing public of the 1820s, Masonry's faux-medievalism, its gothic brew of popery and paganism, was disturbing enough; its hierarchies and deferential titles ("Worshipful Master" and the like), and above all its exclusivity, ran counter to the increasingly democratic spirit of the age.

There is a telling irony in the fact that Andrew Jackson, who had won the popular vote but lost the presidency in 1824, and who received a substantial majority of the popular vote again in 1828, was smeared by the anti-Masons as an elitist and a despot (a famous cartoon portrayed him as King Andrew the First, trampling the Constitution). Before long, notes David Brion Davis, Jackson and the Democrats had triangulated, co-opting "the anti-Masons' egalitarian rhetoric, their hostility to monopolistic privilege, and their appeal to the ballot box as the ultimate arbiter."[44] The emergent Whig Party—widely perceived as the party of industry and finance—would absorb most of the anti-Masons during the 1830s, many of whom, as renters and farmers of relatively humble means, were voting against their own economic interests; they had more in common with Jackson's constituency than with their own party's. Perhaps it is a tribute to the moral seriousness of the denizens of the Burned-Over District, whose sincerely held Christian beliefs would draw many of them not just into anti-Masonry but into abolitionism and the temperance and women's suffrage movements over the next few decades (it's worth remembering that Bible Christianity was more often than not a force for social progressivism in the nineteenth century). Or maybe it is yet another example of the way that the ecumenicism of hatred acts as an intellectual solvent, blurring and eliding precise distinctions.

For all his egalitarian, anti-elitist pretensions, Jackson was a slave owner, a lawyer, and a land speculator. His policies toward Native Americans were nothing short of genocidal, and while his Democratic Party worked hard to extend the franchise to all white males, it also sought—successfully, for the most part—to disenfranchise free blacks in New York, Pennsylvania, Connecticut, North Carolina, and Tennessee by imposing onerous property requirements on them.

Jackson and his Democrats didn't hesitate to make political use of the paranoid style themselves. Sounding themes that would be dear to the hearts of future conspiracy theorists, Jackson set out to "kill" the Second National Bank, calling it a "monster Institution," while raising alarms about the power of the international money interests. "Is there no danger to our liberty and independence in a bank that in its nature has so little to bind it to our country?" he asked when he sent a bill to renew its charter back to the Senate unsigned in 1832.

> Should its influence become concentered . . . in the hands of a self-elected directory whose interests are identified with those of the foreign stockholders, will there not be cause to tremble for the purity of our elections in peace and for the independence of our country in war? . . . Of the course which would be pursued by a bank almost wholly owned by the subjects of a foreign power, and managed by those whose interests, if not affections, would run in the same direction there can be no doubt.[45]

John Tyler, still a Democrat in 1835 (he would be elected vice president as a Whig in 1840), raised the specter of foreign subversion in the form of British support for abolitionism. "Is it come to this," he asked, "that every plotter of mischief from abroad is to be received into our households, to instruct us in our duties as citizens?"[46] But for all that, Jackson and the Democrats mostly resisted the tides of nativism; Irish immigrants would become one of the bulwarks of the party, its source of strength in urban areas. The totalizing framework that conspiracy theories require, the Manichaean poles of opposition—Jacksonian elitists versus egalitarian anti-Masons, or for that matter Jacksonian egalitarians versus elitist, money-power Whigs—is mostly notable by its absence in the real historical record. The closer one looks at this epoch and its principal actors, the more paradoxical and contradictory it seems.

When an unemployed and patently deranged house painter named Richard Lawrence attempted to assassinate him in 1835, Jackson accused the Mississippi senator George Poindexter of arranging the hit. Jackson's opponents countered in the same spirit, accusing Jackson of having orchestrated the attempt himself to discredit his opposition. What were the odds, they asked, that *both* of the shooter's pistols would have jammed?

The economic philosophy that would become known as Jacksonian producerism, which pitted farmers, artisans, and entrepreneurs, who create real wealth, against a parasitic elite of bankers, lawyers, and middlemen, who feed off it, provided a basic template for the populist conspiracy theories that would emerge in the second half of the nineteenth century (and that continue to resonate today). "The aristocracy of our country are well aware that their notions of government are unsound, and in order to prevent the true appellation of aristocracy from being attached to them, they continually contrive to change their party name," the Massachusetts Democrat Frederick Robinson, a Jackson partisan, thundered in a Fourth of July address in 1834.

> But by whatever name they reorganize themselves, the true democracy of the country, the producing classes, ought to be able to distinguish the enemy. Ye may know them by their fruit. Ye may know them by their deportment toward the people . . . the capitalist, the merchant, the lawyer, and all who live without labor, and all who are possessed of property.[47]

Abolitionists—not a few of them anti-Masons—would devise and promote a set of conspiracy theories of their own. William Goodell's *Slavery and Anti-slavery: A History of the Great Struggle in Both Hemispheres* (1852) argued that the slave power had been behind virtually every major event in American history, from 1790 on. The slave power allowed the First National Bank to die in order to exempt the South from the obligation of paying its debts; it contrived the War of 1812 to damage northern trade. The Second National Bank was "a tool of political corruption, and chiefly for the pecuniary and political emolument of the South at the expense and for the management and subjugation of the North." Like the Jesuits had been accused of doing for centuries, like the Jews would be accused of doing at the turn of the next century in *The Protocols of the Elders of Zion*, or like Robert Welch would accuse the all-powerful "Insiders" of doing in the 1950s and 1960s, the slave power was said to play both sides against each other, keeping the national political parties at each other's throats "on the most fallacious and deceptive issues, or upon scarcely any issue at all."

> By this means she diverts attention from the real to the merely nominal issues before the country, while by controlling both par-

ties, she secures her ends through the ascendency of either, makes the one a check upon the other, and manages them through fear or through hope.[48]

Slavery, of course, would turn out to be a far more critical issue in American history than anti-Masonry; the persecution that the Freemasons suffered pales next to that endured by blacks, Native Americans, immigrants, and manual laborers during the same era. If institutional Masonry was sorely stressed, the Masons themselves were not persecuted as persons: they didn't lose their civil liberties; their property wasn't expropriated; they weren't forbidden to marry non-Masons or lynched. Should they choose to forswear their fraternal oaths (as William Wirt did, before he ran for president on the Anti-Masonic ticket in 1832), little stigma was attached to their past. It's tempting to compare the travails of the Masons with what McCarthyism wrought for Communists, ex-Communists, and fellow-traveling pinkos in the 1950s, but the witch-hunt metaphor only goes so far. Even at the height of the anti-Masonic scare, the president of the United States was a Mason.

If there was a religious component to anti-Masonry, displaced economic resentment played a significant role as well. The Erie Canal had brought new money, industry, and an influx of immigrants to northwestern New York, where the anti-Masonic movement began. If the 1820s and 1830s saw rapid territorial and economic expansion, they were also a time of economic instability and insecurity. For the most part, the Masons *did* belong to a privileged establishment—people with professions and land and social standing—and as such, they were well provisioned to endure their years in the wilderness. As painful as it might have been for them to hear and read such terrible things about themselves, most of them realized that if they simply kept their heads down, the storm would inevitably pass. Meanwhile, as so many other persecuted groups have done, they could draw sustenance and consolation from their faith. Robert Morris quotes a "vigorous speaker" who scoffed at the efforts of "this mongrel party called Anti-Masons . . . to upset Freemasonry. Let them upset. They will find they have simply upset a cube—whichever side they turn it on it will stand four-square, solid as ever!"[49]

But demonization and scapegoating are ugly things, and they can't but exact a human toll. Robert Morris followed the story of one of the Masons involved in the Morgan affair who *did* go to prison, Eli Bruce, the Niagara County sheriff. "Young, intelligent, rooted in the confidence of the people, enjoying a responsible position, and on his way to higher honors, Bruce was suddenly stricken down by the Malaria of Anti-Masonry which swept over the land in 1826, and all his hopes, all his expectations, were blighted and brought to naught," Morris eulogized him.[50] Bruce admitted that he'd helped transport Morgan from Canandaigua to Fort Niagara but insisted to the end that he'd believed Morgan was voluntarily expatriating to Canada. He was removed from office by order of Governor De Witt Clinton, tried, convicted, and sentenced to twenty-eight months in what Morris quaintly called "the Masonic Bastille." While serving his term, Bruce kept copious diaries. Morris quotes some of his *pensées:*

> The results of this Anti-Masonic epidemic in western New York have been divisions, separations in families, alienations in church memberships, vacating pulpits, traducing private character, lies unblushingly repeated, absurd tales soberly published, lessening the tone of public morals, polluting domestic circles, inflaming the passions of men, jealousy and distrust. What more can Satan want?[51]

Though his own health was failing, Bruce took up the practice of medicine upon his release. "I seem rapidly striding the downhill of life," he wrote in a letter a few months later.

> I have been very busy both with the healthy and sick. The small-pox has been among us, and created no little alarm and distress. Some ten or fifteen have fallen victims to it. We are yet afflicted with the remains of cholera-morgan. I am again indicted and held to bail for contumacy before Judge Marcy a year ago last June, but the trial troubles me very little. The Anti's are mad because I wouldn't swear five or six clever fellows into jail. I'd see them in Davy Jones' locker first, and then I wouldn't. I go the entire pork for my principles, and they may do their best. I intend to get my diploma of

M.D., next June if possible. Perhaps, however, I shall first be obliged to take another degree in jail.[52]

Bruce wouldn't live that long; he died of cholera (the bacterial variety) the next fall. Whether he was innocent or guilty, after reading his words, one finds it hard to see him as the monster of depravity that the anti-Masonic literature so floridly describes.

But that is how scapegoating works—by systematically dehumanizing its objects, by taking a whole category of human beings and turning them into vermin, germs, or things. As the sociologist James A. Aho wrote in *The Things of the World: A Social Phenomenology*, "The enemy presents itself to me as diabolic—'diabolic' meaning 'that thrown apart' (*dia* = apart + *bolos* = thrown)."

> In other words, it is something alien to me, other than me. If the enemy is "left" . . . then I am "right." I am right-eous. If the enemy is filth, then I am clean; and if the enemy is death, I am life. . . . In marking out, isolating, and destroying the anathema (*ana* = counter + *thema* = themes) in our midst, the mores, values, and customs we share are corrected, purified, rejuvenated. . . . This is precisely the "social function" of enemies. They serve as scapegoats.[53]

If Masons were un-Christian, the anti-Masons were saved; if Masons were un-American, the anti-Masons were patriots.

Like most panics, anti-Masonry didn't last long; by the late 1830s, it was on its last legs. Within a decade, Masonry—albeit with an exaggeratedly "Americanist" and Christian cast—was once again on the ascent. Hosts of other secret societies would spring up (or resurrect themselves) as well: the Foresters, the Good Fellows, the Druids, the Improved Order of Red Men, the Heptasophs, not to mention anti-Catholic and nativist societies such as the American Brotherhood, the Order of United Americans, the Order of the United American Mechanics, the United Sons of America, and the Order of the Star Spangled Banner. There was an implicit irony in the very existence of anti-Catholic secret societies, since secrecy was what was most held against Catholicism; the anti-Masons often bracketed "Masonry, Roman Catholic Faith, Monks, and the Inquisition" together. The select committee that investigated the Morgan disappearance for the New York State Senate in 1829 had specifically compared the Masons to the Jesuits, since both "secured unity of design and secrecy of action which used the most solemn sanctions of the most high God to subserve purposes the most selfish and profane."[54]

A second wave of anti-Masonic feeling swept the nation in the 1870s and 1880s, spearheaded by the National Christian Association, Opposed to Secret Societies, which was formally established in Pittsburgh, Pennsylvania, in 1868. In 1883 the NCA published *The Anti-Masonic Scrap Book: Consisting of Forty-Three Anti-secret Tracts*, which included a brief history, mission statement, and progress report on its activities. Persuasion—sermons, lectures, tracts, a nationally distributed magazine, and public events—was the sole weapon at these new anti-Masons' disposal; there would be no resort to the ballot box this time.

1. We have called the nation's attention to the secret, false worships, displacing the worship of Christ and preying like night vampires upon the vitals of the Republic.

2. We have unveiled the secret orders and shown them to belong to the same family with Jesuitism, the Commune, spirit circle, free-love and Mormonism.

3. We have encouraged and strengthened those denominations which exclude the adherents of secret orders from their Communion.

4. We have encouraged many to renounce and expose, and many to withdraw from lodges, while less substantial men are going into them.

5. We have commissioned and aided a few lecturers and we hope to see such soon in every State.

6. We have through the blessing of God largely stopped the growth of the two leading secret orders, Freemasonry and Odd-Fellowship, as shown by the official statistics of those orders.

7. We have sustained the *Cynosure*, which goes to post-offices scattered through thirty-two States and five Territories from the Pacific coast to the Atlantic, and from Canada and Nova Scotia to the States along the Mexican Gulf.[55]

The National Christian Association's objections to Masonry, appropriately enough, were almost entirely religious. They anathematized Freemasonry as a secular, heretical, or frankly satanic alternative to Protestantism; and as a gateway to spiritualism, free love, and the commune (which, just as Jacobinism was to the anti-Illuminists of the 1790s, were shorthands for the bloody fruits of atheism). It's notable that the word "democracy" does not appear in the NCA's progress report or mission statement even once.

"I have been a Freemason myself," the evangelist Charles Grandison Finney admitted in the opening pages of *The Character, Claims, and Practical Workings of Freemasonry*:

> The lodge where I took my degrees was composed, I believe, mostly of professed Christians. But when I came to join the lodge at Adams I found that the Master of the lodge was a deist. . . . There were in that lodge some as thoroughly irreligious men as I have ever associated with anywhere, and men with whom I never would have associated had they not been Freemasons. . . . I had belonged to the lodge in Adams nearly four years when I was converted to Christ. . . . I soon found that I was completely converted from Freemasonry to Christ. . . . My new life instinctively and irresistibly recoiled from any fellowship with what I then regarded as the "unfruitful works of darkness."[56]

The year before its *Scrap Book* was published, the NCA had erected a thirty-eight-foot-tall monument to William Morgan in the Batavia cemetery ("The Great Lie in Granite," as the Freemasons would call it). According to the September 14, 1882, *Buffalonian*, more than a thousand people turned out for its dedication. A hymn by Alexander Thomson was especially composed for the occasion:

> *And let our Monument proclaim*
> *That Morgan is a martyr's name!*
> *Till heart and home from sea to sea,*
> *Shout from the dark lodge bondage free!*

The Reverend B. T. Roberts of Rochester delivered an invocation that included the lines "We pray that, the colored being freed from slavery, the whites may be emancipated from the evils of secret societies." But Professor Charles A. Blanchard of Wheaton College struck a more somber note in his speech:

> Morgan was not one who was conspicuous for his talent, nor one who shaped the destiny of the nation, nor one who possessed a heaven illumined mind, nor a personal friend of any one of us. . . . He was murdered. . . . When a great movement has resulted in the accomplishment of its object, it has been customary to erect a monument to the man who was prominent in the event. The lodge against which Morgan's blow was aimed, however, still lives and today is ten times greater and more powerful than it was 56 years ago. Its conclaves now fill the air with music and the streets with marching men. Why give a monument to a failure?[57]

Why indeed? For the same reason that missionaries persist in knocking on doors they know will be slammed in their faces; for the same reason that martyrs calmly accept their fates. Because they believe that they are doing God's work; because they are laying up their treasures in heaven.

Almost a century and a half later, wide-scale changes in demographics and lifestyle have largely accomplished in the United States what the anti-Masons so manifestly failed to do. The Freemasons, like most fraternal societies, are rapidly declining. In 1959, there were 4,103,161 members of Grand Lodges in the United States—an all-time high. In 2009, that number had fallen to 1,404,059, roughly a 66 percent drop during a period when the U.S. population increased by almost the same percentage.[58] Nevertheless, the attacks on Masonry continue apace. Some of them are inspired by the same righteous spirit that guided Charles Grandison Finney; some come from a much darker place.

Conspiracists take scant comfort from Masonry's seeming troubles. To many of them, they are just a sinister subterfuge, evidence that the movement is going underground—into occultation, as it were—to begin a new and more dangerous phase of its activities, just as the Templars and the Rosicrucians and the Priory of Sion were all said to do centuries ago. Whether they realize it or not, all of those plumbers and policemen and doctors and lawyers who repair to their meeting places on the second Thursday of every month to socialize and recite their mystical rigmaroles about Hiram Abiff are just window dressing. The *real* Masons, the thinking goes, are invisible and preternaturally powerful and their preferred gathering places don't have signs on their doors. They meet in the boardrooms of banks and multinational corporations, in penthouses and sprawling estates and luxury hotels, and, yes, in the back rooms of synagogues.

Here is how Lieutenant Colonel Gordon "Jack" Mohr explained it in his book *The Hidden Power Behind Freemasonry:*

> Only the "elite" in the "upper echelons" are allowed to see the secret plans. . . . It may interest you to know that most of the lower orders of Freemasonry, do not realize there is a close connection between Masonry and anti-Christ Zionism, but this is an established fact of history which I will seek to prove to you. The Talmudic (Jewish holy book) formulas employed by Freemasonry; the Jewish traditions which run through masonic ceremonies, all point to a Jewish origin, or to the work of Jewish connivers in the lodge. Behind the Zionists' urge to rebuild Solomon's temple, lies a virulent hatred of Christ and all things Christian and is found in the depths of Jewish secret societies.[59]

Mohr goes on for almost two hundred pages, but if you've read the preceding chapter on *The Protocols of the Elders of Zion*, most of what he has to say would sound fairly familiar: Jews and Masons are working together to destroy Christianity, to eliminate America's national sovereignty, and to establish a godless New World Order. The Masonic Covenant practically obliges Master Masons to commit adultery. Oh yes, and this:

> World War II was provoked by the International Jewish-Masonic shysters in the first place, solely out of pathological greed and plain racial spite. . . . The National Socialist regime of Adolf Hitler, whatever may be said against it, had practically eliminated crime and corruption, and had brought about economic and social reforms, which provided jobs and low-interest loans for all. This had prac-

tically put the "usurers, stock exchange speculators, all manner of pimps, all slumlords and other parasites completely out of business."[60]

Though German Freemasonry had been less than welcoming to Jews in the eighteenth and nineteenth centuries, it paid a steep price for its presumed philo-Semitism during the years of the Third Reich. "With characteristic tenacity, [the Jew] championed the cause of religious tolerance . . . and in the Freemason organization, which had fallen completely into his hands, he found a magnificent weapon which helped him achieve his ends," Hitler wrote in *Mein Kampf.*[61] General Erich Ludendorff published a pamphlet called *Vernichtung der Freimaurerei durch Enthüllung ihrer Geheimnisse (Destruction of Freemasonry Through Revelation of Their Secrets)* in 1927, which argued that Freemasonry created "artificial Jews." "It is cheating the people," he wrote, "to fight the Jew while allowing his auxiliary troop, Freemasonry, to function."[62] Reinhard Heydrich, who shared many ideas with Lieutenant Colonel Mohr (though not his Bible religion), tasked a special department in the SS to root out Freemasonry from Germany and later from the countries it conquered.

Texe Marrs sells a three-part video series *(Masonic Lodge over Jerusalem, Thunder over Zion,* and *Cauldron of Abaddon)* that makes much the same point: that "the goal of the Jewish Masonic elite is to establish dictatorial Illuministic Communism and to enslave all of mankind under the thumb of a Jewish master race led by a world messiah who is to rule from Jerusalem."[63] Masonry, he says, is nothing but Jewish Kabbalism through and through—an unholy brew of sorcery and witchcraft.

Anti-Masonry is rife throughout the Islamic world (it was banned in Baathist Iraq on penalty of death; it is specifically condemned in the Hamas charter, along with Lions clubs and Rotary clubs, of all things), because of Freemasonry's presumed Zionist sympathies but also because of its supposed historical ties to the Templar crusaders. In one convoluted conspiracy theory, the immensely wealthy (and satanically evil) Templars took refuge in Scotland after their order was dissolved by Pope Clement V in 1312.[64] Robert the Bruce triumphed at Bannockburn because of the aid he received from Templar knights;

over the next few centuries, as the Templars transformed themselves into the Freemasons, they continued to be a potent power behind the Scottish throne. When James V of Scotland became James I of England, they traveled with him to London. From there, the Masons planted themselves in the heart of the New World; they returned to France and had their revenge on its king when they fomented its revolution in the 1790s. With its symbol of "the Eye of Providence" (the pyramid topped by a single eye that can be seen on the Great Seal of the United States), the story continues, Masonry is clearly a forerunner of the Dajjal, the one-eyed false messiah who plays roughly the same role in some versions of Islamic eschatology that the Antichrist does in Christian millennialism.*

If Andrew Jackson was an important figure in the anti-Masonic movement of the 1820s and 1830s, the late pop star Michael Jackson figures in Islamic anti-Masonry today, according to at least one theorist I encountered on the Internet. The translation is a little spotty, but it gets the idea across well enough:

> Michael Jackson . . . the King of pop regarded as the greatest entertainer of all times . . . may not be known to be linked with the Free Masons. However the cover of his "Dangerous" album had some interesting features on it the Free Masonic symbol of the One Eye can be found and also the picture of a watery Lake behind which laid burning flames. It seems as though anyone entering into the water would really be entering into the fire. The cover also has on it a picture of a bald headed man well known to the occult as Alistair [sic] Crowley. He himself was a Free Mason who became a Satanist and wrote the book "The New Law of Man" which stated in it that it would one day replace the Qur'ân as the law of man.[65]

But what if Michael Jackson wasn't affiliated with the Illuminati but was in fact their victim? Fan Web sites are rife with speculation that, as his sister La Toya put it, Michael Jackson "was murdered and although he died at the hands of Dr. Conrad Murray . . . Dr. Murray was a part of a much larger plan." Murray is reputed to be "a

---

* The concept of the Dajjal postdates Muhammad by several centuries; it is not mentioned in the Koran.

member of the Freemasons according to Fox News," one Web site breathlessly relates, "a centuries-old fraternal order with members including numerous heads of state in the Western World, wealthy business people and local middle-class citizens."[66]

"Yes, the illuminati DID destroy Michael Jackson," a post on Yahoo! replies to an inquiring reader:

> The same group of people bent on world domination for decades are getting ready to "seal the deal." . . . Michael was preparing to use his position and influence to warn the entire world of what these people (the Rothschild, Rockafellers [sic], the International Bank of Settlements, etc) are planning. In particular, their plans to drastically reduce the world's population by mass extermination through a program of forced "vaccinations" against the bogus swine flu.[67]

Michael Jackson isn't the only pop star who has been linked to the Masons and the Illuminati. The hip-hop entrepreneur Jay-Z, a co-founder of Roc-A-Fella Records and the creator of the Rocawear line of apparel—which sells T-shirts emblazoned with pyramids and all-seeing eyes—has long been a subject of intense conspiracist speculation. The rapper Prodigy connects Jay-Z to the Nuwaubian cult (a black nationalist movement that was founded by Dwight D. York in the mid-1970s and that combines equal parts of esoteric Masonry, Moorish Science, Nation of Islam, flying saucer lore, and Christian apocalypticism). "J.Z. knows the truth," Prodigy said, "but he chose sides with evil in order to be accepted in the corporate world."

> J.Z is a God damn lie. I have so much fire in my heart that I will relentlessly attack J.Z, Illuminati, and any-every other evil that exists until my lights are put out. This negativity I speak of is an actual living entity that uses us as food. We must sever ties with it in order to see things for what they really are. This negative energy is created and harnessed by the Illuminati secret government and they will make you spread this energy without you even knowing it. But people like J.Z. are very well aware. He was schooled by Dr. York.[68]

In January 2010, Jay-Z addressed the rumors directly in a radio interview with Angie Martinez. His Illuminati pose was a publicity stunt that had gotten out of control, he admitted sheepishly. "Am I part of some sect or cult? That sounds stupid to me," he protested. "I'm an entertainer at the end of the day. Maybe I'll push your buttons, but you know."[69]

Some contemporary anti-Masons are loyal Roman Catholics who respect the numerous papal injunctions against Freemasonry. Pope Leo XIII's encyclical on Freemasonry, which was promulgated in 1884 (and had much more to do with the Vatican's recent loss of temporal power in Italy as a result of the Risorgimento—Cavour, Mazzini, and Garibaldi were all Freemasons—than anything that was happening in the far-off United States), takes note of earlier papal warnings against "the sect," starting with Clement XII's in 1738. Benedict XIV, Pius VII and VIII, Gregory XVI, and Pius IX had all condemned Freemasonry as well.

"The course of events has demonstrated the prudence of Our predecessors," Leo XIII proclaimed.

> As Our predecessors have many times repeated, let no man think that he may for any reason whatsoever join the masonic sect, if he values his Catholic name and his eternal salvation as he ought to value them. Let no one be deceived by a pretense of honesty. It may seem to some that Freemasons demand nothing that is openly contrary to religion and morality; but, as the whole principle and object of the sect lies in what is vicious and criminal, to join with these men or in any way to help them cannot be lawful.[70]

The pope suggested some Christian sodalities and orders that the laity should be encouraged to join instead, such as the Third Order of Saint Francis and the Society of Saint Vincent de Paul; he held out hope that craft guilds might be revived under Christian auspices. One alternative to the Freemasons that he didn't mention, the Knights of Columbus, had been founded in New Haven, Connecticut, just two years before, specifically as a wholesome alternative to Freemasonry.

Quaesitum est, a declaration on Masonic associations, was issued by the Congregation for the Doctrine of the Faith at the Vatican in 1983 (Cardinal Joseph Ratzinger—the present Pope Benedict XVI—was one of its signatories). "It has been asked whether there has been any change in the Church's decision in regard to Masonic associations since the new Code of Canon Law does not mention them expressly," it began. Its answer is unambiguous:

> The Church's negative judgment in regard to Masonic associations remains unchanged since their principles have always been considered irreconcilable with the doctrine of the Church and, therefore, membership in them remains forbidden. The faithful who enroll in Masonic associations are in a state of grave sin and may not receive Holy Communion.[71]

"I myself have been a forty-five-year student of the satanically inspired, centuries-old conspiracy to use government, education, and media to destroy every vestige of Christianity within our society and establish a new world order," wrote the best-selling minister Tim LaHaye, co-author of the Left Behind series, in his book *Rapture (Under Attack): Will You Escape the Tribulation?* "Having read at least fifty books on the Illuminati, I am convinced that it exists and can be blamed for many of man's inhumane actions against his fellow man during the past two hundred years."[72]

Ralph Epperson has written a string of conspiracist books about the malign influence of Illuminated Masonry in American life, including *The New World Order, The Unseen Hand,* and *Masonry: Conspiracy Against Christianity.* He has been branded as a "crypto-Jew" in some circles because he insists that the belief that the Jews are behind the "conspiracy at work in the world" is "dramatically wrong." The mystery religion at the heart of Masonry was developed in Egypt six thousand years ago, he says, before Judaism even began. The nine adepts who lead the "Great White Brotherhood" are headquartered in Tibet.

Epperson didn't pull this idea out of thin air. The notion of a secret society of enlightened magi is at the root of seventeenth-century Rosicrucianism, which drew on Egyptian Hermeticism, Greek mystery cults, Gnosticism, alchemy, and other occult and mystic traditions in its turn. In the late nineteenth century, the French occultist Joseph Alexandre Saint-Yves d'Alveydre wrote about Agarttha, a country that was located in the caves beneath the Himalayas and that was organized according to the principles of synarchy, or government by secret society. The Theosophists also told about a secret society of immortal beings they called the Ascended Masters. In his book *The Masters and the Path*, C. W. Leadbeater describes these super-beings as men "who, instead of leaving the world entirely, to pursue a life of their own in the divine or superhuman kingdoms, have remained in touch with humanity, through love of it, to assist its evolution in beauty and love and truth." Three of these great ones, he goes on to relate, live in a ravine in Tibet:

> Paths run down the ravine past their houses, and meet at the bottom, where there is a little bridge. Close to the bridge a narrow door . . . leads to a system of vast subterranean halls containing an occult museum of which the Master Kuthumi is the Guardian on behalf of the Great White Brotherhood.[73]

But in case you think that conspiracy theorists spend all their time in libraries, paging through dusty books, consider Svali—the pseudonym of a former Illuminati operative who claims to have escaped the organization in 1996. Svali's story—which brought her a small measure of fame on the Internet—was very much in the tradition of *Michelle Remembers* (1980), the best-selling book of recovered memories by a self-styled victim of satanic cult abuse, which itself was a descendant of *The Awful Disclosures*, published in 1836, the horrifying confessions of Maria Monk, a Canadian woman who'd survived imprisonment in a Catholic convent in Montreal, where she said priests routinely raped the nuns and murdered their babies (I will have much more to say about Maria Monk in the next chapter).

Literally raised in the cult by her Illuminati parents and forced to marry a partner of the Illuminati's choosing, Svali led a seemingly normal life by day as a teacher in a Christian school and a wife and mother of young children. At night she assumed her real identity as the sixth head trainer in the San Diego branch of the Illuminati, where she supervised thirty mind programmers who, utilizing cutting-edge science and medieval torture, reprogrammed the minds of unwitting future Illuminati assets—a virtual zombie army that will be ready to march whenever their masters issue a set of coded commands.

One percent of Americans (more than three million people) are either members of this satanic cult or have been brainwashed by them. Its hierarchy, according to the antifeminist, New World Order conspiracy theorist Henry Makow, Ph.D., who attests to Svali's bona fides on his own Web site, are mostly homosexuals and pedophiles; they carry out animal sacrifices and commit ritual murders. There is almost nothing bad you can think of that doesn't have their fingerprints all over it:

> [The Illuminati] works "hand in glove" with the CIA and Freemasonry. It is Aryan supremacist (German is spoken at the top) but welcomes Jewish apostates. It controls the world traffic in drugs, guns, pornography and prostitution. It may be the hand behind political assassination, and "terrorism," including Sept. 11, the Maryland sniper and the Bali bomb blast.
>
> It has infiltrated government on a local, state and national level; education and financial institutions; religion and the media. Based in Europe, it plans a "world order" that will make its earlier attempts, Nazism and Communism, look like picnics. One other detail: these people are not happy.[74]

Svali wrote articles and self-published a book about her experiences; she also granted numerous interviews. Like Epperson, she believes that the Illuminati are not Jewish:

> The Illuminati SAY they date back to ancient Babylon on the Fields of Shinar around 3,900 B.C, give or take. But this is probably cult programming and boasting. They state that they are founded on the occult base of all ancient mystery religions and occult practices. But they actually seem to be descended from the Knights Templar during the medieval ages, and the Rosicrucians who were also founded back then. I myself have trouble knowing how much of the "cult history" I was taught as a child by my scholarship teachers was merely programming, and how much is accurate truth, so I cannot really be an objective source of information. Like any group, they tend to want to "idealize" their roots.

The UN, she reveals, is a forerunner of the Illuminati's Supreme World Council:

The Illuminati and governmental leaders chose to create the UN early in the past century, and worked hard and against opposition to put it in place (FDR was their man in America who helped the American public accept it). Both he and Eleanor were staunch Illuminists. So is Shirley Temple Black.[75]

Some other facts that Svali relates: The top leaders of the Illuminati can trace their bloodlines to the Hapsburgs, the Rothschilds, and the Merovingians; the Rockefellers are the most important American family. Immoral Hollywood movies, drugs, pornography, and atheism are all helping to condition the public to their future enslavement; when the time is ripe, a planned financial collapse will trigger the military phase of the takeover. The Illuminati perform human sacrifices on special occasions; they devour their victims' hearts while they are still beating. When Svali disappeared off the radar in 2006, it was widely feared that she'd been silenced by her former masters. But then, in 2008, she was reported to be alive and well and "residing safely in an isolated place of refuge with a number of fellow Christian brothers and sisters."[76] As far as anyone knows, she is still underground.

A silly sidebar: Several years ago, a youthful prankster in Utah by the name of John Fenley purchased a long list of domain names, including itanimulli.com, which he redirected to the Web site of the National Security Agency. "Itanimulli," of course, is "Illuminati" spelled backward. Literally thousands of Web-addicted insomniacs have stumbled upon his handiwork; many of them have drawn the obvious conclusion that the NSA and the Illuminati are one and the same. I blogged about Itanimulli a couple of times, and those old posts still account for more than half of my traffic.

Google just about any celebrity's or politician's name alongside the word "Freemasonry" or "Illuminati" and something is likely to pop up. Sarah Palin? Natch. On April 2, 2008, the then Alaska governor issued a proclamation honoring "the Prince Hall Masonic family for its commitment to civic contributions."[77] The question naturally arises: Is she a satanist? Another blog notes Palin's subtle use of a Masonic recognition sign (placing her hand upon her thigh) and draws the obvious conclusions. Laura Bush[78] used that same sign when she met Pope Benedict, who is also a Mason.[79] So is Barack Obama.[80]

And Glenn Beck. "A Mormon is as much a Christian as a Muslim is," JesusSaves 2008, a pseudonymous visitor to a well-trafficked conspiracist forum commented. "Glenn Beck would never dare mention Freemasonry because he is a Freemason. He is paid and paid very well . . . to steer the religious right in the direction they want them to go."[81]

What is it about Freemasonry that can drive an otherwise intelligent and worldly soul like John Quincy Adams into the perseverative distempers of his *Letters on Freemasonry* and people like Jack Mohr, General Ludendorff, and Svali altogether beyond the bounds of reason? One needn't be a raving anti-Semite to entertain the notion that Freemasonry *does* represent a kind of voluntary, "artificial" Judaism—a spiritual/intellectual path, followed by a self-selected minority that vests its hope in a project of ethical and intellectual improvement, rather than in the miracle of divine grace, bought with Christ's blood on the cross.

Freemasonry's ecumenicism, its openness to and acceptance of any and all religious paths—including heretical Gnosticism and the pagan mysteries—might seem like a repudiation of Christianity for those who believe that all who do not come to Christ to be saved must go from him to be damned. At the same time, Masonry's presumption of its own superiority inspires resentment. For all its talk of the "three precious jewels" of "humanity, friendship, and brotherly love," Masonry is an elitist institution—entrée to its fraternity requires a formal invitation and a series of involved initiations; only a small number of its members are privy to its innermost secrets.

If Masons and Jews were merely damned, they would be figures of pity; what's most galling about them to some Christians is their unwonted arrogance. "Therefore be on your guard against the Jews," wrote Martin Luther in *On the Jews and Their Lies.*

> God's wrath has consigned them to the presumption that their boasting, their conceit, their slander of God, their cursing of all people are a true and a great service rendered to God—all of which is very fitting and becoming to such noble blood of the fathers and circumcised saints. . . . And with all this, they claim to be doing right.[82]

"The facts say that Masonic patriotism is no less than sectarian egotism which yearns to dominate everything," Pope Leo XIII wrote in his encyclical on Freemasonry in 1892.

After nineteen centuries of Christian civilization, this sect tries to overthrow the Catholic Church and to cut off its divine sources. It absolutely denies the supernatural, repudiating every revelation and all the means of salvation which revelation shows us. Through its plans and works, it bases itself solely and entirely on such a weak and corrupt nature as ours. Such a sect cannot be anything other than the height of pride, greed, and sensuality.[83]

Given the Masons' ubiquity in conspiracy theory, it is ironic that Masonry's central allegory is itself the story of a "horrid conspiracy." I take this account of the murder of Hiram Abiff and the recovery and reburial of his body from Captain Morgan's *Illustrations of Masonry*, whose author, had he lived to see his book through the press, might have added a poignant personal note or two to the tale. Morgan's body, unlike Hiram Abiff's, was never found or raised.

Masonic tradition informs us that, at the building of King Solomon's temple, fifteen Fellow Crafts, discovering that the temple was almost finished, and not having the Master Mason's word, became very impatient and entered into a horrid conspiracy to extort the Master Mason's word from their Grand Master, Hiram Abiff, the first time they met him alone, or take his life, that they might pass as Masters in other countries, and receive wages as such but, before they could accomplish their designs, twelve of them recanted, but the other three were base enough to carry their atrocious designs into execution. Their names were Jubela, Jubelo, and Jubelum.[84]

Hiram Abiff died rather than reveal the secret. Morgan died because he proposed to expose Masonry's secrets, among them the new word that is whispered into a candidate's ear upon his initiation into the third degree of the Royal Arch. That new word is a pale substitute for the real word, which was known only to Solomon, king of Israel, Hiram, king of Tyre, and Hiram Abiff the widow's son, but it is a dark secret nonetheless. The new word, Morgan revealed, is "Mah-hah-bone," and it must be spoken in a whisper.* A clue to the nature of the old word can be found in the ceremony reenacting the discovery of Abiff's corpse. The participants search on and about his body for the word but "had not discovered anything but a faint resemblance of the letter G on the left breast."

"Nothing but a faint resemblance of the letter G!" the Master cries.

> That is not the Master's word nor a key to it. I fear the Master's word is forever lost! Nothing but a faint resemblance to the letter G! That is not the Master's word nor a key to it. I fear the Master's word is forever lost! Nothing but a faint resemblance of the letter G! That is not the Master's word nor a key to it. O Lord, my God, is there no help for the widow's son?[85]

The Jews, of course, also have a word that they are forbidden to pronounce out loud—the tetragrammaton that spells out the name of God (the Masonic *G*, it is explained elsewhere, stands for both "God" and "Geometry"). And if the Masons have their contract, the Jews have their covenant. Even emancipated, relatively assimilated Jews insist on a degree of separation from the Gentiles they live among; circumcision, dietary restrictions, endogamy, and a separate calendar all work to that end.

The following set of instructions to newly Entered Apprentice Masons (also extracted from William Morgan's book) may appear benign—the Apprentice is told to "submit to legal authority, and conform with cheerfulness" to his country's government—but for those who are inclined to see it that way, they also seem to enjoin a life of divided loyalties and Jesuitical dissimulation:

> In the state you are to be a quiet and peaceable subject, true to your government and just to your country; you are not to countenance disloyalty, but faithfully submit to legal authority, and conform with cheerfulness to the government of the country in which you

---

* Please note that I do not claim to be privy to any Masonic secrets that aren't already in the public domain. If there are secrets that are known only to high-degree Masons, they are not known to me.

live. In your outward demeanor be particularly careful to avoid censure or reproach. Although your frequent appearance at our regular meetings is earnestly solicited, yet it is not meant that Masonry should interfere with your necessary vocations; for these are on no account to be neglected; neither are you to suffer your zeal for the institution to lead you into argument with those, who, through ignorance, may ridicule it.[86]

Though the connections between Masonry and the Knights Templars are more mythological than historical, strictly speaking, it's interesting to note that Philip the Fair expelled the Jews from France and expropriated their money in 1306, only one year before he arrested the Templars en masse and accused them of heresy and Devil worship, helping himself to as much of their vast riches as the Vatican would permit him to take.

If John Quincy Adams's hatred of the Masons was intemperate, his grandson Henry would be driven to distraction by the Jews, whom he blamed for all the financial, political, and cultural problems of the age. "I am myself more than ever at odds with my time," he wrote to Charles Milnes Gaskell on July 31, 1896. "I detest it and everything that belongs to it, and live only in the wish to see an end to it, with all its infernal Jewry."

> I want to put every money-lender to death, and to sink Lombard Street and Wall Street under the ocean. . . . We are in the hands of the Jews. They can do what they please with our values. . . . For three years I have told you that there was only one safe and surely profitable investment and that is gold, locked up in one's private safe. There you have no risk but the burglar. In any other form you have the burglar, the Jew, the Czar, the socialist, and above all, the total, irremediable, radical rottenness of our whole social, industrial, financial, and political system.[87]

The Jews have been hated for millennia because they rejected Christ; since at least the fifteenth century, they have been hated because of their blood. To extreme anti-Semites, Judaism is a race, essentially and intrinsically evil—conversion cannot suffice to erase the curse of its birthright. But Masonry—like heresy, witchcraft, Devil worship, or Communism—is adopted by choice; worse, it is an option that (at least in its early days) was especially alluring to people of education and social standing.

With its quest for "more light," Masonry is basically humanism; its essential premise is the perfectibility of humankind. "The common gavel is an instrument made use of by operative Masons to break off the corners of rough stones, the better to fit them for the builder's use," its ceremonial instructs. "But we, as Free and Accepted Masons, use it for the more noble and glorious purpose of divesting our hearts and consciences of all the vices and superfluities of life, thereby fitting our minds as living and lively stones, for that spiritual building, that house not made with hands, eternal in the heavens."[88]

Freemasonry's allegories might be sententious and windy; its ceremonials stilted and bizarre. But by any rational reckoning, Freemasonry is not only compatible with American democracy; its ideals are implicit in the founding documents of the Republic (thirteen of the Declaration of Independence's fifty-six signers were Masons; nine of the Constitution's thirty-nine signatories were Masons as well). America is neither a Christian nor an anti-Christian polity; officially, at least, it tolerates every religion and none. For all of Masonry's faux medievalism, tyrants and priests have much to fear from its advocacy of freedom of thought and conscience. But out on the paranoid fringes, where resentment and the brooding sense of dispossession hold sway, the ecumenicism of hatred obliterates all of those fine discriminations. The myth of American exceptionalism demands a divine destiny—and, like all memorable narratives, a memorable villain. To the conspiratorial frame of mind, history is a battleground, an arena in which angels and demons are forever grappling. For someone who believes that our fates are determined by the machinations of a secret elect, Freemasonry can't but seem threatening.

Of course Freemasons, like America itself (and like many Jews and Christians, for that matter), aren't always true to their ideals. Ironically—a word that inevitably comes up again and again in a discussion like this—the secessionist, pro-slavery secret society the Knights of the Golden Circle (never the threat to the Union that they were imagined to be) were founded on the model of the Freemasons before the Civil War, as was the racist Ku Klux Klan during

Reconstruction. William Joseph Simmons, the minister who revived the "100 percent Americanist" KKK in 1915, was active in at least a dozen fraternal societies, including the Freemasons. According to William Whalen, the author of *Christianity and American Freemasonry*, "Enthusiasm for the Klan was more widespread among average Masons than among Grand Masters and Masonic leaders, who saw the dangers of too close an association with such an unsavory group. But Klan recruiters concentrated on Masons, since they believed that they were already hostile to Catholics and blacks and not overly fond of Jews."[89]

In *Secret Societies and Subversive Movements*, Nesta Webster conceded that a strictly personal Freemasonry, whose members follow a program of "individual regeneration" rather than wholesale "social reorganization," can be a force for good. But once Masonry's ideals are politicized, as she believed they had been in Europe, they can only lead to such monstrosities as internationalism, Socialism, and universal atheism. "There will never be a Millennium of man's making," she writes. "Only the application of Christian principles to human conduct can bring about a better order of things."[90] Never mind that some idealistic Christians also "politicize" their principles. Anyone who believes otherwise is in the camp of Satan.

And Satan, needless to say, works most of his mischief through the eager agency of the Jews. "I do not think that the Jews can be proved to provide the sole cause of world-unrest," Webster wrote.

> But this is not to underrate the importance of the Jewish peril. Although the existence of an inner circle of Masonic "Elders" remains problematical, Jewry in itself constitutes the most effectual Freemasonry in the world. What need of initiations, or oaths, or signs, or passwords amongst people who perfectly understand each other and are everywhere working for the same end? Far more potent than the sign of distress that summons Freemasons to each other's aid at moments of peril is the call of the blood that rallies the most divergent elements in Jewry to the defence of the Jewish cause.[91]

5.

The Whore of Babylon
and Stealth Jihad

A lot of heat has been coming off of op-ed pages, cable-TV talk shows, and advertorials in recent years on the subject of the endemic anti-Catholic bias in American culture. Much of it has been generated by William Donohue of the Catholic League for Religious and Civil Rights. Just as AIPAC or the ADL might respond to critics of an Israeli policy regarding settlements on the West Bank or evictions in East Jerusalem with a salutary reminder of Hitler and the Holocaust, Donohue reflexively attributes everything from newspaper stories about pedophile priests to Parkinson's patients' complaints about the church's stance on embryonic stem cell research to anti-Catholic bigotry.

"Hollywood is controlled by secular Jews who hate Christianity in general and Catholicism in particular," Donohue notoriously answered, when Pat Buchanan solicited his thoughts about the controversy surrounding Mel Gibson's movie *The Passion of the Christ* on a cable-TV talk show. "Hollywood likes anal sex," Donohue added. "They like to see the public square without nativity scenes. I like families. I like children. They like abortions. I believe in traditional values and restraint. They believe in libertinism. We have nothing in common."[1]

The Catholic League's Web site backs up its beleaguered posture with quotations from Arthur Schlesinger Sr. (anti-Catholicism is "the deepest bias in the history of the American people") and Peter Viereck ("Catholic baiting is the anti-Semitism of the liberals").[2] Both quotations contain more than a germ of truth, but it's worth remembering that they date back to the 1950s.* The past half century has witnessed a vast sea change, both in Americans' attitudes toward Roman Catholicism and in Catholicism itself.

When John F. Kennedy was running for president in 1960, he felt compelled to stand before the Greater Houston Ministerial Association and pledge that he would be his own man. "I am not the Catholic candidate for President," he insisted. "I am the Democratic Party's candidate for President who happens also to be a Catholic. I do not speak for my church on public matters and my church does not speak for me." Kennedy's election would be a watershed in the mainstreaming of American Catholicism, which has proven itself to be as heterogeneous as the rest of the American population. The alliance that was cemented between Protestant Fundamentalism and right-wing Catholicism in the wake of *Roe v. Wade* has been another—one that is every bit as historically unprecedented as Fundamentalism's newfound accord with political Zionism. "What unites Protestant fundamentalists and right-wing Catholics today, in both the religious and political arenas," Susan Jacoby wrote in *The Age of American Unreason*, "is a shared hatred of secularism and the influence of secular values on culture and public life."[3]

The Pentecostalist Sarah Palin provided a case in point when she revisited Kennedy's Houston speech in her book *America by Heart: Reflections on Family, Faith, and Flag.* "I remember being taught," she wrote, that the speech "reconciled public service and religion without compromising either." But she confessed to a certain disappointment when she read it as an adult:

---

* Schlesinger's mot comes from a conversation with John Tracy Ellis and was quoted in Ellis's *American Catholicism* (Chicago: University of Chicago Press, 1956), p. 151; Viereck's is from *Shame and Glory of the Intellectuals* (New Brunswick, N.J.: Transaction, 2007), which was originally published in 1953.

In the best American tradition, [Kennedy] nobly defended religious tolerance and condemned official governmental preference of any faith over any other. But his language was more defensive than is portrayed today, in tone and content. Instead of telling the country how his faith had enriched him, he dismissed it as a private matter meaningful only to him. And rather than spelling out how faith groups had provided life-changing services and education to millions of Americans, he repeatedly objected to any government assistance to religious schools. . . . His vaunted speech didn't represent a successful reconciliation of faith and public office, but an articulate and unequivocal divorce of the two.[4]

Does the notion that taxpayer subsidies to parochial schools are unconstitutional really amount to an "unequivocal divorce" between the spheres of faith and public life? As another Roman Catholic candidate for the U.S. presidency once said, "Let's look at the record"— let's see what Kennedy actually said.

"Whatever issue may come before me as President," Kennedy promised, "on birth control, divorce, censorship, gambling or any other subject, I will make my decision . . . in accordance with what my conscience tells me to be in the national interest, and without regard to outside religious pressure or dictates." Kennedy didn't promise to purge his conscience of the values that were instilled in it by his religious training and beliefs—far from it. He promised that he would abide by its judgments. "If the time should ever come," Kennedy continued, "when my office would require me to either violate my conscience or violate the national interest, then I would resign the office; and I hope any conscientious public servant would do likewise."[5]

Palin's dismay at Kennedy's opposition to public funding for religious schools is something of an anachronism: he was referring to a different controversy than the one over vouchers and school choice that's become a Republican talking point today; he wasn't alluding to school prayer or evolution either (the landmark Supreme Court decisions forbidding school prayer and religious symbols in the public realm were still several years away when Kennedy gave his speech). He was harking back to a battle that was first fought in New York City more than a century before. In 1840, Archbishop John Hughes of New York City protested the sectarian slant of New York City's public school curriculum, which featured readings from the Protestant King James Bible and recitations of Protestant prayers and hymns, and demanded that the state either purge the curriculum of its Protestant bias or provide tax dollars for Catholic schools. Governor William Seward agreed, proposing that public schools be established "in which [immigrants] may be instructed by teachers speaking the same language with themselves and professing the same faith."[6] After rancorous and sometimes violent debate, Seward's proposal was defeated. Compromise legislation stipulated that public schools would adopt a religiously neutral stance instead, restricting their curricula to the three Rs (which gave rise to angry Protestant complaints that Catholics were seeking to ban the Bible and prayer from schools). Similar battles were fought in Philadelphia and Boston. The Catholic parochial school movement arose for two reasons: because a number of public schools continued to press Protestantism on their students (pupils were still reciting the Anglican Lord's Prayer in many schools when Kennedy gave his speech) and, ironically, because the ones that did adopt a neutral stance were considered too secular (thanks largely to Catholic pressure to make them that way).

JFK, who was born in 1917, had more direct experience of anti-Catholic prejudice than many contemporary readers might realize. *The Menace*, an anti-Catholic magazine that was published between 1911 and 1931 in Aurora, Missouri, had 1.4 million weekly subscribers at its peak. "What we are striving for," one of its editorials read, "is to EDUCATE THE PEOPLE of this republic of ours to a CLEARER UNDERSTANDING of the difference between allowing the Roman Catholic to worship God in his own way AND permitting the ROMAN CATHOLIC CHURCH, as a political factor, to put the Bible out of our public schools, elect her servants to office that the Church may prosper and the laws of the nation [be] defied with impunity." *The Menace* maintained that both Lincoln and Warren Harding were victims of Roman Catholic plots—a stunning irony, when one considers what the fate of the country's first Catholic president would be. "Nobody ever got a dollar out of these tax-gatherers from the pope's garden," the editorial concluded, "and nobody ever will except assassins they hire to get presidents out of the way."[7]

Sarah Palin may know whereof she speaks when it comes to resigning from public office, but her views on the First Amendment are hard to parse until you realize that they don't extend to the idea that a wall of separation between church and state is a desirable thing (except, of course, when the issue is Sharia law). She concedes that Kennedy said what he did in Houston out of political necessity—"It seems incredible today that this was even an issue," she explains, "but . . . Catholicism had long been held in suspicion by the Protestant majority, who feared that a Catholic president would secretly take orders from the Pope"[8]—but she clearly feels that what politicians should be assuring us of today is that they do in fact answer to a higher power.

Granted, there are principled arguments that can be made about where the boundary between church and state should be drawn; granted, too, the forces of secularism can be every bit as dogmatic and insensitive and overbearing as those of established religions. But the notion that religious Christians suffer from state-sanctioned discrimination in the United States today is a hard one to swallow, even if the law does still require them to pay for their own religious schooling or, for the time being at least, forbids public schools to teach creationism as science.

And yet historically, America has indeed been a deeply anti-Catholic place. It couldn't have been otherwise, considering that it was colonized during a time when England was at odds with the Catholic Church and involved in internecine warfare with Catholic Spain and France. In its early days, Massachusetts Bay reserved the death penalty for priests and Jesuits. Though Maryland began as a refuge for Catholics, its charter was voided after the Glorious Revolution of 1688, and Anglicanism became its established church; Rhode Island and Pennsylvania followed suit by disenfranchising their Catholics. During the Great Awakening in the 1740s, preachers like George Whitefield preached about the "swarms of monks . . . and friars like so many locusts . . . overspreading and plaguing the nation"; school primers taught children "to abhor that arrant Whore of Rome and all her Blasphemies."[9] Throughout the eighteenth century New York required holders of public office to formally abjure their allegiance to the Catholic Church and disavow the doctrine of transubstantiation; the latter oath inoculated itself against papal guile by adding the following condition, in language that was imported verbatim from the Irish Penal Laws:

I do make this Declaration, and Every Part Thereof, in the Plain and Ordinary Sence, of the Words read to me, as they are Commonly Understood, By English Protestants, Without Any Evasion, Equivocation, or Mental Reservation Whatsoever, and Without any Dispensation, Already Granted me for this Purpose, by the Pope, or any Other Authority Whatsoever, or Without Thinking, that I am or Can be Acquitted, before God or Man, or Absolved of this Declaration, or any Part Thereof, Although the Pope, or any other Person or Persons, or Power Whatsoever, Should Dispence with, or Annul the same, and Declare that it was Null and Void, from the Beginning.[10]

Pope's Day, which is still celebrated in England as Guy Fawkes Day or Bonfire Night, commemorated the discovery of the "Gunpowder Plot," a Catholic conspiracy to blow up the Houses of Parliament during the state opening on November 5, 1605, when the king and the royal family were scheduled to be present. Robert Catesby was the plot's mastermind; Fawkes, a Protestant mercenary, was apprehended in the cellar of the House of Lords, guarding thirty-six barrels of gunpowder. Joshua Coffin's *Sketch of the History of Newbury, Newburyport, and West Newbury, from 1635 to 1845* includes this colorful account of an annual Pope's Day celebration in Massachusetts:

This year, the celebration went off with a great flourish. In the day time, companies of little boys might be seen, in various parts of the town, with their little popes, dressed up in the most grotesque and fantastic manner, which they carried about, some on boards, and some on little carriages, for their own and others' amusement. But the great exhibition was reserved for the night, in which young men, as well as boys, participated. They first constructed a huge vehicle . . . on the front of which, they erected a paper lantern, capacious enough to hold, in addition to the lights, five or six persons. Behind that, as large as life, sat the mimic pope, and several other personages, monks, friars, and so forth. Last, but not least, stood an image of what was designed to be a representation of Old Nick himself, furnished with a pair of huge horns, holding in his hand a pitchfork, and otherwise accoutered, with all the frightful ugliness that their ingenuity could devise. . . . After perambulating the town . . . they concluded their evening's entertainment with a splendid supper; after making, with the exception of the wheels and the heads of the effigies, a bonfire of the whole concern, to which were added, all the wash tubs, tar barrels, and stray lumber, that they could lay their hands on.[11]

On November 5, 1775, General Washington issued orders forbidding soldiers in the Continental army to observe that "ridiculous and childish custom of burning the Effigy of the Pope"—an act that could only insult and alienate the ex-colonies' potential allies in Francophone Canada. "At such a juncture, and in such Circumstances, to be insulting their Religion, is so monstrous, as not to be suffered or excused," he expostulated.[12] Washington's indignation is understandable, but not his surprise. The Quebec Act of 1774, which granted French-Canadian Catholics freedom of worship and allowed them to hold public office without renouncing their faith, had been one of the five so-called Intolerable Acts that sparked the Revolution in the first place.

On March 15, 1790, Washington did for America's Catholics what he would do for the Jews of Newport, Rhode Island, a few months later. In a letter addressed to a committee of lay Catholics who'd congratulated him on his presidency, he expressly and publicly acknowledged their status as patriotic Americans. "As mankind become more liberal they will be more apt to allow that all those who conduct themselves as worthy members of the community are equally entitled to the protection of civil government," he wrote.

> I hope ever to see America among the foremost nations in examples of justice and liberality. And I presume that your fellow-citizens will not forget the patriotic part which you took in the accomplishment of their Revolution, and the establishment of their government; or the important assistance which they received from a nation in which the Roman Catholic faith is professed.[13]

As he was in so many other matters as well, Washington was way ahead of his time.

Still, it's not hard to understand why Catholicism would have vexed even the new Republic's vaunted spirit of liberality, for the Roman Catholic Church was a decidedly unliberal institution. Though papal infallibility didn't become a matter of dogma until 1870, the pope was as authoritarian and un-egalitarian a figure as could be imagined, and he wielded his temporal power through kings. If latter-day anti-Semites had to invent the specter of the Davidic tyrant of a Jewish superstate out of whole cloth, the pope and the institution of the Roman Catholic Church were very much in the world. "The most refined, sublime, extensive, and astonishing constitution of policy that ever was conceived by the mind of man was framed by the Romish clergy for the aggrandizement of their own order," John Adams wrote in 1765, in his "Dissertation on Canon and Feudal Law."

They even persuaded mankind to believe, faithfully and undoubtingly, that God Almighty had entrusted them with the keys of heaven, whose gates they might open and close at pleasure; with a power of dispensation over all the rules and obligations of morality; with authority to license all sorts of sins and crimes; with a power of deposing princes and absolving subjects from allegiance; with a power of procuring or withholding the rain of heaven and the beams of the sun; with the management of earthquakes, pestilence, and famine; nay, with the mysterious, awful, incomprehensible power of creating out of bread and wine the flesh and blood of God himself. All these opinions they were enabled to spread and rivet among the people by reducing their minds to a state of sordid ignorance and staring timidity, and by infusing into them a religious horror of letters and knowledge. Thus was human nature chained fast for ages in a cruel, shameful, and deplorable servitude to him, and his subordinate tyrants, who, it was foretold, would exalt himself above all that was called God, and that was worshipped.

America's Protestant settlers, Adams said, "saw clearly, that popular powers must be placed as a guard, a control, a balance, to the powers of the monarch and the priest, in every government, or else it would soon become the man of sin, the whore of Babylon, the mystery of iniquity, a great and detestable system of fraud, violence, and usurpation."

"A native of America who cannot read and write is as rare an appearance as a Jacobite or a Roman Catholic," Adams added. "That is, as rare as a comet or an earthquake."[14] Twenty-five years later, when Washington wrote his letter, Catholics were more common than comets, but there were still only about 35,000 of them in all of the thirteen states, a little less than 1 percent of the population. Many of them were nonpracticing, and most of them were English. Though their numbers grew continuously—the Louisiana Purchase added some 40,000 at a stroke—it wasn't until the 1830s that the flow of Catholic immigrants swelled into a flood tide. By 1840 the Catholic Church claimed 660,000 members in the United States; by 1900 the number had risen to 7 million, and Catholicism had become the nation's largest single religious denomination (there are more than 60 million Catholics in the United States today).

Even before Catholics began arriving in America en masse, the Second Great Awakening—the wave of enthusiastic Protestantism that swept the country in the first three decades of the nineteenth century—was giving timeworn anti-Papist themes new currency (Catholics were called "Papists" and their religious practice "popery" because they were said to worship the pope rather than Christ).

Thousands of the freshly saved were not only attending revival meetings but reading tracts and journals like the *Anti-Romanist*, *Priestcraft Unmasked*, *Priestcraft Exposed*, and, starting in 1834, the New York Protestant Association's biweekly *Protestant Vindicator* (later called *The American Protestant Vindicator*), which promised to "unfold" Catholicism's "detestable impieties, corruptions, and mischiefs." "Popery ought always to be loathed and execrated," the *Protestant Vindicator*'s mission statement read, "not only by all Christians, but also by every patriot and philanthropist."[15] An early issue reported "that Jesuits are prowling about all parts of the United States in every possible disguise, expressly to ascertain the advantageous situations and modes to disseminate Popery."

A minister of the Gospel from Ohio has informed us that he discovered one carrying on his devices in his congregation; and he says that the western country swarms with them under the names of puppet show men, dancing masters, music teachers, peddlers of images and ornaments, barrel organ players, and similar practitioners.[16]

Richard Hofstadter quoted that passage in "The Paranoid Style in American Politics" for obvious reasons. It's interesting to compare both its spirit and its syntax with the tocsin that Attorney General J. Howard McGrath sounded about the Communist threat in 1950: "They are everywhere—in factories, offices, butcher stores, on street corners, in private business. And each carries in himself the death of our society."[17] It also evokes the "sleeper cell" hysteria that swept the United States in the immediate aftermath of 9/11, which continues unabated today in some quarters. A sensationalistic mid-nineteenth-century best seller, *The Female Jesuit; or, The Spy in the Family*, described how Jesuits enlisted Irish domestics to spy on their Protestant employers:

> Little did these families know that, while they and their children were quietly reposing in the arms of sleep, this apparently innocent waiting maid or chambermaid was, perhaps in the dead hour of night, reducing to paper their conversation of the day previous, and preparing it, at least as much of it as could answer any Jesuitical purpose, to be recorded among the secret archives of the Jesuit college of Stonyhurst, from which they were to be transcopied to those of the parent college in Rome.[18]

If so-called popery symbolized the darkness and cruelty of the old feudal Europe that America's ancestors had fled (and that was still pressing on the new country from its southern and northern margins), it was no longer an abstract hobgoblin by the late 1820s. Real-life Catholic immigrants from Ireland and Germany were more and more in evidence, especially in eastern cities. They were clannish: they clung together in their own communities. They were hungry: they competed for jobs. As America's cities industrialized and rural pioneers set out to tame the frontier (and, more and more overtly, to exterminate the country's indigenous peoples), the national economy went through a series of violent booms and busts. If America was a place where anyone could succeed, it was also a place where many failed.

As patriotic as they might have been, Americans had never been a particularly homogeneous lot, no matter how many generations had passed since their ancestors arrived. As the pace of expansion and change accelerated, the divisions between city and country, slave states and free, artisans and manufacturers, landholders and renters, educated and uneducated, were increasingly hard to ignore. If nothing else, a growing immigrant Catholic population provided natives with a foil to set off their own elusive identities—and an objective correlative that they could fasten their anxieties upon.

Even some of the most enlightened and progressive-minded among the white, native-born citizenry took their innate superiority to enslaved blacks and the growing hordes of non-English immigrants for granted, as witnessed by this much-cited fragment in Ralph Waldo Emerson's notebooks, circa the early 1830s. He begins generously, with a heading about the "duty to our fellow man the Slave." "We are to assert his right in all companies," he begins. But the paragraph that follows is much less high-minded:

> I think it cannot be maintained by any candid person that the African race have ever occupied or do promise ever to occupy any very high place in the human family. Their present condition is the strongest proof that they cannot. The Irish cannot; the American Indian cannot; the Chinese cannot. Before the energy of the Caucasian race all the other races have quailed and done obeisance.[19]

The twenty-two-year-old Walt Whitman assumed the editorship of *The New York Aurora* in 1842, just as the controversy over public funding for Catholic schools was coming to a boil. Whitman flung himself into the battle, deploring the "gang of false and villainous priests whose despicable souls never generate any aspiration beyond their own narrow and horrible and beastly superstition . . . dregs of foreign filth—refuse of convents." "Had it been the reverend hypocrite's head, instead of his windows," he wrote, when St. Patrick's Cathedral was attacked by a Protestant mob and the windows of the bishop's residence were shattered, "we could hardly find it in our soul to be sorrowful."

"There are a thousand dangerous influences operating among us," he editorialized.

> Influences whose tendency is to assimilate this land in thought, in social customs, and, to a degree, in government, with the moth eaten systems of the old world. *Aurora* is imbued with a deadly hatred to all these influences; she wages open, heavy, and incessant war against them.[20]

Whitman's contempt for Catholicism was more political and cultural than racial and religious—there was something of Peter Viereck's "anti-Semitism of the liberals" in it—but still, his choice of words is jarring, coming as they did from the poet who would later so eloquently celebrate the "Nation of many nations" in his verse.

As mentioned earlier in these pages, the nativist Know-Nothing movement began with secret societies—the American Brotherhood, the Order of United Americans, and later the Order of the Star Spangled Banner in New York City; and the Order of United American Mechanics and the United Sons of America in Philadelphia—complete with secret handshakes, whispered shibboleths, and elaborate hierarchies. Like the anti-Masons before them, they would coalesce into a mainstream, national political movement, with a complicated, often contradictory agenda. The name Know-Nothing was coined by Horace Greeley as a pejorative, because its members were supposedly told to answer "I know nothing" when asked about their organizations. By the 1850s, they'd adopted it as an honorific.

"As a result of developments abroad, especially the Irish potato famine, immigrants were arriving in America at a rate never known before or since," wrote the literary historian David Reynolds.

> Between 1845 and 1855, 3 million foreigners swarmed to America's shores, peaking in 1854, when 427,833 arrived. . . . The large majority were Roman Catholic. The Know-Nothings responded to a deep-seated fear that Catholic foreigners would infiltrate American institutions and possibly even take over the government. Since many foreigners, particularly the Irish, supported slavery, the

Know-Nothings appealed to antislavery activists. They also incorporated defenders of the working class.

Above all, they were the party of intense, unabashed Americanism. "America for Americans" was their motto, the Star Spangled Banner was their emblem, and in 1855 the "American Party" became their public name. Their success in the northern elections of 1854 and 1855 was stunning. They elected 8 governors, over 100 congressmen, mayors in three major cities, and thousands of other local officials. They peaked in popularity in June 1855, the month before *Leaves of Grass* appeared, numbering about 1.5 million members.[21]

Whitman himself never admitted to joining the Know-Nothings ("What Know-Nothing would?" as Reynolds pointedly remarks), but if his politics put him in their camp, his poetry implicitly rebuked them. The popular newspaper columnist Fanny Fern reviewed *Leaves of Grass* in *The New-York Ledger* on May 10, 1856. "Walt Whitman," she apostrophized him in his own style, "the effeminate world needed thee."

> Walt Whitman, the world needed a "Native American" of thorough, out and out breed—enamored of *women* not *ladies, men* not *gentlemen;* something beside a mere Catholic-hating Know-Nothing; it needed a man who dared speak out his strong, honest thoughts, in the face of pusillanimous, toadeying, republican aristocracy; dictionary-men, hypocrites, cliques and creeds; it needed a large-hearted, untainted, self-reliant, fearless son of the Stars and Stripes, who disdains to sell his birthright for a mess of pottage.[22]

As mentioned earlier, Samuel F. B. Morse, the son of the Reverend Jedidiah Morse, feared that the Catholic powers of Russia and the Hapsburg Empire were infiltrating an army of conquest into the United States in the guise of impoverished immigrants, most of whom, he wrote in the *New-York Observer* in 1834, are "too ignorant to act at all for themselves, and expect to be guided wholly by others. These others are of course their priests."

The conspirators against our liberties, who have been admitted from abroad through the liberality of our institutions, are now *organized* in every part of the country; they are all subordinates, standing in regular steps of slave and master, from the most abject dolt that obeys the commands of his priest, up to the great master-slave Metternich. . . . They report from one to another, like the sub-officers of an army, up to the commander-in-chief at Vienna (not the Pope, for he is but a subordinate of Austria). There is a similar organization among the Catholics of other countries, and the whole Catholic church is thus prepared to throw its weight of power and wealth into the hands of Austria.[23]

As busy as he was devising his telegraph, Morse would find the time to mount an unsuccessful run for the New York City mayoralty on the ticket of the New York Native American Democratic Association in 1836.

Lyman Beecher (Harriet Beecher Stowe's father) also worried that the "rapid influx of foreign emigrants, the greater part unacquainted with our institutions, unaccustomed to self-government, inaccessible to education, and easily accessible to prepossession, and inveterate credulity, and intrigue," formed a clear and present danger to the Republic. What if, he asked, in his book *A Plea for the West*, "this emigration, self-moved and slow in the beginning, is now rolling its broad tide at the bidding of the powers of Europe hostile to free institutions, and associated in holy alliance to arrest and put them down?"

If the potentates of Europe have no design upon our liberties, what means the paying of the passage and emptying out upon our shores such floods of pauper emigrants—the contents of the poorhouse and the sweepings of the streets?—multiplying tumults and violence, filling our prisons, and crowding our poorhouses, and quadrupling our taxation, and sending annually accumulating thousands to the polls to lay their inexperienced hand upon the helm of our power?

If Beecher loathed Catholicism in the abstract, he didn't propose to persecute American Catholics or forbid them to practice their religion. As he saw it, the solution to the problem—and the salvation of the Republic—lay in education and aggressive acts of outreach. "It is not the striking of the fist which will disarm them, but words and acts of kindness and the warm beating of our heart; while contemptuous treatment will augment hatred of Protestants, and rivet their prejudice, and deliver them over double bound to the power of their priesthood, already too great for their happiness and our safety."[24]

Words and acts of kindness or not, on August 10, 1834, Beecher delivered three of his signature anti-Catholic sermons in Boston; the next day, a mob of Protestants attacked the Ursuline Convent in Charlestown and burned it to the ground. Though many accounts link the two events, it wasn't quite as uncomplicated as that. Tensions had been building for some time. The convent had been the dream of the Reverend John Thayer, the scion of an old Yankee family, who became a Congregationalist minister upon his graduation from Yale. Thayer was in Rome on April 16, 1783, when Saint Benedict Joseph Labre, a mendicant holy man, died. Over the next three months, 136 miraculous cures were credited to his relics. Thayer set out to investigate the phenomenon with an eye to debunking it and converted instead. "I clearly saw that the Catholic Church is established on innumerable and unanswerable proofs," he wrote in his *Account of the Conversion of the Reverend John Thayer, Formerly a Protestant Minister of Boston,* "and that her replies to the reproaches of Protestants are solid and satisfactory."[25] He was ordained in France in 1787 and upon his return to America raised the money to build the convent, the third in the United States. In 1834, it was home to an exclusive academy for girls; only a handful of its forty-seven students were Catholic; most were the daughters of Boston's Unitarian elite. The convent was thus a focus of both anti-Catholic prejudice and class resentment, an inflammatory combination.

In 1831, a charity student named Rebecca Theresa Reed had "escaped" the convent through an unlocked gate and written an exposé of life behind its walls. Though her book, *Six Months in a Convent,* wouldn't be published until 1835, the year after the riot, her story had been circulating locally in the months before the disturbance. More recently—on July 28, 1834, just two weeks before the riot—a nun named Elizabeth Harrison (Sister Mary John) left the convent suffering from "delirium" and sought refuge at the home of a local brickyard boss. After she returned to the convent the next day, rumors flew, fanned by the *Mercantile Journal*, that she was being held there against her will—or that the nuns had murdered her. Signs were hung throughout Boston, reading, "To the Selectmen of Charlestown!! Gentlemen: It is currently reported that a mysterious affair has lately happened at the Nunnery in Charlestown, now it is your duty gentlemen to have this affair investigated immediately[;] if not the Truckmen of Boston will demolish the Nunnery thursday night—August 14."[26]

When the selectmen of Charlestown visited the convent and interviewed Sister Mary John, the mother superior, Sister Saint George, née Mary Anne Moffatt, was rude and combative ("the sauciest woman I ever heard talk,"[27] one of the rioters would later say of her). The night of August 11, when a band of Protestant "brickmakers, sailors, firemen, apprentices, and hooligans, Charlestown's poorest and least educated," gathered outside the gates of the convent and demanded to see Sister Mary John for themselves, the mother superior angrily ordered them to disperse.[28] Two days before, she had threatened a neighbor, who'd warned her of the impending trouble, that "the Right Reverend Bishop's influence over ten thousand brave Irishmen might lead to the destruction of his property and that of others also."[29] At eleven o'clock that night, the crowd tore down the fence and lit bonfires. In her book *Fire and Roses: The Burning of the Charlestown Convent*, Nancy Lusignan Schultz vividly described the mayhem:

> Engine companies from Charlestown and Boston raced to the scene. But many of the firemen had friends in the crowd and escaped nun Rebecca Reed's brother-in-law, Prescott Pond, was a member of Boston Engine No. 13. Instead of fighting the fire, the men from No. 13 provided cover for the rioters as they raced up the hill toward the convent. Stones and bricks shattered the rows of windows in the three-story building and its adjoining wings. A farmhand grabbed a stake to batter in the front door, and the rioters burst into the building. . . . Some of them broke up furniture and heaped it in the center of the large assembly room. Others gleefully hurled musical instruments out the windows, violins, harps, and even pianos.

Amid cheers and jeers, the Bible, the ornaments of the altar, and the cross were tossed on the pyre and with their torches, the rioters ignited a fire.[30]

Then they battered their way into the convent's mausoleum, looking for the bodies of murdered Protestant girls. They pulled the corpses of nuns out of their coffins and threw them on the floor; one of them smashed a skull with a cudgel, and the men collected the teeth for souvenirs. Before the night was over, they'd burned down the barn, the stables, and a farmhouse. The next day they returned and destroyed the gardens.

None of the nuns or students was harmed; thirteen of the rioters were arrested and tried, and only one was convicted (he later received a pardon from the governor). If Boston's Catholics were convinced that the system was tilted against them, the Protestant appetite for stories about captive nuns had barely been whetted. Charles Frothingham's *Convent's Doom: A Tale of Charlestown in 1834*, which justified the attack, became a national best seller; Rebecca Reed's *Six Months in a Convent* sold ten thousand copies in Boston alone in its first week on the market. Sister Saint George's rebuttal, *An Answer to "Six Months in a Convent," Exposing Its Falsehoods and Manifold Absurdities*, was swiftly answered by Reed and her publisher with *Supplement to "Six Months in a Convent," Confirming the Narrative of Rebecca Theresa Reed, by the Testimony of More Than One Hundred Witnesses*.

The year 1836 saw the publication of Maria Monk's *Awful Disclosures of the Hotel Dieu Nunnery*, the horrific confessions of a refugee from Montreal's "Black Nunnery." When she was a novice, Maria Monk related, she was taught to despise the Protestant Bible and venerate sacred relics. After she took her vows, the mother superior had a frank talk with her:

I was now, she told me, to have access to every part of the edifice, even to the cellar, where two of the sisters were imprisoned for causes which she did not mention. I must be informed, that one of my great duties was, to obey the priests in all things; and this I soon learnt, to my utter astonishment and horror, was to live in the practice of criminal intercourse with them. I expressed some of the feelings which this announcement excited in me, which came upon me like a flash of lightning, but the only effect was to set her arguing with me, in favor of the crime, representing it as a virtue acceptable to God, and honorable to me.

And that wasn't the worst of it:

She gave me another piece of information which excited other feelings in me, scarcely less dreadful. Infants were sometimes born in the convent; but they were always baptized and immediately strangled! This secured their everlasting happiness; for the baptism purified them from all sinfulness, and being sent out of the world before they had time to do anything wrong, they were at once admitted into heaven. How happy, she exclaimed, are those who secure immortal happiness to such little beings! Their little souls would thank those who kill their bodies, if they had it in their power![31]

Maria learned to find her way around the cellars of the convent where the dungeons were; she found the open pit where the murdered infants' bodies were covered with quicklime and the trapdoor where the priests emerged from the tunnel that led to the seminary next door. She was there when the pious nun Saint Francis was murdered (she was placed between two mattresses and trampled by a band of priests and nuns, "some . . . with their feet; some with their knees; and others, in different ways, seemed to seek how they might best beat the breath out of her body, and mangle it, without coming in direct contact with it"[32]); she got into mischief with the mad sister Jane Ray (a comic relief character who might have been lifted out of the pages of Ann Radcliffe's *Mysteries of Udolpho*), and much, much more. After she escaped, Monk gave birth to a baby and fled to the United States; eventually, she returned to Montreal, exposing herself to the risk of being abducted and returned to the convent or worse, where she appealed to the governor and the attorney general to investigate. Threatened on all sides, and with all her efforts unavailing, she left Canada for good, determined to make her accusations in print. William K. Hoyte, the head of the Canadian Benevolent Society, accompanied her to New York City, where the two hooked up with the team of writers—the Reverends J. J. Slocum and George Bourne, and Theodore Dwight Jr., anti-Catholic nativists all—who helped her tell her story. Dwight's father has already appeared in these pages as a vocal anti-Illuminist.

The book was a sensation; it sold some 300,000 copies before the Civil War, more than any other book in America except *Uncle Tom's Cabin*. Its market was anti-Catholics, but it appealed to the nation's taste for gothic novels (upon which it was clearly modeled) and also for sadomasochism. As Richard Hofstadter would write in *The Paranoid Style in American Politics*, "Anti-Catholicism has always been the pornography of the Puritans."

> Whereas the anti-Masons had imagined wild drinking bouts and had entertained themselves with fantasies about the actual enforcement of grisly Masonic oaths, the anti-Catholics developed an immense lore about libertine priests, the confessional as an opportunity for seduction, licentious convents and monasteries and the like.[33]

"Eels were repeatedly given to some of us," Maria Monk told her readers, "because we felt an unconquerable repugnance to them, on account of reports we heard of their feeding on dead carcasses in the river St. Lawrence."

> It was no uncommon thing for us to be required to drink the water in which the Superior had washed her feet.* Sometimes we were required to brand ourselves with a hot iron, so as to leave scars; at other times to whip our naked flesh with several small rods, before a private altar, until we drew blood.† I can assert with the perfect knowledge of the fact, that many of the nuns bear the scars of these wounds.[34]

A nativist newspaper called *The Downfall of Babylon* published a tract called *Decisive Confirmation of the Awful Disclosures*, and

---

* Members of the Aum Shinrikyo cult paid a premium to drink their leader Shoko Asahara's bathwater; he also sold them hair clippings that they were told to steep and make into tea.
† Self-mortification, of course, is not unheard of in Catholicism; Maria Monk's "small rods" bear a certain resemblance to the cilice, a spiked chain that some members of Opus Dei are said to fasten around their thighs for part of each day.

then found a Maria Monk of its own, Saint Patrick, née Frances Partridge, who detailed her story in *The Escape of Sainte Frances Patrick, Another Nun from the Hotel Dieu Nunnery of Montreal*. Both books provided detailed descriptions and diagrams of the secret architecture of the convent's cellars and tunnels. Maria's plea that somebody investigate for him- or herself finally bore fruit when a Protestant journalist named William Leete Stone visited the Black Nunnery. Upon his arrival in Montreal, he discovered that it was a "city of skeptics" who "seemed to look upon the intelligent denizens of the United States as laboring under a widely extended monomania."

> There was but one voice upon the subject—protestants and catholics—those of every and all denominations, born and bred upon the spot—men of intelligence and unquestioned piety—those who had passed the open gates of the Hotel Dieu, or looked from their casements over its frowning walls every day of their lives— were all stubborn unbelievers;—and I may add in this place, instead of elsewhere, that I was able to hear of two believers in the "Awful Disclosures" in Montreal, one of whom . . . was evidently afraid to visit the nunnery, lest he should be forced by actual demonstration to change his opinion.[35]

Stone met with the mother superior and found her to be "a lady of dignity and refinement of manner"; the sisters, he reported, had "all the ease, simplicity, dignity, and grace which distinguish the high bred and truly genteel."

> They were all affability and kindness. Cheerfulness was universal, and very unlike the notions commonly entertained of the gloom of the cloister. Their faces were too often wreathed in smiles to allow us to suppose they were soon to assist in smothering their own children, or that those sweet spirits were soon to be trodden out of their bodies by the rough-shod priests of the seminary.[36]

As for the interior of the convent, "neither I nor my companions could discover, from the drawings, the least evidence that the author had ever been within the walls of the cloister."[37] "MARIA MONK IS AN ARRANT IMPOSTOR, AND HER BOOK IN ALL ITS ESSEN-

TIAL FEATURES A TISSUE OF CALUMNIES," he concluded. "However guilty the Catholics may be in other respects, or in other countries," he added, "as a man of honor and professor of the Protestant faith, I MOST SOLEMNLY BELIEVE THAT THE PRIESTS AND NUNS ARE INNOCENT IN THIS MATTER."[38]

Upon his return to New York, Stone interviewed Maria Monk and Frances Partridge, who were accompanied by the Reverend William Craig Brownlee of the *Vindicator* and the Reverends Bourne and Slocum. Neither woman acquitted herself well under his cross-examination, and Brownlee resorted to threats. "Your story is all a humbug," he said, "and if you go to publishing any thing, recollect that we have got a press too!"[39]

Upon further examination, it came out that Maria Monk had learned what she knew of Catholicism when she was a resident of Montreal's Magdalen Asylum for prostitutes, from which she had been expelled when she became pregnant. Within a few years she and her co-writers had fallen out and were squabbling over the spoils of her book in the courts—only a fraction of which ever found their way to her. In 1837, Maria Monk claimed to have been captured by a group of priests who seemingly intended to return her to Canada by a mysterious southern route; somehow she ended up in Philadelphia. William Willcocks Sleigh, a doctor with whom she sought refuge, published a tell-all soon afterward, *An Exposure of Maria Monk's Pretended Abduction and Conveyance to the Catholic Asylum, Philadelphia, by Six Priests on the Night of August 15, 1837, with Numerous Extraordinary Incidents During Her Residence of Six Days in This City.* Unbowed, Maria Monk issued a sequel, *Further Disclosures by Maria Monk.* By then, her estranged mother (a shadowy figure in *The Awful Disclosures*) had come out of the woodwork and was telling reporters that her daughter had been brain damaged as a toddler when a pencil was shoved into her ear; she'd been an incorrigible liar ever since. In 1838, Maria Monk got pregnant again and abruptly fell off the map. This second child, Lizzie St. John Eckel Harper, converted to Catholicism and would have many adventures of her own, which she detailed in *Maria Monk's Daughter* in 1874—a book that never became the runaway best seller that her mother's did. The last time the newspapers took notice of Maria Monk was when she was arrested for pickpocketing a john in a bordello in 1849, when she was thirty-three years old. She died in jail on Blackwell's Island a few months later.

The affinity of paranoia and pornography is not unique to Protestantism; it goes back in the Catholic Church to the Inquisition (whose dungeons and torture chambers provide so many of the lurid tropes of gothic anti-Catholic fiction) and the descriptions of infanticide, cannibalism, bestiality, and orgies that it attributed to its enemies in its witch-hunting manual, the *Malleus maleficarum*. Before that, in the early fourteenth century, the Templars had been accused of trampling, spitting on, and urinating on the cross, of welcoming initiates into their order with obscene kisses on the mouth, navel, and buttocks, and of other homosexual practices. The church father Epiphanius's horrifying description of the Phibionite Gnostics' sexual practices in his *Panarion* dates back further still, to the late fourth century. It's worth quoting at great length, since it contains so many monstrous (and licentious) allegations—and perhaps the world's earliest depiction of what a propagandist today might call a partial-birth abortion:

> I will now come to the place of depth of their deadly story. . . . First they have their women in common. And if a stranger appears who is of the same persuasion, they have a sign, men for women and women for men. When they extend the hand for greeting at the bottom of the palm they make a tickling touch and from this they ascertain whether the person who appeared is of their faith. After they have recognized each other, they go over at once to eating. They serve rich food, meat and wine even if they are poor. When they thus ate together and so to speak filled up their veins to an excess they turn to passion. The man leaving his wife says to his own wife: Stand up and make love with the brother. . . . Then the unfortunates unite with each other, and as I am truly ashamed to say the shameful things that are being done by them. . . . Nevertheless, I will not be ashamed to say those things which they are not ashamed to do, in order that I may cause in every way a horror in those who hear about their shameful practices. After they have had intercourse in the passion of fornication they raise their own blasphemy toward heaven. The woman and the man take the fluid of the emission of the man into their hands, they stand, turn toward

heaven, their hands besmeared with the uncleanness, and pray. . . .
They say: "We offer to thee this gift, the body of Christ." And then
they eat it, their own ugliness, and say: "This is the body of Christ
and this is the Passover for the sake of which our bodies suffer
and are forced to confess the suffering of Christ." . . . They have
intercourse with each other but they teach that one may not beget
children. . . . And if . . . the woman becomes pregnant, then . . .
they pull out the embryo in the time when they can reach it with
the hand. They take out this unborn child and in a mortar pound it
with a pestle and into this mix honey and pepper and certain other
spices and myrrh, in order that it may not nauseate them, and then
they come together, all this company of swine and dogs, and each
communicates with a finger from the bruised child. And after they
have finished this cannibalism finally they pray to God, saying,
"We did not let the Archon of lust play with us but collected the
mistake of the brother." And this they consider to be the perfect
Passah. Many other horrible things are done by them.[40]

What strikes me about all this—and this is a completely off-the-
cuff observation, there are no studies that I am aware of to back this
up, no authorities I can cite in a footnote—is that while almost everyone worries that their enemies are having better sex than they are,
programmatic haters are downright certain of it. While most men
are mildly anxious about how they measure up sexually, haters are
obsessed with what they fancy to be their enemies' superior prow-
ess and potency; worse yet, they are morbidly certain that given half
a chance, their wives and daughters (or their sons, for that matter)
would happily surrender themselves to them. Call it "the Pornography of Resentment." Though they put their women on pedestals,
there is more than a whiff of misogyny in their chivalry.

"The black-haired Jewish youth lies in wait for hours on end,
satanically glaring at and spying on the unsuspicious girl whom he
plans to seduce, adulterating her blood and removing her from the
bosom of her own people," Hitler wrote in *Mein Kampf.*

The Jew uses every possible means to undermine the racial foundations of a subjugated people. In his systematic efforts to ruin girls
and women he strives to break down the last barriers of discrimi-

nation between him and other peoples. The Jews were responsible
for bringing Negros into the Rhineland, with the ultimate idea of
bastardizing the white race which they hate and thus lowering its
cultural and political level so that the Jew might dominate.[41]

American slaveholders, who raped their female chattel with neither compunctions nor consequences ("To debauch a Negro girl
hardly injures an American's reputation," as Tocqueville famously
observed in *Democracy in America*, "to marry her dishonors him"[42]),
suffered nightmares about their male slaves' designs on their wives;
anti-Papists presumed that priests, sworn to celibacy as they were,
cut a Dionysian swath through their dioceses (I am speaking here of
Maria Monk–type depravity, not today's pedophile scandals, which,
however much they may be distorted or exaggerated by people with
an anti-Catholic bias, are all too real).

Some of the antihomosexual literature circulating today has a
wistfully lascivious undertone to it as well. Many of the antigay
tracts produced by groups like Focus on the Family accuse homosexuals of "recruiting" confused teenagers, whose attraction to their
same-sex peers, given time and perhaps a judicious dose of reparative
aversion therapy, would have proven to be no more than a passing
phase. "Who, in going from childhood to puberty and all the strange
new feelings that come with it has never asked 'what is wrong with
me? I can't believe that I should feel this way,'" Griff Ruby asked
readers of the *Daily Catholic*.

> A big part of these new feelings is the "crush" which, at that age
> often follows no rational pattern. Crushes can be felt for father
> figures, mother figures, attractive celebrities, cartoon characters,
> heroes, heroines, and in short anything and anyone. When you have
> a crush on someone you want to be with them, you want to be like
> them, you want to be close to them, you want—well, you don't
> know or can't explain just exactly what it is that you want—but
> you want them. For however long it lasts (which could be minutes
> or weeks) whoever you have a crush on becomes something of a
> god to you.
>
> So, enters here the most crucial factor in the spread of homosex-
> uality that there is, namely the "recruiter." "Gays" are not born,

but made. And they are made so by these recruiters who themselves are already totally enslaved to their perversion.[43]

"We shall sodomize your sons, emblems of your feeble masculin-
ity," begins a flamboyantly satirical "Gay Manifesto" that was published in Boston's *Gay Community News* in 1987.

> We shall seduce them in your schools, in your dormitories, in your
> gymnasiums, in your locker rooms, in your sports arenas, in your
> seminaries, in your youth groups, in your movie theater bath-
> rooms, in your army bunkhouses, in your truck stops, in your all-
> male clubs, in your house of Congress, wherever men are with men
> together. Your sons shall become our minions to do our bidding.[44]

Its author, Michael Swift, called it "an eruption of inner rage, on
how the oppressed desperately dream of being the oppressor." Nevertheless, it is presented on countless Web sites and in books and pamphlets as irrefutable proof of the "gay agenda," much as Taxil's hoax
about Palladism was embraced by anti-Masonic conspiracy theorists
and Maurice Joly's satire on Napoleon III was folded intact into *The
Protocols of the Elders of Zion*.

A couple of years ago, I came across a bizarro-world specimen of
this masochistic overestimation of one's enemy's sexual powers in
the writings of the thirteenth-century Jewish sage Isaac ben Yedaiah.
A woman, he wrote, "will court a man who is uncircumcised in
the flesh and lie against his breast with great passion, for he thrusts
inside her for a long time because of the foreskin, which is a barrier
against ejaculation."

> When an uncircumcised man sleeps with her and then resolves to
> return to his home, she brazenly grasps him, holding on to his geni-
> tals, and says to him, "Come back, make love to me." This is because
> of the pleasure that she finds in intercourse with him, from the sin-
> ews of his testicles—sinew of iron—and from his ejaculation—that
> of a horse—which he shoots like an arrow into her womb. They are
> united without separating and he makes love twice and three times
> in one night. . . . But when a circumcised man desires the beauty of

a woman . . . he will find himself performing his task quickly . . . he arouses her passion to no avail and she remains in a state of desire for her husband, ashamed and confounded. . . . She does not have an orgasm once a year, except on rare occasions, because of the great heat and the fire burning within her.[45]

Ben Yedaiah went on to propose that it was this very penchant for premature ejaculation that accounted for Jewish supremacy in intellectual and spiritual matters (their lackluster sex lives left them with more bandwidth for study and prayer) but that sounds like sour grapes to me.

If bondage pornography is the preferred genre for the expression of racial, gender, and religious resentment, 1950s science fiction movies embodied many of America's deepest fears about the insidious nature of the Communist threat. A spurious "textbook" that the Soviet Union purportedly provided to aspiring sleeper agents in the 1930s, *The Communist Manual of Instructions of Psychopolitical Warfare,* explained how "a good and experienced psychopolitical operator, working under the most favorable circumstances, can, by the use of psychopolitical technologies, alter the loyalties of an individual so deftly that his own companions will not suspect that they have changed."[46] The book was widely circulated in the mid-1950s and can easily be downloaded on the Internet today. Almost certainly concocted by the young L. Ron Hubbard, it resonated perfectly with the nation's paranoid mood.

The young boy in *Invaders from Mars,* who realizes that aliens have seized control of his parents' minds, and Kevin McCarthy's desperate efforts to warn the public about the soulless pods who were replacing his neighbors in *Invasion of the Body Snatchers* both reflected and exacerbated those anxieties. From Jeff Sharlet's *Family*—a fascinating book about the shadowy Dominionists behind the National Prayer Breakfast movement, an elite network of American businessmen and politicians who, if they were liberals and/or Jews, would almost certainly have been singled out as a cult or a conspiracy a long time ago—I learned an interesting piece of trivia about the cult classic movie *The Blob:* it was conceived by a Christian filmmaker, Irvin "Shorty" Yeaworth, at the 1957 National Prayer Breakfast, specifically as a metaphor for creeping Communism.[47] But I have strayed very far indeed from my subject.

Political nativism peaked and then quickly declined in the 1850s, when it became clear that the issue of slavery was a clearer and more present danger than Catholicism. Once the Civil War began, all those unemployed, dirty, diseased, superstitious immigrants, Romanists or not, proved themselves to be indispensable as cannon fodder. Which is not to say that anti-Catholic prejudice—or nativist organizations—disappeared altogether, only that they were edged out of the mainstream for a time.

The long depression of the 1870s wreaked economic devastation in the West, sparking outbreaks of anti-Asian violence. The Chinese Exclusion Act banned both "skilled and unskilled laborers" from emigrating from China; at the same time, it refused resident Chinese aliens the right to be naturalized. The act was renewed and extended in 1892, 1893, and 1902; similar measures were passed targeting the Japanese.

Still the flow of immigrants continued. Between 1880 and 1920, some twenty-three million of them arrived on America's shores, many of them from eastern Europe and southern Italy. Not uncoincidentally, racialist eugenics came into vogue around the same time. Arthur de Gobineau's *Moral and Intellectual Diversity of Races, with Particular Reference to Their Respective Influence in the Civil and Political History of Mankind* had been published in the United States in 1856; it argued that "nations degenerate only in consequence and in proportion to their admixture with an inferior race."[48] William Z. Ripley, the author of the magisterial *The Races of Europe* (1899), warned that immigration was " 'tapping the political sinks of Europe,' bringing a 'great horde of Slavs, Huns and Jews, and drawing large numbers of Greeks, Armenians and Syrians. No people is too mean or lowly to seek an asylum on our shores.' " If these immigrants provided businesses with inexpensive labor, some of them imported revolutionary ideas with them—or adopted them upon their arrival. The Anarchist Exclusion Act of 1903 was passed after President William McKinley was assassinated by a second-generation Polish American.

When all was said and done, there was plenty of hatred left over for American-born blacks, too. After Reconstruction ended in 1877, so-called Jim Crow laws had been enacted throughout the former Confederacy, which formally segregated its schools, businesses, hospitals, public transportation, and cemeteries and banned marriages between whites and people of color. Voting rights were severely restricted; federal laws installed a color bar in the military. Their job accomplished, vigilante hate groups like the Ku Klux Klan, the White Brotherhood, the White League, the Pale Faces, the Constitutional Union Guards, the Black Calvary, the White Rose, the '76 Association, the Men of Justice, and the Knights of the White Camelia faded away (though the KKK would roar back in the next century).

Segregation wasn't just essential for the maintenance of the South's antebellum values; its factory owners saw it as a way to protect its industrial future, by driving a wedge between poor white and black mill workers, who might otherwise have made common cause together. A formal color bar required both an objective and an enduring definition of "blackness": the old slave-era classifications of mulattoes, quadroons, and octoroons were too generous and by legally acknowledging the notion of mixture, they implicitly sanctioned it. In contrast, the legal and anthropological concept of "hypo-descent" automatically assigned a child of a mixed union to the less privileged group. Thus "one drop" rules (that is, one drop of "Negro blood"), as difficult as they were to enforce, became the norm. "The stigma carried by blackness is unique, and is affixed and perpetuated resolutely by the American practice of treating blackness as a monolithic identity that an individual either has or does not have on the basis of the principle that any African ancestry at all determines that one is simply black," David Hollinger wrote in *The American Historical Review*.

The invidiousness of this "one-drop rule" was eloquently encapsulated by Barbara Fields more than twenty years ago: we have a convention "that considers a white woman capable of giving birth to a black child but denies that a black woman can give birth to a white child." One has not been able to say, "I'm one-eighth African American" without giving up socially, if not legally, the seven-eighths part of one's self that is not. You can be one-eighth Cherokee and still be seven-eighths something else, but if you are one-eighth black you are not likely to be counted as white at all.[49]

Barack Obama, the child not only of a mixed-race marriage but of mixed nationalities, has inherited two stigmas; the "birther" controversy not only provides his racist adversaries with politically correct cover but also evokes a panoply of nativist anxieties. When Dinesh D'Souza (a dark-skinned immigrant himself, of course, but fully assimilated, or so he insists) appeared on Glenn Beck's radio show to promote *The Roots of Obama's Rage*, he deflected the birther issue as a red herring—"the Birther thing is a diversion. See, Barack Obama was born August 4th, 1961, and he was born in Hawaii. And the reason we know this, the single best piece of evidence is that there were notices of his birth in two local newspapers"—before turning his focus to Obama's essential un-assimilableness and his profoundly anti-American, anti-Western agenda.

> The problem with the race theory and the problem with so many theories about Obama is we all look at Obama and we try to in a sense project American history onto him. . . . What is Obama's dream? Is it the American dream? Is it Martin Luther King's dream? And the beauty is, we don't have to guess. Obama tells us himself in his book . . . *Dreams from My Father*. . . . This is absolutely critical and in fact I think even Obama's own supporters are misunderstanding him. They think he's a conventional liberal. They think he's like Al Gore: He thinks the planet is too hot, he thinks that energy consumption for the world is too high, he wants to decrease it across the board. But then we see no, he doesn't. He wants to decrease energy consumption by us while increasing energy availability and consumption by them. In other words, he wants to decrease the wealth of the colonizers, the rich West, and increase the availability of wealth and energy. That's why he proposes huge global transfers of wealth from the wealthy west to the rest. So this anticolonial key opens the lock. . . . He's a little bit like the guy in the Schwarzenegger movie who comes home and his whole family has been massacred and he becomes a man on a mission. He's got to go back, he's got to settle scores. . . . This is Barack Obama.[50]

In 1889, Henry Baldwin, a second-generation nativist (his father had been a leader of the Order of United Americans), brought the nation's nativist groups together in a consortium, the National League for the Protection of American Institutions. He presided over conferences in New York and Philadelphia that were attended by representatives of a wide range of organizations:

> The Order of United Americans, the United American Mechanics, the Patriotic Order of the Sons of America, the Order of the American Union, the Daughters of Liberty, the Junior Order of United American Mechanics, the American Patriotic League, the American Protestant Association, the Loyal Orange Institute of the United States, the Templars of Liberty of America, the Red, White and Blue Organization ("Red to Protect Protestantism, White to Protect the Purity of the Ballot Box, Blue Against the Domination of Dictation by Foreign Citizens"), the Patriotic Daughters of America, United Sons of America, United Order of Native Americans, the Sons of Revolution, Loyal Women of America, the United Order of Pilgrim Fathers, the National Association of Loyal Men of American Liberty, and others.[51]

Missing from this impressive roster is the American Protective Association, founded in Clinton, Iowa, in 1887 by a failed farmer, lawyer, and Mason named Henry Bowers as a combination nativist pressure group and fraternal society. In 1893, Bowers was pushed aside by William J. H. Traynor, the publisher of Detroit's *Patriotic American*. Under his leadership—and fueled by the ruinous economy of the early 1890s—the movement grew to more than 500,000 members nationwide. The APA advocated for immigration restriction, taxation of the Catholic Church, and the refusal of diplomatic recognition to the Vatican or "representatives from any ecclesiastical body." *The Awful Disclosures* was reprinted under APA auspices, as were Edith O'Gorman's *Convent Life Unveiled* and Julia McNair Wright's *Priest and Nun;* APA newspapers featured short stories like "A Priestly Liar," the tale of a "libidinous rapist priest with lust in his heart." They found a new Maria Monk in Margaret Shepherd, author of *My Life in the Convent*, and sent her out on the lecture circuit. Shepherd had taken refuge in a nunnery after she was ruined by a priest—only to fall victim to still more "licentious and lecherous priests."[52]

A phony encyclical from Pope Leo XIII was circulated, which characterized Protestant America as "with the worst enemies of the church . . . having seized upon the lands discovered by Christopher Columbus a Catholic and usurped the authority and jurisdiction of the supreme head of the church." Not only did the pope excommunicate America's "obscure heretics" and absolve any Catholics who'd taken "any oath of loyalty to the United States" from "all duty, fidelity, or obedience," but he pronounced the ultimate sentence on America's non-Catholics: "On or about the feast of Ignatius Loyola in the year of our Lord, 1893, it will be the duty of the faithful to exterminate all heretics found within the jurisdiction of the United States of America."[53]

If nothing else, this spectacular libel suggests where Eustace Mullins might have gotten his idea for "Plan Naamah," the Judeo-Masonic Final Solution for fair-haired, blue-eyed Americans that he detailed in *The Curse of Canaan: A Demonology of History:* "Plan Naamah, named after the demonic being who first introduced human sacrifice and cannibalism to the world, is a documented plan for the systematic extermination of all the people of Shem in the United States."

The plan is a simple one; newspapers, radio, and television will announce an imminent attack. . . . Everyone will be instructed to assemble in schools and auditoriums in every town and city in the United States. Only the fair-skinned people of Shem will actually obey this command; others, of Canaanite extraction, will be told that they should return to their homes. Once they have been herded into these buildings, the people of Shem are to be killed, but only according to regulated procedures, that is, with hatchets, clubs, and knives. . . . Should any Canaanite be inadvertently present, he or she will be protected by using the secret password, "Tubal Cain," the brother of Naamah, and the password of the Freemasons. Plan Naamah will remain in effect until the people of Shem have been entirely eliminated throughout the United States. The teams of specially trained killers will be provided by the hordes of "immigrants" who have been imported into the United States during recent years specifically for this program.[54]

Where this secret plan is documented, he does not say. And note the scare quotes around the word "immigrants." But yet again, I digress.

The APA peaked quickly, much as the Know-Nothings had before them—and as the revived KKK would a few decades hence. Roman Catholics had become a considerable power within the Democratic Party (enough so that it was dubbed the party of "rum, Romanism, and rebellion" as early as 1884); the sheer numbers of American Catholics—and their growing prosperity—rendered them less "other" than they'd been, particularly in cities.

The mostly rural populist, agrarian, and Silverite movements, as already mentioned, incorporated anti-English, anti-Catholic, and anti-Semitic tropes into their literature; we've already heard from Georgia's Thomas E. Watson, who would espouse fire-breathing anti-Romanist and anti-Semitic ideas in his magazines *Watson's Jeffersonian Magazine* and *Watson's Magazine*. Many Progressives, Woodrow Wilson and Theodore Roosevelt not excepted, espoused views about race and eugenics that, to put it mildly, would fail to pass muster at even the most latitudinarian of sensitivity-training sessions today. In *The Winning of the West*, Roosevelt rued the malign effects of conquest on the white races, "who speedily sink almost to the level of their barbarous foes, in point of hideous brutality," yet pronounced it of "incalculable importance that America, Australia, and Siberia should pass out of the hands of their red, black, and yellow aboriginal owners, and become the heritage of the dominant world races."[55] When M. W. M. Trotter led a delegation from the National Independent Equal Rights League to the White House to protest segregation in the departments of the federal government in 1913, Woodrow Wilson testily explained that while he wished to see colored people progress "along independent lines," in the meantime racial prejudice must be dealt with pragmatically:

> Segregation is not humiliating but a benefit, and ought to be so regarded by you gentlemen. If your organization goes out and tells the colored people of the country that it is a humiliation, they will so regard it, but if you do not tell them so, and regard it rather as a benefit, they will regard it the same. The only harm that will come will be if you cause them to think it is a humiliation.[56]

Wilson was less backwards when it came to Catholicism. In his book *The New Freedom: A Call for the Emancipation of the Generous Energies of a People,* he lauded the Roman Catholic Church as a "great democracy"—a notion that seems every bit as counterintuitive as the idea that segregation is a boon for black people. "There was no peasant so humble that he might not become a priest," Wilson declared, "and no priest so obscure that he might not become Pope of Christendom."[57]

There was an tremendous surge of anti-German feeling during World War I, aided and abetted by propagandists from the American Protective League; after the armistice, they turned their efforts against the anarcho-syndicalists of the Industrial Workers of the World, and Communists and Socialists. And of course William Joseph Simmons's revived KKK became a major political force for a little over a decade, starting in 1915. When the publicists Edward Young Clarke and Elizabeth Tyler came on board to energize the Klan's recruiting efforts (the Klan was very much a for-profit venture, much as Judson Phillips's Tea Party Nation is today;[58] receipts from membership dues and sales of costumes and regalia and literature represented a significant income stream), they "re-branded" it as a broadly nativist Protestant organization. "To the Negro, Jew, Oriental, Roman Catholic, and alien, were added dope, bootlegging, graft, nightclubs and road houses, violations of the Sabbath, unfair business dealings, sex, marital 'goings on,' and scandalous behavior as the proper concern of the one-hundred-percent American," wrote David Mark Chalmers in *Hooded Americanism*.[59] With more than one thousand recruiters, or Kleagles, working on commission nationwide, its membership swelled into the millions.

Before it crashed and dived in a welter of lawsuits and sex scandals, the KKK was big and powerful enough to have helped elect sixteen U.S. senators, eleven governors, and countless lower-ranking officials throughout the country. Though it had enough political clout to do serious damage to Al Smith's presidential candidacy in 1928 (it issued a "Klarion Kall for a Krusade" against him), it wasn't powerful enough to prevent a Catholic from receiving the Democratic Party's nomination in the first place.

———

In fact Catholicism had become so mainstream by the 1930s that it had produced an incendiary, right-wing populist of its own in Father Charles Edward Coughlin. The Canadian-born Coughlin studied with the Basilian fathers and taught in their schools; he took from them not only their passion for social justice but their detestation of usury ("Usury is the origin of lying; the beginning of ingratitude, unfairness, perjury," Saint Basil famously preached in the fourth century[60]).

In 1926, Coughlin took over the parish in Royal Oak, Michigan, and built a church, the Shrine of the Little Flower. When the Ku Klux Klan burned crosses on its lawn, he was inspired to use the fledgling medium of commercial radio to send them back a message of his own. Though he had been forgotten for decades when he died in 1979, between 1926, when he first began his broadcasts, and 1942, when the church ordered him to cease his non-pastoral activities, his increasingly Fascistic message reached an audience that numbered in the tens of millions. At his peak, he received eighty thousand letters a week (many of them accompanied by contributions); the U.S. Postal Service had to build a special facility just to accommodate his mail. By 1932, Coughlin himself maintained a staff of four personal secretaries and 106 clerks.[61]

Coughlin loathed Communism, but he had equal contempt for an unregulated free market. "My friends, the outworn creed of capitalism is done for," he declared in a broadcast on November 11, 1934. "The clarion call of communism has been sounded. I can support one as easily as the other. They are both rotten!" In the same speech, he laid out a sixteen-point credo for his newly formed National Union for Social Justice:

1. I believe in liberty of conscience and liberty of education, not permitting the state to dictate either my worship to my God or my chosen avocation in life.

2. I believe that every citizen willing to work and capable of working shall receive a just, living, annual wage which will enable him both to maintain and educate his family according to the standards of American decency.

3. I believe in nationalizing those public resources which by their

very nature are too important to be held in the control of private individuals.

4. I believe in private ownership of all other property.
5. I believe in upholding the right to private property but in controlling it for the public good.
6. I believe in the abolition of the privately owned Federal Reserve Banking system and in the establishment of a Government owned Central Bank.
7. I believe in rescuing from the hands of private owners the right to coin and regulate the value of money, which right must be restored to Congress where it belongs.
8. I believe that one of the chief duties of this Government owned Central Bank is to maintain the cost of living on an even keel and arrange for the repayment of dollar debts with equal value dollars.
9. I believe in the cost of production plus a fair profit for the farmer.
10. I believe not only in the right of the laboring man to organize in unions but also in the duty of the Government, which that laboring man supports, to protect these organizations against the vested interests of wealth and of intellect.
11. I believe in the recall of all non-productive bonds and therefore in the alleviation of taxation.
12. I believe in the abolition of tax-exempt bonds.
13. I believe in broadening the base of taxation according to the principles of ownership and the capacity to pay.
14. I believe in the simplification of government and the further lifting of crushing taxation from the slender revenues of the laboring class.
15. I believe that, in the event of a war for the defense of our nation and its liberties, there shall be a conscription of wealth as well as a conscription of men.
16. I believe in preferring the sanctity of human rights to the sanctity of property rights; for the chief concern of government shall be for the poor because, as it is witnessed, the rich have ample means of their own to care for themselves.[62]

Coughlin is unquestionably the father of angry right-wing talk radio, but his concern for the poor and his belief in the power of government to accomplish good starkly distinguish his politics from those of Rush Limbaugh, Mark Levin, Sean Hannity, and Glenn Beck today, who regard the poor much as an earlier generation of conservatives regarded the Soviet Union, as a powerful, implacably determined foe. For them, the unfettered right to hold private property is synonymous with the public good; no possible national emergency, no imaginable moral compulsion could ever override it. Beck ridiculed his critics who compare him to Coughlin.

> Yes, Father Coughlin was against communism. Yes, he was on the radio, like me. Yes, he was against the sitting president, FDR.
> But it's weird, because that's where it ends. . . . Father Coughlin perverted American ideals for his own power and most importantly for social justice. Social justice. Social justice. Social justice.[63]

As Chip Berlet and Matthew N. Lyons explain in *Right-Wing Populism in America*, Coughlin's politics were producerist, in much the same spirit (though not at all the same policy particulars) as Andrew Jackson's and Henry Ford's. "The capitalist or—to coin a more pertinent word—the financialist and the industrialist are really two distinct persons each fulfilling a definite function in our civilization," Coughlin wrote in his book *The New Deal in Money*. "The object of the former is to make money out of money, caring only for profits. The object of the latter—the industrialist—is to make things—shoes, plows, stoves, typewriters, automobiles—out of raw materials. He is essentially a producer. The financialist is essentially a parasite"—a parasite that Coughlin identified with England, Wall Street, the Rothschilds, and Jews in general.[64] Coughlin blasted the eastern Anglo-Saxon elites as well, the "bankers with their grouse hunting estates in Scotland who never traveled west of Buffalo."[65] "The rhetoric of the radio priest," David H. Bennett wrote in *The Party of Fear*, "provided an inverted nativism that served both as a final ritual of assimilation for Catholic and ethnic followers and a way of striking back at ancient oppressors."[66]

Coughlin was an impassioned Roosevelt partisan ("Roosevelt or ruin" and "the New Deal is Christ's Deal" were two of his catchphrases) until he realized that a cabinet appointment would not be coming his way. Secretary of the Treasury Henry Morgenthau answered Coughlin's cries for the remonetization of silver—an economic nostrum that Coughlin had adapted wholesale from agrarian populism—by publicizing the fact that the Shrine of the Little Flower had been investing heavily in the metal itself and thus stood to gain from the policy. Interestingly, Glenn Beck, who exhorts his listeners to hedge themselves against the consequences of the coming financial collapse with "God, gold, and guns," is sponsored by the precious metals vendor Goldline (which also sponsors Mark Levin's, Monica Crowley's, and Laura Ingraham's radio shows).

By the middle of Roosevelt's first term, Coughlin felt personally snubbed and increasingly alienated by the administration's pro–Wall Street leanings at home and its pro-British leanings abroad. In 1935, Coughlin joined forces with Francis Townsend and Gerald L. K. Smith to launch the Union Party. It was a fragile alliance, and it didn't even hold until the election, but Coughlin's choice of partners exemplifies the opposite poles of his politics. Townsend advocated that the government pay everyone over sixty years of age a generous pension supported by sales taxes—an idea that provided the germ of Social Security. The virulently racist and anti-Semitic Smith was the leader of Huey Long's Share Our Wealth movement; in later years, he would become one of the founders of the Christian Identity Church. Had Long not been assassinated in September, he might have been the Union Party's candidate; instead, they ran the North Dakota congressman William Lemke. Though Coughlin bragged that he could personally deliver nine million votes, Lemke received fewer than one million. Roosevelt won by a landslide.

After 1936, the increasingly demagogic Coughlin (he would call Roosevelt "an anti-God and a radical") no longer bothered to mute or moderate his anti-Semitism or his Fascist sympathies.[67] At a Bund rally in the Bronx in 1937, he famously gave a Nazi salute and shouted, "When we get through with the Jews in America, they'll think the treatment they received in Germany was nothing!"[68] In 1938, his newspaper Social Justice published The Protocols of the Elders of Zion ("We are not attributing them to the Jews," Coughlin disingenuously explained, "we are simply insisting upon their factuality, be they plagiarized or not plagiarized, be they satires—or not satires"[69]). Though Coughlin kept enough distance from the paramilitary Christian Front (whose gangs attacked Jews on the streets and promoted boycotts of Jewish-owned businesses) to maintain deniability, its members openly hailed him as their spiritual leader. A 1940 pamphlet by Theodore Irwin described one of their rallies:

> Speakers . . . have the skill and intensity of a Holy Roller with a shot in the arm. They begin by denouncing communism, then identify communists with Jews, who are also maligned as "international bankers" and "war mongers." City, State and federal administrations, unfriendly members of the Dies Committee, the press, and the radio are all assailed as Jew-controlled. Borrowing many phrases from Goebbels, the soapboxers refer to the President as "Rosenfelt" or, more intimately, "Rosie." Often a meeting ends with a pledge of allegiance to the American flag—and the Nazi salute. . . . If you had made a tour of Christian Front assemblages in New York in recent months, you would have been subjected to exhortations such as these: "I am not content to walk in the footsteps of Christ. I want to walk ahead of him with a club." . . . "We must hate! We must get the youth aroused!"[70]

After the attack on Pearl Harbor, Coughlin's following evaporated; the networks no longer carried his radio shows, and wartime censorship took a toll on *Social Justice*, which he was no longer permitted to distribute through the U.S. mail. In May 1942, when Archbishop Edward Mooney threatened to defrock him, Coughlin fell silent.

Perhaps the contemporary figure who resembles Coughlin the most is Pat Buchanan, an inveterate critic of Israel and its "amen corner" in Washington and a stalwart defender of accused Nazis such as John Demjanjuk, Karl Linnas, and Arthur Rudolph. Writing in *The New Republic* in 1990, Jacob Weisberg noted that "Buchanan's politics has its roots in the 1930s isolationism of Father Charles E. Coughlin and Charles A. Lindbergh."

> The hallmarks of this tradition are a fierce and unselective anti-communism, an animosity toward Britain, and an eccentric obsession with the menace of "Jewish internationalism." Buchanan's earliest syndicated columns echo these obsessions. In 1975 he attacked the infamous United Nations resolution equating Zionism with racism. But he laid some of the blame at the door of "West-

ern intellectuals and internationalists, many of them Jews." . . .
This echoes Coughlin, in whose lexicon "intellectual" and "internationalist" were not only cusswords but also synonyms both for Jews and for secular liberals.[71]

There is a certain irony in the fact that Buchanan's signature issue today is nativism. "Whose country is this?" he asked in his December 17, 2010, column. "If no action is taken . . . the border will disappear and America will be a geographical expression, not a country anymore."[72] In a column headlined "Will America Survive to 2050?" he warned that "George Bush may go down in history as the man who not only lost the magnificent lands won for America by James Polk, but, by refusing to do his duty and halt this [Hispanic] invasion, ensured the Balkanization and dissolution of his country."[73]

Something very much like those things was also being said about Buchanan's ancestors when they first arrived in this country. Perhaps that is the ultimate mark of assimilation—when a descendant of immigrants can confidently declare, as Buchanan so emphatically does, that "the Melting Pot is broken."[74]

John Hagee is a gospel singer, the pastor of a Pentecostalist Texas mega-church, a leading Christian Zionist, and a televangelist whose broadcasts are beamed into nearly 100 million homes worldwide. On February 27, 2008, he stood next to John McCain at a joint press conference in San Antonio, Texas, and spoke of his confidence that a McCain "administration will not permit Iran to have nuclear weapons to fulfill the evil dreams of President Ahmadinejad to wipe Israel off the map," adding that McCain has had a "solid, pro-life voting record for the past 24 years"[75] and that he "is a man of principle, who does not stand boldly on both sides of any issue."[76] Hagee's endorsement had been long sought after by McCain; he needed it to help him woo evangelical votes away from Mike Huckabee in the Texas primary, which was just a week away. Like so much else in McCain's hapless 2008 campaign, things quickly went awry.

"There are plenty of staunch evangelical leaders who are pro-Israel, but are not anti-Catholic. John Hagee is not one of them," declared

William Donohue of the Catholic League—whom we met at the beginning of this chapter, railing against the anal-sex- and abortion-loving, family-hating Jews of Hollywood. "Indeed, for the past few decades, he has waged an unrelenting war against the Catholic Church," he continued. "For example, he likes calling it 'The Great Whore,' an 'apostate church,' the 'anti-Christ,' and a 'false cult system.' "[77] A Catholic League fact sheet, "Hagee in His Own Words," documented the minister's most inflammatory sound bites—some of which, to my Jewish ears and eyes, seem more impolitic than strictly libelous:

- "When Adolf Hitler came to power he said, 'I'm not going to do anything in my lifetime that hasn't been done by the Roman Church for the past 800 years, I'm only going to do it on a greater scale and more efficiently.' And he certainly had done just exactly that."

- "Anti-Semitism in Christianity began with the statements of the early church fathers, including Eusebius, Cyril, Chrysostom, Augustine, Origen, Justin, and Jerome. . . . They labeled the Jews as 'the Christ killers, plague carriers, demons, children of the devil, bloodthirsty pagans who look for an innocent child during the Easter week to drink his blood, money hungry Shylocks, who are deceitful as Judas was relentless.' "

- "The Roman Catholic Church, which was supposed to carry the light of the gospel, plunged the world into the Dark Ages. . . . The brutal truth is that the Crusades were military campaigns of the Roman Catholic Church to gain control of Jerusalem from the Muslims and to punish the Jews as the alleged Christ killers on the road to and from Jerusalem."

- "The Spanish Inquisition was perhaps the most cynical plot in the black history of Catholicism, aimed at expropriating the property of wealthy Jews and converts in Spain for the benefit of the royal court and the Roman Catholic Church."

- "Need we be reminded that the loving theology of the New Testament, as translated by the Roman church fathers, is what sponsored the Crusades, the Inquisition, and ultimately produced the Holocaust?"[78]

"Senator Obama has repudiated the endorsement of Louis Farra-khan, another bigot," Donohue concluded. "McCain should follow suit and retract his embrace of Hagee."[79]

Recent left-leaning books like Daniel Goldhagen's *Hitler's Willing Executioners: Ordinary Germans and the Holocaust* (1996), James Carroll's *Constantine's Sword: The Church and the Jews* (2001), and John Cornwell's *Hitler's Pope: The Secret History of Pius XII* (1999) had all said much the same things as the arch-rightist Hagee did: that the Catholic Church had combined supersessionism or replace-ment theology (the notion that Christianity supplanted and nulli-fied Jewish law) with racial and political anti-Semitism to create a climate in which genocide seemed justifiable. Naturally, those books received more than their share of criticism and praise from special pleaders; religious and political scholars found much to argue about in them as well. But Hagee is hardly a disinterested academic; his philo-Semitism is as theologically driven as the Catholic Jew hatred that he purports to expose. Hagee's end-time scenario requires the presence of a Jewish state in the Holy Land and a rebuilt Temple before Christ will return. As much as Hagee loves the idea of a Jew-ish Greater Israel, he no less ardently longs for the bloodbath that will accompany its ultimate obliteration. Only the handful of Jews who convert to Christianity will survive.

In a controversial sermon in 1999, Hagee had declared that Hitler had been a servant of God's will, that the Holocaust was the ful-fillment of God's divine plan to regather the Jews in the Holy Land. When God saw that Theodor Herzl's Zionism had only attracted a few hardy souls, Hagee said, he had dispatched a hunter to flush out the rest:

A hunter is someone with a gun and he forces you. Hitler was a hunter. And the Bible says—Jeremiah writing—*"They shall hunt them from every mountain and from every hill and from the holes of the rocks,"* meaning there's no place to hide. And that might be offensive to some people but don't let your heart be offended. I didn't write it, Jeremiah wrote it. It was the truth and it is the truth. How did [the Holocaust] happen? Because God allowed it to happen. Why did it happen? Because God said my top priority for the Jewish people is to get them to come back to the land of Israel.[80]

The independent researcher Rachel Tabachnick has collected a fact sheet of her own on John Hagee, which is posted at the Web site Talk to Action. It suggests that his abiding friendship toward the Jews, whether based on the controversial doctrine of dual covenantalism or not (dual covenantalism being the notion that God's covenant with Abraham guarantees the Jews' salvation even if they don't accept Christ—a seemingly heretical position that Hagee has boldly stood on both sides of, depending upon who's in the room), comes with significant qualifications and with strings attached.

"When will the divinely imparted spiritual blindness upon the Jewish people end concerning the identity of Jesus Christ as Messiah?" Hagee asked in his book *Jerusalem Countdown: A Warning to the World*. "This spiritual blindness will end when Christ returns to earth and they see the scars in His hands from the Roman crucifixion." Only Orthodox and Conservative Jews give his movement their wholehearted support, Hagee complained to the *San Antonio Express-News* in 2006. The rest of the Jews "have a liberal agenda. And the liberal agenda," he explained, sounding not unlike William Donohue, "is they are pro-abortion. They're pro-homosexual. They're pro-gay marriage—they want men to marry men and women to marry women—and their difference with me is not really what I'm doing with Israel. Their hostility to me is poisoned by their liberalism."

In his book *Day of Deception*, Hagee played a series of variations on some timeworn conspiratorial, anti-Semitic themes, noting that the four largest stockholders of the Federal Reserve "are not even Americans but members of the Rothschild family of Europe." In a 2003 sermon, he described the satanic Illuminati's plan to "rule the world" through the destruction of the world's financial systems. "America's economic problems are not created by market conditions, they are planned and orchestrated to devalue and to destroy the value of the dollar."[81]

That last one is an oft-told story, as we know, but the perfidy of Jewish bankers isn't the sort of thing that one generally talks about in mixed company, certainly not at an interfaith event like the one Hagee organized in Washington, D.C., in the summer of 2010 to commemorate Tisha B'av, when "Rabbi Scheinberg and several other Orthodox rabbis" and "nearly 1,000 Christians and Jews, including the State of Israel's Ambassador to the United States, Michael Oren, sat on the floor and were led in the reading of the book of Lamentations."[82]

Though John McCain ultimately did reject Hagee's endorsement (the furor aroused by the "Hitler was a hunter" quotation was the last straw), Donohue and Hagee became fast friends. In the tradition of Henry Ford, Hagee sent Donohue a letter that "clarified" his positions. "After engaging in constructive dialogue with Catholic friends and leaders," Hagee allowed, "I now have an improved understanding of the Catholic Church, its relation to the Jewish faith, and the history of anti-Catholicism."

> In my zeal to oppose anti-Semitism and bigotry in all its ugly forms . . . I may have contributed to the mistaken impression that the anti-Jewish violence of the Crusades and the Inquisition defines the Catholic Church. It most certainly does not. Likewise, I have not sufficiently expressed my deep appreciation for the efforts of Catholics who opposed the persecution of the Jewish people. It is important to note that there were thousands of righteous Catholics—both clergy and laymen—who risked their lives to save Jews from the Holocaust.[83]

Donohue was instantly mollified. "The tone of Hagee's letter is sincere," he wrote in a press release. "Whatever problems we had before are now history. This case is closed."[84]

A little over a year later, in July 2009, a less repentant-sounding Hagee shared his version of what had transpired between him and Donohue with *U.S. News & World Report*'s Dan Gilgoff:

> Bill Donohue of the Catholic League claimed that I had slighted the Catholic Church while teaching from the Book of Revelation. He was mistaken on this point. But he and I handled this disagreement the way that Christians should. We met. We had fellowship. We learned from one another. A few months after the controversy, he came to our Washington, D.C., Summit as my guest. When I recognized him during my keynote address, he received a rousing ovation from our CUFI [Christians United for Israel] audience. I consider him a friend.
>
> Bill and I decided that we should turn our personal reconciliation into a broader reconciliation. We decided to try to bring Catholics and Protestants together on behalf of Israel.[85]

"Bigot," "false cult system," and "Whore of Babylon" notwithstanding, one can only conclude that the two men's mutual detestation of secular liberalism trumped their not inconsiderable differences—yet another example of the triumphant ecumenicism of hatred, of its capacity to elide precise intellectual and emotional discriminations.

These days, more often than not, the Satan of conspiracists' nightmares appears in Islamic guise. A man who lives near Shanksville, Pennsylvania, has been on a crusade to force the U.S. National Park Service to change the design of the 9/11 memorial that's being erected at the crash site of United Airlines Flight 93, because it is crescent-shaped and points toward Mecca, just like a mosque, and its ninety-three-foot tower resembles a minaret. I know much more about this burning issue than I need to, because he has posted about it extensively on my blog.

In the fall of 2010, Oklahoma voters decided on a ballot initiative to amend the state constitution to ban judges from considering international or especially Sharia law when making rulings (it won handily but was blocked in the courts). The anti-Islamic Web site Logan's Warning only regretted that it didn't go far enough:

> This is a great step in our war with Islam. The reason is that, not only does it protect us from Islam, it will also expose the pro-Sharia Muslims. Personally I would like to take it one step further though. After the law is passed, I would arrest and deport if possible, any Muslim that calls for Sharia Law. All Sharia loving Muslims are to be looked upon as enemies of the state, just like Nazis were.[86]

The former House Speaker Newt Gingrich proposed a federal ban on Sharia law, and Terry Jones, an obscure preacher in Gainesville, Florida, made headlines when he threatened to burn Korans to commemorate the anniversary of September 11. The anti-Islamic bandwagon had started rolling on May 13, 2010, when the *New York Post*'s columnist Andrea Peyser abruptly erupted about "mosque madness at Ground Zero."

"Plans are under way," she wrote, "for a Muslim house of worship, topped by a 13-story cultural center with a swimming pool, in a building damaged by the fuselage of a jet flown by extremists into the World Trade Center." No one on the right had emitted as much as a peep when the project was announced months before, but now a protest was scheduled for June 6, D-day, organized by the "human rights activist" Pamela Geller, who'd co-founded Stop Islamization of America* with the writer Robert Spencer. A month or so later, on July 18, 2010, Sarah Palin added her unmistakable voice to the growing chorus. "Ground Zero Mosque supporters: doesn't it stab you in the heart, as it does ours throughout the heartland?" she tweeted. "Peaceful Muslims, pls refudiate." Later, she edited her words for clarity: "Peaceful New Yorkers, pls refute the Ground Zero mosque plan if you believe catastrophic pain caused @ Twin Towers site is too raw, too real." Even if the people of New York City are inexplicably numb and insensate to their own pain, she seemed to be saying, real heartland Americans suffered and are suffering still from the wound New York received on September 11, 2001. Or something like that, anyway. Palin posted a third and final tweet on the subject: "Peace-seeking Muslims pls understand. Ground Zero mosque is UNNECESSARY provocation. Pls reject it in interest of healing."[87]

One can almost sympathize with Palin's evident confusion. She thinks that America is a Christian polity and that Islam is intrinsically foreign and inimical to its interests. She takes it for granted that al-Qaeda speaks and acts on behalf of all Muslims and that all of Islam's followers (even its "peace-seeking" minority) bear equal responsibility for whatever is done in Islam's name. She doesn't seem to appreciate that there are 600,000 Muslims who live, work, and worship in New York City—more than twice the entire population of Anchorage, Alaska, and more than a hundred times that of Wasilla—and more than a billion and a half in the world, the vast majority of whom are neither Arabs nor Wahhabites.

As the summer wore on, protests against planned mosques had spread to such unlikely locales as Temecula, California, and Murfreesboro, Tennessee. On August 10, 2010, Bryan Fischer, director of issue analysis for Donald Wildmon's fundamentalist Christian American Family Association, poured gasoline on the fire with this blog post:

---

* Geller blogs at Atlas Shrugs, a site that is much trafficked by the Tea Party crowd; she is the author of *The Post-American Presidency: The Obama Administration's War on America* and *Stop the Islamicization of America: A Practical Guide to the Resistance.*

Permits should not be granted to build even one more mosque in the United States of America, let alone the monstrosity planned for Ground Zero. This is for one simple reason: each Islamic mosque is dedicated to the overthrow of the American government.

Each one is a potential jihadist recruitment and training center, and determined to implement the "Grand Jihad."[88]

The "monstrosity" in question was actually to be sited several blocks away from Ground Zero, in the former Burlington Coat Factory. Until Geller and her colleagues began their campaign of demonization, the organization behind it, the Cordoba Initiative, had been considered a model of moderation and cultural outreach. Its founder, Imam Feisal Abdul Rauf, a naturalized U.S. citizen, had been a frequent speaker at international conferences and think tanks, an adviser to the Interfaith Center of New York, and a consultant for George W. Bush's State Department. His book *What's Right with Islam: A New Vision for Muslims and the West* had been praised by *The Christian Science Monitor* as "an invigorating glimpse into the heart and mind of a wise Muslim seeking the higher ground, and a moving example of the impact of the American experience." Nevertheless, he would be widely calumniated in the right-wing press as "an unrepentant militant Muslim, an Islamist fellow traveler . . . [who] openly seeks the Islamization of America."[89]

Though New York City's mayor, Mike Bloomberg, supported the project without reservation, many nationally prominent Democrats showed extraordinary cowardice as the "scandal" took flight. The Senate majority leader, Harry Reid—facing a tough reelection campaign against an anti-immigrant Tea Partier in his home state—opined that it would be better if the Cordoba Initiative built its mosque elsewhere. The Anti-Defamation League's Abe Foxman tried to have his cake and eat it too, insisting on his uncompromising support for religious freedom while demurring that this particular case was "not a question of rights, but a question of what is right."[90] Building a mosque in the same neighborhood where the twin towers once stood counted as a clear wrong, according to his moral calculus.

Commenting on the television show *Fox & Friends* in February 2011 on some Protestant churches that allowed Islamic congregations to use their facilities, Mike Huckabee declared, "As much as I respect the autonomy of each local church, you just wonder, what are they thinking? If the purpose of a church is to push forward the gospel of Jesus Christ, and then you have a Muslim group that says that Jesus Christ and all the people that follow him are a bunch of infidels who should be essentially obliterated, I have a hard time understanding that." Applying the same kind of reasoning that surmises that marriage between two members of the same sex will inexorably lead to marriage between man and beast, he added, "I mean if a church is nothing more than a facility and a meeting place free for any and all viewpoints, without regard to what it is, then should the church be rented out to show adult movies on the weekend? . . . How far does it go?"[91] Islam, adult movies. Nothing hateful about that.

Ironically, Mike Huckabee has had past associations with Christian Reconstructionists, people who—much in the manner of stealth jihadists—are seeking to transform the United States into a theocracy.[92] "I believe it's a lot easier to change the Constitution than it would be to change the word of the living God," Huckabee himself remarked on January 15, 2008, while campaigning for the Republican primary in Michigan. "What we need to do is to amend the Constitution so it's in God's standards rather than try to change God's standards." Obviously, it's difficult for him to summon up a spirit of tolerance for a religion that he regards as an illegitimate rival to his own.

There are a host of "aspects of Shariah that are now beginning to be adopted or accommodated in our country," Frank Gaffney had told Fox News as far back as 2008. "We think far from being frivolous or innocuous or innocent, these represent a form of, what I think [is] best described as stealth Jihad."[93] In the fall of 2010, Gaffney's Center for Security Policy issued a massive report titled *Shariah: The Threat to America.* "The result of months of analysis, discussion and drafting by a group of top security policy experts," the report was intended to provide "a comprehensive and articulate 'second opinion'" on "the preeminent totalitarian threat of our time: the legal-political-military doctrine known within Islam as 'shariah.' "[94] For the report's purposes, Sharia was defined not simply as the body of Islamic law but as an all-out effort to create a worldwide caliphate by any means possible.

If shariah is thus viewed as an alien legal system hostile to and in contravention of the U.S. Constitution, and as one which dictates both violent and non-violent means to a capable audience ready to act imminently, then logically, those who seek to establish shariah in America—whether by violent means or by stealth—can be said to be engaged in criminal sedition, not the protected practice of a religion.

So long as Muslims see the West as "an obstacle to be overcome, not a culture and civilization to be embraced or at least tolerated," they should be treated as either enemy soldiers or subversive spies. Back in the 1920s, Henry Ford was as horrified by the presence of rabbinical courts in New York State as the anti-Sharia forces are today by the prospect of Muslim law worming its way into state, local, and federal statutes. "There is a Jewish court sitting in a public building in the city of New York every week, and other courts, for the sole advantage and use of this people whose spokesmen deny that they are a 'separate people,' are in formation everywhere," he wrote. "Wherever Jewish tendencies are permitted to work unhindered, the result is not 'Americanization,' or 'Anglicization' nor any other distinctive nationalism, but a strong and ruling reversion back to essential 'Judaization.' "[95]

The authors of the *Shariah* report acknowledge that some of the world's Muslims—maybe even most of them—are not ouvert extremists. But they don't vest much credit in them either. Just as the Devil quotes Scripture when it suits his purposes, stealth jihadists will pay lip service to liberal values while secretly working to undermine them. If Catholics are defined as soldiers in the service of the pope who are determined to destroy representative government in whatever country they live in, then there can be no innocent Catholics; if Communists are understood to be slaves of Moscow, then they can only be subversive. So it is with Islam. Moderate-seeming Muslims may be the most suspect of all, since they would be the most ideally positioned to become sleepers.

Some of the anti-Sharia hysteria can be attributed to Christian chauvinism; some to an instinctive, defensive nativism, inflamed by an uncertain economy and the lingering shock of 9/11. Some of it has been fomented by Christian cultural conservatives, some of it by right-wing Jews who regard Israel's traditional enemies with the same indiscriminate loathing that Hitler's Nazis did their ancestors (when Osama bin Laden's killing was announced on May 1, 2011, Debbie Schlussel blogged, "One down, 1.8 billion to go . . . many of 'em inside U.S. borders, with the U.S. government at all levels kissing their asses").[96] Anders Behring Breivik's 1,500 page manifesto, "2008: A European Declaration of Independence," which explains why the forces of Politically Correct Multiculturalism, Marxism, and Shariah compelled him to murder 77 of his fellow Norwegians, contains a generous selection of their writings, much to some of its unwitting contributors' embarrassment.[97] Robert Spencer and Pamela Geller were so distressed at their inclusion that they began to regard themselves as Breivik's true victims. Breivik's "citations of our work," they wrote in a column in the Internet publication *American Thinker*, "have led to an international campaign to blame us for the massacre. *The New York Times*, NBC, the BBC, CNN, the *Washington Post*, many European publications, and a host of others have claimed that we are responsible for creating a climate of 'hate' in which a Breivik was inevitable. This is not only false, but such charges against us challenge fundamental principles of the freedom of speech."[98] It wasn't the first or the last time that extremists have found themselves in the awkward position of having to disavow a follower who took their rhetoric more seriously than they did themselves.

But much of what has been playing out in the political scene over the past few years is displaced Obama hatred, and many of his political rivals have been leveraging it for all it's worth. Obama is a Marxist revolutionary whose middle name is the same as the ex-dictator of Iraq's. He's not white, he's probably not American, and he might not even be a Christian. A Pew Research Center survey conducted in August 2010 found that nearly one in five Americans and more than one in three self-described conservative Republicans believed that Obama is a Muslim.[99]

As the Reverend Gerald Burton Winrod wrote of Franklin Delano Roosevelt three-quarters of a century ago, he is "not one of us."

6.

The New Deal, the Old Right, and the Pseudo-conservative Revolts

ather Coughlin and Huey Long were unusual in that they attacked FDR and the New Deal from both the left and the right; most of Roosevelt's adversaries were firmly in one camp or the other. If FDR's signal achievement was to have charted a mostly centric course through the perilous straits of the global financial crisis and World War II, imposing modest reforms on America's free enterprise system so it would remain intact for its vast peacetime expansion, his enemies demonized him in absolutist terms that sound eerily familiar today. "Whenever a president tries to bring about significant changes, particularly during times of economic unease, then there is a certain segment of the population that gets very riled up," Barack Obama observed on the *Late Show with David Letterman* on September 21, 2009. "FDR was called a socialist and a communist."[1]

He was called worse than that. John T. Flynn's *Country Squire in the White House,* published in 1940, was relatively charitable. It summed up Roosevelt as a basically well-intentioned mediocrity whose gimmicky economic nostrums had left the country in significantly worse shape than he'd found it in and whose appalling determination to provoke an unnecessary war with Hitler was driving the world to the brink of disaster:

> Politics, vacillation, the eternal straining after cleverness, a mind, as H. G. Wells observed of the President, "appallingly open," open indeed at both ends, through which all sorts of half-baked ideas flow, love of the spectacular, preoccupation with war problems and the affairs of Europe, and only a dim perception of the profound problems of economics and finance that dominate our scene, good intentions mixed with confused ethical concepts—these have brought the President to the tragic point where the only thing that can save his regime is to take the country off into a war hysteria.[2]

The isolationist tract *War! War! War!*, published under the pseudonym Cincinnatus in the same year, summoned up more vitriol. Roosevelt wasn't just an amiable but blundering blue blood; he was a would-be Caesar (and a willing tool of the Jews):

> Another World War, plotted by Roosevelt and World Jewry, the Jewish controlled American press and radio, the British-Jewish Empire and the French Empire with a large proportion of their press and banks owned by the Jews, is being fought as these words are put down. . . . The Draft Bill which has been passed is a hideous New York City, Atlantic seaboard, Jewish, Anglophile effort to permanently regiment our American Republic into a totalitarian, militaristic empire, with the immediate purpose of redressing, by an unprovoked war, the Jewish grievances in Europe. It is a new Roosevelt shackle. . . . We have a President who thrives on "emergencies," creating them almost at will and whenever he finds that his schemes for dealing with the previous "emergency" have failed to work. . . . The efforts of the New Dealers to remake our system of government have not succeeded to the extent they plainly wished. They have been slowed up by the Congress, speaking the voice of the people. Therefore, another "emergency"—this time the greatest and most dangerous of all—must be concocted. The war in Europe is that "emergency."[3]

Threescore and ten years later, *WorldNetDaily*'s David Kupelian channeled the same sentiments and almost the same words, when he wrote that "the Obama administration's primary mode of governance is literally to create crises where none actually exist. . . . 'Big Lies' transform people and entire societies, and the most powerful form of 'Big Lie,' at least when it comes to government, is the *manufactured crisis.*"[4] On Veterans Day in 2009, *The American Spectator* noted that "Barack Obama . . . has boundless enmity for America, its key institutions, and its longtime allies."[5] Then there's this syndicated column, from March 2010, which reads like an over-the-top parody from the likes of *The Onion* or the *Weekly World News*'s Ed Anger, but whose author, Gordon Bishop, claims to have been the New Jersey Press Association's 1986 Journalist of the Year:

> After more than a half-century as a columnist and investigative reporter, I've come to the scary conclusion that Barack Hussein Obama, a black African Arab, hates America and plans to destroy capitalism because he is a pro-terrorist Marxist Communist who grew up in an Indonesian Muslim country. . . . Obama's agenda is to transform America into a Socialist Marxist Nation State, as fast as he can. . . . Yes, this egotistic, arrogant dictator wants to control the world. America is just not big enough for this destructive madman.[6]

Walk through any bookstore and you'll find the likes of Stanley Kurtz's *Radical-in-Chief*, which reveals Obama's plans "to ensnare the country in a new socialism,"[7] stacked up on tables alongside Dinesh D'Souza's *Roots of Obama's Rage*, Michelle Malkin's *Culture of Corruption: Obama and His Team of Tax Cheats, Crooks, and Cronies*, Ann Coulter's *Treason: Liberal Treachery from the Cold War to the War on Terrorism*, and David Limbaugh's *Crimes Against Liberty: An Indictment of President Barack Obama.*

The New Hate isn't so different from the Old Hate after all. The concept of the "loyal opposition" is altogether alien to it. It is a question of good and bad, right and wrong, and—for some quite literally—white and black. You can't agree to disagree with a president who usurped his office, an impostor whose partisans have more of Amalek than America in them. If the world is divided between the saved and the damned, the clean and the unclean, how can you stake out any common ground with the other side?

Here's Representative Trent Franks, a Republican from Arizona, at the Tea Party's "How to Take Back America Conference" in St. Louis in September 2009:

> Obama's first act as president of any consequence, in the middle of a financial meltdown, was to send taxpayers' money overseas to pay for the killing of unborn children in other countries. Now, I got to tell you, if a president will do that, there's almost nothing that you should be surprised at after that. We shouldn't be shocked that he does all these other insane things. A president that has lost his way that badly, that has no ability to see the image of God in these little fellow human beings, if he can't do that right, then he has no place in any station of government and we need to realize that he is an enemy of humanity.[8]

An enemy of humanity—we know who that is. "Since what is at stake is always a conflict between absolute good and absolute evil," Hofstadter wrote in *The Paranoid Style in American Politics*, "the quality needed is not a willingness to compromise but the will to fight things out to a finish."[9] You can't split the difference with the Devil.

"As polarized as we have ever been, we Americans are locked in a cultural war for the soul of our country," Pat Buchanan thundered in 1992.

> What is it all about? . . . It is about power; it is about who determines "the norms by which we live, and by which we define and govern ourselves." Who decides what is right and wrong, moral and immoral, beautiful and ugly, healthy and sick? Whose beliefs shall form the basis of law?[10]

"There it was, completely undisguised," Leonard Zeskind wrote of Buchanan's speech in *Blood and Politics: The History of the White Nationalist Movement from the Margins to the Mainstream*. "The question at issue for Buchanan was not *what* the common beliefs of the Republic should be, but *whose* beliefs. Not which ideas should hold hegemony, but which people should rule."[11] Those people, in Buchanan's and many others' view, are white American-born Christians—producers who grow and make things. And they are the very people who are being shunted aside by immigrants and other minorities, thanks to the untiring efforts of godless secularists, un-American internationalists, parasitic financiers, and effete, America-hating intellectuals.

> They have seen their Christian faith purged from schools their taxes paid for, and mocked in movies and on TV. They have seen their factories shuttered in the thousands and their jobs outsourced in the millions to Mexico and China. They have seen trillions of tax dollars go for Great Society programs, but have seen no Great Society, only rising crime, illegitimacy, drug use and dropout rates. . . . America was once their country. They sense they are losing it. And they are right.[12]

Listening to Buchanan, one begins to understand the reason for the birthers' obstinate skepticism. Even if Obama did produce every last scrap of documentation they demand, they still wouldn't believe he is an authentic American; his dark skin and his foreign name belie him.

Of course the vast majority of Americans are more generous-minded than the constituency that Buchanan has courted so assiduously; we are much less racist and xenophobic as a society today than we've ever been. But the politics of hatred pushes Pavlovian buttons that people don't like to acknowledge, even to themselves; worse still, it exerts an irresistible gravitational pull on the center. Pat Buchanan's insurgent primary campaigns in 1992 and 1996 did to the Republicans what George Wallace did to the Democrats when he entered the primaries against LBJ in 1964; they forced Bush and Dole to change some of their positions to protect their right flanks. Bill Clinton's tactic of "triangulation," by which he staked out a place in the so-called middle, compelled him to track rightward as well. The same process is repeating itself today, as mainstream Republicans vie with each other to tap the inexhaustible reservoirs of resentment and alienation that feed the Tea Party, and timorous Democrats try not to draw their fire and bolder ones with less developed senses of shame attempt to co-opt them.

And so it has ever been. In 1943, the Armenian American writer Avedis Boghos Derounian, writing under the pseudonym John

Roy Carlson, lifted the lid off the anti-Roosevelt underground in his best-selling exposé *Under Cover: My Four Years in the Nazi Underworld of America.* Working first for *Fortune* magazine and then for the Friends of Democracy, an antitotalitarian group organized by the Unitarian minister L. M. Birkhead, Carlson fashioned an alternate identity as an Italian American Fascist sympathizer named George Pagnanelli. He established his bona fides by selling Father Coughlin's *Social Justice* on street corners and then by publishing a newsletter of his own he called *The Christian Defender,* "deliberately designed to be one of the coarsest sheets published in New York. The cruder it got, the more it lied, the more it slandered the Jew and assailed Democracy, the more popular it became."[13]

Carlson/Pagnanelli's efforts gave him entrée to the offices of senators and congressmen like John Elliott Rankin ("When you go back to New York, you tell them this. There is only one way to win this fight and that is to expose the international Jewish bankers as the war mongers"[14]) and to a Bund camp in rural New Jersey, where operatives from the paramilitary Christian Mobilizers and the Christian Front joined ranks with Bundists and the KKK in a spectacular cross-burning ceremony. He met with George Sylvester Viereck at Flanders Hall in Scotch Plains, New Jersey, the publisher of Representative Stephen A. Day's *We Must Save the Republic* and other isolationist tracts, and signed on as a sales rep; he labored in a shabby back room behind a midtown barbershop, where star-spangled, 100 percent Americanist hate sheets were printed and packaged and shipped, some of them originating in Erfurt, Germany, where Goebbels's "propaganda mill [ground out] Nazi literature in thirteen different languages," many of them produced domestically: *The American Vindicator,* "published by North Carolina's Senator Robert Rice Reynolds; *Liberation,* published by Silver Shirt Leader William Dudley Pelley; Father Coughlin's *Social Justice;* Reverend Gerald B. Winrod's *Defender;* James True's *Industrial Control Reports;* Robert Edward Edmondson's *Vigilante Bulletin;* Colonel E. N. Sanctuary's, Merwin K. Harr's and Mrs. Elizabeth Dilling's leaflets."[15] Carlson vividly described a Friday luncheon meeting of American Patriots Inc. at the Hotel Iroquois in midtown New York in 1939, whose participants were "distinctly Park Avenue."

As the meeting broke up and the plump, well-fed men and women passed out into the hall . . . I walked out with the crowd.

"Hate! Did you hear what he said? Hate! We must learn to hate!"

Hate was the fascist formula.

Hate was the international cement that held fascism together, and America's fascist leaders built their organizations on a framework of hate. Hate was their handshake and hate their parting word. To join a "one hundred per cent Christian-American-Patriotic" group you didn't have to be Christian or American. Heathens and Mohammedans were welcome. Japanese were eligible. Crooks, thugs, racketeers, step right up. There was just one requirement. Hate! Hate the Niggers, the Jews, the Polacks, the Catholics, the Communists, the Masons, the bankers, the labor unions! Democracy. Hate anything but hate! And call anything you hated by a common name. Rich man, poor man, art, science, logic, politics— tie them together, stick an odious label on them and hate the label for all you're worth.[16]

Carlson was a propagandist, and he was writing during wartime. His book was hardly temperate or balanced; it pounded home the point that many of the antiwar and anti-Roosevelt groups, wrapped in the flag and armored with the cross as they might have been, were fully funded subsidiaries of the Third Reich, whether their rank and file or even their nominal leaders in some cases knew it or not. Of course not all of Roosevelt's adversaries were racists or traitors, any more than all of Obama's are today; the vast majority of isolationists thought they were protecting American blood and treasure. If they were indifferent to the fate of European Jewry, it wasn't because they shared Hitler's murderous agenda but because they didn't care about it; they believed that it would be possible for a Fascist Europe and a democratic America to peacefully coexist (or perhaps join forces in the fight against Soviet Communism). Not all of the antiinterventionists were economic conservatives, either (Flynn wasn't, for example). There was significant isolationist sentiment in the labor movement; there were radical black nationalists who identified with Japan.

As easy as it might have been for a literary man like Derounian/ Carlson to expose such louche characters as Joe McWilliams, the "fuehrer of Yorkville," Senator Robert Rice Reynolds of North Carolina ("Hitler and Mussolini have a date with destiny," he declaimed to the Senate in 1938. "It's foolish to oppose them so why not play ball with them?"[17]), or the society matron Leonora St. George Rogers Schuyler of the Daughters of the American Revolution as the raging anti-Semites that they were, or to establish that Charles Lindbergh and other high-profile figureheads of the America First movement had been at best Hitler's dupes, it was a much harder matter to prove that any of them were guilty of treason in a court of law.

Many of the figures that slouch through the pages of *Under Cover* would be defendants in the so-called Great Sedition Trial of 1944 ("Seldom have so many wild-eyed, jumpy, lunatic fringe characters been assembled in one spot, within speaking, winking, and whispering distance of one another," remarked James Wechsler of the newspaper *PM* as the proceedings began[18])—a legal and arguably a moral train wreck, in which the government attempted to prove that the disparate activities and writings of thirty-odd right-wing extremists met the formal definition of sedition as laid out in the Smith Act of 1940. More specifically, the government needed to prove that these men and women had conspired together "and with officials of the . . . German Reich and . . . members of the Nazi party . . . to interfere with, impair and influence the loyalty, morale and discipline of the military and naval forces" of the nation.[19] Upon the first indictment, in 1942, Congressman John Elliott Rankin was appalled. He read it into the *Congressional Record*, then he ventured some choice comments of his own:

> Mr. Speaker, I hesitate to use the word Jew in any speech in this House for whenever I do a little group of Communistic Jews howl to high heaven. They seem to think it is all right for them to abuse gentiles and to stir up race trouble but when you refer to one of them they cry "anti-Semitism," or accuse you of being pro-Nazi.
>
> Read this indictment and then read it again and ask yourself if the white gentiles of this country have any rights left that the Department of Justice is bound to respect.[20]

When, after many fits and starts, the court finally convened for *United States v. McWilliams* almost two years later, the twenty-eight defendants included William Dudley Pelley, Gerald Winrod, and Elizabeth Dilling, the Fascist philosopher Lawrence Dennis, George Sylvester Viereck (the poet and political philosopher Peter Viereck's father), and the white supremacist George E. Deatherage. Though the prosecution produced box loads of evidence that established their Nazi sympathies, there were no smoking guns to corroborate the charge that they'd actively collaborated either with each other or with the enemy. As weeks turned into months, Geoffrey R. Stone wrote in *Perilous Times: Free Speech in Wartime,* the "trial devolved into a circus that threatened to go on indefinitely. *The Washington Post* predicted that the trial would 'stand as a black mark against American justice for years to come' and urged the government to 'end this sorry spectacle.' On November 30, 1944, before the case was submitted to the jury, an exhausted and miserable Judge Eicher suddenly died."[21]

"With practically no lamentations from any source," *The New York Times* dryly reported, a mistrial was declared, and "the mass sedition trial came to an end."[22] The case would be formally dismissed in 1946. A similar mass trial of Rankin's and Deatherage's ideological heirs would be held in Fort Smith, Arkansas, in 1988, with equally sorry results. The defendants in that case, indicted under Title 18, Section 2384, included Aryan Nations' founder Richard Butler; the Christian Identity leader Robert Miles; the white nationalist theorist Louis Beam, author of the seminal "Leaderless Resistance"; David Lane, the imprisoned member of the Order who coined the two canonical fourteen-word slogans of white nationalism ("We must secure the existence of our people and a future for white children" and "Because the beauty of the white Aryan woman must not perish from the earth"); plus nine lesser soldiers. To their utter astonishment and confusion—for, according to all their own teachings, the American legal system was a compliant creature of ZOG, the Zionist Occupation Government—they were all acquitted.*

---

* In general, mass trials have gone better for the government when it has set its cap against leftists. Eleven Communists were successfully prosecuted under the Smith Act in 1949; by 1957, 140 Communists had been charged and tried. Even so, many of their convictions were overturned by *Yates v. United States* in 1957, which acknowledged that "advocacy of forcible overthrow as mere abstract doctrine is within the free speech protection of the First Amendment."

One of the best-known and certainly one of the most bizarre of the American fifth columnists, William Dudley Pelley, was already in jail by 1944, serving a fifteen-year sentence; he had been charged with and convicted of aiding the enemy in 1942, under the authority of the Espionage Act of 1917. Though Pelley kept himself busy writing about flying saucers, pyramidology, and his new religion, Soulcraft, in his twilight years, he had been almost completely forgotten when he died in Noblesville, Indiana, in 1965. But the legacy of his para-military group, the Silver Legion of America, a.k.a. the Silver Shirts, would live on in the racialist Christian Identity Church and other related movements. "Posse Comitatus," wrote David Neiwert in *The Eliminationists*, "which advocated forming 'citizen militias' back in the 1970s . . . was cofounded by Identity leader William Potter Gale and Mike Beach, a former Silver Shirt. It, in turn, gave birth to the Patriot/militia movement of the 1990s."[23]

Christian Identity began with British Israelism, the belief that the people of western Europe are descended from the Ten Lost Tribes—and that the people who call themselves Jews today are the descendants of Khazars or Edomites rather than Hebrews. Some Christian Identity churches adopted the Gnostic dual-seed doctrine, in which Cain's father wasn't Adam but the Devil, whose half-human progeny, the Jews, have been conspiring against the white race since time immemorial—a state of affairs that will soon end in an orgy of apocalyptic violence. In 1984, the white supremacist Louis Beam wrote about "the millenniums of warfare between the Aryan and the Jew":

> The victories each has in turn known, when spread over the centu-ries, equal stalemate. However, Aryan technology has shrunk the whole earth to the size of one battlefield. The eternal war, which can most properly be called a Conflict Of The Ages, has taken a final turn. The age-long conflict approaches, the last battle—Ragnarök, Armageddon—is about to be fought, and there will be only one survivor of this struggle.[24]

Pelley believed that World War II heralded the beginning of this final conflict. Excarnate beings that he was in "clairaudient" communication with told him that after decades of bloodletting, the Second Coming would occur on September 17, 2001.

Pelley wasn't a Nazi precisely—the system he proposed for America was a corporate theocracy, with white citizens owning shares in the state, blacks relegated to service occupations and held as wards of the government, closely regulated to make sure they didn't attempt miscegenation, and Jews confined to one ghetto city per state, which he called "Beth Havens"—but there was no question whose side he was on. Pelley's ultimate plan for the Jews was to "painlessly, humanely" sterilize them, so that the "race as a race gradually dies out."[25]

"In 1933," Pelley wrote in *Dupes of Judah: The Inside Story of Why the World War Was Fought*, "a buck private of the German army whose first name was Adolf came to the chancellorship of the German Fatherland and shoveled the whole mob of burglars, shysters, criminals, and blackguards out." Why would Americans want to step in, as they did in the last war, and help the Jews regain control of Europe?

> That's precisely what the big Sephardic Jew, Rossocampo-Rosenvelt, now sitting in the White House as of New Year's Eve, 1938–39, is striving his best to have happen with all the official powers at his command!
>
> And around him, thicker than flies about a honey-pot, sit the kith and kin of the same Ashkenazic Mob that only twenty-five years ago were paying ten grand to a Serbian kike to shoot an Archduke and precipitate the whole of it. Fine business, say I! And if I stick my head out and say I know a few things that the rest of America hasn't yet learned, I'm a Nazi Spy, an agent of Hitler, a Jew-Baiter. I'm "anti-American" because I don't want to see the growing boys of today shipped overseas to fight any more Ashkenazic-Sephardic fights in a wholesale bamboozlement![26]

Like Lyndon LaRouche, another conspiracy-obsessed megalomaniac, Pelley was born into an old New England family that had ties to the shoe business; like L. Ron Hubbard, who also founded a religion, writing was his first career. Unlike Hubbard, who wrote pulp science fiction (and unlike his own father, a part-time preacher and a restless, only intermittently successful businessman, who kept his family constantly on the move), Pelley enjoyed considerable mainstream success. His novels were critically acclaimed best sellers; he won two O. Henry Awards for his short stories; he covered the Russian Revolution for *The Saturday Evening Post* and wrote screenplays for Lon Chaney movies. In addition to his well-paid literary efforts, he had investments in a chain of restaurants, a real estate firm, and an advertising agency. But all of that changed in 1927, when he decided to take a sabbatical so he could "browse, ponder, meditate, and study." He divested himself of his business interests, moved to a bungalow in the hills outside Pasadena with his police dog, Laska, and commenced work on "The Urge of Peoples," a racial history of the world.

One night in the spring of 1928, he had an incredible experience that he would write about in a much-talked-about magazine article, "Seven Minutes in Eternity," which he later adapted into a book. One moment, he was lying in his bed in his bungalow, musing over the mystery of race—"How did it come about in Nature that one man's skin was black, another's white, another's red, another's yellow? How did it happen that a Chinaman would be a Chinaman for a thousand generations never mind where he lived?"—the next, in a scenario that could have been ripped out of the pages of one of Whitley Strieber's books about alien abductions, from the autobiography of Saint Teresa, or for that matter from a clinician's account of a hypnagogic hallucination, he was "plunging down a mystic depth of cool blue space not unlike the bottomless sinking sensation that attends the taking of ether for anesthetic."

At first he thought he was dying. When he came to, he was lying nude on a white marble pallet. Blinking against the "queer opal light," he saw two "kindly faced young men in white uniforms" standing over him. When he asked them where he was, they exchanged good-humored glances. " 'Don't try to see everything *in the first seven minutes!'* was all the answer they offered." They brought him to a "roofed-in Roman garden, about fifteen feet high and thirty feet square." Off to one side, a columned passageway led off into the interminable distance. After he bathed in a pool of immaculate water, he sat on a bench while one of the kindly faced men—whom he now realized was a soldier he'd known, a Southerner of good family who'd been killed in World War I—began to answer his questions.

First of all, his old friend told him, this wasn't his first visit to this strange place. "You left this plane or condition to go down into earth-life and function as the person you know yourself to be. . . . Everyone has lived before—hundreds of times before. People still in earth-life will live hundreds of times again—as they may have need of the mortal experiences."

Then he solved the enigma of race. It was all about Karma:

> You wondered what races were. I'll tell you what they are. They're great classifications of humanity epitomizing gradations of spiritual development, starting with the black man and proceeding upward in cycles to the white. Each race is an earthly classroom to which people go to get certain lessons in specific things. When they've acquired the experiences from those lessons they come back into this condition and rest, absorbing the increment from those experiences into their characters and thus "developing."[27]

Pelley stayed in contact with his dead friend for the rest of his life. Though he would write millions more words, he was now a man with a mission.

By 1930, he was living in Asheville, North Carolina, writing religious tracts and political pamphlets and books, teaching correspondence courses through his unaccredited Galahad College, and building a national religious movement he called the League for the Liberation, which mixed themes from his father's fire-and-brimstone Christianity and the New Thought and Ascended Master Theosophy that he'd discovered on his own. In 1933, Hitler's rise to power "supplied the key that unlocked a staggering sequence in my own progression," Pelley later wrote.[28] "When a certain young house painter comes to the head of [the German state] . . . you take that as your time symbol for bringing the work of the Christ Militia into the open!"[29]

The League for the Liberation became the Silver Legion, a religio-political crusade premised completely on anti-Semitism, and that was specifically organized to be the nucleus of a new Christ Commonwealth. The Luciferian Jews, an oriental race with "Dark Souls," created Communism, Pelley believed. Moses was the "Stalin of his day"; Jesus wasn't Jewish but a Galilean descended from immigrant Gauls.

Pelley's new America would be divided into nine administrative divisions, including Departments of Public Enlightenment, Patriotic

Probity, Crime Erasement, and Public Morals and Mercy. Like Hitler's Brownshirts, the Silver Legion's members wore uniforms, which he sold them for $6—a cap, blue corduroy pants, a tie with a membership number stamped on it, and a silver shirt with a red *L* stitched onto the breast, signifying love, loyalty, and liberation. Members were required to familiarize themselves with a number of foundational texts, including *The Protocols of the Elders of Zion* and Pelley's own *No More Hunger,* which laid out the debt-free monetary system that he'd largely derived from Frederick Soddy's 1926 book, *Wealth, Virtual Wealth, and Debt: The Solution of the Economic Paradox.* Pelley claimed that his vision was completely compatible with the Constitution, with Christian ideals of social justice, and with patriotism.

The Silver Shirts numbered only about fifteen thousand at their peak (though some accounts claim there were as many as a hundred thousand of them); Pelley's magazine *Liberation* had about fifty thousand subscribers. When he ran for president as the candidate of his own Christian Party in 1936, he only got on the ballot in Washington State, where he collected a mere sixteen hundred votes. Though some Silver Shirts did stockpile arms and their rhetoric and activities could be disturbingly militant (in Salt Lake City in 1933, for example, Silver Shirts kidnapped and beat a suspected Communist; the San Diego Silver Legion, led by Willard W. Kemp, "was an elite, clandestine, military order divided into squads of five men apiece, each of whom knew only his leader and the other three men in his group . . . Kemp always carried a Springfield rifle and four fully loaded ammunition belts"[30]), they never posed a significant threat to public safety. But as Scott Beekman wrote in *William Dudley Pelley: A Life in Right-Wing Extremism and the Occult,* there were as many as one hundred other Fascist or proto-Fascist groups operating in the United States alongside them. The year 1933 saw "the creation not just of the Silver Shirts but also the White, Blue, and Khaki Shirts and the refocusing of older groups such as the Anglo-Saxon Federation, the Industrial Defense Association of Edward Hunter, and Winrod's Christian Defenders."

Pelley . . . cultivated relationships with, among others, C. Leon de Aryan of *The Broom* magazine, American White Guard leader and convicted forger Henry D. Allen, the "Wichita Fuehrer" Gerald

Winrod, Reverend Gerald L. K. Smith, Colonel Edward Emerson, Harry Jung, James True (the inventor of the patented "kike killer" billy club), Royal Scott Gulden of the Order of '76, and various Bund leaders.... Usually these friendships ended either when Pelley tried to "absorb" their organizations into his own or when his esoteric religious beliefs became too much for his compatriots to stomach.[31]

In Detroit, the Black Legion, a paramilitary revenant of the KKK, "provided fellowship and community for Americans who lacked character references for the Elks and Odd Fellows," Geoffrey S. Smith noted in his book *To Save a Nation: American "Extremism," the New Deal, and the Coming of World War II.*

Neophytes seeking entrance first stood before a loaded revolver aimed at their heart and promised "to be torn from limb to limb and scattered to the carrion" if they betrayed the organization's existence. Then, according to ritual, they were asked if they believed in a Supreme Being and if they could shoot, ride, drink, and lie. If accepted, new members would swear to uphold "Americanism, Protestantism, and womanhood," purchase a dark robe for seven dollars, and commence the good fight against Jews, Negroes, aliens, Catholics, and Communists.[32]

Malcolm X believed that his father, Earl Little, was murdered by members of the Black Legion.

In 1939, when Pelley was about to be arrested for violating the terms of a suspended sentence he'd received in 1935 for fraud, the Asheville, North Carolina, police circulated a wanted poster to law enforcement agencies throughout the forty-eight states. Its description of Pelley reads like a call to central casting for a character actor to play a crazed mentalist:

Wanted: William Dudley Pelley. Age, approximately fifty years; height, five feet, seven inches; weight, 130 pounds; has black hair mixed with gray; heavy eyebrows; wears mustache and a Vandyke; has dark gray eyes, very penetrating; has straight Roman nose; wears nose glasses; dresses neatly; distinguished looking; good talker; highly educated; interested in psychic research.[33]

Smith argues that antiwar activists like Pelley and the jackbooted Bundist Fritz Kuhn did such damage to the reputation of the isolationist movement that they might as well have been Roosevelt's allies. Their pro-Nazi activities "brought into clearer focus the moral issue that loomed beneath the surface of the growing debate on American foreign policy."

> Many citizens who might otherwise have remained convinced that the war in Europe could not possibly affect the country's safety saw firsthand the obscenity of secular anti-Semitism as patterned on the Nazi model. In America Jews were guaranteed religious and civil liberty, and Pelley's assertion that their lives were worthless—a suggestion later carried to a horrible extreme in Germany—strengthened American resolve to aid England and France in resisting totalitarian aggression.[34]

Pelley was without a doubt a first-class crackpot, but his ideas continue to circulate in the conspiracist fringe and especially within the white power movement today. Google "Benjamin Franklin" and "Jew" and you will read about Franklin's efforts to ban Jews from the American Republic; Google "Rothschild" and "Abraham Lincoln" and you will learn that the sixteenth president was killed by international Jewry (I mentioned both of these canards in the first chapter of this book). A bathetic post on the white power Web site Stormfront eulogizes Pelley as a man who was tormented by the thought of the "kosher one-world promised by Karl Marx" but whose "living martyrdom in the belly of the Jew beast won him a place of honor in the hearts of fellow fighters who came after him. He did not fail, as he thought, any more than a brave soldier who does his best when captured by the enemy fails."[35]

One somehow suspects that Pelley never for a moment believed that he had failed—he had too highly developed a sense of self-importance to have permitted himself any such doubts. In a book he published in 1955, he revealed that he'd received a clairaudient communication in 1929 that detailed all that would happen in the world over the next thirty years: the stock market crash, Hitler's rise and fall, and his own ordeal. "The course of Bolshevism was depicted, my own battle with its political infiltrations in this country, and the penal sentence I must pay for striving to counteract its evil designs on our own Christian Republic." But, in words that echo Brigham Young's famous prophecy about the Constitution hanging by a thread, he foresaw his ultimate vindication as well:

> In the denouement of national political and economic affairs in the closing years of my life, when Constitutionalism was due to hang by the frailest of threads, something I wrote or uttered was suddenly to be picked up by the nation's press—I should go to bed with the cares of the nation on my shoulders, to arouse in the morning and discover the country behind me to a man. And it would be the recommendations I made in that period of influence that should lead our beloved America up and out of the lowlands of subversion and despair.[36]

Charles Lindbergh didn't know Pelley personally, but when Pelley was put on trial for sedition in 1942, his defense team called Lindbergh as a character witness because, as the prosecutor Oscar R. Ewing recalled in an oral history interview in 1969, Lindbergh "had been making speeches along the same line as Pelley's articles in his magazines."

> Lindbergh, as you may recall, was opposed to our getting into the war. He felt that the German Air Force was so strong that they would crush us right away. Well, the fact that Lindbergh had been subpoenaed as a witness by the defense caused a lot of national interest in the case. As it turned out, I objected to most of the defense counsel's questions and the Judge sustained my objections. Such questions were obviously irrelevant. When I refused to cross-examine, nothing that Lindbergh had said helped the defense or hurt the prosecution.[37]

The little that Lindbergh did say (he was on the stand for less than twenty minutes) was strictly pro forma, although he did allow that "the majority of the people of this country were opposed to getting into war—that is, before we were attacked."[38]

Lindbergh's popularity was at its nadir in 1942; even so, it was painful for many to see the once-golden hero brought down to the same level as the altogether odious Pelley; the awkwardness of his plight earned him a small share of sympathy. Lindbergh's biographer A. Scott Berg quotes an editorial from *The Roanoke Times:*

> The effort of Pelley's counsel to drag Lindbergh into the proceedings was unfair to Lindbergh and does not seem to have helped their client in the least. We have taken the view all along that Lindbergh was a misguided and mistaken young man, but we have never had the slightest reason to doubt [his] patriotism or to feel that he would for one moment put any other country's interests above that of his own country.[39]

But with the benefit of hindsight, it's hard not to concede that the famous aviator had more in common with Pelley than he—or his loyal supporters—might have cared to admit.

Not that Lindbergh was a traitor, a would-be führer (as Harold Ickes unfairly called him in 1939—and as the novelist Philip Roth witheringly characterized him in his novel *The Plot Against America*), or a programmatic anti-Semite. Lindbergh showed tremendous courage and commitment in his service during World War II; as media shy as he was, there can be no doubt that he acted out of principle when he lent his celebrity to the America First movement. There was the not inconsiderable matter of filial loyalty, too. Lindbergh's father had been a U.S. congressman from Minnesota's Sixth Congressional District. An agrarian radical, a longtime critic of the banking interests, and a vociferous opponent of the Federal Reserve, the senior Lindbergh had ruined his political career when he voted against America's entry into World War I. In his book *Why Is Your Country at War?* he acknowledged that "trespass upon our rights on the high seas makes our cause just" but insisted that it had not been "wise to enter the war" or even necessary. He accused a conspiratorial elite of forcing the enemy's hand:

> I believe the problem could have been settled without war or sacrifice of national honor. . . . I believe that I have proved that a certain "inner circle," without official authority and for selfish purposes, adroitly maneuvered things to bring about conditions that would

make it practically certain that some of the belligerents would violate our international rights and bring us to war with them.[40]

The younger Lindbergh believed that history was repeating itself
in the 1930s. His first "Neutrality Talk," broadcast on September
15, 1939, was delivered as FDR was more and more clearly signaling
his intention to enter World War II on England's side. Lindbergh had
seen the German war machine close-up during his many visits to the
country as an honored guest of the Luftwaffe; he genuinely believed
that if the United States entered the war "fighting for Democracy
abroad, we may end by losing it at home." Americans mustn't be
"misguided by this foreign propaganda to the effect that our frontiers
lie in Europe . . . An ocean is a formidable barrier," he urged. The
stakes just weren't that high: it wasn't as if Hitler posed an existential
threat to Western civilization, such as Genghis Khan had to medieval
Europe or Xerxes to classical Greece. "This is not a question of band-
ing together to defend the white race against foreign invasion," he
added. "This is simply one more of those age-old struggles within our
family of nations—a quarrel arising from the errors of the last war."[41]

At an America First rally in Des Moines, Iowa (the date, for collectors of spooky coincidences, was September 11, 1941—the same
day ground was broken for the Pentagon), Lindbergh uttered out loud
for the first time what one of today's journalists might have coyly
called the *J* word. "The three most important groups who have been
pressing this country toward war are the British, the Jewish and the
Roosevelt administration," he said.

> It is not difficult to understand why Jewish people desire the over-
> throw of Nazi Germany. The persecution they suffered in Germany
> would be sufficient to make bitter enemies of any race.
>
> No person with a sense of the dignity of mankind can condone
> the persecution of the Jewish race in Germany. But no person of
> honesty and vision can look on their pro-war policy here today
> without seeing the dangers involved in such a policy both for us
> and for them. Instead of agitating for war, the Jewish groups in this
> country should be opposing it in every possible way for they will be
> among the first to feel its consequences.
>
> Tolerance is a virtue that depends upon peace and strength.

History shows that it cannot survive war and devastations. A few far-sighted Jewish people realize this and stand opposed to intervention. But the majority still do not.

Their greatest danger to this country lies in their large ownership and influence in our motion pictures, our press, our radio and our government. . . . We cannot blame them for looking out for what they believe to be their own interests, but we also must look out for ours. We cannot allow the natural passions and prejudices of other peoples to lead our country to destruction.[42]

In his biography *Lindbergh*, A. Scott Berg relates that upon reading the draft of her husband's speech, Anne Morrow Lindbergh was thrown into a "black gloom." "The ugly cry of anti-Semitism will be joyfully pounced upon and waved about," she confided to her diary. It's "so much simpler to brand someone with a bad label than to take the trouble to read what he says."[43] Lindbergh countered that the point was not what the effect would be on him but whether or not what he said was true.

Though his longtime friend Harry Guggenheim maintained that "Slim has never had the slightest anti-Semitic feeling,"[44] and Lindbergh himself was convinced that he'd spoken with both compassion and circumspection, his wife's forebodings were swiftly confirmed. "It seems," the disappointed Lindbergh wrote in his own diary on September 15, "that almost any problem can be discussed in America except the Jewish problem. The very mention of the word 'Jew' is cause for a storm."[45] Justly or unjustly, his name would forever after be linked with the word "anti-Semitism." Though Berg defends Lindbergh against the charge, he notes that when he examined Lindbergh's original diaries, he found passages that had been deleted from their published versions. "As with the later publication of Anne's diaries," he relates, "the bulk of these omissions centered on one subject: the Jews."

"None of the cuts contains any overt denigrations of Jews," Berg adds. "In fact most of the references express Lindbergh's affinity and admiration for them." But the one example he quotes hardly buttresses his case. On April 10, 1939, when Lindbergh was sailing home from Europe, his ship encountered rough seas. "The steward tells me that most of the Jewish passengers are sick," Lindbergh wrote.

Imagine the United States taking these Jews in addition to those we already have. There are too many in places like New York already. A few Jews add strength and character to a country, but too many create chaos. And we are getting too many. This present immigration will have its reaction.[46]

Compare Lindbergh's sentiments, if you would, with this crude Bundist ditty, quoted in Geoffrey S. Smith's *To Save a Nation:*

Oh Abie sails over the ocean;
Und Izzy sails over the sea
So the shrine of each patriot's devotion
Has to take in the damned refugee!

Go back, go back!
Back where you came from across the sea!
Go back, go back!
And leave my own country to me.

On each ocean liner they're coming
By steerage and cabin and "first"!
Great Britain and France get the best ones
And send Uncle Sammy the worst![47]

Lindbergh was hardly a gutter anti-Semite like Pelley or Gerald L. K. Smith or the Bund's Fritz Kuhn; neither, for all that he admired Germany's "proud and virile" spirit, was he a Fascist. He and the vast majority of his fellow America Firsters were model citizens. Yale University Law School's America First Committee included such future luminaries as Gerald Ford and Potter Stewart. Herbert Hoover, Alice Roosevelt Longworth, Chester Bowles, and Kingman Brewster were all prominent isolationists as well. Yet Lindbergh clearly did regard America's Jews as aliens—admirable in many ways, no doubt, but not really citizens, no matter what their legal status might have been. He believed that they were here on sufferance and that their status would change for the worse if the United States was defeated by Hitler—an outcome that he seemed to regard as inevitable. The prospect of a solidly Fascist Europe, an intolerable horror for the more farsighted FDR, was one that Lindbergh could contemplate with apparent equanimity.

Though Lindbergh didn't consort with Pelley and his extremist peers, wrote Geoffrey S. Smith, "he did nothing to repudiate them either. And in the long run it was this omission that proved important." Absent any condemnation from Lindbergh, Smith continues, the American Fascists hastened to attach themselves to his coattails.

> Lauded by *Social Justice*, Lindbergh was also named to Pelley's "patriotic honor roll." The vice-president of the German-American Bund, meanwhile, August Klapprott, agreed with a lesser functionary, Hermann Schwarzmann, in hoping that the former flying ace would become "*Führer* of our great political party"; the *Free American* commended him for giving the American people "a douche of good, American common sense"; and the *Christian Front News* supported his battle against vast armies of the night, composed of "war mongers, political parasites, financial shylocks, and munitions moguls." Every countersubversive, it seemed, was climbing aboard the Lindbergh bandwagon, and further support was also lent by Park Avenue fascist John B. Snow, Boris Brasol, and Count Anastase Vonsiatsky. In Berlin, understandably, the official word praised Lindbergh as "the most potent enemy" of American Jews.[48]

In the fall of 2010, James P. Duffy published a curious book called *Lindbergh vs. Roosevelt: The Rivalry That Divided America*. Duffy set out to do much the same thing that I have been doing in these pages—to show how the climate of political hatred and vilification that we are experiencing today in Obama's America is nothing new; that there were parallels back in the days of the New Deal and World War II. Except that Duffy sees a mirror version of the world that I do. In his telling, Lindbergh was the victim of a "venomous smear campaign by the White House and the president's supporters"; he was unfairly demonized "for simply taking an opposing position." With Obama's election, in Duffy's view, an "elitist" returned to the White House "who has filled his administration with other elitists and his favorite 'experts.' This president doesn't want to change Washington but America itself." When "hundreds of thousands united in the grassroots tea party movement" to resist him, the "name-calling and demonizing began."

> People who protested Obama's policies were "racists," "Nazis," and "unpatriotic." Speaker of the House Nancy Pelosi called tea parties an "Astroturf" operation, implying its adherents were shills being organized and manipulated by some higher authority. Meanwhile, other critics made the opposite charge—that tea partiers were an unruly, violence-prone mob.
>
> A special dose of malice was reserved for former governor and vice presidential candidate Sarah Palin, radio and TV host Glenn Beck, and talk radio king Rush Limbaugh. . . . For me, it was Lindbergh's fate playing out again, but with different victims. He had dared to speak out against the policies of a president the Left revered, and he was maligned in much the same way as Obama's opponents are today.[49]

Duffy's overall historical narrative—about how Lindbergh and Roosevelt first clashed in 1934 over the administration's ill-considered decision to cancel its contracts with private airmail carriers and turn the job over to the inadequately equipped, ill-trained pilots of the U.S. Army Air Corps (costing the fledgling airlines millions in profits and a dozen army pilots their lives), and then again five years later over the much larger issue of lend-lease and the war—is generally factual. Roosevelt clearly did detest Lindbergh. "We will get that fair-haired boy," he purportedly told his press secretary in 1934, when Lindbergh sent a telegram of protest simultaneously to the White House and the media, words that his budget director Lewis Douglas later said made him "shudder" with the "brutal unscrupulousness of it."[50] At a press conference in 1941, FDR pointedly compared Lindbergh to Clement L. Vallandigham, a former congressman who was imprisoned and then expelled to Confederate territory during the Civil War because of his Copperhead activities.

Roosevelt played rough; there can be no question about that. For all of his gentility and charm, his politics were as ruthless as those of any big-city machine boss. Even progressives justly accused FDR of Caesarism; he overreached his constitutional powers on more than one occasion, and he made promises on the campaign trail in 1940 that he surely knew he couldn't keep—"While I am talking to you mothers and fathers, I give you one more assurance. I have said this before, but I shall say it again and again and again: Your boys are not going to be sent into any foreign wars." For as long as FDR needed Stalin, he measured him against a different human rights standard than he did Hitler and turned a blind eye on his equally heinous crimes.

But Duffy implies that FDR's attacks on Lindbergh were not only waspish and hurtful but altogether gratuitous, that Lindbergh had done nothing to provoke them, and that Lindbergh's "downfall" in the public's eyes was due entirely to the lies that were told about him, not to anything that he had done or said on his own account.

Duffy spends a whole chapter documenting examples of FDR's, his mother's, and his half brother's casual anti-Semitism and of Roosevelt's "expedient" attitude toward the Holocaust, despite the pleas of Henry Morgenthau and other prominent Jews for him to do more. Why do Jews grant so much credit to a president who supported quotas for Jewish students at Harvard and allowed the *St. Louis* to sail back to Europe with its doomed passengers, Duffy asks, and yet still tar Lindbergh—"who in the 45 years I lived with him," his wife told Herbert Mitgang, "I never heard . . . make a remark against Jews, not a crack or a joke"—as a Nazi Jew baiter? "The Roosevelt smear campaign," Duffy concludes, "destroyed Lindbergh's reputation as an American patriot and even as a decent human being. Today, when we speak of the politics of personal destruction, we should consider the interventionists' attacks on Charles Lindbergh as Exhibit A."[51]

But if Lindbergh was right about the airmail contracts in 1934, he was on the wrong side of history where World War II was concerned. He believed that England was doomed; he doubted that the United States could prevail against the Axis; and he rather hoped that the United States and the Third Reich could work out a modus vivendi. Though he didn't make cracks about Izzy und Abie in front of his wife (one suspects that Lindbergh wasn't exactly a font of jests anywhere else either) and he claimed to be appalled by the Nuremberg Laws, he seemingly didn't lose too much sleep over what the likely fate of Europe's Jews would be—not to mention Romanies, Slavs, homosexuals, Jehovah's Witnesses, and mentally retarded—if Hitler had been given free rein to complete the agenda he set in *Mein Kampf*. The stakes were incredibly high, high enough in Roosevelt's estimation to justify secret negotiations and disingenuous political sloganeering, high enough to justify a very high level of name-calling against Hitler's witting or unwitting enablers.

"In the end," Duffy declares, "the question we must ask is this: Why Lindbergh? Why does the liberal-left in this country continue relentlessly attacking him long after his death in 1974? The clear answer is that he is condemned because he dared to speak out, not once, but twice, against a liberal icon, Franklin D. Roosevelt." And then Duffy brings up the Tea Party again—and takes writers like me to task.

> Like Lindbergh, the tea partiers make an argument that deserves to be discussed on its own merits. But it is difficult for them to make their case when they constantly have to defend themselves from spurious allegations of racism. Those who are orchestrating this campaign know very well that an easy way to kill a message is to ignore it and discredit the messenger. After all, it worked against Charles Lindbergh.[52]

Far be it from me to offer Duffy advice about the craft of writing revisionist histories, but I submit that in likening the Tea Party to America First, he is not exactly covering it with glory. And his comparisons of Obama to FDR aren't likely to bring his fellow partisans much comfort either. Roosevelt, after all, was reelected three times. Amusingly enough, back in 2005, when President George W. Bush was being accused of having lied the nation into war in Iraq, Jonah Goldberg of *Liberal Fascism* fame wrote a column in the *Los Angeles Times* under the headline "A Lie for a Just Cause." "The evidence that FDR lied," he said, "is far greater than the evidence that Bush did."

> Does this make FDR a bad president? No. While I have my problems with FDR, most historians are right to be forgiving of deceit in a just cause. World War II needed to be fought, and FDR saw this sooner than others.
>
> Even the most cursory reading of any presidential biography will tell you that statesmanship requires occasional duplicity. . . . This isn't to say that the public's trust should be breached lightly, but

there are other competing goods involved in any complex situation. . . . If Bush succeeds . . . the painful irony for Bush's critics is that he will go down in history as a great president, even if he lied, while they will take their paranoia to their graves.[53]

But as Lindbergh himself might have observed, with a name like Goldberg you'd hardly expect him to say anything else.

Duffy's solicitude for "victims" of liberal hatred such as Lindbergh in the past, and Glenn Beck, Rush Limbaugh, and Sarah Palin in the present, seems oddly misplaced. Surely politics—especially its insurgent varieties—is no field for the fainthearted. Beck and Limbaugh are professional provocateurs; both of them can give as good as they get. Palin is a self-described Pit Bull with Lipstick, a Mama Grizzly, and a barracuda whose slogan is "don't retreat—RELOAD!" Or perhaps not—the evidence seems to suggest that all of their feelings are easily bruised.

In January 2011, a twenty-two-year-old man brought a legally purchased semiautomatic pistol to a "Congress on Your Corner" event at a shopping mall in Tucson, where, in a matter of seconds, he killed six people and wounded a dozen others, including Representative Gabrielle Giffords, who was shot through the head. Among the dead were a minister, a federal judge, and a nine-year-old girl (who, for collectors of coincidences, was born on September 11, 2001). As it happened, back in March 2010, Sarah Palin had targeted Giffords's and other vulnerable Democrats' districts and posted the map on her Facebook page. "We'll aim for these races and many others," she wrote. "This is just the first salvo in a fight to elect people across the nation who will bring common sense to Washington."[54] Giffords expressed her alarm on March 25, 2010, during an appearance on MSNBC's *Daily Rundown*. "We're on Sarah Palin's targeted list," she said. "But the thing is that the way that she has it depicted has the crosshairs of a gunsight over our district. When people do that . . . they've got to realize there's consequences to that action."[55]

Within hours of the shooting, Markos Moulitsas of the liberal Web site Daily Kos had tweeted, "Mission accomplished, Sarah Palin"; other left-leaning commentators piled on as well.[56] "We don't have proof yet that this was political," *The New York Times*'s Paul Krugman blogged, "but the odds are that it was . . . and for those wondering why a Blue Dog Democrat, the kind Republicans might be able to work with, might be a target, the answer is that she's a Democrat who survived what was otherwise a GOP sweep in Arizona, precisely because the Republicans nominated a Tea Party activist. (Her father says that 'the whole tea party' was her enemy.)"[57] That evening, the Pima County sheriff, Clarence Dupnik, who had made national headlines when he refused to enforce the profiling provisions of SB 1070, Arizona's notorious anti-illegal immigration law,[58] gave a press conference in which he called his state a "mecca for prejudice" and went on to assign some of the blame for the shooting to "the vitriolic rhetoric that we hear day in and day out from people in the radio business and some people in the TV business."[59] A few days later, he singled out Rush Limbaugh by name as one of the worst offenders. "In my judgment he is irresponsible," he said. He "uses partial information, sometimes wrong information. . . . [He] attacks people, angers them against government, angers them against elected officials and that kind of behavior in my opinion is not without consequences."[60]

But what *were* the shooter's politics? It's hard to say. Jared Lee Loughner had posted a string of YouTube videos that left little doubt that he was mentally disturbed; they also suggested that he was familiar with some of the paranoid memes that one encounters in the writings of the right-wing Patriot movement (or to be fair, at ecumenical clearinghouses for conspiracy theory like Alex Jones's radio show and Web site and the movie *Zeitgeist*). Loughner spoke of "currency that's not backed by gold and silver" and that's illegal under the Constitution; some of his allusions suggested that he was familiar with the far-out theories of David Wynn Miller, in which the government uses grammar to "enslave" people, and even of the "phantom time hypothesis" proposed by Heribert Illig, who maintains that three hundred years of the Middle Ages never occurred ("The date is also wrong," Loughner muttered in one of his videos, "it's impossible for it to be that date, it's mind control"[61]). Or maybe it was just that his clinical condition predisposed him to share some of those writers' obsessions. *Mein Kampf* appeared on a list of his favorite books, but so did *The Communist Manifesto*, *Animal Farm*, and *The Wizard of Oz*.

The push back from the Right was, well, vitriolic. Not long after Markos Moulitsas sent out his vindictive tweet, Pamela Geller of

Atlas Shrugs (who would later take tremendous issue with the idea that her and her counter-jihadist colleagues' rhetoric had inflamed Norway's Anders Breivik) seized on a Twitter post from a "high school pal" of Loughner's who described him as "left wing, quite liberal." "I strongly recommend that left wing defamers and smear merchants tamp down their evil rhetoric and false accusations," she began.

> Left wing politicians blaming the tea party (before the gunman was named), left wing hate sites blaming Sarah and Rush et al for one of their murderous own. It's always one of their own.
>
> They count on the right to do what is proper and decent and maintain a respectful silence (which we always do) while they foam at the mouth with conspiracy theories and outrageous accusations. They expect us to cede them the field, so that by the time we get around to correcting the record, the lies, and the smears—the narrative—is already fixed in America's psyche. Those days are over. This slaughterer was a liberal. This is what they teach, this is the poisonous fruit of their indoctrination. Clearly, Loughner is sick, mentally ill—but suckling at the lefty teat is deadly poison for the soul.[62]

It's always one of their own. The turnabout continued as Rush Limbaugh took to the airwaves and told his listeners that Sheriff Dupnik was "a fool" and that Jared Lee Loughner enjoyed the full support of the Democratic Party:

> The Democrat party is attempting to find anybody but him to blame. [Loughner] knows if he plays his cards right, he's just a victim. He's the latest in a never-ending parade of victims brought about by the unfairness of America, the bigotry, racism, sexism, homophobia of America, the mean-spiritedness of America . . . he understands he's got a political party doing everything it can, plus a local sheriff doing everything that they can to make sure he's not convicted of murder.[63]

Glenn Beck commiserated with Sarah Palin via an e-mail that he shared with his TV viewers, in which he urged her to "look into protection for her family" because "an attempt on you could bring the republic down."[64]

A few days later Sarah Palin upstaged the president's scheduled address to the nation with a quasi-presidential video of her own that she posted on her Facebook page. Seated before a fireplace and an American flag, she spoke of her sympathy for the innocent victims of the tragedy and of her steadfast faith in "our exceptional nation . . . a light to the rest of the world." But mostly, as they say, it was all about her. "I've spent the past few days reflecting on what happened and praying for guidance," she said.

> I listened at first puzzled, then with concern, and now with sadness, to the irresponsible statements from people attempting to apportion blame for this terrible event. . . . Acts of monstrous criminality stand on their own. They begin and end with the criminals who commit them, not collectively with all the citizens of a state, not with those who listen to talk radio, not with maps of swing districts used by both sides of the aisle, not with law-abiding citizens who respectfully exercise their First Amendment rights at campaign rallies. . . . Especially within hours of a tragedy unfolding, journalists and pundits should not manufacture a blood libel that serves only to incite the very hatred and violence they purport to condemn. That is reprehensible.[65]

Palin wasn't the first to use the highly charged term "blood libel" in that way; the conservative pundit and blogger Glenn Reynolds had invoked it in *The Wall Street Journal* a few days earlier. "So as the usual talking heads begin their 'have you no decency?' routine aimed at talk radio and Republican politicians," he'd written, "perhaps we should turn the question around. Where is the decency in blood libel?"[66] But coming from as divisive a figure as Sarah Palin, and with the added irony that Representative Giffords is Jewish, it ignited a firestorm. "The term 'blood libel' is not a synonym for 'false accusation,'" Simon Greer, president of Jewish Funds for Justice, expostulated.

> It refers to a specific falsehood perpetuated by Christians about Jews for centuries, a falsehood that motivated a good deal of anti-

Jewish violence and discrimination. Unless someone has been accusing Ms. Palin of killing Christian babies and making matzoh from their blood, her use of the term is totally out of line.[67]

There were many more condemnatory editorials, including one or two from Jewish neoconservatives who intimated that maybe Sarah Palin wasn't hewn from presidential timber after all. "Shows her inflam. tendency=critics pt. she's not serious, cert. not pres. - more G.Beck than Reagan,"[68] tweeted *The Washington Post*'s Jennifer Rubin, who had analyzed Jewish antipathy to Sarah Palin at length in *Commentary* in January 2010.[69] As the days went by, an equal number of op-eds popped up defending her. Revving up their search engines, right-leaning journalists, bloggers, and political operatives found innumerable examples of cases where Democratic politicians had also used "blood libel" in its nonsectarian sense—for example, in 2000, during the Florida recount, when a Florida Democrat characterized Republican accusations that Al Gore was preventing servicemen and servicewomen from having their votes counted as "almost a blood libel."[70]

They were right of course—overblown hyperbole is the coin of the realm in right- and left-wing politics alike—and about a week later the U.S. representative Steve Cohen, a Democrat from Tennessee, proved their point beyond a shadow of a doubt when he took to the House floor to defend Obama's health-care act, which the Republican-controlled Congress was about to vote to repeal. "They say it's a government takeover of health care," he fulminated to the C-SPAN cameras and a mostly empty chamber. "A big lie."

> Just like Goebbels, you say it enough, you repeat the lie, you repeat the lie, you repeat the lie, and eventually, people believe it, like "blood libel." That's the same kind of thing. The Germans said enough about the Jews and the people believed it and you had the Holocaust.

Fox News's Greta Van Susteren was outraged—not at Cohen's dubious analogy, or its trivialization of the Holocaust, but for Sarah Palin's sake. "They took Governor Sarah Palin to the woodshed for using the term 'blood libel,'" she sputtered. "Well, are those same people going to do the same to Congressman Cohen?"[71]

Other right-wing writers Googled for Democratic calls for violence, and they didn't come up dry. If Harry Reid's opponent Sharron Angle had intimated that citizens might resort to "Second Amendment remedies . . . if this Congress keeps going the way it is" during a radio interview with Lars Larson in January 2010, adding that "the first thing we need to do is take Harry Reid out,"[72] Barack Obama had boasted to a cheering throng at a political fund-raiser in Philadelphia in 2008 that he knew the proper way to deal with Republican attacks. "If they bring a knife to the fight, we bring a gun," he'd said. "Because from what I understand folks in Philly like a good brawl. I've seen Eagles fans."[73] How thuggish was that?

Michelle Malkin posted an eight-part "comprehensive, illustrated primer" on the "progressive climate of hate" on her Web site, including such exhibits as "Abort Sarah Palin" bumper stickers, "Kill Bush" T-shirts, an exhortation on a Web site for people opposed to Proposition 8 (the California Marriage Protection Act) to take to the streets and "burn their fucking churches to the ground and tax the tarred timbers," YouTube videos of unruly protesters at antiwar rallies and outside of AIG executives' homes, and a mug shot of a student who was arrested in Indianapolis for throwing an ice cream pie at William Kristol.[74] Clearly the Right hasn't cornered the market on incivility or hatred.

While words alone can't kill, and First Amendment protections of speech—even vile, offensive, and hurtful speech—are sacrosanct, there's no denying that words have extraordinary—and dangerous—power. Right wing or left wing or middle of the road, anyone who commands a national soapbox, whether as a citizen crusader like Charles Lindbergh, professional pundits like Jonah Goldberg and Paul Krugman, edgy political entertainers like Bill Maher and Ann Coulter, candidates for elected office like Sharron Angle and Barack Obama, or even tawdry merchandisers of inflammatory bumper stickers and T-shirts ("Abort Sarah Palin" no less than "Jesus Hates Obama"), needs to be mindful of what he or she says. Just as Lindbergh's notoriety as an isolationist made it more likely that his outstretched arm in photographs would be retrospectively misconstrued as a Hitler salute,* politicians and pundits who fetishize guns, allude repeatedly to Jefferson's tree of liberty, and reflexively accuse their opponents of treason need to either tamp down their rhetoric or grow thicker hides if they don't want to be accused of crying fire in a crowded theater when someone shoots a congressperson or parks a Ryder truck filled with fertilizer in front of a federal office building.

Dallas, Texas, had been no less of a mecca for hatred in November 1963 than Arizona was in 2011. The evening of the Tucson massacre, the blogger Andrew Sullivan† posted as his "Quote for the Day" a long passage from William Manchester's *Death of a President:*

> In that third year of the Kennedy Presidency a kind of fever lay over Dallas County. Mad things happened. Huge billboards screamed "Impeach Earl Warren." Jewish stores were smeared with crude swastikas. Fanatical young matrons swayed in public to the chant, "Stevenson's going to die—his heart will stop, stop, stop and he will burn, burn burn!" Radical Right polemics were distributed in public schools; Kennedy's name was booed in classrooms; junior executives were required to attend radical seminars. Dallas had become the mecca for medicine-show evangelists of the National Indignation Convention, the Christian Crusaders, the Minutemen, the John Birch and Patrick Henry societies.[75]

Manchester went on to describe the "Wanted for Treason" handbills that were circulated two days before Kennedy's arrival in Dallas. Beneath a presidential portrait was a list of his seven indictable offenses, many of which could be transferred, with only minor topical adjustments, to a Tea Party broadside today:

---

* In fact he was giving the so-called Bellamy salute, named after Francis Bellamy, the author of the Pledge of Allegiance. Americans didn't start putting their hands on their hearts when they saluted the flag until 1942, when they decided that they didn't want to look like Nazis. Interested readers can learn about this and more in Jeffrey Owen Jones and Peter Meyer's book *Pledge: A History of the Pledge of Allegiance.*

† Sullivan has some experience of his own in the verbal incontinence department—he has never quite lived down his own intemperance less than a week after 9/11, when he wrote in the London *Sunday Times* that "the middle part of the [United States]—the great red zone that voted for Bush—is clearly ready for war. The decadent Left in its enclaves on the coasts is not dead—and may well mount what amounts to a fifth column" ("Why Did It Have to Be a Perfect Morning?" London *Sunday Times,* September 16, 2001).

1. Betraying the Constitution (which he is sworn to uphold): He is turning the sovereignty of the U.S. over to the communist controlled United Nations. He is betraying our friends (Cuba, Katanga, Portugal) and befriending our enemies (Russia, Yugoslavia, Poland).

2. He has been WRONG on innumerable issues affecting the security of the U.S. (United Nations-Berlin wall-Missile removal-Cuba-Wheat deals-Test Ban Treaty, etc.).

3. He has been lax in enforcing Communist Registration laws.

4. He has given support and encouragement to the Communist inspired racial riots.

5. He has illegally invaded a sovereign State with federal troops.

6. He has consistently appointed Anti-Christians to Federal office . . . Upholds the Supreme Court in its Anti-Christian rulings . . . Aliens and known Communists abound in Federal offices.

7. He has been caught in fantastic LIES to the American people (including personal ones like his previous marriage and divorce).

Number seven referred to Kennedy's rumored secret marriage to the socialite Durie Malcolm. Back before JFK's myriad infidelities were widely known, that was what passed for personal scandal in Camelot.

Then there was the ominously black-bordered "Welcome Mr. Kennedy to Dallas" ad that ran in *The Dallas Morning News* on November 22. "Mr. Kennedy," it began, in a singularly inhospitable tone, "despite contentions on the part of your administration, the State Department, the Mayor of Dallas, the City Council, and members of your party, we free-thinking and America-thinking citizens of Dallas still have, through a Constitution largely ignored by you, the right to address our grievances, to question you, to disagree with you and to criticize you."[76]

"It's déjà vu all over again," Sam Kashner, the author of a *Vanity Fair* cover story on the making of *The Death of a President*, told an interviewer in 2009, when asked about the parallels between Kennedy's and Obama's America.

It's really scary out there. Remember, it was President Kennedy who told his wife . . . before leaving for Dallas, "We're heading into nut country." . . . The nuts are back. With Oswald, I think his political sympathies were as mixed-up as he was. . . . Regardless of where he was on the political spectrum, he was more mentally ill than politically adept. Still, it was that over-heated climate of hate that kind of helped hatch his crazy plan.[77]

Three years before the Tucson shooting, when George W. Bush still occupied the White House, Jeffrey Lord had seized on the same passage in Manchester's book to illustrate a strikingly different proposition—that it is liberals who are the standard-bearers of hatred today. "Any observer of the fever swamps of the American left this November week of 2007 will recognize instantly that the assessments and conclusions Manchester reached about the Dallas of 1963 are dead-on assessments of today's modern liberalism," he wrote in *The American Spectator*. "What better description of the atmosphere permeating today's Democratic Party than Manchester's of Dallas, a place that he charged was filled with 'something unrelated to conventional politics—a stridency, a disease of the spirit, a shrill, hysterical note suggestive of a deeply troubled society?' "[78]

Back in 1964, Ezra Taft Benson had summoned much the same aggrieved spirit as James P. Duffy did on Lindbergh's behalf, and as Pamela Geller, Sarah Palin, Michelle Malkin, and Rush Limbaugh did for themselves in the hours and days after the shooting in Tucson. "It was communism that sowed the seeds of treason in the mind of President Kennedy's accused assassin," wrote Benson. But "communist leaders spread the word that the slaying of the President must have been the work of American conservatives."

Moscow has conducted a three-year propaganda campaign to make American conservatives look like hysterical fanatics. It has called them "rightists," "extremists," and even "fascists." . . . Even after Oswald was captured and identified as a Moscow-associated communist, there were those who insisted that any who had opposed the President during his term of high office was guilty of that same "spirit of hate" as that which led to the President's death. This line of thinking was expressed by a number of prominent persons through the press, radio, and TV. To me it was incomprehensible.[79]

It's not exactly edifying, all this back-and-forth and name-calling, and for any parent of a teenager it's bound to have a painfully familiar ring: "I'm not shouting! *You're shouting!*"

One important takeaway is that extreme partisanship, especially when it comes to "culture war" issues like desegregation, guns, immigration, affirmative action, gay marriage, abortion, the right to die, evolution, school prayer, and even global warming, is not so much about ideas as it is about identity. On some chthonic, prerational level, many people—especially those who are already anxious about their shifting status—experience political criticism existentially, as a challenge to their very right to be the person they know themselves to be. From that perspective, there's nothing disingenuous about Benson's incomprehension. As Benson saw it, Kennedy had been bending over backward to indulge Negroes—a people that Benson's Latter-Day Saints still regarded as accursed and less than fully human "sons of Cain"; worse still, Kennedy and his minions were fellow travelers, if not Communists themselves. "America is big enough to make room for many different kinds of thinking," Benson allowed, "but many liberals have claimed to see virtues in socialism and communism which I, for one, have not been able to find."

> To promote their ideas, American liberals have become a highly organized, hardcore establishment in the United States and they have been excusing their appeasement and coddling of communism on the ground that they were being "tolerant," "broadminded," and "working for peace."[80]

And yet even after the likes of Oswald killed the president— *Oswald*, who had defected to the U.S.S.R., for God's sake, and who'd also tried to kill General Edwin Walker, a right-winger if there ever was one—the East Coast elites continued to cast aspersions on patriotic members of the John Birch Society. It was enough to turn anyone into a conspiracy theorist.

The palindromically named classicist and budding white nationalist Revilo P. Oliver, one of the original contributors to William F. Buckley's *National Review* and a member of the elite Council of the John Birch Society, was nowhere near as nonplussed by the backlash against conservatives in the wake of the Kennedy assassination as Benson was; he recognized the phenomenon for what it was: the carefully orchestrated, entirely intentional consequence of the event. A trained philologist and a research analyst at a cryptology unit of the Signal Corps during World War II, he well knew how to read between the lines. "Marxmanship in Dallas," the much-talked-about two-part article he contributed to the John Birch Society's publication *American Opinion*, cut to the heart of what really happened at Dealey Plaza.

In a nutshell, Oliver contended that Kennedy's assassination was a Communist plot that was foiled by the providential intervention of J. D. Tippit, the Dallas policeman who stopped Oswald on the street and was murdered for his trouble. Alas, JFK was not "sanctified by a bullet"; he was both a victim of the Communists and a Communist himself; his assassination was strictly a fratricidal affair. "So long as there are Americans," Oliver continued, throwing a bucket of cold water on the whole Camelot myth, Kennedy's "memory will be cherished with execration and loathing." The scant bit of comfort one can take from his killing, he wrote, is the knowledge that the conspiracy, as pervasive and powerful as it is, is not infallible.

Oliver listed three possible motives for Kennedy's assassination: (1) that he was about to "turn American" and had to be stopped ("For this comforting hypothesis," he said, "there is no evidence now known"); (2) "that the assassination was a result of one of the rifts that not infrequently occur within the management of the Communist Conspiracy, whose satraps sometimes liquidate one another without defecting from the Conspiracy, just as Persian satraps, such as Tissaphernes and Pharnabazus, made war on one another without revolting or intending to revolt against the King of Kings"; or (3) that "the Conspiracy ordered the assassination as part of systematic preparation for a domestic take-over. If so, the plan, of course, was to place the blame on the 'right-wing extremists' (if I may use the Bolshevik's code-word for informed and loyal Americans)."

> It is easy to see what could have happened, had everything gone smoothly. . . . There could have been a complete break-down of law and order. . . . What is more, the great nest of traitors in Washington could have begun a pseudo-legal reign of terror, for which the infamous "Sedition Trial" in Washington in 1944 was obvi-

ously a small-scale and premature pilot-study. In an atmosphere of hysteria, maintained by the anti-American television, radio, and press, all the leading American patriots could have been dragged in chains to Washington. . . . There could have been a national Saturnalia of *legalized* violence under cover of which the International Conspiracy could have gained a control of the whole nation.

Oliver is careful to use Jack Ruby's Jewish name, "Jakob Rubenstein," throughout his piece ("It may be significant that, when observed on the street, [Oswald] was walking directly toward the apartment of the Jakob Rubenstein (alias Jack Ruby) who later silenced him"); he does the same when he provides a list of other "rabid rats of Bolshevism" who turned on one another, noting that Zinoviev's real name was Apfelbaum, Kirov's Kostrikov, and Kamenev's Rosenfeld. Though Oliver doesn't say so in so many words, the Communist conspiracy is really the Jewish conspiracy; we are back in *The Protocols of the Elders of Zion* territory.

Oliver reserves special venom for the members of the Warren Commission, "an illegal and unconstitutional" board of inquiry that "was improvised with the obvious hope that it could be turned into a Soviet-style kangaroo court." He singles out Warren himself for special abuse—"so notorious as chief of the quasi-judicial gang engaged in subverting the Constitution of the United States that many thousands of the finest and most prominent American citizens have for two years been demanding with increasing insistence his impeachment and trial"—as well as T. Hale Boggs, "the loud-mouthed agitator who disgraces the State of Louisiana in Congress"; Allen Dulles, "one of the founders of the malodorous Council on Foreign Relations"; and John J. McCloy, "of the Council on Foreign Relations, the Ford Foundation, the World Brotherhood, and other mysteriously powerful organizations whose un-American or anti-American activities should have been investigated by Congress long ago."

McCloy is reputed to be the principal author of the present plan to disarm the United States and prepare it for occupation by Soviet troops and associated savages of the "United Nations," which he, as an assistant of Alger Hiss, helped to design and foist on the American people.[81]

Oliver's article "touched off the expected furor" at the University of Illinois, *Newsweek* reported at the time. A future Pulitzer Prize winner, then a student journalist, received what was likely his first mention in a national magazine:

> But while deploring the taste of Oliver's article, officials held that his teaching role on the campus was not affected. Student editor Roger Ebert wrote in the *Daily Illini:* "Only a strong and free society could permit Professor Oliver his own freedom." The hubbub hardly fazed the professor [who] blandly explained, "If you are a patriotic American, you must expect to meet all kinds of defamation, both open and snide."[82]

A few months after his article appeared, Oliver would be subpoenaed by that selfsame Warren Commission. He testified on September 9, 1964; the transcript includes an awkward colloquy about the "vignettes of various members of the commission" that appeared in his article. The assistant counsel Albert E. Jenner assured Oliver that "no member of the Commission has any hurt feelings whatsoever with respect to this article or any statement in it"; mostly they sought information about his sources.[83]

How, for example, did Oliver know that rehearsals for Kennedy's funeral were held a week before the assassination—a piece of circumstantial evidence that strongly suggested that forces within the government knew what was coming? He didn't; after the funeral, the *Clarion-Ledger* of Jackson, Mississippi, had run an interview with an army captain from the area who'd worked with the horses and who mentioned that at the time of the assassination, his unit "had just finished a funeral rehearsal because there was grave concern for President Hoover's health" (Hoover would die in the fall of 1964). Oliver also relied on articles in the *National Enquirer,* "America's Liveliest Newspaper,"* and especially on the research of the Staten Island–based anti-Red crusader Frank Capell, the publisher of the ultra-right-wing newsletter the *Herald of Freedom.* Capell's published books

---

* Though it had long since transformed itself into a sensation-mongering tabloid, the *National Enquirer* and its publisher had been indicted for sedition in 1942 for its pro-Fascist and isolationist editorials.

include *The Threat from Within, Treason Is the Reason,* and *Henry Kissinger, Soviet Agent;* his *Strange Death of Marilyn Monroe* would be the first book to connect Robert Kennedy and Marilyn Monroe, who he said was murdered by Communists.

Oliver's prose style weds high-flown erudition and Mencken-esque invective with gutter racism and blatant Fascism (a few years after "Marxmanship in Dallas" appeared, he would join William Luther Pierce in the neo-Nazi National Alliance); for all of his insistence that he was a true patriot, his writings epitomized what Richard Hofstadter dubbed "pseudo-conservatism"—a term he adopted from Theodor Adorno's *Authoritarian Personality* because it underlined the decidedly un-conservative character of the anti-Communist Far Right of the 1950s and early 1960s, its "serious and restless dissatisfaction with American life, traditions, and institutions," and its "profound if largely unconscious hatred of our society and its ways."[84]

Thomas Jefferson was "not a moron, and cannot have meant anything so absurd as is sometimes supposed" when he wrote the words "all men are created equal," Oliver explained in 1982. In his telling, Jefferson's ideas about democracy were proposed and designed for a racially homogeneous people; they should only be taken to mean that every *Englishman* is equal before the law. "If we wish to institute such a true democracy," Oliver concludes, "we shall first have to create the conditions in which it is possible."

> The proponents of democracy will have to begin by deporting, vaporizing, or otherwise disposing of the swarms of Jews, Congoids, Mongoloids, and mongrels that now infest our territory and are becoming ever more numerous and audacious in their unappeasable hatred of us. I cannot suggest offhand a convenient way of effecting that indispensable *epuration* of the population, but I am willing to believe that it could still be carried out.[85]

"Epuration" means "purification"; it is a rarely used word nowadays, whose strongest associations go back to the postwar purges of Fascists in France and Italy. "Vaporize" is a word that Oliver had used before.

In "Conspiracy or Degeneracy," the infamous speech that he delivered before the New England Rally for God, Family, and Country on

July 2, 1966 (in which, oddly enough, he took a strong stance *against* conspiracy theory), Oliver had proposed a thought experiment that proved the last straw for Robert Welch:

> The conspiracy that is destroying us, we are told, is a conspiracy of Communists or of Illuminati or of Jews. Now most of the authors who offer us one or another of those three identifications expound their view in a manner that is less than cogent. Most of them either overstate or oversimplify their case, and some of them, I am sorry to say, give the impression that they are no more intelligent than "Liberal intellectuals." Most of the writers on this subject are either so fascinated by their own discoveries or so anxious to convince a maximum number of readers that they imply that the conspiracy they identify is the root of all evil—that is if it were abolished, mankind—all mankind, mind you—would enter, instanter, on a Golden Age of peace and domestic tranquility and happiness. If only by some miracle all the Bolsheviks or all of the Illuminati or all the Jews were vaporized at dawn tomorrow, we should have nothing more to worry about. The trouble with that beatific vision, of course, is that every educated man knows that it just can't be so.[86]

"I do not in the least object to [the] implication that I am sadly deficient in veneration for the world-conquering Sheenies who have occupied and rule what was once a White Man's country," Oliver noted in "Contemporary Journalists," a 1985 essay in response to George Johnson's book *Architects of Fear: Conspiracy Theories and Paranoia in American Politics*, "but I do resent the libelous imputation that I adopted one of the simple-minded simplifications to which I specifically objected."[87]

7.

White Supremacy and Black Separatism—Exceptional Hatreds, Separate but Equal

Revilo Oliver taught in both the classics and the modern languages departments of the University of Illinois and claimed to be fluent in eleven languages. William F. Buckley, who had ended their friendship by at least the early 1960s, called him "without exception, the single most erudite man I have ever known."[1] And yet Oliver has been "erased from the history of the American right," as "Nesta Bevan"* wrote in *Taki's Magazine* in 2009.[2]

There's really no mystery as to why Oliver's memory has been allowed to fade. He despised Christianity almost as ardently as he did Judaism; he was openly contemptuous of democracy as well. He couldn't even be bothered to pay obeisance to the legend of Ronald Reagan. "The 'conservative movement,'" he wrote dyspeptically in 1989, "succeeded when the old ham actor was installed in the White House to consummate the bankruptcy of the United States while

---

* Surely a pseudonym, as Bevan is the maiden name of the famous conspiracy theorist Nesta Webster, who died in 1960.

taxing his serfs to give every holy family in the Holy Land $5000 every year, provide God's Own with the weapons they need to beat into submission to God's Law the wicked Palestinians . . . create a legal basis for Jewish terrorism in the United States, and import into this country hundreds of thousands of anthropoid pests, in preparation for Integration, when the occasionally troublesome White people will have been replaced by a fetid mass of half a billion coffee-colored mongrels with the minds of rats."[3]

Hateful doesn't even begin to describe Oliver's racialism, which is expressed in impolitic, frankly Hitlerian terms that would shock even many a hard-core segregationist. His reflexive use of epithets like "sheeny" and "nigger" alone put him beyond the pale. Fringe theorists have their political uses—particularly if they can make racism sound like an expression of patriotic principle, a higher form of freedom—but if Robert Welch was too far-out for William F. Buckley, who saw to it that Barry Goldwater "dissociated himself" from him (if not from the John Birch Society) when he mounted his run at the presidency in 1964, then Revilo P. Oliver was too far-out for Robert Welch, who sincerely deplored expressions of racial and religious prejudice, even if the themes that animated the John Birch Society—adamant support for states' rights on issues pertaining to segregation, *Protocols of the Elders of Zion*-esque conspiracy theories, accusations of treachery within the government—seemingly put him in the bigots' camp.

In our own day, there are indications that a critical mass of mainstream Republicans may be increasingly eager to dissociate themselves from Glenn Beck, whose speculations about the progressivist-Islamist nexus in the wake of the uprising against Hosni Mubarak in Egypt in February 2011 roused William Kristol to editorialize in *The Weekly Standard* that "hysteria is not a sign of health."

When Glenn Beck rants about the caliphate taking over the Middle East from Morocco to the Philippines, and lists (invents?) the connections between caliphate-promoters and the American left, he brings to mind no one so much as Robert Welch and the John Birch Society. He's marginalizing himself, just as his predecessors did back in the early 1960s.[4]

Less than two months after Kristol's piece ran, on April 6, 2011, Glenn Beck and Fox News jointly announced that he would cease to be an on-air Fox News personality when his contract expired at the end of the year, though his Mercury Radio Arts company would co-develop and otherwise collaborate with Fox on a variety of new programs. But that Beck might fade into the same twilight of obscurity that Father Coughlin did, however devoutly his longtime enemies on the left and his erstwhile friends on the right might both wish it, is a doubtful surmise. Beck was a big star on syndicated radio before he was hired by Fox, and, Fox personality or not, he has no intention of forswearing the spotlight. Beck "has managed to monetize virtually everything that comes out of his mouth," *Forbes* reported in April 2010.

He gets $13 million a year from print (books plus the ten-issue-a-year magazine *Fusion*). Radio brings in $10 million. Digital (including a newsletter, the ad-supported Glennbeck.com and merchandise) pulls in $4 million. Speaking and events are good for $3 million and television for $2 million.[5]

By adding still more products to the mix (The Blaze.com Web site and newsletter; the subscription-based GBTV network) and eliminating various middle men, Beck hopes to make even more money as a free agent. Still, Beck and his audience are as much a liability as an asset to the Republican Party. Having retaken the House in the 2010 midterms, and with their eyes firmly set on the Senate and the White House in 2012, they need to do more than stoke the passions of their angry base; they have to look like a plausible majority party to the rest of the country. Carrying the country to the brink of default, as they almost did in the summer of 2011 during the "debate" over the debt ceiling, was a dangerous exercise in brinksmanship that threatened to alienate the very investor class that used to be the most reliable Republican stalwarts. Nativism is a devastatingly effective way to rouse anger and resentment and fear, but as many politicians have learned to their grief, it can be a two-edged sword: immigrants and their children vote too.

———

Willis Carto was a right-wing media figure too, but he kept a much lower profile than Glenn Beck. A former salesman for Procter & Gamble and an ex–loan officer at the Household Finance Corporation, Carto lived a dual life for decades as a putatively mainstream proponent of conservative causes, which he supported through the Liberty Lobby, a Washington, D.C.–based pressure group, and an avid anti-Semite and white supremacist. His Institute for Historical Review was a think tank dedicated to Holocaust denial; he also published a long list of anti-Semitic and racist journals, newsletters, and magazines, including the Noontide Press and *The American Mercury*, which was founded by George Jean Nathan and H. L. Mencken in the 1920s but had begun its transmogrification into a racist hate sheet in the 1950s (one of its last owners, before Carto purchased it, was Gerald Winrod, the Jayhawk Nazi; George Lincoln Rockwell, the future founder of the American Nazi Party, was also associated with it for a while).

Back in 1960, when the Southland was plastered with "Impeach Earl Warren" billboards but the Cold War consensus still held so firmly that the vast majority of Americans had no idea how divided their country really was, Carto paid a visit to a prisoner in the San Francisco County Jail who had been arrested for passport violations. "Even though the man upon whom I was calling was locked in equality with petty thieves and criminals," Carto later related (in an essay that is widely reputed to have been at least partially ghostwritten by Revilo P. Oliver), "I knew that I was in the presence of a great force. . . . I could feel History standing aside me."

Carto's description of the forty-three-year-old Francis Parker Yockey, whose eyes were "dark, with a quick and knowing intelligence," and "bespoke great secrets and knowledge and such terrible sadness," is lushly romantic.[6] Reading it, one might well expect the secret Yockey bore in his burning breast to be something a bit more, I don't know, *spiritual* than his conviction of the innate superiority of the Aryan race. Yockey, Carto tells us, was a concert-quality amateur musician, a writer of genius, a gifted financier, and the possessor of "the precious gift of a sense of humor."[7] He graduated from Notre Dame Law School with honors in 1938 and, despite his objections to the war, had served in the military until 1942, when he received a medical discharge (the diagnosis was dementia praecox). He was working as a county prosecutor in Wayne County, Michigan, when he was invited to serve on the Nuremberg war crimes tribunal in 1946. The experience, as Yockey later related, would scar him for life; it was as if he'd looked on the face of pure evil. He was referring, of course, to the Allied prosecutors, who, Yockey maintained, used torture, doctored evidence, ex post facto legalisms, and monstrous lies about so-called atrocities to justify their cruel vendettas against the innocent Nazis they were determined to railroad. "I am a lawyer, not a journalist," Yockey told his bosses when he resigned. "You'll have to write your own propaganda."[8]

After a brief visit to the United States, Yockey returned to Europe again, where he would spend most of the rest of his brief life, trying to save the Old World from the dark fate America's victorious Jews had planned for it. He founded the neo-Fascist European Liberation Front, whose manifesto, "The Proclamation of London," would be released in 1949. "The European struggle," it said, "is the fight for the liberation of our sacred soil and our Western soul."

> The propaganda of the American-Jew and the Jewish-American deceives no one. With their talk of a struggle between "East" and "West" they hope to entice the marginal minds of Europe into cooperation with them. But to us, the West is a word containing a divinely-emanated Mission, a sacred word, and it does not refer to America, to Russia, or to the Jew, but solely to the sacred soil of Europe and to the European organism.[9]

The "Proclamation" includes a concise summary of Yockey's magnum opus, *Imperium: The Philosophy of History and Politics*, which he'd written at an inn in Brittas Bay, Ireland, in 1947, without the benefit of a library or even notes. It was published in two volumes in 1948 in England, under the pseudonym Ulick Varange. "Ulick is an Irish given name, derived from Danish, and means 'reward of the mind,'" Carto explains. "Varange, of course, refers to the Varangians, that far-roving band of Norse heroes led by Rurik who . . . came to civilize Russia in the 9th Century."[10]

Carto sat through Yockey's court appearances (presided over by the former rabbi turned judge Joseph Karesh) until, on June 17, 1960, he heard the terrible news: somehow Yockey had gotten hold of a dose of cyanide and killed himself in his cell—a story that didn't fool Carto for a moment. Yockey hadn't died by his own hand, he instantly realized: he'd been murdered because he'd written a book. He was the victim not just of America's perverted justice system but of a group "so powerful . . . that men dare not speak its name above a whisper, unless in terms of the most groveling praise," a group that "is able to dictate to the government the exact procedure which is to be used in disposing of troublemakers like Francis Parker Yockey." In Carto's telling, a wise old journalist comforted Yockey's grief-stricken sister outside the courtroom. "Your brother is a martyr," he told her. "The first of a long line of them if we are to take back our country from those who have stolen it from us."

Imperium is written at a high level of abstraction; it owes profound intellectual debts to Spengler and the German idealist tradition as well as to racialist histories like Houston Stewart Chamberlain's *Die Grundlagen des neunzehnten Jahrhunderts (The Foundations of the Nineteenth Century)*. Its first five hundred pages propose that race is an emergent idea or "will to power" that transcends mere biology and heredity; it's not until one is well into the book that one begins to appreciate the particular implications of Yockey's political vision. Carto characterizes Yockey as a "sincere patriot" "whose every thought and effort was in behalf of his fellow man." But I suspect that Carto and Yockey construed both patriotism and altruism in a somewhat narrower sense than most people do.

For Yockey, race consciousness amounts to the same thing as power and will: "The center of gravity of ascendant life is on the side of instinct, will, race, blood."

Life which places rationalistic ideals of "individualism," "happiness," "freedom" before the perpetuation and increase of power is *decadent*. Decadent means—moving toward extinction, extinction of higher Life in particular, and finally even of the life of the race. The intellectual of the great city is the type of the man without race. In every Civilization, he has been the inner ally of the outer barbarian.[11]

Does this mean that "individualism," "happiness," and "freedom"—as in "life, liberty, and the pursuit of happiness"?—are bad things? Precisely. And just who are these big city intellectuals?

America, Yockey explains, began as two opposing ideas proposed by two opposing groups of founders. Washington, Hamilton, and Franklin believed in "the healthy and natural organic ranking of the population from the top down, with a monarch and aristocracy at the top, educated from birth to the idea of service of the National-Idea." But for "under-types" like Samuel Adams, Jefferson, and Paine, the Revolution was a class war, and the independence idea was "only a technique for actualizing the equality ideals of Rationalistic literature."

> The implementation of these equality ideals has always taken the form of jealousy, hatred, and social destruction, in America and in Europe. The class-warrior . . . hated monarchy, leadership, discipline, quality, aristocracy, anything superior and creative.

Class war, Yockey assures us, is a bad thing: "an autopathic Culture-disease which arises with the beginnings of the Civilization-crisis, and is only finally liquidated with the end of that crisis and the beginning of the second phase of Civilization, the Resurgence of Authority."[12] America was particularly vulnerable to this disorder because (1) it had been a colony and was hence isolated from the positive influence of the mother country's blood and soil; and (2) from the very beginning it welcomed sub-cultural and extra-cultural forces into its midst, namely the Jews, who invented the notion of the "melting pot" to serve their own destructive purposes (it is almost humorous to read Yockey's solemn allusions to Benjamin Franklin's speech against the Jews at the Constitutional Convention, as if it were a historical fact and not one of William Dudley Pelley's malicious inventions).

> The word "American" was changed . . . to mean an immigrant who had improved his personal circumstances by coming to America, and to exclude the native American who was displaced by the immigrant. If the latter showed resentment, he was called "un-

American." Thus native American movements like the second Ku Klux Klan, formed in 1915, as an expression of the reaction of the American organism to the presence of the foreign matter, were more or less successfully called "un-American" by the propaganda organs in America, which even by that time had come under strong Culture-distorting influences.[13]

The "Jewish Culture-State-Nation-Religion-People-Race" regards the Western idea as "a sinister force working against the Jewish Messiah idea"; one of the tools they use to foment its destruction is the so-called Negro problem.[14] The Negroes, Yockey relates, had been a "contented, primitive people" until the misbegotten War of Secession deprived them of their security and delivered them "to financial slavery in an industrial civilization with whose problems they could in no way cope":

> The converting of the Negro into a wage slave has demoralized him completely, made him into a discontented proletarian, and created in him a deep racial bitterness. The soul of the Negro remains primitive and childlike in comparison with the nervous and complicated soul of Western man, accustomed to thinking in terms of money and civilization. The result is that the Negro has become a charge of white society.[15]

Imperium's story begins with a God's-eye view of the world, from far out in the astral regions, where we "are allowed to look upon a hundred generations as the earthbound look upon the life-span of a fruit-fly."[16] Its narrative climaxes in the 1930s, when the lies of the culture distorters inflamed the world into an unnecessary, unjust war with the peace-loving Axis. Those lies continued unabated, Yockey tells us, even after Europe lay prostrate:

> This propaganda announced that 6,000,000 members of the Jewish Culture-Nation-State-Church-People-Race had been killed in European camps, as well as an indeterminate number of other people. The propaganda was on a world-wide scale, and was of a mendacity that was perhaps adapted to a uniformized mass, but was simply disgusting to discriminating Europeans. The

propaganda was technically quite complete. "Photographs" were supplied in millions of copies. Thousands of the people who had been killed published accounts of their experiences in these camps. Hundreds of thousands more made fortunes in post-war black-markets. "Gas-chambers" that did not exist were photographed, and a "gasmobile" was invented to titillate the mechanically-minded.

But what did they have to gain by so misleading everyone?

The American masses, both military and civilian, were given this mental poison in order to inflame them to the point where they would carry out without flinching the post-war annihilation-program. In particular: *it was designed to support a war after the Second World War, a war of looting, hanging, and starvation against defenseless Europe.*

All along, the war was the fulfillment of the parasitical Jews' plan for revenge. Since there was no anti-Semitism in Japan, the occupation there was benign; Europeans, in contrast, were brutalized. The Holocaust was a lie—the real horror was the "peace."

When defeated Europe—and in particular, the most vital part of it, the bearer of the grand European Idea of the 20th century—lay at the feet of this totally alien conqueror from a Culture of the past, no feelings of magnanimity, chivalry, generosity, mercy, were in his exultant soul. There was only there the gall which he had been drinking for a thousand years while he had bided his time under the arrogance of the alien Western peoples whom he had always considered, and still considers, barbarians, *goyim*.[17]

But it didn't have to end that way. *Imperium* concludes with a stirring vision of a western Europe that is recalled to its true destiny, when the imperium idea is able to reconquer "the world-supremacy which the jealous little opponents of the Hero flung to the winds."[18] Arable Russian land to the east, ripe for conquest, will provide the imperium with the Lebensraum it so desperately needs. All that is required is the "setting free of the Western soul from its domination by traitors and parasites" and "the liquidation of the tyranny of 19th century ideas."

> This means the complete cleansing of the Western soul from every form of Materialism, from Rationalism, Equality, social chaos, Communism, Bolshevism, liberalism, Leftism of every variety, Money-worship, democracy, finance capitalism, the domination of Trade, nationalism, parliamentarism, feminism, race-sterility, weak ideals of "happiness" and the like, of every form of class war. Replacing these ideals is the strong and manly Idea of the Age of Absolute Politics: Authority, Discipline, Faith, Responsibility, Duty, Ethical Socialism, Fertility, Order, State, Hierarchy—the creation of the Empire of the West.[19]

It's not very subtle, when you get right down to it. Mel Brooks's fanatical playwright Franz Liebkind might have tried to set *Imperium*'s closing pages to music.

Carto might not have liked it when Jews and blacks and culture distorters of other sundry hues impugned his and Yockey's patriotism, but I don't think I'd be going particularly far out on a limb if I suggested that their apotheoses of authority, state, and hierarchy, not to mention their boundless contempt for trade and money-mindedness, and most of all for democracy, place them well outside the American mainstream. For all of Glenn Beck's, Rush Limbaugh's, Newt Gingrich's, Ann Coulter's, and Sarah Palin's many foibles, it's hard to imagine any of them sharing a platform with a Yockey-ite; one suspects that the prototypical Tea Partier would be as nauseated by *Imperium*'s militaristic racialism as any progressive would. Unlike his idol Spengler, Yockey never did reach a large popular or academic readership. Perhaps the last time his name received wide play in the mainstream media was in 1999, when the white supremacist John William King, sentenced to death for the dragging murder of James Byrd Jr. in Jasper, Texas, issued a statement to the press that ended with a quotation from Yockey: "The promise of success is with the man who is determined to die proudly when it is no longer possible to live proudly." King's pride hasn't prevented him from taking full advantage of the appeals process that the judicial system makes available to him; he is still alive as of this writing, desperately trying to shift the blame for James Byrd's murder to his co-defendants and to Byrd himself.

Still, white nationalists like Yockey, Willis Carto, Revilo Oliver, William Luther Pierce, David Duke, Kevin MacDonald, Ben Klassen, the author of *The White Man's Bible,* and even the relatively clubbable Jared Taylor, a graduate of Yale University, the editor of the journal *American Renaissance,* and the founder of the "racial realist" school of thought (which eschews anti-Semitism), bring a welcome clarity to political discourse. All of their politics can be reduced to two interlocking themes: "I hate you because of who you are" and "I demand my birthright." Resentment, jealousy, prejudice—they're all explicitly acknowledged. If a southern Republican presidential hopeful like Haley Barbour is compelled to tread a perilous path between the Scylla of outmoded racism and the Charybdis of political correctness, praising segregationist traditions while not quite endorsing them, white nationalists suffer from no such compunctions.

With white nationalists, you understand that you have reached the ground zero of hatred, the reductio ad absurdum of conspiracy theory. Everything—*everything*—is explained with reference to a fluke of DNA; history is seen as a dialectic between opposing poles of, well, black and white. Except it's not quite that simple. The smarter racists have long understood that if blacks are as intellectually, morally, and physically subpar as they make them out to be, then their nearly unbroken string of victories over the past few generations hardly does credit to whites. If whites are as innately superior as they say they are, then why have they been reduced, as they insist they have been, to a pitiful, powerless minority in their own lands? This is perhaps the biggest reason that *Protocols of the Elders of Zion*–style anti-Semitism, dreamed up by Russian Orthodox monarchists over a century ago, has proven so adaptable in federalist, Protestant America—because it proposes a different enemy, one who is as old as history. As the neo-Nazi George Lincoln Rockwell explained it in his book *White Power* (1967), "The Negro masses are biologically inferior and easily manipulated. But the Jews can't as easily manipulate White men, so they are doing everything possible to destroy the idea that there is any such thing as 'race,' with the intention of breeding the White man (especially the Nordic) out of existence."

To destroy the hated Whites and thus advance their violent world revolution, the Jews promote the endless breeding, arming, and organizing of the colored world. They move hordes of Blacks into urban areas, forcing them into competition with Whites, and then, when the Blacks fail, the Jews convince them that they are being "oppressed." This produces riots and finally armed rebellion both in America and elsewhere. As a result of this Jewish promotion of colored breeding, the colored birthrate is skyrocketing while the best of the Whites are killing each other off in fratricidal wars and by birth control. The end will be world racial warfare, in which the swarming colored races will be pitted against the minority of Whites for survival. Either the colored swarms, led and inflamed by the Jews, will overwhelm the White minority and inherit a ruined world, or we will smash them. It's "them or us."[20]

Many black nationalists have turned to the *Protocols* as well for an explanation of their plight, as have the hard-core Islamists who provide cannon fodder for al-Qaeda, and some 9/11 Truthers who believe that al-Qaeda was just a convenient patsy. It almost makes you wonder why all these groups don't simply join forces and make common cause against the Jews.

In fact, some of them have.

Between 1930 and 1960, during the same period that the Third Reich rose and fell and Francis Parker Yockey conceived his enduring hatred for his hopelessly Judaized native land, Elijah Muhammad was slowly building the Nation of Islam into a religio-political movement that, however small it might have been in numbers, was beginning to command serious international attention. The Nation of Islam owed more to Marcus Garvey's Pan-Africanism and to the Masonic-inspired Moorish Science Temple than it did to Koranic Islam; it imported chunks of apocalyptic Christianity and pop science whole as well (its eugenic theories are and were every bit as discreditable as those of its white counterparts).

Noble Drew Ali (né Timothy Drew), who founded the Moorish Science Temple in Newark, New Jersey, in 1913, had authored a text he called "The Holy Koran," which taught that the Negroes of the United States are really Asiatic Moors from Morocco. Until they surrender their slave identities, he said, American blacks can never hope to be free. Ali died in 1929. Identifying himself as Ali's reincarnation, W. D. Fard, a former door-to-door clothing salesman of obscure origins—he claimed to have been born in Mecca; the FBI said he was from New Zealand and tracked down some fifty other aliases for him, including David Ford and Wali Farad Muhammad—founded the Allah Temple of Islam in Detroit in 1930. In 1932, a member named Robert Karriem (his given name was Harris) confessed to killing a boarder named James Smith on a wooden altar in his home in the expectation that the victim would be transformed into the "Savior" in accordance with a fifteen-hundred-year-old prophecy. In the aftermath of the scandal, Fard changed his religion's name to the Nation of Islam; Harris was later declared insane and committed to the Ionia State Mental Hospital.[21] Rumors persisted for decades that members of the Nation of Islam were required to kill four Caucasian devils before they could go to Mecca. In fact there is an esoteric teaching to that effect, but it is meant to be understood symbolically, with the demons representing the "Four Beasts" of Revelation, who are said to "stand between the destruction of the present world and the emergence of the New World."[22] In 1934, Fard abruptly disappeared. His disciple Elijah Muhammad (born Elija Pool in Georgia in 1897, he had added terminal letters to both his names in 1926, becoming Elijah Poole, to signal a new start after he was arrested for public drunkenness; he changed his name again when he began to follow Fard) took over the reins of the movement.[23] Fard, Muhammad revealed, was Allah incarnate, the "Great Mahdi or Messiah . . . also the Son of Man and the Saviour."[24]

Like all religions, the Nation of Islam provided a mythological framework for first and last things. Its creation story told of a mad scientist, Dr. Yakub, who bred a soulless, bleached race of devils on the island of Patmos six thousand years ago: the Caucasian or the white man, a creature that was morally and physically inferior to black people but infinitely crueler and destined to rule the world for a time. Trillions of years before that, in a sci-fi version of the Tower of Babel story, another black scientist had set off a devastating explosion because of his frustration that he couldn't make all the people in the world speak the same language. The earth and the moon were separated in the blast; the sole survivors of the catastrophe, the tribe of Shabazz, made a new start on what became the earth. Muhammad taught that another worldwide disaster, in which the white man will be destroyed and only a handful of righteous blacks (the book of Revelation's 144,000) will survive, was destined to occur between 1970 and the turn of the millennium. A flying saucer (the Old Testament's Ezekiel's wheel) would be the source of the destruction. The date of Armageddon had been postponed for a few generations, Muhammad said, to give America's blacks the opportunity to return to their true faith.

Black Nationalism: A Search for an Identity in America (1962), the Nigerian scholar E. U. Essien-Udom's sociological study of the Nation of Islam and other American black nationalist movements circa 1960, makes for fascinating reading today, because it provides a kind of time capsule. Based on personal observation and interviews, as well as archival and scholarly research, Essien-Udom captures Elijah Muhammad and his world at a critical inflection point—just moments before everything in it and around it changed beyond recognition. The Freedom Summer and the Birmingham bombings, not to mention the Civil Rights Act of 1964 and the long, hot summer of 1968, were still years away. Medgar Evers was alive; James Meredith was a student at Jackson State, an all-black college, still sending applications to the University of Mississippi; Stokely Carmichael had just matriculated at Howard University. Martin Luther King was famous, of course, but not yet the iconic figure he would become; Malcolm X was the loyal minister of Elijah Muhammad's New York City mosque; Louis Farrakhan is only mentioned once in the entire book and then only tangentially, as the former calypso singer who became Minister Louis X of Boston and recorded "A White Man's Heaven Is a Black Man's Hell," a tuneful introduction to the tenets of the Nation of Islam that can be heard on YouTube to this day.[25] Revelations of Elijah Muhammad's personal peccadilloes (the numerous affairs and illegitimate children, the luxurious lifestyle he and his family maintained at his followers' expense) were still in the future—as was Muhammad's outreach to the neo-Nazi George Lincoln Rockwell, who would praise him at a 1961 Nation of Islam rally as "the Adolf Hitler of the black man."[26]

Elijah Muhammad's detestation of white people and especially of Jews—an attitude that would within a few short years become ubiquitous throughout the civil rights movement—was and is deplorable, but at least before 1960 it served a practical purpose in that it helped to inculcate a sense of separateness in his followers, without which, Muhammad believed, there could be no true freedom. His message was not so much about the despicableness of white people per se, or of Jews qua Jews, as the animus that they allegedly bore toward blacks:

> We know today that we are having trouble trying to sit in class-rooms with white people, is that right? If they hate us and despise us so much that they don't want their children educated in the same classroom with you and I, then what should we do? Should we continue to beg for freedom justice and equality from people who don't want to even sit beside you in an educational institution or ride with you on the same vehicle? Should we continue to beg for freedom, justice and equality from a people that have all of these written in their Constitution and then fail to give it to us?[27]

The Nation of Islam's highest purpose was less to be found in the granular details of its catch-as-catch-can religiosity, its racialized space-opera variations on Seventh-Day Adventist end-time scenarios, or its dubious anthropological theories, than in the rigidly mandated way of life that it imposed upon its members—a framework on which to erect a new set of values, a new ethos. Elijah Muhammad didn't so much endorse racism as acknowledge it as an inescapable fact of life. "Don't look for strange people, members of another race that are not members of your own nation for friendship. They are not your friends, you will be greatly disappointed. . . . Be like white people; they are in unity with all their kind."[28] Utopian dreams of a future black home-land, schadenfreude about the white devils' ultimate comeuppance, conspiracy theories about history and politics all have their place, but when all is said and done, there is much more of Booker T. Washing-ton than Frantz Fanon in his teachings:

> It is only fear that keeps you and I from becoming a great nation, just fear. . . . Your leaders are preaching the wrong thing. They are not preaching the Gospel of self-independence. . . . It is not injustice for a white man to tell you and I tomorrow morning he doesn't have a job for us and that he will go and hire all of his kind. He could eas-

ily say to you and I that we have had near a hundred years to make jobs for ourselves. Go make one for yourself. . . . Stop quarreling and fighting among yourselves. Don't make the whole world look down on you as a crazy people. Go on, love one another. Do good to each other.[29]

As in so many other religions—particularly evangelical Christianity—the conversion experience was of paramount importance. When one joined the Nation of Islam, one left one's old self behind—both one's Christian or slave name and the stereotypical, self-destructive behaviors that were the most insidious legacies of slavery. Converts forswore drinking, drugging, adultery, and flashy clothes; they adopted a serious, disciplined mien; they learned to respect their spouses and aspired to become model breadwinners and providers. Every would-be convert was required to copy a letter of application and send it to national headquarters. Only when the letter was rendered flawlessly was a convert admitted to instruction, and only after one was initiated in the "Actual Facts" did he or she receive his or her "original" name. Elijah Muhammad enforced dress codes (dark-colored suits and ties for men; white gowns for women) and provided his followers with long lists of forbidden and encouraged foods. Pork was verboten, as was catfish, possum, and squirrel; white turnips, asparagus, and whole-wheat bread were permitted, but collard greens, black-eyed peas, and corn bread were *tref*. Only eat white potatoes in moderation, he cautioned, as they are fattening; chicken is not forbidden, but squabs are healthier. Though the Nation of Islam's schools were woefully underfunded in the 1950s, education was a huge priority. Men and women alike were urged to aspire to learn good trades and even to attend college.

Everything, as I said, was about to change: the militancy of the Black Panthers would soon make Elijah Muhammad's brand of reactive racialism seem almost quaint; the intensity of Louis Farrakhan's anti-Semitism would eventually rival Revilo Oliver's. I don't intend to defend the Nation of Islam: there was and is too much in it that is cultish, anti-intellectual, and revanchist; hatred can only beget more hate. But when one compares the Nation of Islam with the white power movement at that critical cusp, when Eisenhower's supposedly complacent America was teetering on the brink of the revolutionary 1960s (a revolution that is being refought to this day on the air-waves of Fox News and in the speeches of Tea Partiers), one can't but take note of the former's relatively healthy-minded openness to self-criticism. If Elijah Muhammad had no use at all for white people or Jews, he saw much that he could constructively criticize in his own people. "Where is your intelligence? You have none. You care less. Why? Because you are blind, deaf, and dumb."[30] He exhorts them; he shames them; he loves them in the exasperated way that the God of the Old Testament loved his stiff-necked Hebrews. "My beloved, I, Elijah Muhammad, who must speak if it kills me and who will die rather than lie, tell you this. . . ."[31] There is as much of the psychologist in him as the seer or the politician.

"The process by which whites have been able to create and sustain the Negro's image of his own inferiority is known in common parlance as 'brainwashing,'" E. U. Essien-Udom wrote.

> In Muhammad's teaching, this process is known as "tricknowledgy." It would appear to the observer that it takes another kind of "tricknowledgy" to undo the former. . . . [Muhammad's] eschatology or other doctrines of "racial supremacy" are gimmicks meant for the consumption of his followers and for combating the "enemy within"—the Negro's "mentality." If this is correct, the frequent comparison of the Muslim movement with the Ku Klux Klan or with the White Citizens' Council misses the point and has only a superficial relevance. Although alike in the crudity of their racial diatribes, they differ significantly in their objectives—for instance, the Muslims do not seek to deprive their fellow citizens of their political rights.[32]

One looks in vain, when reading the writings of white nationalists, for any like efforts at self-improvement. Yockey didn't plead with white Americans to stay in school, to improve their personal hygiene, to include more nutritious foods in their diets. George Lincoln Rockwell might have bemoaned his white compatriots' misguided guilt, their irrational dread of being mistaken for bigots, the congenital softheartedness that made them fall for the fallacy that all men are created equal under God, but in his eyes their biggest failing of all was their lack of amour propre. "We must have an all-White America," he declared in "What We Stand For: Goals and Objectives of the National Socialist White People's Party."

> An America in which our children and our grandchildren will play and go to school with other White children; an America in which they will date and marry other young people of our own race; an America in which all their offspring will be beautiful, healthy White babies—never raceless mongrels. We must have an America without swarming black filth in our schools, on our buses and in our places of work; an America in which our cultural, social, business and political life is free of alien, Jewish influence; an America in which White people are the sole masters of our own destiny.

"Flush down the drain the poisonous Jewish and negroid degeneracy which today passes for art and music and literature," weed out and destroy "every threat to our racial integrity, every form of organized crime and vice, every element which threatens public terror or chaos," and all will be well.[33] Ban Chuck Berry and white Americans will listen to Beethoven and Wagner on their transistor radios; drive the Jewish money changers out of the temple and each and every white producer will rise to his natural level.

Elijah Muhammad might have been the rankest of charlatans, but his methods and his agenda were canny and complex. Though he demanded that the United States cede territory for a black homeland, he had no illusions that it ever would. "They will never give us three or four states," he admitted, "but that don't hinder you and me from asking for it."[34] Black supremacy wasn't an end in itself but a "gimmick," a form of rhetorical shock therapy, or, as Plato might have put it (though it's admittedly difficult to imagine Plato giving much thought to the likes of the Nation of Islam), a "noble lie" that was in service to a set of relatively attainable aspirations. If the utter destruction of white people remained a fantasy, a movement of tens, hundreds of thousands, or even millions of black people who purchased goods and services from one another, taught their children in their own schools, and in general avoided social, economic, political, cultural, and sexual intercourse with their former slave masters was well within the bounds of the possible.

White supremacy, in contrast, though it begins with the same base of hatred, simply mixes equal measures of mysticism and rank sentimentality into its noxious formula. It presumes that the superiority of white "racial values" is self-evident and weeps for their undoing; any practical energy it unleashes is devoted to tearing its enemy down rather than building its own self up. "Anybody who is forced to live with masses of Negroes (not a few select Negro doctors or lawyers, but the real, black, average Negro) will quickly form the opinion that Negroes are a very low form of humanity, and we cannot mix with them without reverting to the jungle and the filth in which they live," Commander Rockwell wrote in *White Power*.

> Nothing on this planet is so precious to us, and should be so precious to the world, as the White "Master-Race" heredity that, alone, can produce and maintain justice, order, culture and White civilization.
>
> Those Jews aid ape-like Negroes who plot to destroy that precious pool of White blood, and the "liberals" who help them in that plot, are murderers and exterminators of a whole race,—the greatest race which has ever walked the face of this planet.[35]

White power's boundless regard for its own whiteness comes across as a kind of grotesque kitsch ("Sentimentality," wrote Norman Mailer, "is the emotional promiscuity of those who have no sentiment"). The white power proponent is like a bore in a bar who insists on telling you how much money he had before his ex-wife and her Jewish lawyer fleeced him, or the floozy on the next stool over who can't stop talking about how exceptionally beautiful she used to be.

Which brings me to one of the leading tropes of the Tea Party today, American exceptionalism—a term that first gained currency in 1929, when Josef Stalin condemned the so-called "heresy of American Exceptionalism," the notion that the United States' unique economic circumstances inoculated it from the social contradictions that led to social collapse and revolutions.[36] During the 2008 presidential campaign, hardly a day went by that John McCain and Sarah Palin didn't offer testimonials to their abiding faith in American exceptionalism—or implicitly criticize Obama for his lack thereof. It made a huge impression on me, because I had somehow neglected to include the word in my book 'Isms & 'Ologies. I'd like to make up for that oversight now.

Long before Stalin, Alexis de Tocqueville had used the word "exceptional" in relation to Americans in *Democracy in America*, though when you read what he said in context, you quickly realize that he wasn't using the word as today's conservatives do, as a shorthand for America's innate superiority. Rather, he was marveling at Americans' stubborn materialism, their manifest lack of interest in the arts or ideas, in much the same spirit as any latte-sipping, NASCAR-hating snob:

> The position of the Americans is therefore quite exceptional, and it may be believed that no democratic people will ever be placed in a similar one. Their strictly Puritanical origin—their exclusively commercial habits—even the country they inhabit, which seems to divert their minds from the pursuit of science, literature, and the arts—the proximity of Europe, which allows them to neglect these pursuits without relapsing into barbarism—a thousand special causes, of which I have only been able to point out the most important—have singularly concurred to fix the mind of the American upon purely practical objects. His passions, his wants, his education, and everything about him seem to unite in drawing the native of the United States earthward: his religion alone bids him turn, from time to time, a transient and distracted glance to heaven. Let us cease then to view all democratic nations under the mask of the American people, and let us attempt to survey them at length with their own proper features.[37]

I did define the phrase "American providentialism" in 'Isms & 'Ologies, which connotes much more of what conservatives do when they invoke exceptionalism, except that it does so in a highly qualified, provisional way. The notion of providentialism goes back to "A Model of Christian Charity," the sermon that John Winthrop preached aboard the *Arabella* in 1630, which contained the famous line "For we must consider that we shall be as a city upon a hill. The eyes of all people are upon us." Winthrop proposed that the American Puritans, like the Hebrews in the Old Testament, had entered a covenant with God, that they had "taken out a Commission." If they hoped to be able to meet such a demanding obligation, he said, they "must be knit together in this work as one man."

> We must entertain each other in brotherly Affection, we must be willing to abridge ourselves of our superfluities, for the supply of others necessities, we must uphold a familiar Commerce together in all meekness, gentleness, patience and liberality, we must delight in each other, make others Conditions our own, rejoice together, mourn together, labor and suffer together, always having before our eyes our Commission and Community in the work, our Community as members of the same body.

"Abridge ourselves of our superfluities, for the supply of others necessities"? Sounds like "social justice," as Glenn Beck might say—and you know what *that* means.

If the Puritans kept their side of the bargain, Winthrop said, God would grant them such strength that "ten of us shall be able to resist a thousand of our enemies" and their new country would prosper. Should they default in any way, "we shall be made a story and a by-word through the world, we shall open the mouths of enemies to speak evil of the ways of God and all professors for Gods sake; we shall shame the faces of many of God's worthy servants, and cause their prayers to be turned into Curses upon us till we be consumed out of the good land whither we are going."[38] When Winthrop spoke of the city on a hill, he meant that they would be exposed to critical scrutiny at all times—that everyone in the world and God himself would be watching them, ready to pounce the moment they did anything wrong. He was talking about America's unprecedented *potential* for greatness, not its intrinsic perfection.

Somewhere along the way, this punitively worded, nonnegotiable contract with the Almighty became a blank check, and the city on the hill turned into an earthly paradise. "I've spoken of the shining city all my political life," Ronald Reagan remarked in his Farewell Address, which he delivered from the Oval Office on January 11, 1989. "In my mind it was a tall proud city built on rocks stronger than oceans, wind-swept, God-blessed, and teeming with people of all kinds living in harmony and peace, a city with free ports that hummed with commerce and creativity." No longer a byword for responsibility and reciprocity, the city on the hill had become a place you might read about in a pamphlet prepared by the chamber of commerce of a coastal city that's trying to entice new businesses to relocate there; it had devolved from a biblical charge to behave better to a cliché for patriotic after-dinner speakers.

Just as white supremacists believe that the less melanin they have in their skin, the smarter and stronger and better-looking they are (a faith they cleave to no matter what doubts they might harbor about their dwindling status and declining prospects), exceptionalism is the conviction that America is morally, legally, militarily, spiritually, and economically superior to any other land. Just saying as much—witnessing to it out loud, like a subway evangelist praising Jesus's name during rush hour—is enough to make some of America's intrinsic awesomeness rub off on you.

"There is something special about this country," *The American Spectator's* Quin Hillyer wrote on the eve of the 2008 presidential election. "The United States is exceptional."

> We are blessed by the good Lord, and in turn we have done more, far more, than any other people to spread freedom across the globe, and prosperity across the globe, and human rights across this great good Earth. We are a particularly good people—and John McCain understands all this and believes it with every fiber of his being, down to his very marrow, in a way that is deeply spiritual in nature. There is nothing fake about McCain's belief in American Exceptionalism. His belief in this is as genuine, and as deeply felt, as is a son's love for his father. He will defend this country, fight for this country, with every last breath in his body.[39]

On July 4, 2010, Ken Blackwell defined American exceptionalism in his column in *Townhall* magazine as "the belief that America is something special. We are a shining beacon of light throughout the world and throughout the annals of history. We are the exception, not the rule." What constitutes America's specialness, he goes on to explain, is "our right to worship according to the dictates of our conscience," "our right to bear arms," "our right not to be deprived of life, liberty or property without due process," and especially our "economic freedom."[40]

In April 2009, at the G-20 summit in France, when a correspondent from the *Financial Times* asked him if he subscribed "to the school of American exceptionalism that sees America as uniquely qualified to lead the world," Barack Obama rained on the parade. "I believe in American exceptionalism," he replied, "just as I suspect that the Brits believe in British exceptionalism, and the Greeks believe in Greek exceptionalism."

Never mind that Great Britain gave us the Magna Carta, habeas corpus, bicameral legislatures, John Locke, Adam Smith, and Edmund Burke. Forget that the Greeks endowed the world with its first great democracy, not to mention a matchless literary and philosophical legacy. Disregard the salutary reflection that both empires, for all the high opinion they held of themselves, for all the military, cultural, and economic power they once wielded, have long since gone the way of all flesh. "President Obama's reference to British or Greek exceptionalism suggests a belief that the United States doesn't stand alone with a particular greatness but that every nation is great in its own way and America is simply one of many nations with something cool to offer," Monica Crowley scolded in *The Washington Times*. "In Mr. Obama's kaleidoscopic left-wing view, no nation is better than any other, no country can tell another country not to have nuclear weapons, and we're all socialists now."[41] Quoting Obama's words in her book *America by Heart*, Sarah Palin could only conclude that Obama "doesn't believe in exceptionalism at all. He seems to think it is just a kind of irrational prejudice in favor of our way of life. To me that is appalling."[42] "America is exceptional," Rick Santorum insisted, "and Americans are concerned that there are a group of people in Washington who don't believe that anymore." "To deny American exceptionalism," Mike Huckabee added, "is in essence to deny the heart and soul of this nation."

Writing in *The Washington Post*, Karen Tumulty noted that all these recent conservative disquisitions on exceptionalism—and I could have quoted many, many more—have "a more intellectual sheen than the false assertions that Obama is secretly a Muslim or that he was born in Kenya." Then she quotes William Galston of the

Brookings Institution, who said that writing about exceptionalism provides "a respectable way of raising the question of whether Obama is one of us."[43]

And there you have it—the core proposition of the not-so-New Hate: that there are those of us who are really "us" and those of us who are essentially "other"—aliens, interlopers, pretenders, and culture distorters, parasites and freeloaders, who bear the blame for the fact that being a white Anglo-Saxon Protestant American no longer suffices to make one the cynosure of the world.

Back on November 19, 1955, in the mission statement he prepared for the first issue of the *National Review*, William F. Buckley derided the presiding liberal orthodoxy of his day, which, he said, had as much as ceded the field to "the jubilant single-mindedness of the practicing Communist, with his inside track to history." The *National Review*, Buckley vowed, would stand "athwart history, yelling Stop, at a time when no one is inclined to do so, or to have much patience with those who so urge it."[44] Patron saint of the conservatives as he might have been, in John Judis's memorable phrase, Buckley was much more of a pragmatist than that. He knew that the wheels of history never do stop turning, no matter how devoutly one might wish they did; he recognized that ideological purity (or any other kind of purity, for that matter) was not to be found in our fallen world. "No sense running Mona Lisa in a beauty contest," he replied, when an interviewer asked whom he was supporting for president in 1967. "I'd be for the most right, viable candidate who could win."[45]

The New Hate is at once the expression of a quixotic desire to turn back the clock to a mythical golden age when women and minorities and gays and foreigners were less troublesome than they are today, when the government only gave and never took, and a cynical ploy to up the turnout of Republican voters. Most of the time it's reflexive and vindictive to its core. And the vast majority of its proponents, even in the heat of the moment—dressed up in colonial costume, with powdered wigs on their heads and "Say No to Socialism" placards in their hands—know better, too.

No one in New England in 1798 really believed that Jefferson was plotting to bring Jacobinism to the United States, any more than Maria Monk's readers thought that the convent down the street was a nest of debauchery. Senator Joseph McCarthy never really believed that George Marshall was a Communist or even a Communist tool. For all the prevalence of anti-Semitic stereotypes, even the most vicious of Jew haters are more likely to deny that the Holocaust really happened than they are to defend it. Though millions of Americans claim to believe that Obama is a Muslim and a foreigner, and some of them hate him merely because of the color of his skin, most of them know that the real issue isn't what Obama is but what they increasingly fear they're not.

And thus it has always been.

Afterword to the Vintage Edition

When the hardcover edition of this book came out in February 2012, the Republican presidential hopefuls had already been debating each other for more than six months. It had been like a season of *American Idol*, *Dancing with the Stars*, or *Survivor*. One contender after the other had emerged from the pack to challenge the odds-on favorite, only to stumble and fall. All Mitt Romney had to do, it seemed, was wait for his rivals' inevitable self-destruction. But if his ultimate victory was a foregone conclusion, there was no denying that the GOP as a whole seemed decidedly lukewarm to him—and the Tea Party and the religious right actively disliked him.

As *The New Hate* made its way into the world, the Tea Party's latest champion, Clinton-era House speaker Newt Gingrich, was beginning to be eclipsed by Rick Santorum, the former senator from Pennsylvania. Gingrich staked his claim to the party's right wing: "The centerpiece of this campaign," he said in his victory speech in South Carolina, "is American exceptionalism versus the radicalism of Saul Alinsky. . . . The founding fathers of America are the source from which we draw our understanding of America. [Obama] draws his from . . . radical left-wingers and people who don't like the classical America."[1] Months before, Gingrich had proclaimed that he'd entered the race lest his grandchildren be forced to live in "a secular atheist country, potentially one dominated by radical Islamists."[2]

Not to be outdone, Santorum inveighed against "the intolerance of the left, the intolerance of the secular ideology. It is a religion unto itself." He continued, "Just like we saw from the days of the atheists of the Soviet Union, it is completely intolerant of dissent. They fear dissent. Why? Because the dissent comes from folks who use reason, common sense, and divine revelation and they want no part of any of those things. . . . They want their worldview to be imposed without question, and if you question them, you're haters, you're bigots, and you should be as a result of that ostracized from the public square."[3]

Santorum wasn't the first or the last right-winger to call out the left for being too quick to accuse the right of being haters. Many of my critics have accused me of doing just that. And I would have indeed been remiss had I suggested that the right enjoys anything like a monopoly on nastiness. Comedian Bill Maher referred to Sarah Palin with a crude anatomical vulgarity; MSNBC suspended talk show host Ed Schultz after he flung another four-letter epithet at Laura Ingraham. As noted in these pages, left-wing pundits like Markos Moulitsas and Paul Krugman rushed to blame Sarah Palin and the Tea Party for the shooting spree in Tucson that killed six and wounded many more, including Representative Gabrielle Giffords, despite the absence of any evidence connecting the gunman to the right.

There are plenty of other examples: Rosie O'Donnell called for "guilty bankers" to be "sent to reeducation camps, and if that doesn't help, then be beheaded"; the *New York Times* columnist Maureen Dowd coined the phrase "extra-chromosome conservatives" without regard to the pain she might have caused people with Down's syndrome and their families. These and more can be found in the Conservapedia's extensive entry on "liberal hate speech."[4] Michelle Malkin also collects specimens of left-wing bile at her Web site under the rubric of "The Progressive 'Climate of Hate'" (her daily newsletter never fails to include an ad hominem "Hate Tweet of the Day").[5]

But however waspish and mean-spirited left-wing comedians, pseudonymous Internet commenters, and the occasional rabble-rousing talk show host might be, liberal policy makers as a breed tend to be rather circumspect compared to their peers across the aisle, often to their constituents' frustration. In contrast, the polarizing "with us or against us" rhetoric that I call the New Hate—in which whole groups of people are demonized and accused of treason—are routine talking points of Republican Party leaders and elected officials.

Many disagree with me about this, I know, and I respectfully invite them to write books of their own. Some already have. See, for example, Ann Coulter's *Demonic: How the Liberal Mob Is Endangering America*, which purports to expose the liberal penchant for bullying and name-calling. Coulter notes that "it's important to liberals to express contempt for an adversary. Belittling people is pleasurable for them as well as tactically useful. Instead of 'counterrevolutionaries,' liberals' opponents are called 'haters,' 'those who seek to divide us,' 'tea baggers,' and 'right-wing hate groups.' Meanwhile, conservatives call liberals 'liberals'—and that makes them testy."[6] Some conservatives also call liberals demonic, but I suppose that's quibbling.

What I *will* concede is that there isn't all that much that is new about either the haters I describe in these pages or the objects of their loathing. In some ways my book's title is ironic. Tea Partiers, radio talkers, best-selling authors like Coulter, anti-Islamic activists like Pam Geller and Robert Spencer, Evangelicalist culture warriors like the Family Research Council's Tony Perkins and the American Family Association's Bryan Fischer, bloggers at conservative sites like *RedState*, Glenn Beck's *The Blaze*, *WorldNetDaily*, and Breitbart .com are still fighting battles that many of us civilians supposed had been settled decades ago.

A case in point: on April 10, 2012, Allen West, the Republican representative from Florida's Twenty-second Congressional District, informed the audience at a town hall meeting that "about seventy-eight or eighty-one" of the Democrats in the U.S. Congress "are members of the Communist Party." He paused meaningfully, according to the transcript provided by Tucker Carlson's conservative *Daily Caller*, before adding, "It's called the Congressional Progressive Caucus."[7] A media firestorm ensued, in which West's comments were widely compared to the accusations that Joseph McCarthy had made about Communists in the State Department and other parts of the government in the 1950s. In a press conference a few days later, West clarified his remarks, giving reporters a history lesson in the process. "If you would take the time to study the political spectrum of ideologies," he schooled them, "you'd understand that at the turn of the [twentieth] century, American Communists renamed themselves as progressives. If you study the Woodrow Wilson administration, people referred to the Woodrow Wilson administration as a *progressive* administration."

In other words, even before the U.S. Communist Party existed (it was founded after the Bolshevik Revolution, in 1919), Theodore Roosevelt and Woodrow Wilson were working secretly to carry out its agenda. "There's a very thin line between Communism, progressivism, Marxism, socialism—or even, as Mark Levin has said, statism," West continued. "It's about nationalizing production, it's about creating and expanding the welfare state. It's about this idea of social and economic justice. And you hear that being played out—you know, with fairness, fair share, economic equality, shared sacrifice, ad nauseum, ad infinitum. And it's also about the creation of a secular state."[8]

Like Gingrich and Santorum, West is appalled by the Jeffersonian notion of a "secular state"; he dismisses "social and economic justice," "fairness," and "shared sacrifice" as transparently risible canards. As bizarre as they might seem to some readers, West's ideas were staples of the anti-Roosevelt right in the 1930s; John Birchers affirmed them in the 1950s and 1960s; and even more to the point, you can hear them on Glenn Beck's and Mark Levin's radio shows every day. They resonate with a goodly enough portion of the voting public that West has been able to leverage the controversy to raise money. "I'm the number one target of liberals and their friends in the media who are going completely nuts about my comments at a recent Townhall meeting," he e-mailed supporters. "Please stand with me by making a contribution today."[9]

West's views may be extreme, but he is a political star with a growing national reputation. Partly, no doubt, because he is an African American—and as such would presumably inoculate the GOP ticket against imputations of racism—he has been talked up as a potential vice presidential nominee in the 2012 election. "Top of my list is Allen West," Sarah Palin told Sean Hannity when he asked her who she liked for the job.

I love that he has that military experience. He is a public servant willing to serve for the right reasons. He understands the Constitution. He understands our national foreign policy issues that must be addressed. . . . No matter who it is . . . the media will make things up about them and their record and their reputations and their families . . . so they might as well get someone who is passionate and strong.[10]

West's witch hunting might seem a tad anachronistic two decades and counting after the collapse of the Berlin Wall and more than sixty years after McCarthy brandished his famous list of turncoats. But he is not alone. A just-published book by Brian Sussman, *Eco-Tyranny: How the Left's Green Agenda Will Dismantle America*, reveals that environmentalism is not only bad for business; it's quite literally a Communist plot. There's a sinister reason that Earth Day is celebrated on April 22, he says: it's Lenin's birthday.[11]

And then—as always—there is the old standby of race hatred. On February 26, 2012, George Zimmerman, a part-Hispanic neighborhood watch volunteer, shot and killed Trayvon Martin, an unarmed black teenager, in the gated community in Sanford, Florida, where Martin's father's girlfriend lived. The police took Zimmerman at his word that he had acted in self-defense and released him after only a superficial investigation. A month later, as the controversy was reaching its tipping point, President Obama addressed it, saying, "I think every parent in America should be able to understand why it is absolutely imperative that we investigate every aspect of this, and that everybody pulls together—federal, state, and local—to figure out exactly how this tragedy happened." He added, "If I had a son, he would look like Trayvon Martin."[12] Newt Gingrich was apoplectic. "Any young American of any ethnic background should be safe period," he scolded the president. "We should all be horrified no matter what the ethnic background. Is the president suggesting that if it had been a white who had been shot that would be okay because it didn't look like him?"[13]

Within a few more weeks, the story had devolved into a media circus of O. J. Simpson–esque proportions, with the New Black Panther Party putting a bounty on the gunman's head, neo-Nazis pledging to patrol the streets of Sanford, and Reverend Terry Jones, who'd enjoyed his fifteen minutes of notoriety when he threatened to burn a Koran to commemorate 9/11, planning a rally in Sanford on Zimmerman's behalf. Zimmerman has since been indicted, but the story will continue to simmer during the months leading up to the election.

And there is sexism too. Just a few months ago, a number of leading Republicans decided that it would be politically advantageous for them to restoke an issue that dates back to the days of Margaret Sanger. It began when Catholic bishops protested a provision in the Obama health-care plan that required Catholic hospitals and universities to cover contraceptive services without charging a deductible. Obama, they said, was forcing church officials to violate their consciences. Pledging congressional action, House Speaker John Boehner called the mandate "an unambiguous attack on religious freedom in our country."[14] Even after Obama announced a compromise—insurance companies would pick up the costs themselves, and not charge them back to Catholic institutions—partisan conservatives and religious activists continued to pour oil on the flames. "This was an unexpected gift," Ralph Reed, chairman of the evangelical Faith and Freedom Coalition, acknowledged candidly, as he and his group joined the protests.[15] If Mitt Romney wasn't a draw for religious voters, perhaps a timely revival of the culture wars would do the trick.

When Sandra Fluke, a third-year law student at Georgetown University law school and the former president of its Students for Reproductive Justice, told a congressional committee about a lesbian friend who couldn't afford the prescription birth control pills she needed to control her ovarian cysts and lost an ovary as a result, she was subjected to a vicious public sliming, spearheaded by Rush Limbaugh.

"On the Wednesday, Thursday and Friday editions of his talk show," *The New York Times* reported,

> Mr. Limbaugh attacked Ms. Fluke as sexually promiscuous and politically motivated—"an anti-Catholic plant," he said at one point. On Wednesday, he called her a "slut" who "wants to be paid to have sex"; on Thursday, he said she was "having so much sex, it's amazing she can still walk"; and on Friday, after Senate Democrats beat back a Republican challenge to the new policy, he said Ms.

Fluke had testified that she was "having sex so frequently that she can't afford all the birth-control pills that she needs."[16]

Even more over-the-top was Limbaugh's grotesque proposition: if "Miss Fluke and the rest of you Feminazis" expect us to pay you to have sex, "we want something for it," he said. "We want you to post the videos online so we can all watch." (Those words were later erased from the official transcript of Limbaugh's show; the *Atlantic Wire* preserved them.)[17]

Limbaugh offered a tepid apology on March 3, as an ad hoc campaign to pressure advertisers to pull their sponsorship began to yield results. (A similar effort had done tremendous damage to Glenn Beck's Fox TV show after he spoke of President Obama's "deep hatred for white people.") Other conservatives doubled down. "She is banging it five times a day," Pam Geller declared on her Web site, *Atlas Shrugs*. "Calling this whore a slut was a softball. Obama calls her and tells Sandra slut Fluke that her parents should be so proud of her. He's a pimp."[18] The blogger Ace of Spades called Fluke "a shiftless rent-a-cooch from East Whoreville."[19] "There is no doubt in my mind, in my investigator's mind," Bill O'Reilly opined on his *O'Reilly Factor*, "that this woman, from the very beginning, was what they call 'run' by very powerful people. . . . So I'm going to say—and I can't prove it beyond a reasonable doubt, I think I will be able to—that this was run out of the White House. The White House ran this."[20]

On March 13, a Web site called *The Graph* informed its readers that Sandra Fluke has a Jewish boyfriend, Adam Mutterperl. And not just any Jew—a rich one, with connections to radical politics. It is the same nexus of wealth, revolutionary ideology, and Judaism that *The Protocols of the Elders of Zion* tells of:

> The Mutterperl family, via Adam's great grandfather Sol's handbag fortune, established the "Mutterperl Scholarship Endowment Fund" in 1951 for Brandeis University. This school, as some people call it, is named for Louis Brandeis, a secular Jew, Zionist, and United States Supreme Court Justice appointed by Woodrow Wilson. Brandeis was a self-proclaimed socialist. Herbert Marcuse, the famous Frankfurt School Marxist, came to Brandeis in 1954, three years after the Mutterperl fund was created. Brandeis University is

one of the nation's leading petri dishes for anti-American and neo-Marxist thought.[21]

Others looked not to the Jews but to Nazis and Reds. On April 14, Bishop Daniel R. Jenky of the Roman Catholic diocese of Peoria, Illinois, declared that "Hitler and Stalin, at their better moments, would just barely tolerate some churches remaining open, but would not tolerate any competition with the state in education, social services, and health care. In clear violation of our First Amendment rights, President Obama—with his radical, pro-abortion and extreme secularist agenda, now seems intent on following a similar path."[22]

Putting matters into perspective, the Fluke case will probably be remembered more for the blowback it caused the right than any lasting damage it did to the left (Romney's gender gap in the polls widened dramatically as the controversy intensified). Also, as Sarah Palin, Monica Lewinsky, Laura Ingraham, Linda Tripp, and Michele Bachmann have all experienced themselves, misogyny crosses party lines—unfortunately, the left can give as good as it gets in that department. But the Fluke firestorm shed a lurid light on the close associations between prudery and prurience, not to mention paranoia, that have long been a feature of American politics.

Even if the most egregious of the New/Old Hate is espoused by only a noisome and opportunistic fringe, the Internet and twenty-four-hour cable news have given it a wider reach than it's ever had—and mainstream politicians are not shy about co-opting its most demagogic themes. Some of those memes are quite sticky, as they say in marketing. Once a politician adds one of them to his or her brand, it's hard to erase it later on. In an effort to bring the GOP's base on board, Mitt Romney, for example, espoused ideas about immigration during the debates that might have given even a Know-Nothing pause. Though he now needs to broaden his appeal to the more centrist undecideds who determine the outcome of general elections (not to mention otherwise conservative Hispanic voters), he is under tremendous pressure to stick to his guns. "If Romney flip-flops on immigration issues, the resulting demoralization of conservative voters could leave America with a liberal Republican or Democrat in the White House as well as Democrats being in control of both chambers of Congress!" William Gheen, the president of Americans for

Legal Immigration PAC (ALIPAC), declared recently. "That could be enough to finally kill America."[23] As Barney Frank ruefully observed when he announced his imminent retirement from Congress, "The House consists half of people who think like Michele Bachmann and half of people who are afraid of losing the primary to people who think like Michele Bachmann."[24]

This, to me, is the most insidious effect of the New Hate. As marginal as Allen West and Michele Bachmann might be, the GOP's willingness to accommodate them exerts an irresistible gravitational pull on the political middle, dragging everybody else rightward as well.

The Allen West, Trayvon Martin, and Sandra Fluke incidents all occurred within months of *The New Hate*'s publication. As I write these words, conspiracy theories linking Obama and Bill Ayers to the untimely death of Andrew Breitbart are taking shape, and a film called *Dreams from My Father? A Story of Reds and Deception* is giving new currency to the old story that Obama's father was the Communist writer Frank Marshall Davis, infuriating diehard birthers (Davis was an American). And on it goes. As the presidential campaign gets under way in earnest, who knows what other tempests will erupt? Considering the fact that one candidate is a black man with an Islamic name and the other a wealthy Mormon who desperately needs to prove himself to the Tea Party and the Evangelicalist right, it's likely to be déjà vu all over again—and again and again and again.

—Arthur Goldwag,
June 2012

NOTES

A NOTE ON SOURCES

Except in a few cases, where they are documented at the bottom of the page or in the text itself, every direct quotation is sourced in the endnotes. I refer to many books, especially in the historical chapters, some of them, like Richard Hofstadter's *Paranoid Style in American Politics;* Chip Berlet and Matthew N. Lyons's *Right-Wing Populism in America: Too Close for Comfort;* and Seymour Martin Lipset and Earl Raab's *Politics of Unreason: Right-Wing Extremism in America, 1790–1977,* canonical works of scholarship; some of them (Milton William Cooper's *Behold a Pale Horse,* Nesta Webster's *Secret Societies and Subversive Movements,* and Gary Allen's *None Dare Call It Conspiracy* leap to mind) more like specimen samples than sources per se.

Inevitably in a book of this kind, I also draw on ephemera like newspaper and magazine articles, pamphlets, blogs, and, in the case of louche characters like the white supremacists Revilo P. Oliver, George Lincoln Rockwell, Eustace Mullins, and Francis Parker Yockey, hate Web sites (not the most reliable places, to be sure) that offer access to their writings in digital form. I provide URLs when I am quoting from Internet sources; but I must also offer the caveat that some of these sites have an unnerving propensity to disappear or turn into something else without warning. Major talk show hosts like Glenn Beck and Rush Limbaugh post transcripts of their programs on their official Web sites; the watchdog group Media Matters for America maintains an extensive, searchable online archive of some of the more egregious examples of the New Hate; the Southern Poverty Law Center, People for the American Way, and the ADL have useful databases as well, all of which I have used and refer to in the notes.

Conspiracists and haters may well quote me out of context to accuse me of cutting and pasting indiscriminately from the Internet. That's not at all my practice, but without Google Books and other online resources it would have been much harder for me to find the texts of out-of-print volumes by neglected and forgotten authors like Robert Morris, the nineteenth-century Masonic apologist who wrote a biography of William Morgan, or for that matter by William Morgan himself.

I am grateful to my late friend Amina Rachman—very possibly the only person in the world who had deep personal ties to both Malcolm X and the Nation of Islam and liberal Judaism—who told me about E. U. Essien-Udom's book *Black Nationalism* (and loaned me her copy). I learned much from our conversations over the years and I treasure her memory. The independent researcher Ernie Lazar, a ubiquitous and preternaturally patient commenter at right-wing hate sites, has posted many fascinating tidbits about the Far Right on my blog; his extensive databases on Cleon Skousen and Eustace Mullins were particularly eye-opening.

The selected bibliography includes titles that I explicitly refer to in the text as well as many others that are pertinent. It is not exhaustive, but it provides a starting point for anyone who wants to explore, as I put it in my introduction, the role of organized hatred in the historical arc of American politics. I have provided copyright dates and publishers for those hard-to-find books that I accessed on the Internet. Many of them can also be obtained in scanned, print-on-demand editions, with all the vagaries of spelling and pagination that they entail.

INTRODUCTION: BIRTHERS, BIRCHERS, AND DEATH PANELS

1. Affidavit of Susan Daniels, *Barnett v. Obama*, No. 09-cv-00082 (C.D. Cal. October 1, 2009), http://www.scribd.com/doc/20509291/KEYES-v-OBAMA -78-4-Exhibit-Affidavit-PI-Susan-Daniels-Obama-s-use-of-SS-number-of -the-deceased-Taitz-Orly-Entered-10-01-2009-Gov-uscourts.
2. Exhibit Dossier 4, *Barnett v. Obama*, No. 09-cv-00082 (C.D. Cal. October 1, 2009), http://www.scribd.com/doc/20042509/KEYES-v-OBAMA-69-5 -Exhibit-Dossier-4-Gov-uscourts-cacd-435591-69-5.
3. Jess Henig, with Joe Miller, "Born in the U.S.A.: The Truth About Obama's Birth Certificate," FactCheck.org, August 21, 2008, http://www.factcheck .org/elections-2008/born_in_the_usa.html.
4. Joshua Green, "What Donald Trump's Birther Investigators Will Find in Hawaii," *Atlantic Online*, April 12, 2011, http://www.theatlantic .com/politics/archive/2011/04/what-donald-trumps-birther -investigators-will-find-in-hawaii/237198/.
5. Lisa Schiffren, "Obama's Political Origins," *The Corner* (blog), *National Review Online*, February 19, 2008, http://corner.nationalreview.com/post /?q=NmM2NDQ3ZWQ1YWM0Y2QyZTUxMDdkY2M2OTJlNGE5MWE.
6. "Is Obama the Secret Son of Malcolm X?," *Israel Insider*, November 4, 2008, http://israelinsider.net/profiles/blogs/is-obama-the-secret-son-of.
7. Andy Martin, "Barack Obama Is Not Barack Obama (Real Father Is Frank Marshall Davis)," *Free Republic*, October 22, 2008, http://www.freerepublic .com/focus/f-news/2112829/posts.
8. W. Cleon Skousen, "The Campaign to Abolish the Constitution," *Law and Order*, March 1971, http://www.latterdayconservative.com/articles /w-cleon-skousen/the-campaign-to-abolish-the-constitution.
9. *Glenn Beck*, Fox News, September 2, 2009. Video available at "Beck Links Mussolini, 'Completely Unrelated' Obama 'Indoctrination Next Week,'" *Media Matters*, September 2, 2009, http://mediamatters.org/mmtv/20090 9020037.
10. Max Blumenthal, "Behind the Obama-Hitler Slur," *Daily Beast*, August 24, 2009, http://www.thedailybeast.com/blogs-and-stories/2009-08-24 /behind-the-obama-hitler-slur/.
11. Mark Frauenfelder, "Jay Kinney Reviews *Zeitgeist: The Movie*," *Boing*

Boing, August 6, 2007, http://boingboing.net/2007/08/06/jay-kinney-reviews-z .html.
12. Hofstadter, *Paranoid Style in American Politics*, p. 14.
13. Willis E. Stone, "Organized Tax Protests," *Lima Ohio News*, January 22, 1959, p. 21.
14. "Gates, Buffet, Winfrey Attend Secret NYC Population Control Summit," *Final Hour*, May 25, 2009, http://thefinalhour.blogspot.com/2009/05 /gates-buffett-winfrey-attend-secret-nyc.html.
15. Frank, *Wrecking Crew*, pp. 108–10.
16. Anti-Defamation League, *Rage Grows in America: Anti-government Conspiracies*, p. 1, November 2009, http://www.adl.org/special_reports /rage-grows-in-America/default.asp.
17. Brian Fitzpatrick, "Now Look Who *Else* Is Infiltrating CPAC," *WorldNet Daily*, January 4, 2011, http://www.wnd.com/?pageId=247341.
18. David Catanese, "Tea Party Nation: The Left's Killed 'A Billion People'" Politico, August 7, 2011, http://www.politico.com/blogs/davidcatanese /0811/Tea_Party_Nation_The_lefts_killed_.html.
19. Hofstadter, *Paranoid Style in American Politics*, p. 29.

CHAPTER 1: THE PARANOID STYLE OF HATRED

1. Bishop, *Big Sort*, p. 6.
2. Michelle DeArmond, "Inland GOP Mailing Depicts Obama's Face on Food Stamp," *Press-Enterprise*, October 16, 2008.
3. "Official Apologizes for Obama Chimpanzee E-Mail," CNN.com, April 19, 2011, http://articles.cnn.com/2011-04-19/politics/california.apology_1 _e-mail-apology-scott-baugh?_s=PM:POLITICS.
4. Ingraham, *Obama Diaries*, p. 101.
5. Dinesh D'Souza, "How Obama Thinks," *Forbes*, September 27, 2010.
6. Robert Costa, "Gingrich: Obama's 'Kenyan, Anti-colonial' Worldview," *The Corner* (blog), *National Review Online*, September 11, 2010, http:// www.nationalreview.com/corner/246302/gingrich-obama-s-kenyan -anti-colonial-worldview-robert-costa.
7. *The Rush Limbaugh Show*, September 15, 2009. Audio and transcript available at "Limbaugh: '[I]n Obama's America, the White Kids Now Get Beat Up with the Black Kids Cheering,'" *Media Matters*, http://mediamatters.org /mmtv/200909150017.
8. "Limbaugh Says Obama's Economic 'Role Model' Is Robert Mugabe, Who 'Took the White People's Farms,'" Media Matters, August 4, 2011, http:// mediamatters.org/mmtv/201108040018.
9. *The Rush Limbaugh Show*, July 2, 2010. Audio and transcript available at http://www.rushlimbaugh.com/home/daily/site_070210/content/01125106 .guest.html.
10. George Washington to Bryan Fairfax, August 24, 1774.
11. Quoted in Perlstein, *Before the Storm*, p. 124.
12. Letter to the Inhabitants of Canada, May 29, 1775, *Journals of the Continental Congress*, Avalon Project, Yale Law School, http://avalon.law.yale.edu /18th_century/contcong_05-29-75.asp.
13. Joseph Boven, "Bachmann Calls for Constitutional Conservative Takeover to Free 'Nation of Slaves,'" *Colorado Independent*, July 10, 2010, http://coloradoindependent.com/57145/bachmann-calls-for-constitutional -conservative-takeover-to-free-nation-of-slaves.

14. Davis, "Some Themes of Countersubversion: An Analysis of Anti-Masonic, Anti-Catholic, and Anti-Mormon Literature," in *Fear of Conspiracy*, p. 19.

15. Dixon, *Clansman*, p. 289.

16. Bennett, *Party of Fear*, p. 218.

17. "The 45 Questions Most Frequently Asked About the Jews with the Answers by Pelley" (1939), *Come and Hear*, http://www.come-and-hear.com/supplement/pelley.html.

18. "The Jews Who Run Clinton and the U.S.," Bible Believers, http://www.biblebelievers.org.au/clilist.htm.

19. "Full Text: Bin Laden's 'Letter to America,'" *Guardian*, November 24, 2002, http://www.guardian.co.uk/world/2002/nov/24/theobserver.

20. Beekman, *William Dudley Pelley*, p. 92.

21. Edmondson collected his pamphlets in *I Testify*.

22. *Revealer*, October 15, 1936. The article is reprinted at a number of conspiratorial Web sites (often with extensive annotations), including one belonging to the anti-Semitic Christian Party, http://www.fathersmanifesto.net/fdr2.htm.

23. Morgan, *Illustrations of Masonry*, p. x.

24. Samuel F. B. Morse, "A Foreign Conspiracy Against the Liberties of the United States," in Davis, *Fear of Conspiracy*, p. 99.

25. Ibid., p. 189.

26. Ibid., pp. 315–16.

27. Smoot, *Invisible Government*, http://www.gutenberg.org/files/20224/20224-h/20224-h.htm#chapter07.

28. Sonia Sotomayor, "Lecture: A Latina Judge's Voice," *New York Times*, May 14, 2009, http://www.nytimes.com/2009/05/15/us/politics/15judge.text.html?pagewanted=5&_r=1.

29. *The Rush Limbaugh Show*, May 29, 2009. Audio and transcript available at http://www.rushlimbaugh.com/home/daily/site_052909/content/01125106.guest.html.

30. "*Daily Show*: 'Back of the Bus' Non-story Is a 'Fox News Exclusive,'" *Media Matters*, November 2, 2010, http://mediamatters.org/blog/201011020008.

31. Chuck Baldwin, "Why Are Internment Camps Being Built?," *News with Views*, August 11, 2009, http://www.newswithviews.com/baldwin/baldwin527.htm.

32. *Fox & Friends*, July 28, 2009. Video available at "Beck: 'Obama Has Exposed Himself as a Guy' with 'Deep-Seated Hatred for White People,'" *Media Matters*, July 28, 2009, http://mediamatters.org/mmtv/200907280008.

33. Johnston, *Politics of Healing*, p. 111.

34. Grant, *Passing of the Great Race*, p. xxix.

35. *Good Housekeeping*, February 1921.

36. 1924 Immigration Act, Pub. L. No. 68-139, 43 Stat. 153 (May 26, 1924), http://web.archive.org/web/20080210025205/http://www.historicaldocuments.com/ImmigrationActof1924.htm.

37. *Congressional Record*, 68th Cong., 1st sess., vol. 65, pp. 5961–62 (April 9, 1924).

38. Rand, *Virtue of Selfishness*, p. 135.

39. J. L. DeWitt, *Final Report: Japanese Evacuation from the West Coast, 1942*, U.S. War Department, http://www.archive.org/details/japaneseevacuatioodewi.

40. *Congressional Record*, House, 77th Cong., 2nd sess., vol. 88, pt. 1, p. 1419 (February 18, 1942).

41. Malkin, *In Defense of Internment*, pp. xxxiv–xxxv.
42. U.S. Department of Homeland Security, "Rightwing Extremism: Current Economic and Political Climate Fueling Resurgence in Radicalization and Recruitment," April 7, 2009, http://www.fas.org/irp/eprint/rightwing .pdf.
43. Michelle Malkin, "Confirmed: The Obama DHS Hit Job on Conservatives Is Real," April 14, 2009, http://michellemalkin.com/2009/04/14 /confirm-the-obama-dhs-hit-job-on-conservatives-is-real/.
44. Nathanael Kapner, "Is the Bailout a Rothschild Trick?," *Real Zionist News*, September 25, 2008, http://www.realjewnews.com/?p=288.
45. Christopher Jon Bjerknes, "Ron Paul and the Rothschild Agenda," *Jewish Racism*, April 21, 2009, http://jewishracism.blogspot.com/2009/04 /ron-paul-and-rothschild-agenda.html.
46. David Duke, "Racism: Rand Paul and Rachel Maddow," June 4, 2010, http:// www.davidduke.com/general/racism-rand-paul-and-rachel-maddow-part-ii _18316.html.
47. "Libertarian Party of Kentucky: Rand Paul Is Not a Libertarian or a libertarian," *Independent Political Report*, May 26, 2010, http://www .independentpoliticalreport.com/2010/05/libertarian-party-of-kentucky -rand-paul-is-not-a-libertarian-or-a-libertarian/.
48. Jason Zengerle, "GQ Exclusive: Rand Paul's Kooky College Days (Hint: There's a Secret Society Involved)," *The Wire* (blog), *GQ*, August 9, 2010, http://www.gq.com/blogs/the-q/2010/08/gq-exclusive-rand-pauls -crazy-college-days-hint-theres-a-secret-society-involved.html.
49. Matt Lewis, "Bad News for Rand Paul? 'Aqua Buddha' Prank Victim Is Back," *Politics Daily*, October 19, 2010, http://www.politicsdaily.com/2010 /10/19/bad-news-for-rand-paul-aqua-buddha-prank-victim-is-back/.
50. Nihar Patel, "Palin-Truman," *Daydreaming* (blog), NPR, September 5, 2008, http://www.npr.org/blogs/daydreaming/2008/09/palintruman.html.
51. Robert F. Kennedy Jr., "Governor Palin's Reading List," *Huffington Post*, September 15, 2008, http://www.huffingtonpost.com/robert-f-kennedy-jr /governor-palins-reading-l_b_126478.html.
52. Alden Whitman, "Free-Swinging Critic Dies," obituary of Westbrook Pegler in *New York Times*, June 25, 1969.
53. "Our Mission," The 9/12 Project, http://the912-project.com/test/about /about-the-912-project/.
54. Zaitchik, *Common Nonsense*, p. 219.
55. Ibid., p. 223.
56. Drew Zahn, "Glenn Beck Under Fire for Touting Nazi Author's Book," *WorldNetDaily*, June 7, 2010, http://www.wnd.com/index.php?fa=PAGE .view&pageId=163877.
57. "Elizabeth Dilling's Cautionary Work—*The Plot Against Christianity* Is Now Online," August 20, 2007, http://www.davidduke.com/general/ elizabeth-dillings-cautionary-work-the-plot-against-christianity-is -now-online_2635.html.
58. Dilling, *Roosevelt Red Record*, in Davis, *Fear of Conspiracy*, pp. 274–76.
59. Ezra Taft Benson, *Civil Rights, Tool of Communist Deception* (Salt Lake City: Deseret Book Company, 1968). Excerpt available at http://www .ldsinfobase.net/liberty/ETB_67oct.html.
60. *Glenn Beck*, Fox News, March 23, 2010. Transcript available at Glenn Beck, "What Is 'Social Justice'?" FoxNews.com, March 23, 2010, http://www .foxnews.com/story/0,2933,589832,00.html.

61. "Glenn Beck: Are You a Sept. 12th Person?" December 18, 2008, http://www .glennbeck.com/content/articles/article/198/19403/.

62. *The Glenn Beck Program* (radio), May 7, 2010. Audio available at "Beck: 'The Most Racist People to Ever Live in America Were the Progressives,'" *Media Matters*, May 7, 2010, http://mediamatters.org/mmtv/201005070020.

63. *Glenn Beck*, Fox News, October 15, 2009. Video and transcript available at "Beck Falsely Claimed Anita Dunn 'Worships' 'Her Hero' Mao Zedong," *Media Matters*, October 15, 2009, http://mediamatters.org/research/2009 10150044.

64. Video of Glenn Beck rally, available at "Glenn Beck: 'We Need to Start Thinking Like the Chinese,'" http://www.youtube.com/watch?v=rtCQoIY2lrs.

65. Jonathan Allen and Meredith Shiner, "Tea Partiers Descend on Capitol Hill," *Politico*, November 5, 2009, http://www.politico.com/news/stories /1109/29183.html.

66. Sarah Palin, "Statement on the Current Health Care Debate," http://www .facebook.com/note.php?note_id=113851103434.

67. Timothy Noah, "The Medicare-Isn't-Government Meme," *Slate*, August 5, 2009, http://www.slate.com/id/2224350/.

68. Frank, *What's the Matter with Kansas?*, pp. 8–10.

69. Hofstadter, "The Pseudo-conservative Revolt—1954," in *Paranoid Style in American Politics*, p. 52.

70. Hofstadter, "Pseudo-conservatism Revisited—1965," in ibid., p. 87.

71. Hofstadter, "Pseudo-conservative Revolt—1954," p. 54.

72. Ibid., p. 63.

73. Frank, *What's the Matter with Kansas?*, p. 122.

74. "White Citizens' Council Aimed to Maintain 'Southern Way of Life,'" *Jackson Sun*, 2003, http://orig.jacksonsun.com/civilrights/sec2_citizencouncil .shtml.

75. Andrew Ferguson, "The Boy from Yazoo City: Haley Barbour, Mississippi's Favorite Son," *Weekly Standard*, December 27, 2010.

76. "Governor Barbour's Statement Regarding *Weekly Standard* Article," December 21, 2010, http://www.governorbarbour.com/news/2010/dec/12.21 .10govbarbourweeklystandard.html.

77. Blumenthal, *Republican Gomorrah*, pp. 131–32.

78. Gail Lumet Buckley, *American Patriots: The Story of Blacks in the Military from the Revolution to Desert Storm* (New York: Random House, 2001), p. 323.

79. Eric Pianin, "A Senator's Shame: Byrd, in His New Book, Again Confronts Early Ties to KKK," *Washington Post*, June 18, 2005, http://www.washington post.com/wp-dyn/content/article/2005/06/18/AR2005061801105_pf.html.

80. Pat Buchanan, "A Brief for Whitey," March 21, 2008, http://buchanan.org /blog/pjb-a-brief-for-whitey-969.

81. Eric S. Wyatt, "New Report: Ron Paul's Newsletters Contain Racial and Homophobic Ranting," *Digital Journal*, January 9, 2008, http://www .digitaljournal.com/article/248564/New_Report_Ron_Paul_s_Newsletters _Contain_Racial_and_Homophobic_Ranting.

82. Quoted in Perlstein, *Before the Storm*, p. 248.

83. "Reparations by Way of Health Care Reform," *Investor's Business Daily*, July 27, 2007, http://www.investors.com/NewsAndAnalysis/Article/483402 /200907271844/Reparations-By-Way-Of-Health-Care-Reform.aspx.

84. "Steele: Expect Republicans to Raise Questions About Kagan," *Political Ticker* (blog), CNN.com, http://politicalticker.blogs.cnn.com/2010

/05/10/steele-expect-republicans-to-raise-questions-about-kagan/?fbid
=iNSzuvF3u5F.

85. The supposed text of the Extreme Oath of the Jesuits, sometimes credited
to Charles Didier's *Anselmo: The Grand Master of the Secret Order* (1843),
can be found at any number of anti-Catholic Web sites, such as http://www
.biblebelievers.org.au/jesuits.htm.
86. Ibid.

CHAPTER 2: WHAT IS "CONSPIRACY THEORY"?

1. Frank, *Wrecking Crew*, p. 141.
2. Corsi, *America for Sale*, p. 13.
3. John Hawkins, *Human Events*, January 2007.
4. Cooper, *Behold a Pale Horse*, p. 2.
5. Popper, *Open Society and Its Enemies*, vol. 2, p. 104.
6. Quoted in Lipset and Raab, *Politics of Unreason*, p. 255.
7. Comment by Rapier, August 26, 2009, under post by The Cynic, "Edward
Kennedy Dead," *NowPublic*, August 25, 2009, http://www.nowpublic.com
/world/edward-kennedy-dead.
8. Cooper, *Behold a Pale Horse*, pp. 92–93.
9. David Knowles, "Rick Sanchez Fired from CNN After Radio Rant,"
Surge Desk (blog), AolNews.com, October 1, 2010, http://www.aolnews
.com/surge-desk/article/rick-sanchez-fired-over-remarks-on-jews-media
-jon-stewart/19657894.
10. Eric Deggans, "Ex-CNN Anchor Rick Sanchez Releases Statement, Says
Comments 'Never Intended to Suggest Any Sort of Narrow-Mindedness,'"
The Feed (blog), October 6, 2010, http://www.tampabay.com/blogs/media
/content/ex-cnn-anchor-rick-sanchez-releases-statement-says-comments
-never-intended-suggest-any-sort-.
11. "Personal Statement of Frank Weltner, Librarian," http://www.jewwatch
.com/jew-history-jewwatch-frank-weltner-personal.html.
12. Eco, *Six Walks in the Fictional Woods*, p. 134.
13. "Zionist Jews Spreading Sin and Sickness Through America Like a Wildfire," *The French Connection*, May 5, 2008, http://www.iamthewitness.com
/doc/Zionists.spreading.sin.and.sickness.through.America.like.a.wildfire
.htm.
14. "Freemasonry's Connection to the Homosexual Movement," H.O.M.E.,
Heterosexuals Organized for a Moral Environment, http://www.home60515
.com/23.html.
15. Berlet and Lyons, *Right-Wing Populism in America*, p. 10.
16. Ashleigh Banfield, "Exclusive: Donald Trump Would Spend $600 Mil-
lion of His Own Money on Presidential Bid," ABC News, March 17,
2011, http://abcnews.go.com/Politics/donald-trump-president-trump
-weighs-sheen-palin-obama/story?id=13154163&page=1.
17. Gail Collins, "Donald Trump Gets Weirder," *New York Times*, April 1,
2011.
18. "Donald Trump Responds," letter to *New York Times*, April 8, 2011.
19. Michael D. Shear, "Huckabee Questions Obama Birth Certificate," *The
Caucus* (blog), *New York Times*, March 1, 2011, http://thecaucus.blogs
.nytimes.com/2011/03/01/huckabee-questions-obama-birth
-certificate-claims-he-was-raised-in-kenya/.
20. David Ray Griffin, "9/11 and the American Empire: How Should Religious Peo-

ple Respond?" 911Review.com, http://www.911review.com/articles/griffin/madison.html.

21. Hitler, *Mein Kampf*, p. 200.

22. Cass Sunstein and Adrian Vermeule, "Conspiracy Theories," Harvard Public Law Working Paper No. 08-03, http://papers.ssrn.com/sol3/papers.cfm?abstract_id=1084585.

23. Glenn Greenwald, "Obama Confidant's Spine-Chilling Proposal," *Salon*, January 15, 2010, http://www.salon.com/news/opinion/glenn_greenwald/2010/01/15/sunstein.

24. Aaron Klein, "Top Obama Czar: Infiltrate All Conspiracy Theorists," *WorldNetDaily*, January 14, 2010, http://www.wnd.com/?pageId=121884.

25. Zaitchik, *Common Nonsense*, pp. 119, 121.

26. "The Science of Climate Change: Senate Floor Statement by U.S. Sen. James M. Inhofe (R-Okla.), Chairman, Committee on Environment and Public Works," July 28, 2003, http://inhofe.senate.gov/pressreleases/climate.htm.

27. Charlie Martin, "Climategate Meets the Law: Senator Inhofe to Ask for DOJ Investigation," *Pajamas Media*, February 23, 2010, http://pajamasmedia.com/blog/climategate-and-the-law-senator-inhofe-to-ask-for-congressional-criminal-investigation-pajamas-mediapjtv-exclusive/?singlepage=true.

28. Jeff Poor, "Congresswoman Claims to Have Asked Gore About Global Warming on 19-Degree Inauguration Day," Business & Media Institute, January 27, 2009, http://www.businessandmedia.org/articles/2009/20090127124512.aspx.

29. Kevin Diaz, "Obama's Energy Cap-and-Trade Plan Has Bachmann Talking About a Revolution," *StarTribune*, updated March 24, 2009, http://www.startribune.com/politics/state/41719957.html.

30. Hofstadter, *Paranoid Style in American Politics*, pp. 35–36.

31. Bradford W. Scharlott, "Palin, the Press, and the Fake Pregnancy Rumor: Did a Spiral of Silence Shut Down the Story?" Download available at http://www.mediafire.com/?ad6juf531guj4ru.

32. Berlet and Lyons, *Right-Wing Populism in America*, p. 13.

33. Robertson, *New World Order*, p. 6.

34. Lipset and Raab, *Politics of Unreason*, p. 7.

35. Kramer, *Lone Patriot*, p. 77.

36. Perlstein, *Before the Storm*, pp. 112–13.

37. Lipset and Raab, *Politics of Unreason*, p. 14.

38. Ford, *International Jew*, sec. 19, p. 150.

39. Allen, *Richard Nixon*, p. 310.

40. "Absent Without Leave," Snopes.com, June 19, 2009, http://www.snopes.com/rumors/israel.asp.

41. Cliff Kincaid, "President Bush's New World Order Legacy," *Accuracy in Media*, June 1, 2007, http://www.aim.org/aim-column/president-bushs-new-world-order-legacy/.

42. Southern Poverty Law Center, "New SPLC Report: 'Patriot' Groups, Militias Surge in Number in Past Year," March 2, 2010, http://www.splcenter.org/get-informed/news/splc-report-number-of-patriot-groups-militias-surges-by-244-in-past-year.

43. Mark Potok, "The Year in Hate & Extremism, 2010," *Intelligence Report*, no. 141 (Spring 2011), http://www.splcenter.org/get-informed/intelligence-report/browse-all-issues/2011/spring/the-year-in-hate-extremism-2010.

44. Joseph McCarthy, "Speech at Wheeling, West Virginia, February 9, 1950,"

Congressional Record, 81st Cong., 2nd sess., February 20, 1950, http://en.wikisource.org/wiki/%22Enemies_from_Within%22.

45. "Reaction of President Harry Truman to Loyalty Investigation, 'News Conference at Key West,'" March 30, 1950, in *Public Papers of the Presidents of the United States* (Washington, D.C., 1950), http://historymatters.gmu.edu/d/8078.
46. *Glenn Beck*, Fox News, June 24, 2010. Transcript available at "'Glenn Beck': Vilified by History, Was McCarthy Wrong?," FoxNews.com, June 25, 2010, http://www.foxnews.com/story/0,2933,595324,00.html.
47. "You Don't Need to Be a Weatherman," GlennBeck.com, July 21, 2010, http://www.glennbeck.com/content/articles/article/198/43291/.
48. *Glenn Beck's Common Sense*, pp. 63–68.
49. Paine, *Collected Writings*, p. 666.
50. House Committee on Un-American Activities, *Preliminary Report on Neo-Fascist and Hate Groups*, December 17, 1954, http://debs.indstate.edu/u588n4_1954.pdf.
51. Paine, *Collected Writings*, p. 822.
52. Zaitchik, *Common Nonsense*, p. 198.
53. Lacey Rose, "Glenn Beck Inc.," *Forbes*, April 26, 2010.
54. Hofstadter, "Pseudo-conservatism Revisited—1965," in *Paranoid Style in American Politics*, p. 90.
55. "Constitution Hanging by a Thread Statements," The Historians Corner, *BYU Studies* 19, no. 3, (1979), p. 390, http://webcache.googleusercontent.com/search?q=cache:H9kEDNnrywcJ:emp.byui.edu/venemag/CONSTITUTIONHANGINGBYATHREAD.DOC+Joseph+Smith+hanging+by+a+thread&cd=1&hl=en&ct=clnk&gl=us&client=firefox-a.
56. Bertrand Russell, "An Outline of Intellectual Rubbish," in *Basic Writings of Bertrand Russell*, vol. 10, p. 70.

CHAPTER 3: HENRY FORD AND THE PROTOCOLS OF THE ELDERS OF ZION

1. *Yale Forest School News* 11, no. 2 (April 1923), p. 8.
2. Rosemary R. Davies, "The Rosenbluth Affair," *Forest History* 14, no. 3 (October 1970), p. 19.
3. *New York Times*, October 4, 1924.
4. *Yale Forest School News* 11, no. 2 (April 1923), p. 8.
5. *New York Times*, April 16, 1921.
6. *Yale Forest School News* 11, no. 1 (January 1923), p. 3.
7. *Yale Forest School News* 11, no. 2 (April 1923), p. 11.
8. "The Many Lives of Robert Rosenbluth, 1887–1962, a Review by the Webmaster of the New York Correction History Society," n.d., http://www.correctionhistory.org/html/chronicle/newhampton/bluevistas05.html.
9. As quoted in the *Eighteenth Annual Report of the American Jewish Committee* (1924), p. 453, http://www.ajcarchives.org/AJC_DATA/Files/1925_1926_8_AJCAnnualReport.pdf. Much of the AJC report also appeared as a letter in the October 14, 1924, *New York Times*.
10. Davies, "Rosenbluth Affair," p. 20.
11. *Eighteenth Annual Report of the American Jewish Committee*, p. 456.
12. *Yale Forest School News* 11, no. 2 (April 1923), p. 6.
13. Davies, "Rosenbluth Affair," p. 19.
14. Most quotations from *The International Jew* are from the print-on-demand

edition published by General Books in 2009, which includes only the first twenty articles. The rest of the articles are available in various places online; when I quote from them, I provide a URL.

15. Ford, *International Jew*, sec. 2, p. 16, and sec. 1, p. 2.
16. Wallace, *American Axis*, p. 19.
17. *Eighteenth Annual Report of the American Jewish Committee*, pp. 458–59.
18. Ford, *International Jew*, sec. 7, p. 53.
19. Wallace, *American Axis*, p. 10.
20. "If I Were President," *Collier's*, August 24, 1923.
21. Ford, *International Jew*, sec. 20, p. 158.
22. *Chicago Tribune*, March 8, 1923.
23. Henry Ford, "The Gentle Art of Changing Jewish Names," *Dearborn Independent*, November 12, 1921. The unabridged article can be found at http:// www.churchoftrueisrael.com/Ford/original/ij70.html.
24. Baldwin, *Henry Ford and the Jews*, p. 3.
25. "Letter to the Jews of Newport," August 18, 1790, in *The Papers of George Washington: Digital Edition*, Alderman Library, University of Virginia, http://gwpapers.virginia.edu/.
26. From *The Papers of Ulysses S. Grant*, vol. 7, *December 9, 1862, to March 31, 1863* (Carbondale: Southern Illinois University Press, 1979), p. 56.
27. Population figures from the American Jewish Historical Society, http:// www.jewishvirtuallibrary.org/jsource/US-Israel/usjewpop1.html.
28. Lee, *Henry Ford and the Jews*, p. 148.
29. Clark, *Shylock*, pp. 56–60.
30. Hofstadter, *Age of Reform*, p. 81.
31. Donnelly, *Caesar's Column*, pp. 35–36.
32. Thomas Watson, "The Rich Jews Indict a State! The Whole South Traduced: In the Matter of Leo Frank," *Watson's Magazine*, October 1915, http:// leofrank.org/library/watsons-magazine-1915/5-october.pdf.
33. Berlet and Lyons, *Right-Wing Populism in America*, p. 52.
34. Ford, *International Jew*, sec. 16, p. 125.
35. Baldwin, *Henry Ford and the Jews*, p. 209.
36. Quoted in Wallace, *American Axis*, p. 29.
37. The letter was widely reprinted and published as a pamphlet by the AJC. These extracts were taken from Wallace, *American Axis*, which published its full text on pages 31–33.
38. Gerald L. K. Smith, introduction to *The International Jew*, reprint available at JR's Rare Books and Commentary, "A White Nationalist Literary Resource," http://www.jrbooksonline.com/intro_by_gerald_smith.htm.
39. Bennett and Marcus, *We Never Called Him Henry*.
40. Wallace, *American Axis*, p. 35.
41. "Since Henry Ford Apologized to Me," lyrics by Ballard MacDonald, Billy Rose, and David Stamper (Shapiro, Bernstein & Co., 1922).
42. "Ford Repudiates Bias Against Jews," *New York Times*, January 7, 1942.
43. Ford, *International Jew*, sec. 7, p. 53.
44. Jardim, *First Henry Ford*, p. 143.
45. Richards, *Last Billionaire*, p. 163.
46. "Poor Mr. Ford," manuscript, Josephine Fellows Gomon Papers, University of Michigan Library, http://quod.lib.umich.edu/cgi/f/findaid/findaid-idx?c =bhlead;idno=umich-bhl-85710;view=reslist;didno=umich -bhl-85710;subview=standard;focusrgn=C01;cc=bhlead;byte=46269823.
47. Statistics from the Department of Agriculture, "The 20th Century Transfor-

mation of U.S. Agriculture and Farm Policy," *Electronic Information Bulletin*, no. 3 (June 2005), http://www.ers.usda.gov/publications/eib3/eib3.htm.
48. Murray, *Aldous Huxley*, p. 252.
49. Huxley, *Brave New World*, p. 228.
50. Quoted in Wistrich, *Laboratory for World Destruction*, p. 222.
51. Quoted in Laqueur, *History of Zionism*, p. 86.
52. Herzl, *Jewish State*, p. 12.
53. Ford, *International Jew*, chap. 16.
54. Kiš, "The Book of Kings and Fools," in *Encyclopedia of the Dead*, pp. 136–37.
55. Ibid., p. 172.
56. Quoted in Richard S. Levy, introduction to *A Lie and a Libel*, by Segel, pp. 29–30.
57. Fry, *Waters Flowing Eastward*, pp. 150–51.
58. Ibid., p. 55.
59. Segel, *A Lie and a Libel*, p. 54.
60. Wagner, "Judaism in Music" (1850), in *Theatre*, p. 79.
61. Disraeli, *Coningsby*, vol. 2, pp. 201–4.
62. Disraeli, *Lord George Bentinck*, pp. 109–11.
63. Ford, *International Jew*, October 30, 1920, full article available at http://www.iamthewitness.com/books/Henry.Ford/The.International.Jew/ij37.html.
64. Levy, introduction to *A Lie and a Libel*, by Segel, pp. 16–18.
65. Eco, *Foucault's Pendulum*, p. 476.
66. Philip Graves, "The Protocols of Zion, an Exposure," *London Times*, August 16–18, 1921, http://emperors-clothes.com/antisem/graves-tran.htm.
67. Segel, *A Lie and a Libel*, p. 68.
68. Henry Makow, "Maurice Joly Plagiarized 'Protocols of Zion' (Not Vice Versa)," July 30, 2008, http://www.savethemales.ca/maurice_joly_plagiarized_proto.html.
69. "Taxil Hoax Canard Refuted," *Freemasonry Watch*, http://www.freemasonrywatch.org/luciferquotes.html.
70. Lewin, *Report from Iron Mountain*, pp. 33–34.
71. Obituary for L. C. Lewin, *New York Times*, January 30, 1999.
72. Paula Demers, "Iron Mountain, a Hoax or Betrayal?" (1999), http://www.theforbiddenknowledge.com/hardtruth/iron_mountain.htm.
73. Segel, *A Lie and a Libel*, p. 96.
74. Michael Hagemeister, "*The Protocols of the Elders of Zion*: Between History and Fiction," *New German Critique* 35, no. 1 (2008).
75. D. J. R. Bruckner, "Talk with George Steiner," *New York Times*, May 2, 1982.
76. Webster, *Secret Societies and Subversive Movements*, pp. 412–13.
77. Carr, *Pawns in the Game*, http://jesus-is-savior.com/Evils%20in%20Government/Communism/pawnsinthegame.pdf.
78. Recordings of William Pierce's radio broadcasts can be found at http://resistancereport.com/selected.htm. *The New Protocols* was originally aired on October 30, 1999.
79. Marrs, *Rule by Secrecy*, p. 242.
80. Cumbey, *Planned Deception*, pp. 90–99.
81. Lyndon LaRouche, "The Cult Origins of Zionism," *New Solidarity*, December 8, 1978, http://laroucheplanet.info/pmwiki/pmwiki.php?n=Library.CultOriginsofZionism.
82. The Charter of Allah: The Platform of the Islamic Resistance Movement

(Hamas), 1988, http://www.thejerusalemfund.org/www.thejerusalemfund
.org/carryover/documents/charter.html.

83. Bronner, *Rumor About the Jews*, p. x.

84. Anti-Defamation League, "Anti-Semitism on Arab TV: Satellite Network
Recycles Protocols of the Elders of Zion," January 9, 2004, http://www.adl
.org/special_reports/protocols/protocols_recycled.asp.

85. Ford, *International Jew*, June 18, 1921, http://www.iamthewitness.com
/books/Henry.Ford/The.International.Jew/ij57.html.

86. "Louis McFadden on the Federal Reserve," *Congressional Record*, June 10,
1932, pp. 12595–603, http://www.modernhistoryproject.org/mhp/Article
Display.php?Article=McFadden1932.

87. "Franklin D. Roosevelt, the Apostle of Irredeemable Paper Money," speech
of Louis T. McFadden of Pennsylvania in the House of Representatives,
January 24, 1934, http://www.wakeupfromyourslumber.com/blog/fester
/mcfadden-exposes-fdrs-protocols-gold-swindle.

88. Ron Paul, "Abolish the Fed," LewRockwell.com, September 10, 2002, http://
www.lewrockwell.com/paul/paul53.html.

89. Paul Joseph Watson and Steve Watson, "Obama Regulatory Reform Plan Officially Establishes Banking Dictatorship in United States," PrisonPlanet.com,
June 18, 2009, http://www.prisonplanet.com/obama-regulatory-reform-plan
-officially-establishes-banking-dictatorship-in-united-states.html.

90. Rabbi Rabinovitch's speech of January 12, 1952, *Curierul Conservator*
(Romanian Christian publication), http://www.scribd.com/doc/11736412
/Rabbi-Rabinovichs-Speech-of-January-12th-1952-Discurs-despre-o-agenda
-oculta.

91. Paul F. Boller Jr. and John George, *They Never Said It: A Book of Fake
Quotes, Misquotes, and Misleading Attributions* (New York: Oxford University Press, 1989), pp. 13–16.

92. Ellen Cardona, "Pound's Anti-Semitism at St. Elizabeths: 1945–1958," http://
www.flashpointmag.com/card.htm.

93. Ernie Lazar, "Eustace Mullins and the Conspiratorial Extreme Right," February 3, 2010, http://sites.google.com/site/ernie124102/mullins.

94. Ibid.

95. Jeansonne, *Women of the Far Right*, p. 89.

96. Lazar, "Mullins."

97. Mullins, *Murder by Injection*, p. 204.

98. Mullins, *Biological Jew*, quotation drawn from online edition at *Radical
Press*, http://www.radicalpress.com/?page_id=1244.

99. Mullins, *Secrets of the Federal Reserve*, p. 83 (originally published as *Mullins on the Federal Reserve* by Kasper & Horton in 1952). I have drawn all
quotations from a 1985 edition, available at http://www.arcticbeacon.com
/books/Eustace_Mullins-SECRETS_of_the_Federal_Reserve_Bank.pdf.

100. Perlstein, *Before the Storm*, p. 113.

101. Mullins, *Secrets of the Federal Reserve*, pp. 43–44.

102. House, *Philip Dru, Administrator*, p. 148.

103. McManus, *Insiders*, p. 9.

104. *Glenn Beck*, Fox News, July 15, 2010. Video available at http://www.youtube
.com/watch?v=bqAzxHmbzaY&feature=player_embedded#!.

105. "Beck Promoted the Work of an Anti-Semitic 9/11 Truther," *Media Matters*,
September 22, 2010, http://mediamatters.org/research/201009220060.

106. Benjamin H. Freedman, *Zionism: The Hidden Tyranny*, undated pamphlet, easily available online, for example at http://www.iamthewitness

.com/audio/Benjamin.H.Freedman/Benjamin.H.Freedman_The.Hidden
.Tyranny.pdf.
107. Douglas Reed, *Controversy of Zion*, pp. 232–33.
108. John Coleman, "King Makers, King Breakers: The Cecils" (1985), excerpted at http://mailstar.net/house-schiff.html.
109. Ford, *International Jew*, November 27, 1920, http://www.iamthewitness.com/books/Henry.Ford/The.International.Jew/ij25.html.
110. Hume's Ghost blogs at *The Daily Doubter*, http://dailydoubt.blogspot.com/.
111. Victor Thorn, "Who Is Behind Barack Obama's Rise to Stardom?," August 17, 2009, http://www.davidduke.com/general/victor-thorn-examines-the-jewish-connections-behind-barack-obamas-rise-to-power_11632.html.
112. Michelle Goldberg, "Glenn Beck's Anti-Semitic Attacks," *Daily Beast*, November 10, 2010, http://www.thedailybeast.com/blogs-and-stories/2010-11-10/glenn-becks-anti-semitic-attack-on-george-soros/.
113. Anti-Defamation League, "Glenn Beck's Comments About Reform Judaism Demonstrate 'Bigoted Ignorance,'" February 23 and 24, 2011, http://www.adl.org/PresRele/DiRaB_41/5983_41.htm.
114. Nicholas Graham, "'Tea Party' Leader Melts Down on CNN: 'Obama Is an Indonesian Muslim Turned Welfare Thug,'" *Huffington Post*, September 15, 2009, http://www.huffingtonpost.com/2009/09/15/tea-party-leader-melts-do_n_286933.html.

CHAPTER 4: THE APRON, THE TROWEL,
AND THE KNIFE IN THE BACK—
FREEMASONRY AND THE GREAT CONSPIRACY

1. Barruel, *Memoirs Illustrating the History of Jacobinism*, vol. 4, pp. 493–94.
2. Pipes, *Conspiracy*, p. 70.
3. Robison, *Proofs of a Conspiracy Against All the Religions and Governments of Europe*, p. 108.
4. Ibid., p. 111.
5. Ibid., p. 121.
6. Barruel, *Memoirs Illustrating the History of Jacobinism*, vol. 3, p. 353.
7. Ibid., vol. 1, p. vi.
8. Robert Welch, "More Stately Mansions," in Davis, *Fear of Conspiracy*, p. 333.
9. Winrod, *Adam Weishaupt*, pp. 4–5.
10. Ibid., pp. 21–29.
11. Quoted in Webster, *Secret Societies and Subversive Movements*, p. 256.
12. Cooper, *Behold a Pale Horse*, pp. 78–79.
13. "Benjamin Franklin Was in Hellfire and Responsible Murders?," AboveTopSecret.com forum, string begins on November 20, 2008, http://www.abovetopsecret.com/forum/thread413176/Home," *American Heritage*,
14. Tom Huntington, "Benjamin Franklin's
April/May 2006.
15. *Works of Robert G. Ingersoll*, vol. 5, (1818), text can be found at http://www.deism.com/paine_essay_m1.htm.
16. Thomas Paine, "Origin of Freemasonry, Three Degrees of the Ancient and
17. Pike, *Morals and Dogma of t??y*, p. 321.
Accepted Scottish Rite of Fre
18. Crowley, *Book of the Law*, ·

19. *Searchlight* 14, no. 9 (September 1962), p. 4, http://edgarcayceaustralia.com/pdf02/SL1409.pdf.

20. Robert Anton Wilson, *Cosmic Trigger 1*, p. 4.

21. "The Belmont Brotherhood," essay attributed to Nicholas Bove Jr., retrieved at the Watch Unto Prayer Web site, http://watch.pair.com/belmont.html.

22. Stauffer, *New England and the Bavarian Illuminati*, p. 159.

23. Ibid., p. 92.

24. Barruel, *Memoirs Illustrating the History of Jacobinism*, vol. 4, p. 244.

25. Doctoral thesis by Peggy Pawlowski, cited at http://www.bavarian-illuminati.info/?p=332.

26. Quoted in Terry Melanson, "Illuminati Conspiracy Part One: A Precise Exegesis on the Available Evidence," http://www.conspiracyarchive.com/NWO/Illuminati.htm.

27. Stauffer, *New England and the Bavarian Illuminati*, p. 57.

28. Text of the Sedition Act of 1798 can be found in U.S. Congress, *United States Statutes at Large*, 5th Cong., 2nd sess., vol. 1, chap. 74, http://en.wikisource.org/wiki/United_States_Statutes_at_Large/Volume_1/5th_Congress/2nd_Session/Chapter_74.

29. Stauffer, *New England and the Bavarian Illuminati*, p. 183.

30. Ibid., p. 177.

31. Ibid., p. 216.

32. Ibid., p. 217.

33. Ibid., p. 223, quoting Abraham Bishop's "Oration on the Extent and Power of Political Delusion."

34. Stauffer, *New England and the Bavarian Illuminati*, p. 220.

35. *Writings of Thomas Jefferson*, vol. 7, *1795–1801*, p. 419.

36. Palmer, *Morgan Affair and Anti-Masonry*, p. 21.

37. Finney, *Character, Claims, and Practical Workings of Freemasonry*, p. 18.

38. Ibid., p. 12.

39. Cross, *Burned-Over District*, p. 117.

40. Robert Morris, *William Morgan*, p. 301.

41. Ibid., p. 307.

42. "Debates at the Anti-Masonic Convention," in Davis, *Fear of Conspiracy*, pp. 79–80.

43. John Quincy Adams, *Letters on the Masonic Institution*, pp. 245, 68, 109.

44. Davis, *Fear of Conspiracy*, pp. 66–67.

45. "President Jackson's Veto Message Regarding the Bank of the United States," July 10, 1832, Avalon Project, Yale Law School, http://avalon.law.yale.edu/19th_century/ajton01.asp.

46. John Tyler, "From the Sinks of Europe a Plotter Has Come," in Davis, *Fear of Conspiracy*, p. 1

47. Frederick Robinson, "Jacksonian Attack on Monopoly," in ibid., pp. 70–71.

48. William Goodell, "Role of the Slave Power in American History," in ibid., pp. 118–19.

49. Robert Morris, *William Morgan*, p. 318.

50. Ibid., p. 208.

51. Ibid., p. 227.

52. Ibid., p. 245.

53. Aho, *Things of the World*, p.

54. Bennett, *Party of Fear*, pp. 49

55. The Acacia Press is preparing a reprint of the *Anti-Masonic Scrap Book*;

I found this excerpt posted at http://users.crocker.com/~acacia/text_amsb
.html.

56. Finney, *Character, Claims, and Practical Workings of Freemasonry*, p. 1.

57. "Morgan's Monument," September 14, 1882, http://buffalonian.com/hnews/
1882morgansmonument.html.

58. Masonic statistics from Masonic Service Association of North America,
http://www.msana.com/msastats.asp.

59. Mohr, *Hidden Power Behind Freemasonry*, p. 19.

60. Ibid., p. 138.

61. Hitler, *Mein Kampf*, p. 178.

62. Sven G. Lunden, "The Annihilation of Freemasonry," *American Mercury*, February 1941, http://www.thegod720.com/Annihilation%20of%20
Freemasonry%20%286%20pgs%29.pdf.

63. Texe Marrs, "Zionist Secret Society Conducts Luciferian Rituals Deep in
Cave Under City of Jerusalem: Masonic Jews Plot to Control World," *Intelligence Examiner Report* (blog), *Power of Prophecy*, http://www.texemarrs
.com/042003/masonic_jews_plot_world_control.htm.

64. Cf. A. Millar, "Freemasonry in the Mind of the Islamist," March 23, 2009,
Hudson Institute, http://www.hudson-ny.org/421/freemasonry-in-the-mind
-of-the-islamist, and Thomson, *Dajjal.*

65. "Dajjal Is Here," thread on Islamic Awakening forum, May 12, 2004, http://
forums.islamicawakening.com/f20/dajjal-here-freemasonry-90/.

66. "Joe Jackson, La Toya: Freemason's Conspiracy to Murder Michael," *Follow the Money* (blog), posted by Seeker401, February 17, 2010, http://
seeker401.wordpress.com/2010/02/17/joe-jackson-latoya-freemasons
-conspiracy-to-murder-michael/.

67. "Did the Illuminati Kill Michael Jackson?," Yahoo Answers, http://answers
.yahoo.com/question/index?qid=20090626052200AALeEFA.

68. "Jay-Z's 'Run This Town' and the Occult Connections," http://vigilantcitizen
.com/?p=1948.

69. "Jay-Z Speaks on the Illuminati and His Religious Beliefs," Necole Bitchie,
January 13, 2010, http://necolebitchie.com/2010/01/13/jay-z-speaks-on-the
-illuminati-and-his-religious-beliefs/.

70. "Inimica Vis, Encyclical of Pope Leo XIII on Freemasonry," December 8,
1892, http://www.vatican.va/holy_father/leo_xiii/encyclicals/documents
/hf_l-xiii_enc_08121892_inimica-vis_en.html.

71. "Quaesitum Est, Declaration on Masonic Associations, Sacred Congregation for the Doctrine of the Faith," November 26, 1983, http://www.ewtn
.com/library/CURIA/CDFMASN2.HTM.

72. LaHaye, *Rapture (Under Attack)*, p. 138.

73. Leadbeater, *Masters and the Path*, p. 20.

74. Henry Makow, "Illuminati Defector Details Pervasive Conspiracy," October 14, 2002, http://www.savethemales.ca/141002.html.

75. These quotations are selected from an eighteen-part interview with Svali
posted at CentrExNews.com, http://web.archive.org/web/20030609103208
/http://centrexnews.com/columnists/svali/archive.html. Svali's writings
and a link to her self-published book can be found at http://www.suite101
.com/articles.cfm/ritual_abuse; http://www.projectcamelot.org/svali.html
provides further links and updates.

76. Ed Koni, "Svali Is Alive!," October 11, 2008, http://svalispeaks.wordpress
.com/2008/10/11/svali-is-alive-update-on-her-whereabouts/.

77. "Sarah Palin and the Freemasons and the Order of Eastern Stars," posted at *End*

Times Prophetic Words (blog), April 2, 2008, http://endtimespropheticwords .wordpress.com/2008/10/05/sarah-palin-and-the-freemasons-and-order-of -eastern-stars/.

78. "Palin's Freemason Recognition Sign Use," *The F.W.* (blog), November 1, 2008, http://freemasonry-watch.blogspot.com/2008/11/palins-freemason -recognition-sign-use.html.

79. "Proof Pope Benedict Is a Freemason: Facilitating Mystery Babylon Masonic Third Temple Ecumenicalism," posted on YouTube by FreetheMasons, July 7, 2011, http://www.youtube.com/watch?v=1yOjjqqOtmA.

80. "Senator Barack Obama Is a 32nd Degree Prince Hall Mason," End Times Christianity, September 28, 2008, http://www.endtimeschristianity.com /cgi-bin/webbbs_files/webbbs_config.pl?noframes;read=1281.

81. "A Prophetic Prediction Concerning Glenn Beck," posted by JesusSaves2008 at AboveTopSecret.com forum, June 4, 2010, http://www.abovetopsecret .com/forum/thread558849/pg1.

82. Luther, *On the Jews and Their Lies*, http://www.humanitas-international .org/showcase/chronography/documents/luther-jews.htm.

83. Pope Leo XIII, "Custodi di quella fede—On Freemasonry," a letter to the Italian people, December 8, 1892, http://www.catholicnewsagency.com /document.php?n=351.

84. Morgan, *Illustrations of Masonry*, p. 86.

85. Ibid., pp. 83–84.

86. Ibid., p. 15.

87. Quoted in Mendes-Flohr and Reinharz, *Jew in the Modern World*, p. 467.

88. Morgan, *Illustrations of Masonry*, p. 25.

89. Whalen, *Christianity and American Freemasonry*, p. 22.

90. Webster, *Secret Societies and Subversive Movements*, p. 343.

91. Ibid., p. 467.

CHAPTER 5: THE WHORE OF BABYLON
AND STEALTH JIHAD

1. *Scarborough Country*, MSNBC, December 8, 2004. Transcript available at http://www.msnbc.msn.com/id/6685898/.

2. "Is the Catholic League Necessary?," Catholic League for Religious and Civil Rights Web page, http://www.catholicleague.org/about.php.

3. Jacoby, *Age of American Unreason*, p. 198.

4. Palin, *America by Heart*, p. 185.

5. John F. Kennedy, "Address to the Greater Houston Ministerial Association," September 12, 1960.

6. Quoted in Kevin Baker, "Religious Education: Confronting an Issue as Old as Public Schools," *American Heritage*, May 2001.

7. Quoted in Lockwood, *Anti-Catholicism in American Culture*, p. 37.

8. Palin, *America by Heart*, p. 183.

9. Bennett, *Party of Fear*, p. 20.

10. "An American's Oath of Abjuration in 1763, Sworn to by Henry Ludington When Appointed to the Office of Sub-sheriff," *Connecticut Magazine, an Illustrated Monthly* 12, nos. 1–3 (1907), p. 263; also see "Laws in Ireland for the Suppression of Popery," http://library.law.umn.edu/irishlaw/oaths .html.

11. Joshua Coffin, *A Sketch of the History of Newbury, Newburyport, and West Newbury, from 1635 to 1845* (Boston: S. G. Drake, 1845), pp. 249–51.

12. George Washington, General Orders, November 5, 1775, Cambridge, George Washington Papers at the Library of Congress, 1741–1799, edited by John C. Fitzpatrick, http://memory.loc.gov/cgi-bin/query/r?ammem/mgw: @field%28DOCID+@lit%28gw040073%29%29.

13. George Washington to Roman Catholics in America, March 15, 1790, in *The Papers of George Washington, Presidential Series,* vol. 5, pp. 299–301, transcript at http://www.consource.org/index.asp?bid=582&documentid=58331.

14. *Political Writings of John Adams,* pp. 5–9, 12.

15. Leckie, *American and Catholic,* p. 110.

16. Hofstadter, *Paranoid Style in American Politics,* p. 20.

17. Sherry, *In the Shadow of War,* p. 174.

18. Luke, *Female Jesuit,* p. vii.

19. Emerson, *Journals and Miscellaneous Notebooks,* vol. 16, p. 152.

20. *Collected Writings of Walt Whitman: The Journalism,* vol. 1, *1834–1846,* pp. 102–6.

21. Greenspan, *Cambridge Companion to Walt Whitman,* pp. 86–87.

22. Complete transcript of Fanny Fern's *New York Ledger* review of *Leaves of Grass* can be found at the Walt Whitman Archive, Contemporary Reviews, http://www.whitmanarchive.org/criticism/reviews/leaves1855/anc.00026 .html.

23. Samuel F. B. Morse, "A Foreign Conspiracy Against the Liberties of the United States," in Davis, *Fear of Conspiracy,* pp. 97–98.

24. Beecher, *Plea for the West,* pp. 51–68.

25. *Account of the Conversion of the Reverend John Thayer,* p. 15.

26. Carmine A. Prioli, "The Ursuline Outrage," *American Heritage,* February/March 1982.

27. Schultz, *Fire and Roses,* p. 5.

28. Ibid., p. 3.

29. Franchot, *Roads to Rome,* pp. 144–45.

30. Schultz, *Fire and Roses,* pp. 5–7.

31. *Awful Disclosures of Maria Monk,* pp. 24–25.

32. Ibid., p. 63.

33. Hofstadter, *Paranoid Style in American Politics,* pp. 21–22.

34. *Awful Disclosures of Maria Monk,* p. 129.

35. William L. Stone, *Maria Monk and the Nunnery of the Hotel Dieu,* pp. 10–11.

36. Ibid., p. 25.

37. Ibid., p. 26.

38. Ibid., p. 33.

39. Ibid., p. 45.

40. Quoted in Benko, *Pagan Rome and the Early Christians,* pp. 65–66.

41. Hitler, *Mein Kampf,* pp. 185–86.

42. Tocqueville, *Democracy in America,* p. 358.

43. Griff Ruby, "The Selling of Sodomy: Homosexuality's Dirty Secret," *Daily Catholic,* March 10, 2006.

44. Herman, *Antigay Agenda,* p. 85.

45. Quoted in Biale, *Eros and the Jews,* p. 94.

46. Goff, *Soviet Art of Brainwashing,* http://www.fhu.com/articles/brain washing1.html.

47. Sharlet, *Family,* p. 181.

48. Gobineau, *Moral and Intellectual Diversity of Races,* p. 454.

49. David A. Hollinger, "Amalgamation and Hypodescent: The Question of Eth-

noracial Mixture in the History of the United States," *American Historical Review* 108, no. 5 (December 2003).

50. Glenn Beck, September 15, 2010, interview with Dinesh D'Souza. Transcript at http://www.glennbeck.com/content/articles/article/196/45475/.

51. Bennett, *Party of Fear*, p. 170.

52. Ibid., p. 175.

53. Transcripts and a facsimile of this forgery ("Encyclical: A Letter from Pope Leo XIII to the Romish World") can be found at http://threshingfloor-radio.com/wp-content/uploads/Encyclical.pdf.

54. Mullins, *Curse of Canaan*, p. 146.

55. Quoted in Edmund Morris, *Rise of Theodore Roosevelt*, p. 477.

56. Quoted in *Crisis*, July/August 2000, http://bit.ly/gI1Iv4.

57. Woodrow Wilson, *New Freedom*, p. 85.

58. Zachary Roth, "Tea Party Convention Organizer Used 'Our Passion for the Movement to Build His Start-Up,'" *Talking Points Memo*, January 13, 2010, http://tpmmuckraker.talkingpointsmemo.com/2010/01/tea_party_convention_organizer_used_our_passion_fo.php.

59. Chalmers, *Hooded Americanism*, p. 33.

60. Saint Basil the Great, Homily 2 on Psalm 14, *Against Usury*, http://early churchtexts.com/main/basilofcaes/homily_on_psalm_14_usury.shtml.

61. Carpenter, *Father Charles E. Coughlin*, p. 32.

62. "The National Union for Social Justice," speech delivered by Coughlin on November 11, 1934, transcript at Social Security Online History, http://www.ssa.gov/history/fcspeech.html.

63. "Glenn Beck: Father Coughlin Comparison 'Laughable,'" FoxNews.com, March 12, 2010, http://www.foxnews.com/story/0,2933,589110,00.html.

64. Coughlin, *New Deal in Money*, p. 118.

65. Quoted in Bennett, *Party of Fear*, p. 259.

66. Ibid.

67. Quoted in ibid., p. 262.

68. Rudin, *Christians & Jews, Faith to Faith*, p. 88.

69. Quoted in Richard Bernstein, review of *Radio Priest Charles Coughlin: The Father of Hate Radio*, by Donald Warren, *New York Times*, July 10, 1996.

70. Irwin, "Inside the 'Christian Front,'" http://www.ajcarchives.org/AJC_DATA/Files/THR-CF7.PDF.

71. Jacob Weisberg, "The Heresies of Pat Buchanan," *New Republic*, October 22, 1990.

72. Pat Buchanan, "Is This Our America Anymore?," December 17, 2010, http://buchanan.org/blog/is-this-our-america-anymore-4582.

73. Pat Buchanan, "Will America Survive to 2050?," August 25, 2006, http://buchanan.org/blog/pjb-will-america-survive-to-2050-57.

74. Ibid.

75. Elisabeth Bumiller, "Mega-church Pastor in Texas Backs McCain," *New York Times*, February 27, 2008.

76. Michael D. Shear, "Hagee Endorses McCain," *The Trail* (blog), *Washington Post*, February 27, 2008, http://voices.washingtonpost.com/44/2008/02/hagee-endorses-mccain-1.html.

77. Catholic League, "McCain Embraces Bigot—Links to Anti-Catholic Hagee Video," February 28, 2008, http://www.catholicleague.org/release.php?id=1393.

78. Catholic League, "Hagee in His Own Words," http://catholicleague.net/printer.php?p=Catalyst&id=2393.

79. Catholic League, "McCain Embraces Bigot."

80. Sam Stein, "McCain Backer Hagee Said Hitler Was Fulfilling God's Will," *Huffington Post*, May 21, 2008, http://www.huffingtonpost.com/2008/05/21/mccain-backer-hagee-said_n_102892.html.

81. Rachel Tabachnick, "Hagee vs. Hagee, in His Own Words," *Talk to Action* (blog), May 21, 2010, http://www.talk2action.org/story/2010/5/21/162959/223/Front_Page/Hagee_vs_Hagee_In_His_Own_Words.

82. John Hagee, "Washington Summit," Christians United for Israel, http://www.cufi.org/site/PageServer?pagename=events_washington_summit.

83. John Hagee to William Donohue, May 12, 2008, http://www.catholicleague.org/images/upload/image_200805130112.Donohue051208.pdf.

84. Catholic League, "Hagee Regrets Offending Catholics, Controversy Ends," May 13, 2008, http://www.catholicleague.org/release.php?id=1436.

85. Dan Gilgoff, "Exclusive: Pastor John Hagee on Zionism and John McCain," *U.S. News & World Report*, July 20, 2009, http://www.usnews.com/news/blogs/god-and-country/2009/7/20/exclusive-pastor-john-hagee-on-zionism-and-john-mccain.html.

86. "Oklahoma Set to Ban Shariah, Muslims Not Happy," *Logan's Warning* (blog), June 8, 2010, http://loganswarning.com/2010/06/08/oklahoma-set-to-ban-sharia-muslims-not-happy/.

87. Michael Howard Saul, "Mayor Has Strong Words for Palin," *Wall Street Journal*, July 20, 2010, http://online.wsj.com/article/SB10001424052748703720504575377570672971874.html?mod=WSJ_hpp_MIDDLTopStories.

88. Bryan Fischer, "No More Mosques, Period," *Rightly Concerned*, August 10, 2010, http://action.afa.net/Blogs/BlogPost.aspx?id=2147497353.

89. Jeffrey T. Kuhner, "Radical Islam's Conquest of America: Welcome to the United States of Arabia," *Washington Times*, August 5, 2010, http://www.washingtontimes.com/news/2010/aug/5/radical-islams-conquest-of-america/.

90. Anti-Defamation League, "Statement on Islamic Community Center near Ground Zero," July 28, 2010, http://www.adl.org/PresRele/CvlRt_32/5820_32.htm.

91. Bob Allen, "Huckabee Draws Heat for Anti-Islam Remarks," *Associated Baptist Press*, February 21, 2011, http://www.abpnews.com/content/view/6144/53/.

92. See "Exposing Huckabee's Dominionist Sympathies," at *Religious Right Watch*, January 19, 2008, http://www.religiousrightwatch.com/2008/01/exposing-huckab.html; and Alex Koppelman and Vincent Rossmeier, "Huckabee's Radical Religious Friends," *Salon*, January 18, 2008, http://www.salon.com/news/feature/2008/01/18/huckabee_connections/.

93. Catherine Herridge, "AIG Bailout Promotes Shariah Law, Lawsuit Claims," FoxNews.com, December 22, 2008, http://www.foxnews.com/story/0,2933,471004,00.html.

94. Center for Security Policy, *Shariah: The Threat to America, an Exercise in Competitive Analysis, Report of Team "B" II* (2010), http://europenews.dk/files/Shariah%20-%20The%20Threat%20to%20America%20%28Team%20B%20Report%29%2009142010.pdf.

95. Ford, *International Jew*, pp. 87–88.

96. Debbie Schlussel, "Whoa: Osama bin Laden Dead but Won't Make Much Diff Amid Growing Islamic Threat to West," May 1, 2011, http://www.debbieschlussel.com/36592/whoa-osama-bin-laden-dead-but-wont-make-much-diff-amid-growin-islamic-threat-to-west.

97. "2083: A European Declaration of Independence," http://info.public intelligence.net/AndersBehringBreivikManifesto.pdf.
98. Pamela Geller and Robert Spencer, "Norway, Free Speech, and the Counter-jihad," *American Thinker*, August 14, 2011, http://www.americanthinker .com/2011/08/norway_free_speech_and_the_counterjihad.html.
99. Jon Cohen and Michael D. Shear, "Poll Shows More Americans Think Obama Is a Muslim," *Washington Post*, August 19, 2010, http://www.washingtonpost .com/wp-dyn/content/article/2010/08/18/AR2010081806913.html.

CHAPTER 6: THE NEW DEAL, THE OLD RIGHT,
AND THE PSEUDO-CONSERVATIVE REVOLTS

1. "Obama Right That Roosevelt Was Called a Socialist and Communist," *Politifact* (blog), *St. Petersburg Times*, September 22, 2009, http:// politifact.com/truth-o-meter/statements/2009/sep/22/barack-obama /obama-roosevelt-socialist-communist/.
2. Flynn, *Country Squire in the White House*, p. 122.
3. Cincinnatus, *War! War! War!* (1940; repr., Metairie, La.: Sons of Liberty, 1984), pp. 188–212.
4. David Kupelian, "Why Team Obama Thrives on Creating Crises," *WorldNet Daily*, March 17, 2010, http://www.wnd.com/index.php/index.php?pageId =128141.
5. Mark Hyman, "The Man Who Despises America," *American Spectator*, November 11, 2009, http://spectator.org/archives/2009/11/11/the-man-who -despises-america/.
6. Gordon Bishop, "Obama Hates America and Its Constitution," *Western Front America*, March 28, 2010, http://westernfrontamerica.com/2010/04 /07/obama-hates-america-constitution/.
7. Kurtz, *Radical-in-Chief*, p. viii.
8. Brian Montpoli, "Rep. Trent Franks: Obama Is Enemy of Humanity," *Political Hotsheet* (blog), CBSNews.com, September 29, 2009, http://www .cbsnews.com/8301-503544_162-5350756-503544.html.
9. Hofstadter, *Paranoid Style in American Politics*, p. 31.
10. Pat Buchanan, "The Cultural War for the Soul of America," http://buchanan .org/blog/the-cultural-war-for-the-soul-of-america-149.
11. Zeskind, *Blood and Politics*, p. 293.
12. Pat Buchanan, "Traditional Americans Are Losing Their Nation," *World NetDaily*, October 20, 2009, http://www.wnd.com/index.php?fa=PAGE .view&pageId=113463.
13. Carlson, *Under Cover*, p. 72. A free e-book can be downloaded at http:// spitfirelist.com/books/under_cover1b.pdf.
14. Ibid., p. 234.
15. Ibid., p. 31.
16. Ibid., pp. 48–50.
17. Jeansonne, *Women of the Far Right*, p. 35.
18. Belknap, *American Political Trials*, p. 181.
19. Quoted in *Life*, January 17, 1944.
20. Zeskind, *Blood and Politics*, pp. 149–50.
21. Geoffrey R. Stone, *Perilous Times*, p. 274.
22. Frederick R. Barkley, "Sedition Trial's Wrangles Come to an Abrupt Close," *New York Times*, December 9, 1944.

23. Neiwert, *Eliminationists*, p. 90.

24. Quoted in Kaplan, *Encyclopedia of White Power*, p. 17.

25. American Jewish Congress report on Pelley, April 14, 1939, http://www .ajcarchives.org/AJC_DATA/Files/THR-SS2.PDF.

26. A free download of *Dupes of Judah* is available at http://www.archive.org /stream/TheDupesOfJudah/DupesOfJudahJr#page/no/mode/2up.

27. Pelley, *Seven Minutes in Eternity with the Aftermath*, pp. 9–15.

28. Beekman, *William Dudley Pelley*, p. 81.

29. Quoted in David Lobb, "Fascist Apocalypse: William Pelley and Millennial Extremism," Department of History, Syracuse University (paper presented at the Fourth Annual Conference of the Center for Millennial Studies, November 1999).

30. Geoffrey S. Smith, *To Save a Nation*, p. 62.

31. Beekman, *William Dudley Pelley*, p. 98.

32. Geoffrey S. Smith, *To Save a Nation*, p. 62.

33. A paraphrase appears on p. 145 of Smith; a facsimile of the actual poster (from which I quoted directly) can easily be located on the Internet, for example at http://toto.l.b.unca.edu/findingaids/mss.pelley/default_pelley _william_dudley.htm.

34. Ibid., p. 148.

35. A. V. Schaeffenberg, *The Life of William Dudley Pelley*, http://www.come -and-hear.com/supplement/life-of-pelley/index.html.

36. Pelley, *Undying Mind*, pp. 145–46.

37. "Interview with Oscar R. Ewing," conducted by J. R. Fuchs, Truman Library, http://www.trumanlibrary.org/oralhist/ewing1.htm.

38. Berg, *Lindbergh*, p. 445.

39. Ibid.

40. Lindbergh, *Why Is Your Country at War?*, p. 6. A free download is available at http://books.google.com/books?id=qzAWAAAAYAAJ&printsec=front cover&dq=Why+is+Your+Country+at+War%3F+Lindbergh&hl=en&ei =l-M3Tfb-AoH7lweg9ZH_Bg&sa=X&oi=book_result&ct=result&resnum =1&ved=0CCMQ6AEwAA#v=onepage&q&f=false.

41. Quoted from "War and Peace, Hero Speaks," *Time*, September 25, 1939, http://www.time.com/time/magazine/article/0,9171,761950-1,00.html.

42. From a transcript posted at http://www.charleslindbergh.com/americanfirst /speech.asp.

43. Berg, *Lindbergh*, p. 425.

44. Ibid., p. 421.

45. Quoted in Geoffrey S. Smith, *To Save a Nation*, p. 179.

46. Berg, *Lindbergh*, pp. 385–86.

47. Geoffrey S. Smith, *To Save a Nation*, p. 151.

48. Ibid., pp. 178–79.

49. Duffy, *Lindbergh vs. Roosevelt*, pp. x–xi.

50. Ibid., p. 17.

51. Ibid., p. 201.

52. Ibid., pp. 218–19.

53. Jonah Goldberg, "A Lie for a Just Cause," *Los Angeles Times*, November 17, 2005.

54. Sarah Palin, "Don't Get Demoralized, Get Organized! Take Back the 20," March 23, 2010, http://www.facebook.com/note.php?note_id=373854973434.

55. The Daily Rundown, MSNBC, March 25, 2010, http://rundown.msnbc .msn.com.

56. Markos Moulitsas Twitter status, January 8, 2011, http://twitter.com /markos/status/23821038362034176.

57. Paul Krugman, "Assassination Attempt in Arizona," *Conscience of a Liberal* (blog), *New York Times*, January 8, 2011, http://krugman.blogs.nytimes .com/2011/01/08/assassination-attempt-in-arizona/.

58. See Edgar Sandoval, "Arizona Sheriff Clarence Dupnik Refuses to Enforce State's New 'Racist' Immigration Law," *New York Daily News*, April 30, 2010, for example.

59. Michael Martinez, "Shooting Throws Spotlight on State of U.S. Political Discourse," CNN.com, January 10, 2011, http://www.cnn.com/2011/US/01 /09/arizona.shooting.rhetoric/index.html.

60. Sarah Netter, "Arizona Sheriff Blasts Rush Limbaugh for Spewing 'Irresponsible' Vitriol," ABC News, January 10, 2011, http://abcnews.go.com/Politics /arizona-sheriff-blasts-rush-limbaugh-spewing-irresponsible-vitriol /story?id=12583285.

61. Nicholas Graham, "Loughner Genocide Video Released by Pima Community College," *Huffington Post*, January 15, 2011, http://www.huffingtonpost .com/2011/01/15/loughner-genocide-video-r_n_809489.html.

62. Pamela Geller, "Jared Loughner's High School Pal Twitter Page Describes Arizona Shooter as 'Left Wing, Quite Liberal,'" *Atlas Shrugs*, January 8, 2011, http://atlasshrugs2000.typepad.com/atlas_shrugs/2011/01/jared -loughner-high-school-pal-twitter-page-describes-arizona-shooter -loughner-left-wing-quite-liber.html.

63. "Rush Limbaugh: Jared Loughner Has 'Full Support' of Democratic Party," *Huffington Post*, January 11, 2011, http://www.huffingtonpost.com/2011 /01/11/rush-limbaugh-jared-loughner-full-support-democrat_n_807543 .html.

64. "Beck: An Attempt on Palin's Life 'Could Bring the Republic Down,'" *The Hill*, January 10, 2011, http://gop12.thehill.com/2011/01/beck-attempt-on-palins -life-could-bring.html.

65. "Sarah Palin on 'America's Enduring Strength,'" *The Corner* (blog), *National Review Online*, January 12, 2011, http://www.nationalreview.com/corner /256942/sarah-palin-americas-enduring-strength-nro-staff.

66. Glenn Reynolds, "The Arizona Tragedy and the Politics of Blood Libel," *Wall Street Journal*, January 10, 2011.

67. James Oliphant, "Sarah Palin's Charge of 'Blood Libel' Spurs Outcry from Jewish Leaders," *Los Angeles Times*, January 12, 2011.

68. Jennifer Rubin Twitter status, January 12, 2011, http://twitter.com /JRubinBlogger/status/25187179152023552#.

69. Jennifer Rubin, "Why Jews Hate Palin," *Commentary*, January 2010.

70. Jim Geraghty, "The Term 'Blood Libel': More Common Than You Might Think," *National Review Online*, January 12, 2011, http://www.national review.com/campaign-spot/256955/term-blood-libel-more-common -you-might-think.

71. *On the Record with Greta Van Susteren*, Fox News, January 19, 2011. Transcript available at "'Blood Libel' Double Standard? Will Democrat Be Criticized like Palin for Nazis-GOP Comments?," FoxNews.com, January 19, 2011, http://www.foxnews.com/on-air/on-the-record/transcript /039blood-libel039-double-standard-will-democrat-be-criticized-palin-nazis -gop-comments.

72. Greg Sargent, "Sharron Angle Floated Possibility of Armed Insurrection," *The Plum Line* (blog), *Washington Post*, January 15, 2010, http://voices

.washingtonpost.com/plum-line/2010/06/sharron_angle_floated_possibil
.html.

73. Ben Smith, "Obama Brings a Gun to a Knife Fight," *Politico*, June 14, 2008, http://www.politico.com/blogs/bensmith/0608/Obama_brings_a_gun_to_a_knife_fight.html.

74. Michelle Malkin, "The Progressive Climate of Hate: An Illustrated Primer, 2000–2010," January 10, 2011, http://michellemalkin.com/2011/01/10/the-progressive-climate-of-hate-an-illustrated-primer-2000-2010/.

75. Manchester, *Death of a President*, p. 44.

76. Reproductions of both the handbill and the ad can be found at http://www.law.uga.edu/dwilkes_more/jfk_24blownaway.html.

77. Christopher Bateman, "Q&A: Sam Kashner on the Definitive J.F.K. Assassination Book," *VF Daily* (blog), *Vanity Fair*, August 31, 2009, http://www.vanityfair.com/online/daily/2009/08/vf-daily-do-you-think.html.

78. Jeffrey Lord, "JFK, Bush, and the Politics of Hate," *American Spectator*, November 23, 2007.

79. Ezra Taft Benson, "The Internal Threat Today," in Davis, *Fear of Conspiracy*, pp. 340–41.

80. Ibid., p. 340.

81. Revilo P. Oliver, "Marxmanship in Dallas," *American Opinion: An Informal Review*, February 1964. The piece can also be found on the Internet, at http://www.revilo-oliver.com/rpo/Marxmanship1.html.

82. *Newsweek*, February 24, 1964.

83. "The Testimony of Professor Revilo Pendleton Oliver Before the Warren Commission, 9th September, 1964," http://www.revilo-oliver.com/rpo/Warren_Commission_Testimony.html.

84. Hofstadter, *Paranoid Style in American Politics*, pp. 9, 14, 43, 74.

85. Revilo P. Oliver, "Who's for Democracy?," from a pamphlet called *Populism and Elitism*, published by *Liberty Bell Magazine* in 1982. Available at http://www.revilo-oliver.com/rpo/democrac.htm.

86. Audio of the speech can easily be found on the Internet, for example at Kevin Alfred Strom's "Revilo P. Oliver, The Life and Works of a Great American Thinker and Writer," http://www.revilo-oliver.com/news/1966/07/conspiracy-or-degeneracy/.

87. Revilo P. Oliver, "Contemporary Journalists," *Liberty Bell Magazine*, February 1985, http://www.faem.com/oliver/rpo028.htm.

CHAPTER 7: WHITE SUPREMACY AND BLACK SEPARATISM—EXCEPTIONAL HATREDS, SEPARATE BUT EQUAL

1. William F. Buckley Jr., *Cruising Speed: A Documentary* (New York: Putnam, 1971), p. 111.

2. Nesta Bevan, "The Forgotten Conservative," *Taki's Magazine*, September 22, 2009.

3. Revilo P. Oliver, "The New Order Changeth, Too," *Liberty Bell Magazine*, July 1989, http://www.revilo-oliver.com/rpo/conserva.htm.

4. William Kristol, "Stand for Freedom," *Weekly Standard*, February 14, 2011.

5. Lacey Rose, "Glenn Beck Inc.," *Forbes*, April 8, 2010, http://www.forbes.com/forbes/2010/0426/entertainment-fox-news-simon-schuster-glenn-beck-inc.html.

6. Willis Carto, introduction to *Imperium*, by Yockey, p. xiv.

7. Ibid., p. x.

8. Ibid., p. xii.

9. Francis Parker Yockey, "The Proclamation of London 1949," http://home .alphalink.com.au/~radnat/fpyockey/proclamation.html.

10. Carto, introduction to *Imperium*, by Yockey, p. xxiii.

11. Yockey, *Imperium*, pp. 294–95.

12. Ibid., pp. 493–94.

13. Ibid., p. 498.

14. Ibid., p. 511.

15. Ibid., pp. 513–14.

16. Ibid., p. 4.

17. Ibid., p. 546.

18. Ibid., p. 615.

19. Ibid., p. 617.

20. Rockwell, *White Power*, chap. 14. Available as a free e-book at the White Nationalist Web site Church of True Israel, http://www.churchoftrueisrael .com/rocwell/whitepower/.

21. Gardell, *In the Name of Elijah Muhammad*, pp. 55–56.

22. Essien-Udom, *Black Nationalism*, p. 227.

23. Daniel Pipes, "How Elijah Muhammad Won," *Commentary*, June 2000.

24. Essien-Udom, *Black Nationalism*, p. 125.

25. "Farrakhan: A White Man's Heaven Is a Black Man's Hell," video posted at YouTube, http://www.youtube.com/watch?v=cb8xKGaTJhg.

26. "The Messenger Passes," *Time*, March 10, 1975.

27. Elijah Muhammad's 1959 speech, quoted in Essien-Udom, *Black Nationalism*, p. 254.

28. Ibid., p. 260.

29. Ibid., p. 256.

30. Ibid., p. 258.

31. Ibid., p. 257.

32. Ibid., p. 336.

33. Reprinted at the American Nazi Party Web site, http://www.american naziparty.com/rockwell/materials/articles/stand.php.

34. Essien-Udom, *Black Nationalism*, p. 261.

35. Rockwell, *White Power*, chap. 10.

36. Donald Pease, "Exceptionalism" in Bruce Burgett, Glenn Hendler (eds.), *Keywords for American Cultural Studies* (New York: NYU Press, 2007), p 108.

37. Tocqueville, *Democracy in America*, pp. 455–56.

38. John Winthrop, "A Model of Christian Charity" (1630), http://religious freedom.lib.virginia.edu/sacred/charity.html.

39. Quin Hillyer, "McCain's Best Argument," *American Spectator*, October 30, 2008, http://spectator.org/archives/2008/10/30/mccains-best-argument/ print.

40. Ken Blackwell, "Liberty and American Exceptionalism," *Townhall*, July 4, 2010, http://townhall.com/columnists/kenblackwell/2010/07/04/liberty _and_american_exceptionalism/page/full/.

41. Monica Crowley, "American Exceptionalism," *Washington Times*, July 1, 2009, http://www.washingtontimes.com/news/2009/jul/01/american -exceptionalism/.

42. Palin, *America by Heart*, p. 69.

43. Karen Tumulty, "American Exceptionalism: An Old Idea and a New Political

Battle," *Washington Post*, November 29, 2010, http://www.washingtonpost
.com/wp-dyn/content/article/2010/11/28/AR2010112804139.html. Huckabee and Santorum are quoted by Tumulty as well.

44. William F. Buckley Jr., "Our Mission Statement," *National Review*, November 19, 1955, http://www.nationalreview.com/articles/223549/our-mission
-statement/william-f-buckley-jr.

45. Barry Popik, "Origin of the 'Buckley Rule' and the Brand New 'Limbaugh Rule,'" RedState.com, September 14, 2010, http://www.redstate
.com/barrypopik/2010/09/14/origin-of-the-buckley-rule-and-the-brand
-new-limbaugh-rule/

AFTERWORD

1. Christopher Santarelli, "Gingrich Tells Supporters on to 'Florida and
Beyond' in South Carolina Victory Speech," *The Blaze*, January 21, 2012,
http://www.theblaze.com/stories/gingrich-tells-supporters-on-to-florida-
and-beyond-in-south-carolina-victory-speech/.

2. Kendra Marr, "Gingrich Talks Faith—Not Affairs—at Cornerstone Church
in Texas," *Politico*, March 27, 2011, http://www.politico.com/news/
stories/0311/52023.html.

3. Eric Kleefeld, "Santorum Speaks to Texas Pastors, Receives Laying-On
of Hands," *Talking Points Memo*, February 8, 2012, http://livewire.talk-
ingpointsmemo.com/entries/santorum-speaks-to-texas-pastors-receives-
laying-on.

4. http://conservapedia.com/liberal_hate_speech.

5. Michelle Malkin, "The Conservative 'Climate of Hate': An Illustrated Primer,"
Michelle Malkin (blog), January 10, 2011, http://michellemalkin.com/2011/01/
10/the-progressive-climate-of-hate-an-illustrated-primer-2000-2010/.

6. Ann Coulter, *Demonic*, p. 278.

7. Steven Nelson, "'Stupid Reporter' Took 'Communist' Allegation Out of
Context, Says Allen West's Campaign," *Daily Caller*, April 11, 2012, http://
dailycaller.com/2012/04/11/stupid-reporter-took-communist-allegation-
out-of-context-says-allen-wests-campaign/#ixzz1sba3vaEP.

8. Eric Kleefeld, "Allen West Raising Money Off 'Communist' Controversy
Against Progressive Dems," *Talking Points Memo*, April 13, 2012, http://
livewire.talkingpointsmemo.com/entries/allen-west-raising-money-off-
communist-controversy-against.

9. Marc Caputo, "Allen West Doubles Down, Turns Commie Comment into
Fundraising Pitch," *Naked Politics* (blog), *Miami Herald*, April 13, 2012,
http://miamiherald.typepad.com/nakedpolitics/2012/04/allen-west-double-
down-turns-commie-comment-into-fundraising-pitch.html#storylink=
cpy.

10. Mackenzie Weinger, "Sarah Palin's 'Rogue' Pick for VP: Allen West,"
Politico, March 4, 2012, http://www.politico.com/news/stories/0412/74808
.html.

11. Kevin DeAnna, "Do You Know Why Earth Day Is April 22?," *WorldNet
Daily*, April 19, 2012, http://www.wnd.com/2012/04/do-you-know-why-
earth-day-is-april-22/.

12. Krissah Thompson and Scott Wilson, "Obama on Trayvon Martin: 'If I Had
a Son, He'd Look Like Trayvon,'" *Washington Post*, March 23, 2012, http://
www.washingtonpost.com/politics/obama-if-i-had-a-son-hed-look-like-
trayvon/2012/03/23/gIQApKPpVS_story.html.

13. Devin Dwyer and Elicia Dover, "Gingrich Calls Obama's Trayvon Martin Remarks 'Disgraceful,'" ABC News, March 23, 2012, http://abcnews.go.com/blogs/politics/2012/03/gingrich-calls-obamas-trayvon-martin remarks-disgraceful/.

14. John Parkinson, "Boehner Calls HHS Contraception Mandate an 'Attack on Religious Freedom,' Pledges Congressional Action," ABC News, February 8, 2012, http://abcnews.go.com/blogs/politics/2012/02/boehner-calls-contraception-rule-an-attack-on-religious-freedom-pledges-congressional-action/.

15. Erik Eckholm, "Both Sides Eager to Take Birth Control Coverage Issue to Voters," *New York Times*, February 15, 2012, http://www.nytimes.com/2012/02/16/us/politics/both-sides-eager-to-take-contraception-mandate-debate-to-voters.html?_r=1.

16. Brian Stelter, "Limbaugh Apologizes for Attack on Student in Birth Control Furor," *New York Times*, March 3, 2012, http://thecaucus.blogs.nytimes.com/2012/03/03/rush-limbaugh-apologizes-for-verbal-attack/?hp.

17. Elspeth Reeve, "Rush Scrubs 'Slut' Comment, Demand for Fluke Sex Tapes," *Atlantic Wire*, March 8, 2012, http://www.theatlanticwire.com/politics/2012/03/rush-scrubs-demand-for-fluke-sex-tapes/49643/.

18. Pamela Geller, "Slutgate: Contact Carbonite—Drop Ed Schultz UPDATE: 7 Companies to Boycott," *Atlas Shrugs*, March 4, 2012, http://atlasshrugs2000.typepad.com/atlas_shrugs/2012/03/contact-carbonite-drop-ed-schultz.html.

19. "Blogger Ace of Spades Calls Sandra Fluke 'A Shiftless Rent-A-Cooch from East Whoreville,'" *Media Matters*, March 2, 2012, http://mediamatters.org/iphone/blog/201203020019.

20. Alex Alvarez, "Bill O'Reilly Asks 'Who Is Running Sandra Fluke?' . . . It 'All Goes Back to the White House,'" *Mediaite*, March 8, 2012, http://www.mediaite.com/tv/bill-oreilly-asks-who-is-running-sandra-fluke-it-all-goes-back-to-white-house/.

21. Brooks Bayne, "Update #2: Sandra Fluke's Boyfriend, Adam 'Cutie Pants' Mutterperl, and His Radical Socialist Family," *The Graph*, March 13, 2012, http://thegraph.com/2012/03/sandra-flukes-boyfriend/.

22. Eric Kleefeld, "Bishop of Peoria Compares Obama and Contraception Mandates to Hitler and Stalin," *Talking Points Memo*, April 19, 2012, http://2012.talkingpointsmemo.com/2012/04/bishop-of-peoria-compares-obama-and-contraception-mandates-to-hitler-and-stalin.php.

23. "Mitt Romney Change on Illegal Immigration Issue Could Spell Doom for America," ALIPAC press release, April 19, 2012, http://news.yahoo.com/mitt-romney-change-illegal-immigration-issue-could-spell-130412066.html.

24. Jason Zengerle, "In Conversation: Barney Frank," *New York*, April 15, 2012, http://nymag.com/news/features/barney-frank-full-transcript-2012-4.

SELECTED BIBLIOGRAPHY

Adams, John. *The Political Writings of John Adams: Representative Selections.* Edited by George A. Peek Jr. Indianapolis: Hackett, 2003.

Adams, John Quincy. *Letters on the Masonic Institution.* Boston, 1847.

Aho, James A. *The Things of the World: A Social Phenomenology.* Santa Barbara, Calif.: Praeger, 1998.

Allen, Gary. *None Dare Call It Conspiracy.* Cutchogue, N.Y.: Buccaneer Books, 1976.

————. *Richard Nixon: The Man Behind the Mask.* Boston: Western Islands, 1971.

Amato, John, and David Neiwert. *Over the Cliff: How Obama's Election Drove the American Right Insane.* San Francisco: PoliPoint, 2010.

Baldwin, Neil. *Ford and the Jews: The Mass Production of Hate.* New York: Public Affairs, 2001.

Barruel, Augustin. *Memoirs Illustrating the History of Jacobinism: A Translation from the French of the Abbé Barruel by Robert Clifford.* London, 1797.

Beck, Glenn. *Arguing with Idiots: How to Stop Small Minds and Big Government.* New York: Threshold, 2010.

————. *Glenn Beck's Common Sense: The Case Against an Out-of-Control Government, Inspired by Thomas Paine.* New York: Threshold, 2009.

————. *An Inconvenient Book: Real Solutions to the World's Biggest Problems.* New York: Threshold, 2009.

————. *The Overton Window.* New York: Threshold, 2010.

————. *The Real America: Messages from the Heart and the Heartland.* New York: Gallery, 2005.

Beecher, Lyman. *A Plea for the West.* New York: Leavitt, Lord, 1835.

Beekman, Scott. *William Dudley Pelley: A Life in Right-Wing Extremism and the Occult.* Syracuse, N.Y.: Syracuse University Press, 2005.

Belknap, Michal R., ed. *American Political Trials.* Westport, Conn.: Praeger, 1994.

Benko, Stephen. *Pagan Rome and the Early Christians.* Bloomington: Indiana University Press, 1986.

Bennett, David H. *The Party of Fear: The American Far Right from Nativism to the Militia Movement.* Chapel Hill: University of North Carolina Press, 1988.

Bennett, Harry Herbert, and Paul Marcus. *We Never Called Him Henry.* Robbinsdale, Minn.: Fawcett, 1951.

Berg, A. Scott. *Lindbergh.* New York: Putnam, 1998.

Berlet, Chip, and Matthew N. Lyons. *Right-Wing Populism in America: Too Close for Comfort.* New York: Guilford, 2000.

Biale, David. *Eros and the Jews: From Biblical Israel to Contemporary America.* New York: Basic Books, 1992.

Bishop, Bill. *The Big Sort: Why the Clustering of Like-Minded America Is Tearing Us Apart.* Boston: Houghton Mifflin, 2008.

Blumenfeld, Samuel. *NEA: Trojan Horse in American Education.* Boise, Idaho: Paradigm, 1984.

Blumenthal, Max. *Republican Gomorrah: Inside the Movement That Shattered the Party.* New York: Nation Books, 2009.

Bronner, Stephen Eric. *A Rumor About the Jews: Antisemitism, Conspiracy, and the Protocols of Zion.* Oxford: Oxford University Press, 2003.

Brown, Dan. *The Lost Symbol.* New York: Doubleday, 2009.

Buchanan, Patrick J. *The Death of the West: How Dying Populations and Immigrant Invasions Imperil Our Country and Civilization.* New York: St. Martin's Press, 2002.

———. *Suicide of a Superpower: Will America Survive to 2025?* New York: St. Martin's Press, 2011.

Capell, Frank A. *The Strange Death of Marilyn Monroe.* Zarephath, N.J.: Herald of Freedom, 1964.

———. *Treason Is the Reason: 847 Reasons for Investigating the State Department.* Zarephath, N.J.: Herald of Freedom, 1965.

Carlson, John Roy [Avedis Boghos Derounian]. *Under Cover: My Four Years in the Nazi Underworld of America.* New York: Dutton, 1943.

Carpenter, Ronald H. *Father Charles E. Coughlin: Surrogate Spokesman for the Disaffected.* Westport, Conn.: Greenwood, 1998.

Carr, William Guy. *Pawns in the Game.* Hollywood, Calif.: Angriff Press, 1958.

Carroll, James. *Constantine's Sword: The Church and the Jews.* Boston: Houghton Mifflin, 2001.

Chalmers, David Mark. *Hooded Americanism: The History of the Ku Klux Klan.* Durham, N.C.: Duke University Press, 1981.

Clark, Gordon. *Shylock: As Banker, Bondholder, Corruptionist, Conspirator.* Washington, D.C.: American Bimetallic League, 1894.

Cohn, Norman. *Warrant for Genocide: The Myth of the Jewish World Conspiracy and the Protocols of the Elders of Zion.* London: Serif, 1997.

Coogan, Kevin. *Dreamer of the Day: Francis Parker Yockey and the Postwar Fascist International.* New York: Autonomedia, 1999.

Cooper, Milton William. *Behold a Pale Horse.* Flagstaff, Ariz.: Light Technology, 1991.

Corsi, Jerome. *America for Sale: Fighting the New World Order, Surviving a Global Depression, and Preserving USA Sovereignty.* New York: Threshold, 2009.

———. *The Obama Nation: Leftist Politics and the Cult of Personality.* New York: Threshold, 2008.

———. *Where's the Birth Certificate? The Case That Barack Obama Is Not Eligible to Be President.* Washington, D.C.: WorldNetDaily Books, 2011.

Coughlin, Charles Edward. *The New Deal in Money.* Royal Oak, Mich.: Radio League of the Little Flower, 1933.

Coulter, Ann. *Demonic: How the Liberal Mob Is Endangering America*. New York: Crown Forum, 2011.

———. *Godless: The Church of Liberalism*. New York: Three Rivers Press, 2007.

———. *How to Talk to a Liberal, if You Must: The World According to Ann Coulter*. New York: Three Rivers Press, 2005.

———. *Slander: Liberal Lies About the American Right*. New York: Three Rivers Press, 2003.

———. *Treason: Liberal Treachery from the Cold War to the War on Terrorism*. New York: Three Rivers Press, 2004.

Cross, Whitney R. *The Burned-Over District: The Social and Intellectual History of Enthusiastic Religion in Western New York, 1800–1850*. Ithaca, N.Y.: Cornell University Press, 1950.

Crowley, Aleister. *The Book of the Law*. 1904. Newburyport, Mass.: Red Wheel, 2004.

Cumbey, Constance. *A Planned Deception: The Staging of a New Age "Messiah."* Detroit: Pointe, 1985.

Davis, David Brion, ed. *The Fear of Conspiracy: Images of Un-American Subversion from the Revolution to the Present*. Ithaca, N.Y.: Cornell University Press, 1971.

Day, Stephen A. *We Must Save the Republic: A Brief for the Declaration of Independence and the Constitution of the United States*. Scotch Plains, N.J.: Flanders Hall, 1941.

Dilling, Elizabeth. *The Plot Against Christianity*. 1964. Torrance, Calif.: Noontide Press, 1983.

———. *The Red Network: A "Who's Who" and Handbook of Radicalism for Patriots*. 1934. Charleston, S.C.: Nabu Press, 2010.

———. *The Roosevelt Red Record and Its Background*. 1936. Palmdale, Calif.: Christian Book Club of America, 2003.

Disraeli, Benjamin. *Coningsby; or, The New Generation*. 1844. Charleston, S.C.: Forgotten Books, 2010.

———. *Lord George Bentinck: A Political Biography*. 1852. Charleston, S.C.: BiblioBazaar, 2007.

Dixon, Thomas. *The Clansman*. New York: Grosset & Dunlap, 1905.

Donnelly, Ignatius. *Caesar's Column*. Chicago: F. J. Shulte, 1890.

D'Souza, Dinesh. *The Roots of Obama's Rage*. Washington, D.C.: Regnery, 2010.

Duffy, James P. *Lindbergh vs. Roosevelt: The Rivalry That Divided America*. Washington, D.C.: Regnery, 2010.

Eco, Umberto. *Foucault's Pendulum*. San Diego: Harcourt, 1989.

———. *Six Walks in the Fictional Woods*. Cambridge, Mass.: Harvard University Press, 1994.

Edmondson, Robert Edward. *I Testify: Amazing Memoir-Exposure of International Secret War-Plotting*. Bend, Ore.: Robert Edward Edmondson, 1953.

Eisner, Will. *The Plot: The Secret Story of the Protocols of the Elders of Zion*. With an introduction by Umberto Eco. New York: Norton, 2006.

Emerson, Ralph Waldo. *The Journals and Miscellaneous Notebooks*. Cambridge, Mass.: Harvard University Press, 1976.

Epperson, Ralph. *Masonry: Conspiracy Against Christianity*. Tucson, Ariz.: Publius, 1998.

———. *The New World Order*. Tucson, Ariz.: Publius, 1990.

———. *The Unseen Hand: An Introduction to the Conspiratorial View of History*. Tucson, Ariz.: Publius, 1985.

Essien-Udom, E. U. *Black Nationalism: A Search for an Identity in America.* Chicago: University of Chicago Press, 1962.

Finney, Charles G. *The Character, Claims, and Practical Workings of Freemasonry.* 1869. Chicago: National Christian Association, 1924.

Flynn, John T. *Country Squire in the White House.* New York: Doubleday, Doran, 1940.

Ford, Henry. *The International Jew.* Dearborn, Mich.: Dearborn Publishing, 1920–22.

Franchot, Jenny. *Roads to Rome: The Antebellum Protestant Encounter with Catholicism.* Berkeley: University of California Press, 1994.

Frank, Thomas. *What's the Matter with Kansas? How Conservatives Won the Heart of America.* New York: Holt, 2004.

———. *The Wrecking Crew: How Conservatives Ruined Government, Enriched Themselves, and Beggared the Nation.* New York: Holt, 2009.

Freddoso, David. *Gangster Government: Barack Obama and the New Washington Thugocracy.* Washington, D.C.: Regnery, 2011.

Fry, L. [Paquita de Shishmareff]. *Waters Flowing Eastward: The War Against the Kingship of Christ.* 1931. New Orleans: Flanders Hall, 1988.

Gardell, Matthias. *In the Name of Elijah Muhammad: Louis Farrakhan and the Nation of Islam.* Durham, N.C.: Duke University Press, 1996.

Geller, Pamela. *The Post-American Presidency: The Obama Administration's War on America.* New York: Threshold, 2010.

———. *Stop the Islamization of America: A Practical Guide to the Resistance.* Washington, D.C.: WorldNetDaily Books, 2011.

Gingrich, Newt. *To Save America: Stopping Obama's Secular-Socialist Machine.* Washington, D.C.: Regnery, 2011.

Gobineau, Arthur de. *The Moral and Intellectual Diversity of Races.* Philadelphia: J. B. Lippincott, 1856. (Reprint is available from Nabu Press.)

Goff, Kenneth. *The Soviet Art of Brainwashing: Communist Psychopolitics and the Slaughter of Western Culture.* Torrance, Calif.: Noontide Press, 1979.

Goldberg, Jonah. *Liberal Fascism: The Secret History of the American Left, from Mussolini to the Politics of Meaning.* New York: Doubleday, 2008.

Goldhagen, Daniel. *Hitler's Willing Executioners: Ordinary Germans and the Holocaust.* New York: Alfred A. Knopf, 1996.

Grant, Madison. *The Passing of the Great Race; or, The Racial Basis of European History.* 1916. New York: Scribner, 1922.

Greenspan, Ezra, ed. *The Cambridge Companion to Walt Whitman.* New York: Cambridge University Press, 1995.

Griffin, David Ray. *Cognitive Infiltration: An Obama Appointee's Plan to Undermine the 9/11 Conspiracy Theory.* Northampton, Mass.: Olive Branch Press, 2010.

———. *The New Pearl Harbor: Disturbing Questions About the Bush Administration and 9/11.* Northampton, Mass.: Olive Branch Press, 2004.

———. *The New Pearl Harbor Revisited: 9/11, the Cover-Up, and the Exposé.* Northampton, Mass.: Olive Branch Press, 2008.

Griffin, G. Edward. *The Creature from Jekyll Island: A Second Look at the Federal Reserve.* Westlake Village, Calif.: American Media, 1994.

Hagee, John. *Day of Deception.* Nashville: Thomas Nelson, 1997.

———. *Jerusalem Countdown: A Warning to the World.* Lake Mary, Fla.: A Strange Company, 2006.

Hall, Manly P. *The Secret Teachings of All Ages: An Encyclopedic Outline of Masonic, Hermetic, Qabbalistic, and Rosicrucian Symbolical Philosophy.* 1928. Radford, Va.: Wilder, 2007.

Herman, Didi. *The Antigay Agenda: Orthodox Vision and the Christian Right.* Chicago: University of Chicago Press, 1997.

Herzl, Theodor. *The Jewish State.* 1896. Hales Corners, Wis.: Voasha, 2008.

Hitler, Adolf. *Mein Kampf.* 1925. Translated by James Murphy. London: Hurst & Blackett, 1942.

Hofstadter, Richard. *The Age of Reform.* New York: Vintage, 1955.

———. *The American Political Tradition.* New York: Vintage, 1948.

———. *Anti-intellectualism in America.* New York: Vintage, 1963.

———. *The Paranoid Style in American Politics and Other Essays.* New York: Vintage, 2008.

House, Edward Mandell. *Philip Dru, Administrator: A Story of Tomorrow.* 1912. Appleton, Wis.: Robert Welch University Press, 1998.

Huckabee, Mike. *A Simple Government: Twelve Things We Really Need from Washington (and a Trillion That We Don't!).* New York: Sentinel, 2011.

Huxley, Aldous. *Brave New World.* New York: Harper, 1932.

Icke, David. *The Biggest Secret: The Book That Will Change the World.* 2nd ed. Ryde, U.K.: David Icke Books, 1999.

———. *Children of the Matrix: How an Interdimensional Race Has Controlled the World for Thousands of Years—and Still Does.* Ryde, U.K.: David Icke Books, 2001.

———. *The David Icke Guide to the Global Conspiracy (and How to End It).* Ryde, U.K.: David Icke Books, 2007.

Ingersoll, Robert G. *The Works of Robert G. Ingersoll.* New York: C. P. Farrell, 1900.

Ingraham, Laura. *The Obama Diaries.* New York: Threshold, 2010.

Irwin, Theodore. "Inside the 'Christian Front.'" *Forum* 103 (March 1940).

Jacoby, Susan. *The Age of American Unreason.* New York: Pantheon, 2008.

Jardim, Anne. *The First Henry Ford: A Study in Personality and Business Leadership.* Cambridge, Mass.: MIT Press, 1970.

Jeansonne, Glen. *Women of the Far Right: The Mothers' Movement and World War II.* Chicago: University of Chicago Press, 1996.

Jefferson, Thomas. *The Writings of Thomas Jefferson.* New York: Knickerbocker Press, 1892–97.

Johnson, George. *Architects of Fear: Conspiracy Theories and Paranoia in American Politics.* Los Angeles: Tarcher, 1983.

Johnston, Robert D. *The Politics of Healing: Histories of Alternative Medicines in Twentieth-Century North America.* New York: Routledge, 2004.

Joly, Maurice. *The Dialogue in Hell Between Machiavelli and Montesquieu: Humanitarian Despotism and the Conditions of Modern Tyranny.* 1864. Translated by John Waggoner. Lanham, Md.: Lexington Books, 2003.

Jones, Jeffrey Owen, and Peter Meyer. *The Pledge: A History of the Pledge of Allegiance.* New York: St. Martin's Press, 2010.

Kaplan, Jeffrey, ed. *The Encyclopedia of White Power: A Sourcebook on the Radical, Racist Right.* Walnut Creek, Calif.: AltaMira Press, 2000.

Kiš, Danilo. *The Encyclopedia of the Dead.* New York: Farrar, Straus and Giroux, 1989.

Knobel, Dale T. *America for the Americans: The Nativist Movement in the United States.* New York: Twayne, 1996.

Kramer, Jane. *Lone Patriot: The Short Career of an American Militiaman.* New York: Pantheon, 2002.

Kurtz, Stanley. *Radical-in-Chief: Barack Obama and the Untold Story of American Socialism.* New York: Threshold, 2010.

Laqueur, Walter. *A History of Zionism: From the French Revolution to the Establishment of the State of Israel.* New York: Schocken, 2003.

LaHaye, Tim. *Rapture (Under Attack): Will You Escape the Tribulation?* New York: Multnomah, 1998.

LaHaye, Tim, and Jerry B. Jenkins. *Left Behind: A Novel of the Earth's Last Days.* Wheaton, Ill.: Tyndale House, 1995.

Leadbeater, C. W. *The Masters and the Path.* 1925. New York: Cosimo Classics, 2007.

Leckie, Robert. *American and Catholic: A Narrative of Their Role in American History.* New York: Doubleday, 1970.

Lee, Albert. *Henry Ford and the Jews.* New York: Stein & Day, 1980.

Lewin, Leonard C. *Report from Iron Mountain: On the Possibility and Desirability of Peace.* New York: Dial Press, 1967.

Limbaugh, David. *Crimes Against Liberty: An Indictment of President Barack Obama.* Washington, D.C.: Regnery, 2010.

Lindbergh, Charles A. *Why Is Your Country at War?* Washington, D.C.: National Capital Press, 1917.

Lipset, Seymour Martin, and Earl Raab. *The Politics of Unreason: Right-Wing Extremism in America, 1790–1977.* Chicago: University of Chicago Press, 1978.

Lockwood, Robert P. *Anti-Catholicism in American Culture.* Huntington, Ind.: Our Sunday Visitor, 2000.

Luke, Jemima Thompson. *The Female Jesuit; or, The Spy in the Family.* New York: M. M. Dodd, 1851. (Reprint is available from Nabu Press, 2010.)

Luther, Martin. *On the Jews and Their Lies.* 1543. Philadelphia: Fortress Press, 1971.

Malkin, Michelle. *Culture of Corruption: Obama and His Team of Tax Cheats, Crooks, and Cronies.* Washington, D.C.: Regnery, 2010.

———. *In Defense of Internment: The Case for "Racial Profiling" in World War II and the War on Terror.* Washington, D.C.: Regnery, 2004.

———. *Unhinged: Exposing Liberals Gone Wild.* Washington, D.C.: Regnery, 2005.

Manchester, William. *The Death of a President.* New York: Harper & Row, 1967.

Marrs, Jim. *Rule by Secrecy: The Hidden History That Connects the Trilateral Commission, the Freemasons, and the Great Pyramids.* New York: HarperCollins, 2000.

McManus, John F. *The Insiders.* Appleton, Wis.: John Birch Society, 1993.

Mendes-Flohr, Paul R., and Jehuda Reinharz. *The Jew in the Modern World: A Documentary History.* New York: Oxford University Press, 1995.

Moffatt, Mary Anne Ursula. *An Answer to "Six Months in a Convent," Exposing Its Falsehoods and Manifold Absurdities.* Boston: J. H. Eastburn, 1835.

Mohr, Gordon "Jack." *The Hidden Power Behind Freemasonry.* Burnsville, Minn.: Weisman, 1993.

Monk, Maria. *Awful Disclosures of Maria Monk . . . in the Hotel Dieu Nunnery at Montreal.* London: Houlston & Stoneman, 1851. (Reprints are available through Kessinger and other publishers.)

Morgan, William. *Illustrations of Masonry by One of the Fraternity.* Chicago: Ezra A. Cook, 1827.

Morris, Edmund. *The Rise of Theodore Roosevelt.* New York: Coward, McCann & Geoghegan, 1979.

Morris, Robert. *William Morgan; or, Political Anti-Masonry, Its Rise, Growth, and Decadence.* New York: Robert Macoy, 1883.

Mullins, Eustace. *The Biological Jew.* Staunton, Va.: Faith and Service Books, 1968.

———. *The Curse of Canaan: A Demonology of History.* Staunton, Va.: Revelation Books, 1987.

———. *Murder by Injection: The Story of the Medical Conspiracy Against America.* Staunton, Va.: National Council for Medical Research, 1988.

———. *The Secrets of the Federal Reserve.* Carson City, Nev.: Bridger House, 1985.

———. *This Difficult Individual: Ezra Pound.* New York: Fleet, 1961.

Murray, Nicholas. *Aldous Huxley: A Biography.* New York: St. Martin's Press, 2002.

Neiwert, David. *The Eliminationists: How Hate Talk Radicalized the American Right.* San Francisco: PoliPoint, 2009.

Oliver, Revilo P. *Against the Grain.* York, S.C.: Liberty Bell, 2004.

———. *All America Must Know the Terror That Is Upon Us.* Bakersfield, Calif.: Conservative Viewpoint, 1966.

———. *America's Decline: The Education of a Conservative.* London: Londinium Press, 1981.

———. *Christianity and the Survival of the West.* Cape Canaveral, Fla.: Howard Allen, 1973.

Paine, Thomas. *Collected Writings.* New York: Library of America, 1995.

Painter, Nell Irvin. *The History of White People.* New York: Norton, 2010.

Palin, Sarah. *America by Heart: Reflections on Family, Faith, and Flag.* New York: HarperCollins, 2010.

———. *Going Rogue: An American Life.* New York: HarperCollins, 2009.

Palmer, John C. *The Morgan Affair and Anti-Masonry.* 1924. Whitefish, Mont.: Kessinger, 1992.

Pelley, William Dudley. *Dupes of Judah: The Inside Story of Why the World War Was Fought.* Asheville, N.C.: Pelley, 1939.

———. *Seven Minutes in Eternity with the Aftermath.* New York: Robert Collier, 1929.

———. *Undying Mind.* Noblesville, Ind.: Soulcraft Chapels, 1955.

Perlstein, Rick. *Before the Storm: Barry Goldwater and the Unmaking of the American Consensus.* New York: Hill and Wang, 2001.

Pierce, William Luther. *The Turner Diaries.* New York: Barricade Books, 1978.

Pike, Albert. *Morals and Dogma of the First Three Degrees of the Ancient and Accepted Scottish Rite of Freemasonry.* Charleston, S.C.: Supreme Council of the Southern Jurisdiction, A.A.S.R., 1871. (Reprints are available from Kessinger, Theophania, and other publishers.)

Pipes, Daniel. *Conspiracy: How the Paranoid Style Flourishes and Where It Comes From.* New York: Free Press, 1997.

Popper, Karl. *The Open Society and Its Enemies.* 2 vols. New York: Routledge, 1945.

The Protocols of the Learned Elders of Zion. Translated by Victor Marsden. With a foreword by Texe Marrs. Austin, Tex.: RiverCrest, 2011.

Quigley, Carroll. *The Anglo-American Establishment.* Rancho Palos Verdes, Calif.: GSG & Associates, 1981.

————. *Tragedy and Hope: A History of the World in Our Time.* Hollywood, Calif.: Angriff, 1975.

Rand, Ayn. *The Virtue of Selfishness.* New York: Signet, 1964.

Rauf, Feisal Abdul. *What's Right with Islam: A New Vision for Muslims and the West.* New York: HarperOne, 2005.

Reed, Douglas. *The Controversy of Zion.* Durban, South Africa: Dolphin Press, 1978.

Reed, Rebecca Theresa. *Six Months in a Convent.* 1835. Charleston, S.C.: Nabu Press, 2010.

Richards, William C. *The Last Billionaire: Henry Ford.* New York: Scribner, 1976.

Robertson, Pat. *The New World Order.* Dallas: Word Publishing, 1991.

Robison, John. *Proofs of a Conspiracy Against All the Religions and Governments of Europe, Carried on in the Secret Meetings of Free Masons, Illuminati, and Reading Societies.* 1797. Whitefish, Mont.: Kessinger Publishing, 2003.

Rockwell, George Lincoln. *This Time the World.* New York: Parliament House, 1963.

————. *White Power.* 1967. Champaign, Ill.: John McLaughlin, 1996.

Rudin, James. *Christians & Jews, Faith to Faith: Tragic History, Promising Present, Fragile Future.* Woodstock, Vt.: Jewish Lights, 2011.

Russell, Bertrand. *The Basic Writings of Bertrand Russell.* New York: Routledge, 2009.

Schlafly, Phyllis. *The Betrayers.* Alton, Ill.: Pere Marquette Press, 1968.

————. *A Choice Not an Echo.* Alton, Ill.: Pere Marquette Press, 1964.

————. *The Supremacists: The Tyranny of Judges and How to Stop It.* Dallas: Spence, 2004.

Schultz, Nancy Lusignan. *Fire and Roses: The Burning of the Charlestown Convent, 1834.* New York: Free Press, 2000.

Segel, Binjamin. *A Lie and a Libel: The History of the Protocols of the Elders of Zion.* Translated by Richard S. Levy. Lincoln: University of Nebraska Press, 1995.

Sharlet, Jeff. *The Family: The Secret Fundamentalism at the Heart of American Power.* New York: HarperCollins, 2008.

Shea, Robert, and Robert Anton Wilson. *The Illuminatus! Trilogy.* New York: Dell, 1975.

Sherry, Michael S. *In the Shadow of War: The United States Since the 1930s.* New Haven, Conn.: Yale University Press, 1995.

Sinclair, Upton. *The Flivver King: A Story of Ford-America.* Detroit: United Automobile Workers, 1937.

Skousen, W. Cleon. *The Five Thousand Year Leap: Twenty-Eight Ideas That Changed the World.* Washington, D.C.: National Center for Constitutional Studies, 1981.

————. *The Making of America: The Substance and Meaning of the Constitution.* Washington, D.C.: National Center for Constitutional Studies, 1985.

————. *The Naked Capitalist.* Salt Lake City: W. Cleon Skousen, 1970.

————. *The Naked Communist.* Salt Lake City: Ensign, 1958.

Smith, Geoffrey S. *To Save a Nation: American "Extremism," the New Deal, and the Coming of World War II.* Rev. ed. Chicago: Ivan R. Dee, 1992.

Smith, Samuel B. *The Escape of Sainte Frances Patrick, Another Nun, from the Hotel Dieu Nunnery of Montreal.* New York: Office of the Downfall of Babylon, 1836.

Smoot, Dan. *The Invisible Government*. Dallas: Dan Smoot Report, 1962.

Soddy, Frederick. *Wealth, Virtual Wealth, and Debt: The Solution of the Economic Paradox*. London: Allen & Unwin, 1926.

Spencer, Robert. *The Politically Incorrect Guide to Islam and the Crusades*. Washington, D.C.: Regnery, 2005.

———. *Stealth Jihad: How Radical Islam Is Subverting America Without Guns or Bombs*. Washington, D.C.: Regnery, 2008.

———. *The Truth About Muhammad: Founder of the World's Most Intolerant Religion*. Washington, D.C.: Regnery, 2007.

Stauffer, Vernon. *New England and the Bavarian Illuminati*. New York: Columbia University Press, 1918.

Steiner, George. *The Portage to San Cristóbal of A.H.* London: Faber & Faber, 1981.

Stone, Geoffrey R. *Perilous Times: Free Speech in Wartime, from the Sedition Act of 1798 to the War on Terrorism*. New York: W. W. Norton, 2004.

Stone, William L. *Maria Monk and the Nunnery of the Hotel Dieu, Being an Account of a Visit to the Convents of Montreal and Refutation of the "Awful Disclosures."* New York: Howe & Bates, 1836.

Stormer, John. *None Dare Call It Treason*. Florissant, Mo.: Liberty Bell Press, 1964.

Taibbi, Matt. *The Great Derangement: A Terrifying True Story of War, Politics, and Religion at the Twilight of the American Empire*. New York: Spiegel & Grau, 2008.

Thayer, John. *An Account of the Conversion of the Reverend John Thayer, Formerly a Protestant Minister of Boston, Written by Himself*. Hartford, Conn., 1832.

Thomson, Ahmad. *Dajjal: The Antichrist*. London: Ta-Ha, 1997.

Tocqueville, Alexis de. *Democracy in America*. Translated by George Lawrence. New York: Harper & Row, 1966.

Wagner, Richard. *Prose Works*, vol. 3, *The Theatre*. 1907. Translated by William Ashton Ellis. Whitefish, Mont.: Kessinger, 2007.

Wallace, Max. *The American Axis: Henry Ford, Charles Lindbergh, and the Rise of the Third Reich*. New York: St. Martin's Press, 2003.

Webster, Nesta H. *The French Revolution: A Study in Democracy*. 1919. Charleston, S.C.: Nabu Press, 2010.

———. *Secret Societies and Subversive Movements*. 1924. Escondido, Calif.: Book Tree, 2000.

———. *World Revolution: The Plot Against Civilization*. 1921. Charleston, S.C.: Nabu Press, 2010.

Welch, Robert W., Jr. *The Blue Book of the John Birch Society*. 1958. Boston: Western Islands, 1961.

———. *The Life of John Birch*. 1954. Boston: Western Islands, 1960.

———. *The Politician*. 1956. Belmont, Mass.: Belmont, 1964.

Whalen, William Joseph. *Christianity and American Freemasonry*. 3rd ed. San Francisco: Ignatius Press, 1998.

Whitman, Walt. *The Collected Writings: The Journalism*. Edited by Herbert Bergman et al. New York: P. Lang, 1998.

Wilson, Robert Anton. *Cosmic Trigger 1: Final Secret of the Illuminati*. Tempe, Ariz.: New Falcon, 1977.

Wilson, Woodrow. *The New Freedom: A Call for the Emancipation of the Generous Energies of a People*. New York: Doubleday, Page, 1913.

Winrod, Gerald. *Adam Weishaupt: A Human Devil*. Wichita, Kans.: Defender, 1935.

Wistrich, Robert S. *Laboratory for World Destruction: Germans and Jews in Central Europe.* Lincoln: University of Nebraska Press, 2007.

Wolfe, Lucien. *The Myth of the Jewish Menace in World Affairs; or, The Truth About the Forged Protocols of the Elders of Zion.* New York: Macmillan, 1921.

Yockey, Francis Parker. *Imperium: The Philosophy of History and Politics.* 1948. Torrance, Calif.: Noontide Press, 1962.

Zaitchik, Alexander. *Common Nonsense: Glenn Beck and the Triumph of Ignorance.* Hoboken, N.J.: John Wiley & Sons, 2010.

Zeskind, Leonard. *Blood and Politics: The History of the White Nationalist Movement from the Margins to the Mainstream.* New York: Farrar, Straus and Giroux, 2009.

INDEX

Pr
by United States
lor Publisher Services